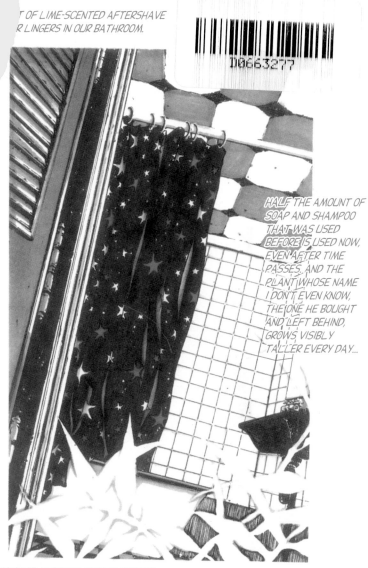

...T OF LIME-SCENTED AFTERSHAVE ...R LINGERS IN OUR BATHROOM.

HALF THE AMOUNT OF SOAP AND SHAMPOO THAT WAS USED BEFORE IS USED NOW, EVEN AFTER TIME PASSES, AND THE PLANT WHOSE NAME I DON'T EVEN KNOW, THE ONE HE BOUGHT AND LEFT BEHIND, GROWS VISIBLY TALLER EVERY DAY...

AT THIS RATE, IT SEEMS POSSIBLE THAT THE ONCE LIME-SCENTED BATHROOM COULD TURN INTO A JUNGLE.

I FELT IRRITABLE.

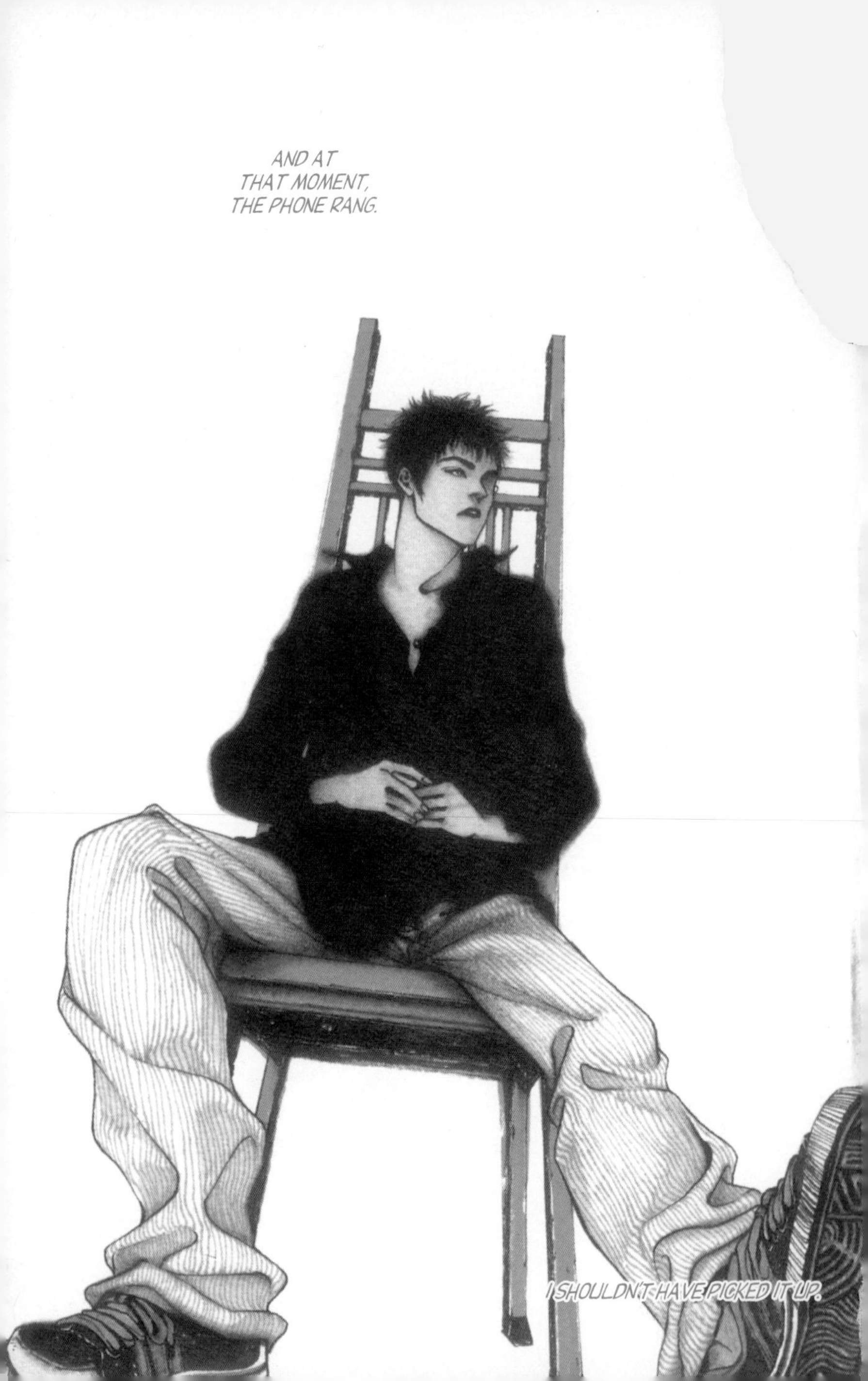
AND AT THAT MOMENT, THE PHONE RANG.
I SHOULDN'T HAVE PICKED IT UP.

Martin & John

By
Hee-Jung Park

TOKYOPOP®

HAMBURG // LONDON // LOS ANGELES // TOKYO

Martin and John Vol.1
Created by Hee Jung Park

Translation - Soo-Kyung Kim
English Adaptation - Ailen Lujo
Copy Editor - Jessica Chavez
Retouch and Lettering - Star Print Brokers
Production Artist - Vicente Rivera, Jr.
Cover Design - Monalisa De Asis

Editor - Stephanie Duchin
Digital Imaging Manager - Chris Buford
Pre-Production Supervisor - Lucas Rivera
Production Manager - Elisabeth Brizzi
Managing Editor - Vy Nguyen
Creative Director - Anne Marie Horne
Editor-in-Chief - Rob Tokar
Publisher - Mike Kiley
President and C.O.O. - John Parker
C.E.O. and Chief Creative Officer - Stu Levy

A **TOKYOPOP** Manga

TOKYOPOP and 🐵 are trademarks or registered trademarks of TOKYOPOP Inc.

TOKYOPOP Inc.
5900 Wilshire Blvd. Suite 2000
Los Angeles, CA 90036

E-mail: info@TOKYOPOP.com
Come visit us online at www.TOKYOPOP.com

ISBN: 978-1-4278-1018-2

First TOKYOPOP printing: July 2008
10 9 8 7 6 5 4 3 2 1
Printed in the USA

Martin & John

1

Hee-Jung Park

FIND SOMEONE ELSE...

FIND SOMEONE WHO CAN ACCEPT THAT LOVE
OF YOURS WITHOUT RESERVATIONS.
SOMEONE LIKE THAT...

#0
MARTIN & JOHN

Starting with that, a boring episode...

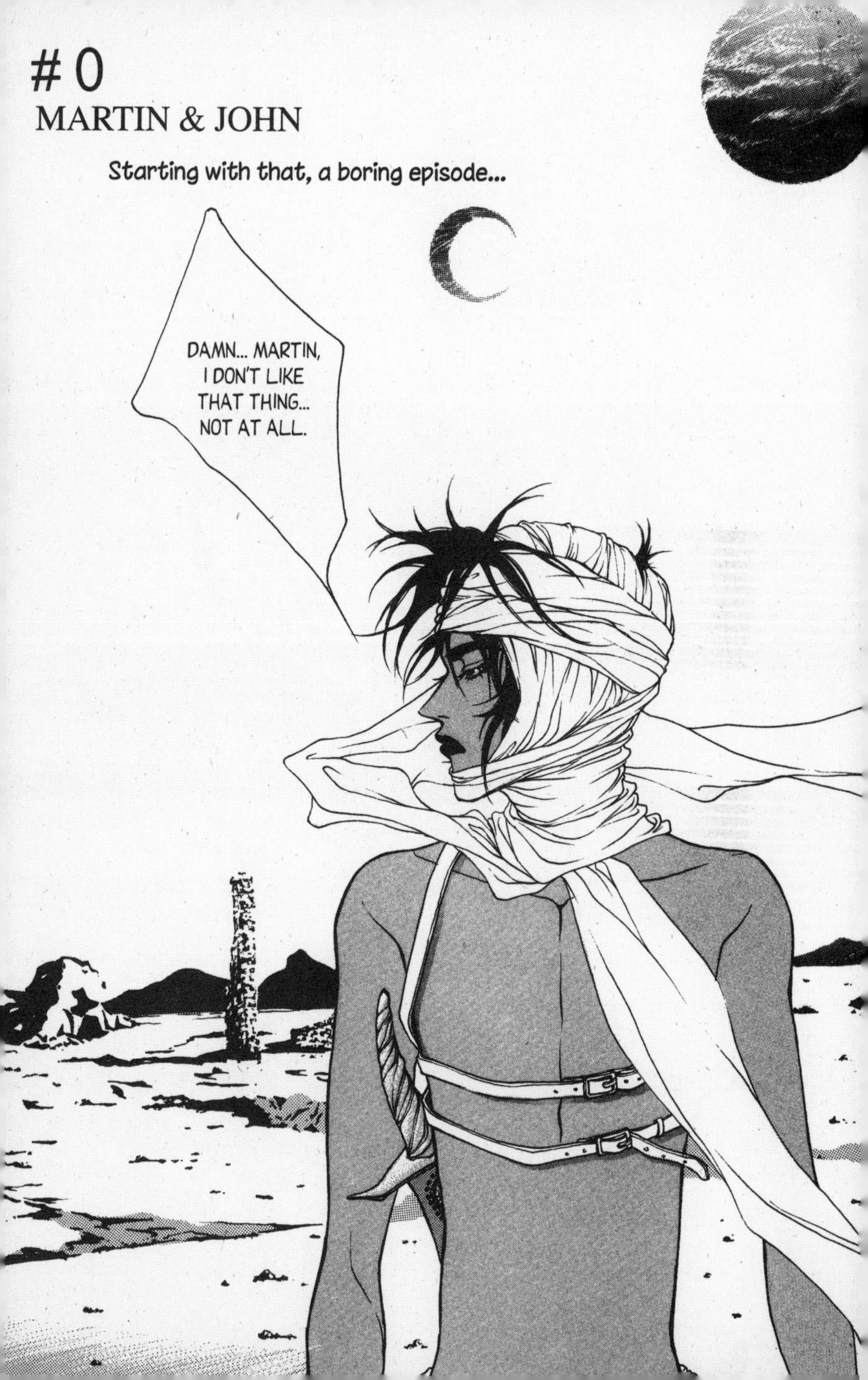
DAMN... MARTIN, I DON'T LIKE THAT THING... NOT AT ALL.

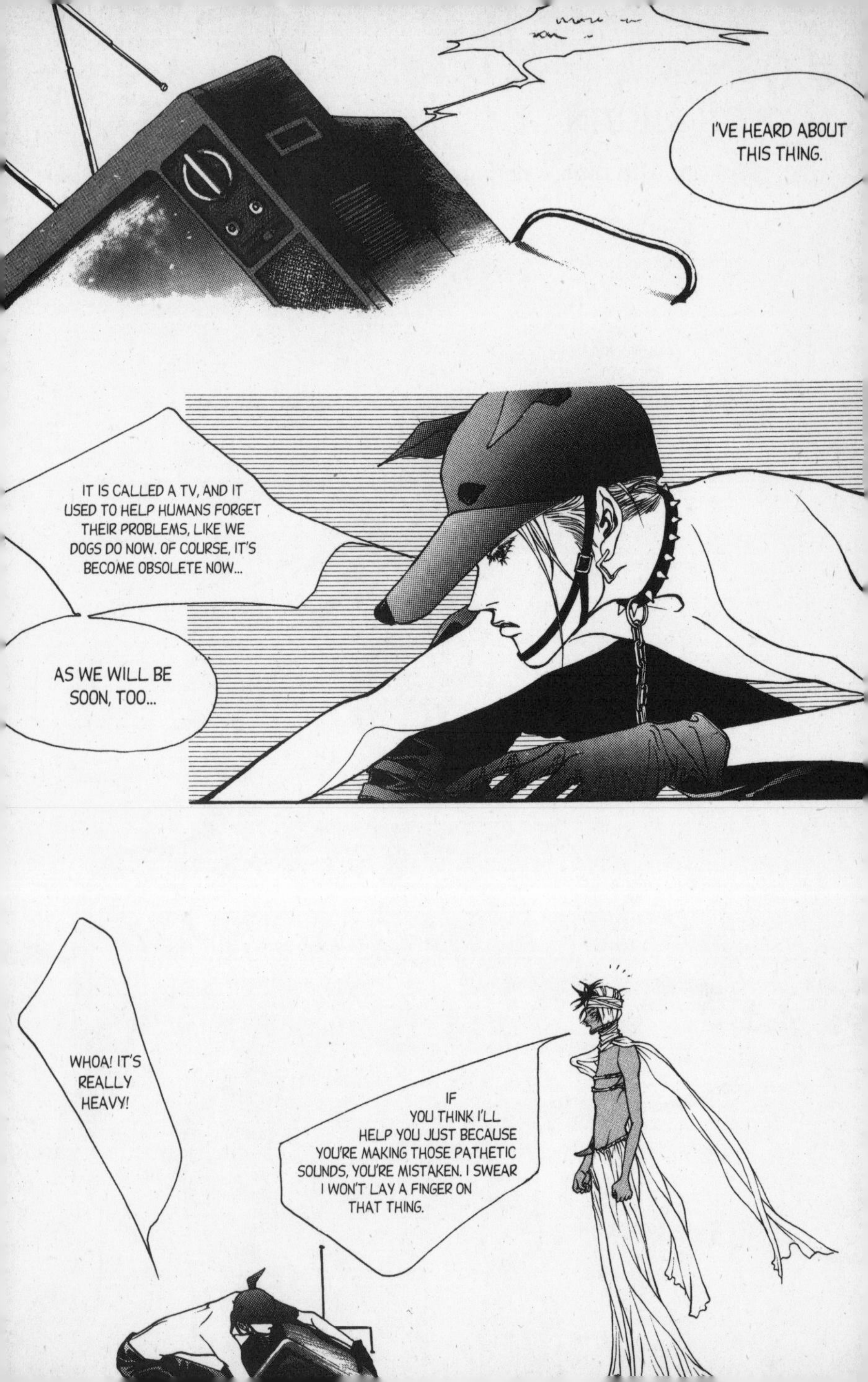
I'VE HEARD ABOUT THIS THING.
IT IS CALLED A TV, AND IT USED TO HELP HUMANS FORGET THEIR PROBLEMS, LIKE WE DOGS DO NOW. OF COURSE, IT'S BECOME OBSOLETE NOW...
AS WE WILL BE SOON, TOO...
WHOA! IT'S REALLY HEAVY!
IF YOU THINK I'LL HELP YOU JUST BECAUSE YOU'RE MAKING THOSE PATHETIC SOUNDS, YOU'RE MISTAKEN. I SWEAR I WON'T LAY A FINGER ON THAT THING.

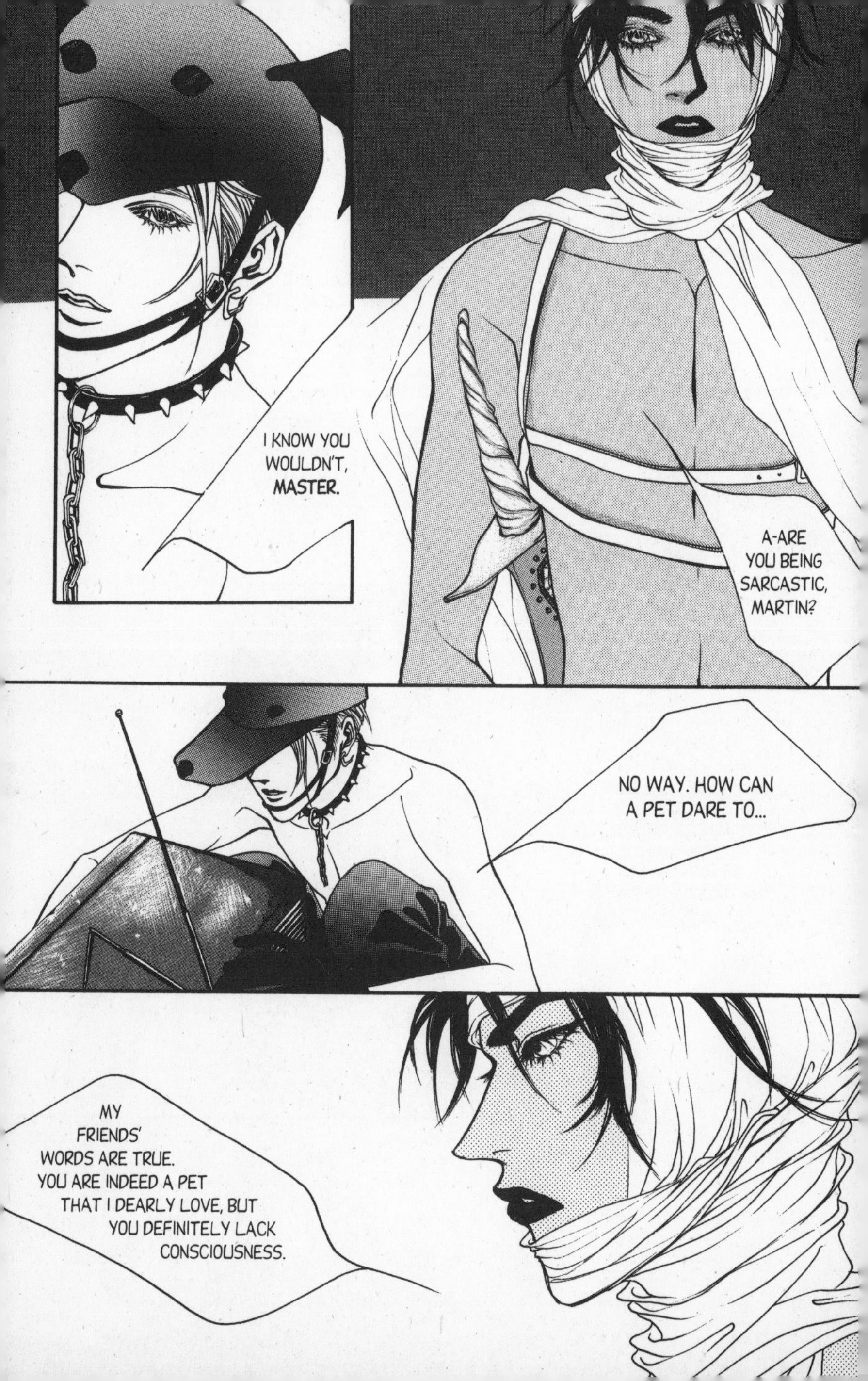
I KNOW YOU WOULDN'T, MASTER.
A-ARE YOU BEING SARCASTIC, MARTIN?
NO WAY. HOW CAN A PET DARE TO...
MY FRIENDS' WORDS ARE TRUE. YOU ARE INDEED A PET THAT I DEARLY LOVE, BUT YOU DEFINITELY LACK CONSCIOUSNESS.

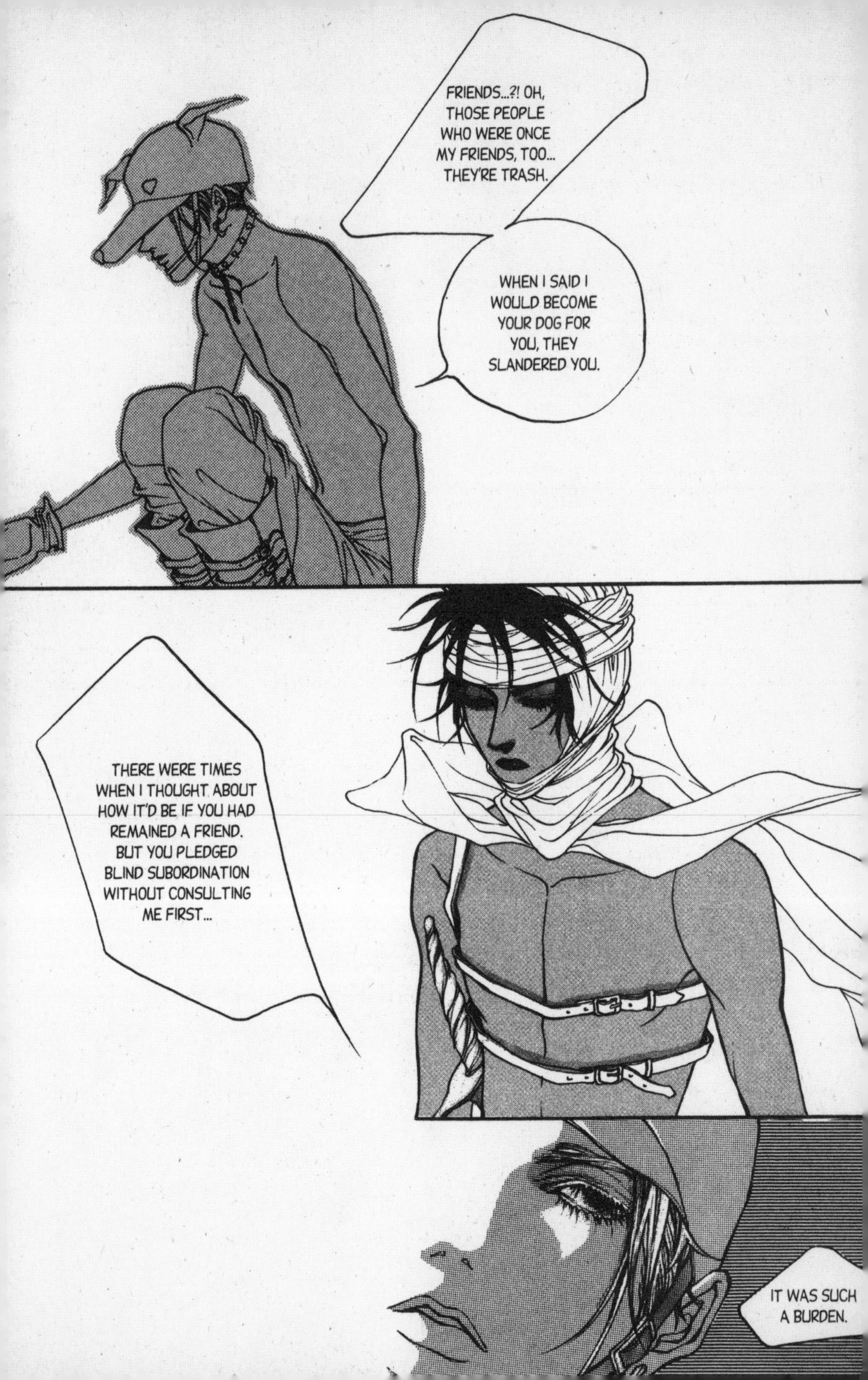
FRIENDS...?! OH, THOSE PEOPLE WHO WERE ONCE MY FRIENDS, TOO... THEY'RE TRASH.
WHEN I SAID I WOULD BECOME YOUR DOG FOR YOU, THEY SLANDERED YOU.
THERE WERE TIMES WHEN I THOUGHT ABOUT HOW IT'D BE IF YOU HAD REMAINED A FRIEND. BUT YOU PLEDGED BLIND SUBORDINATION WITHOUT CONSULTING ME FIRST...
IT WAS SUCH A BURDEN.

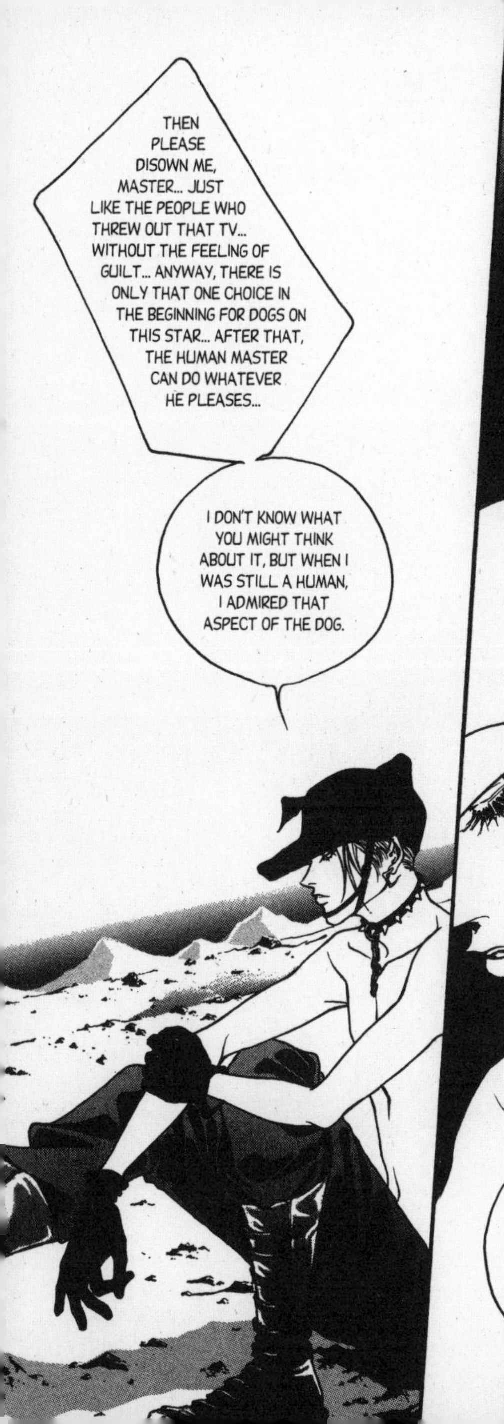
THEN PLEASE DISOWN ME, MASTER... JUST LIKE THE PEOPLE WHO THREW OUT THAT TV... WITHOUT THE FEELING OF GUILT... ANYWAY, THERE IS ONLY THAT ONE CHOICE IN THE BEGINNING FOR DOGS ON THIS STAR... AFTER THAT, THE HUMAN MASTER CAN DO WHATEVER HE PLEASES...
I DON'T KNOW WHAT YOU MIGHT THINK ABOUT IT, BUT WHEN I WAS STILL A HUMAN, I ADMIRED THAT ASPECT OF THE DOG.
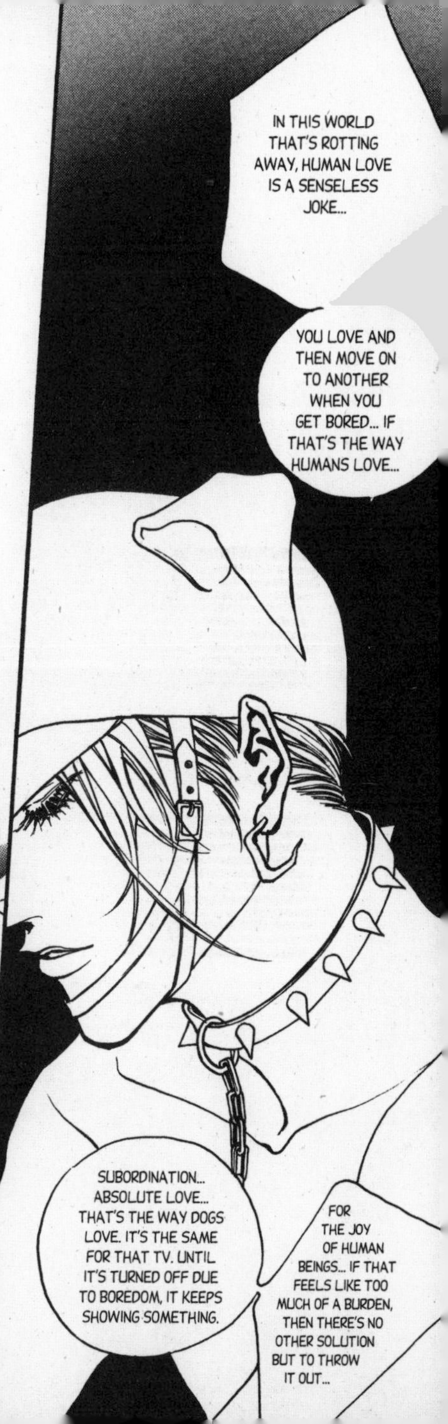
IN THIS WORLD THAT'S ROTTING AWAY, HUMAN LOVE IS A SENSELESS JOKE...
YOU LOVE AND THEN MOVE ON TO ANOTHER WHEN YOU GET BORED... IF THAT'S THE WAY HUMANS LOVE...
SUBORDINATION... ABSOLUTE LOVE... THAT'S THE WAY DOGS LOVE. IT'S THE SAME FOR THAT TV. UNTIL IT'S TURNED OFF DUE TO BOREDOM, IT KEEPS SHOWING SOMETHING.
FOR THE JOY OF HUMAN BEINGS... IF THAT FEELS LIKE TOO MUCH OF A BURDEN, THEN THERE'S NO OTHER SOLUTION BUT TO THROW IT OUT...

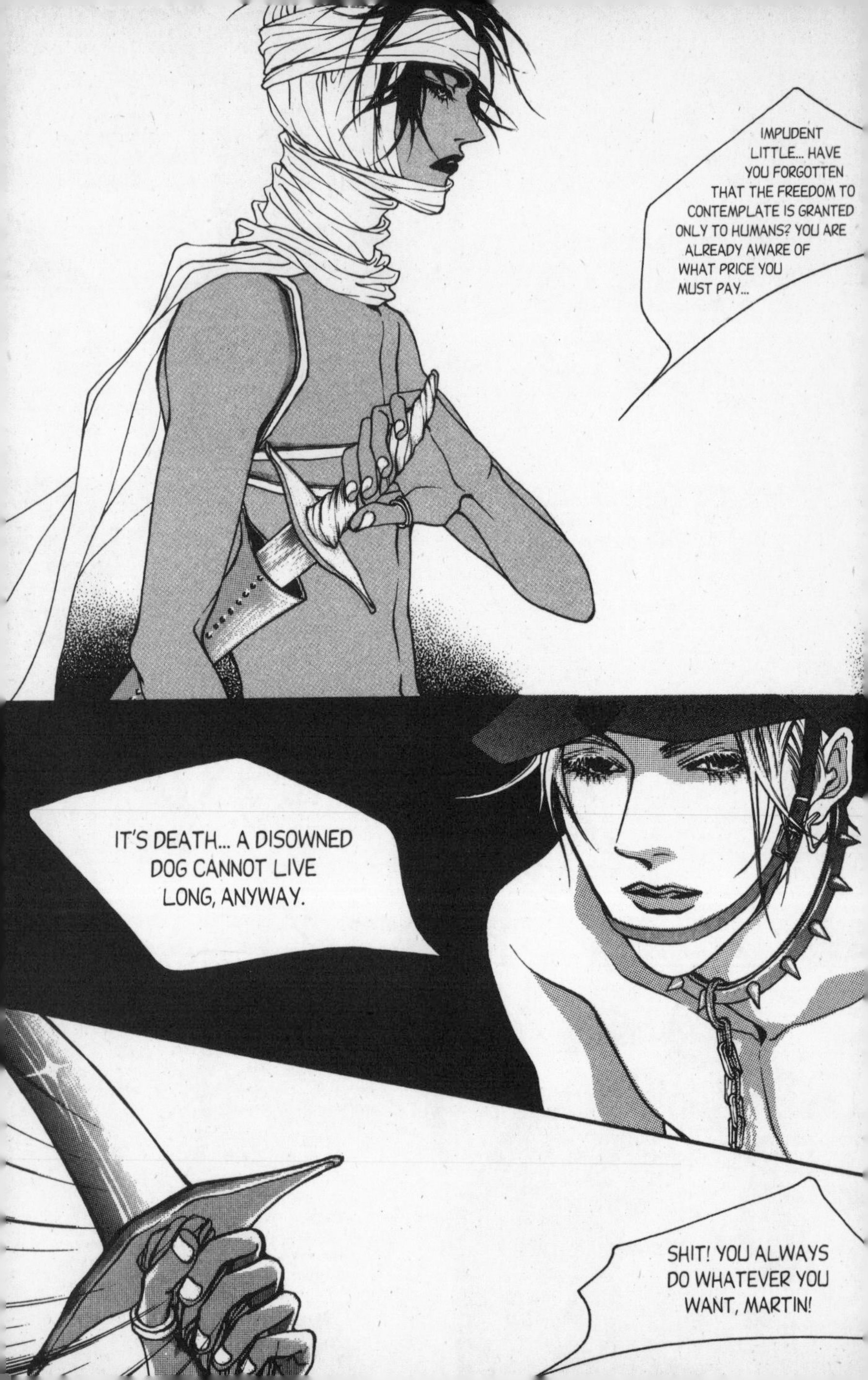
IMPUDENT LITTLE... HAVE YOU FORGOTTEN THAT THE FREEDOM TO CONTEMPLATE IS GRANTED ONLY TO HUMANS? YOU ARE ALREADY AWARE OF WHAT PRICE YOU MUST PAY...
IT'S DEATH... A DISOWNED DOG CANNOT LIVE LONG, ANYWAY.
SHIT! YOU ALWAYS DO WHATEVER YOU WANT, MARTIN!

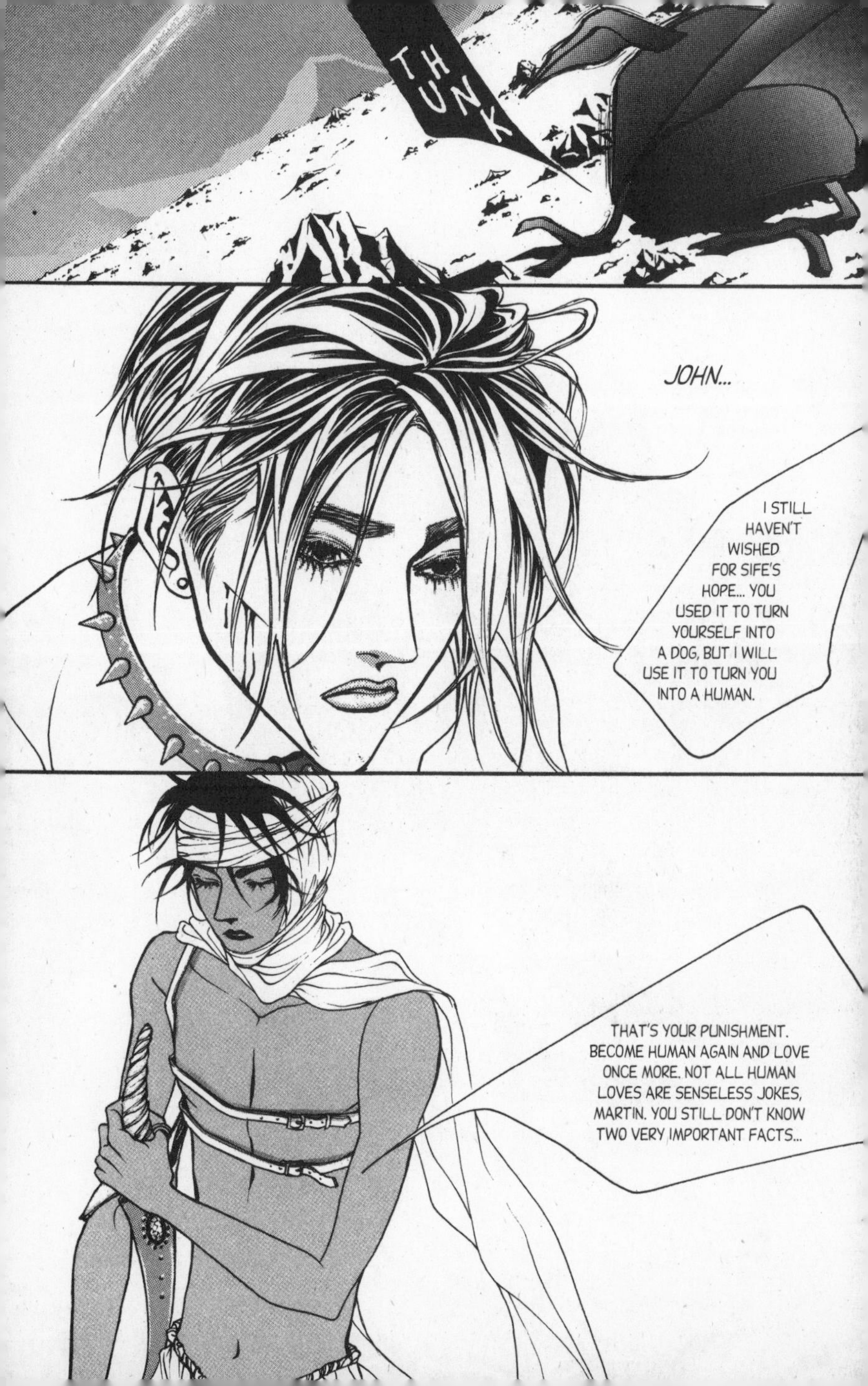
THUNK
JOHN...
I STILL HAVEN'T WISHED FOR SIFE'S HOPE... YOU USED IT TO TURN YOURSELF INTO A DOG, BUT I WILL USE IT TO TURN YOU INTO A HUMAN.
THAT'S YOUR PUNISHMENT. BECOME HUMAN AGAIN AND LOVE ONCE MORE. NOT ALL HUMAN LOVES ARE SENSELESS JOKES, MARTIN. YOU STILL DON'T KNOW TWO VERY IMPORTANT FACTS...

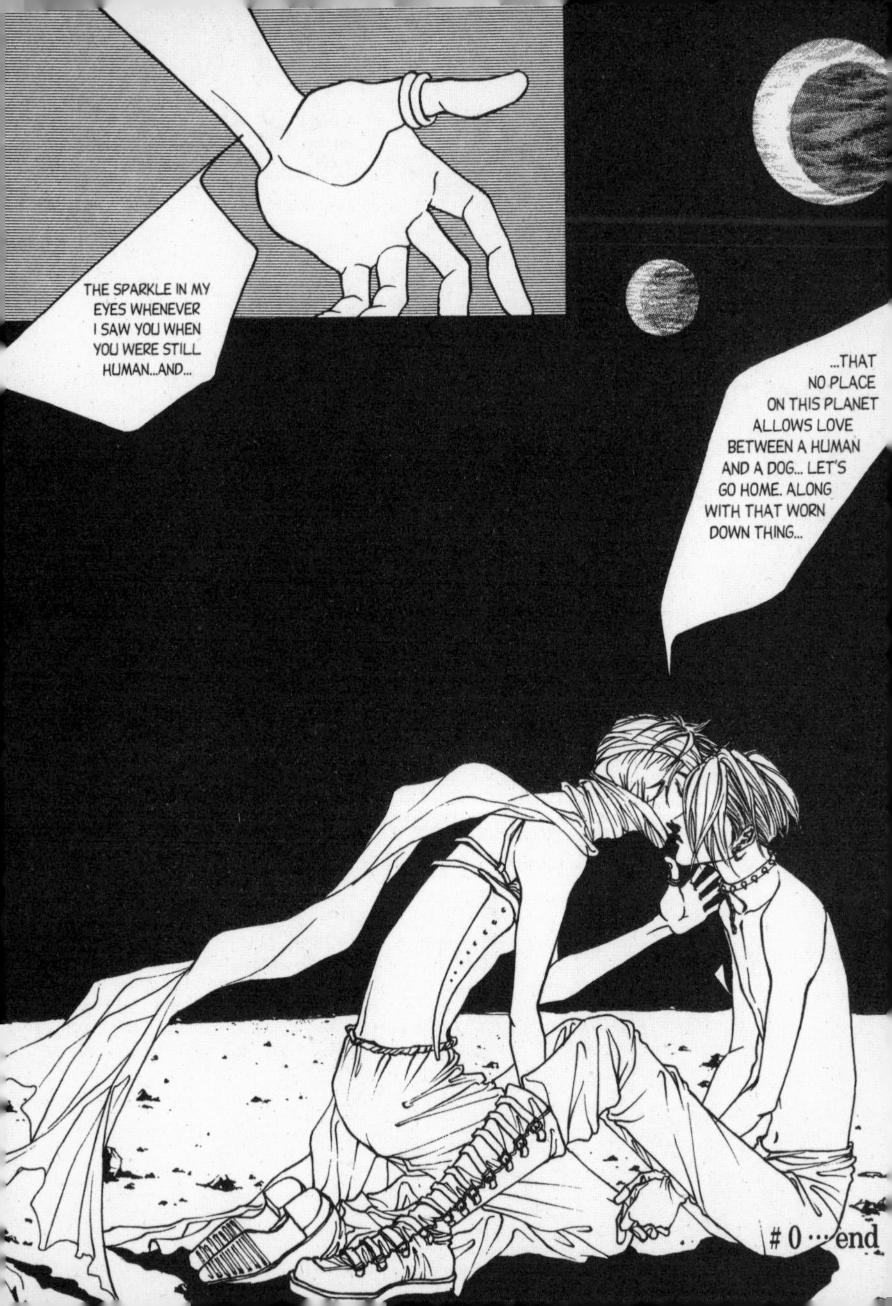
THE SPARKLE IN MY EYES WHENEVER I SAW YOU WHEN YOU WERE STILL HUMAN...AND...
...THAT NO PLACE ON THIS PLANET ALLOWS LOVE BETWEEN A HUMAN AND A DOG... LET'S GO HOME. ALONG WITH THAT WORN DOWN THING...
0 ... end

#1

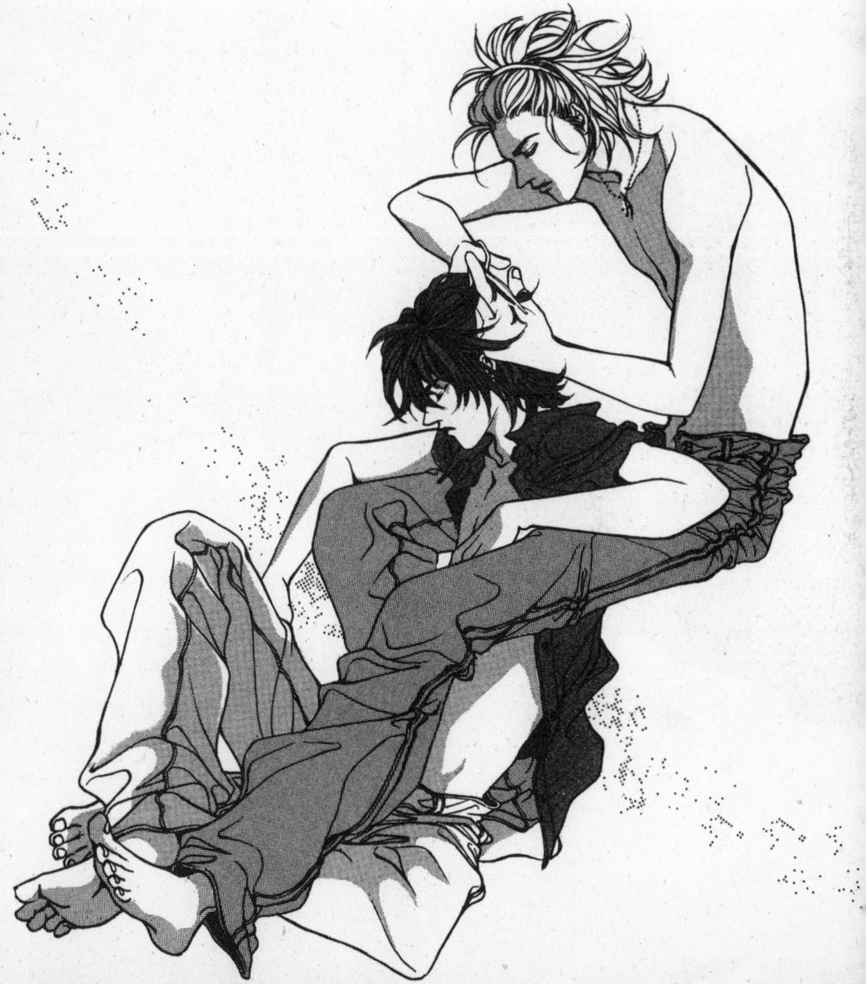

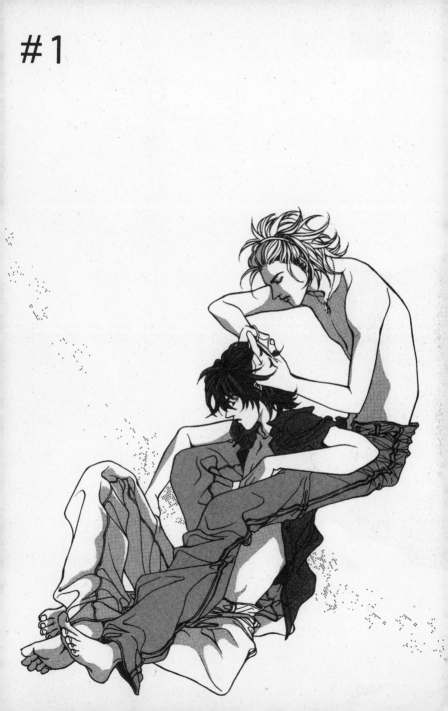

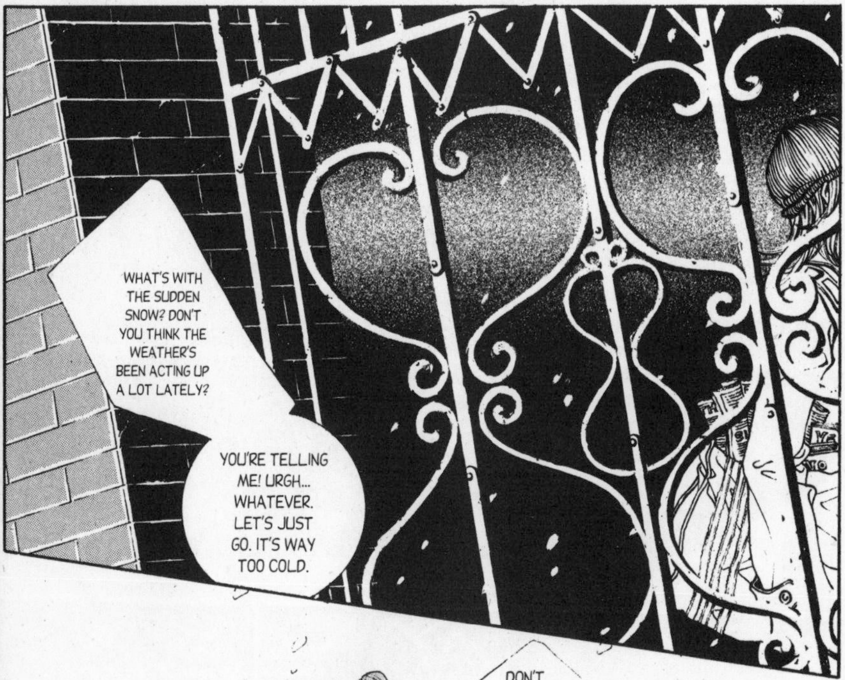
WHAT'S WITH THE SUDDEN SNOW? DON'T YOU THINK THE WEATHER'S BEEN ACTING UP A LOT LATELY?
YOU'RE TELLING ME! URGH... WHATEVER. LET'S JUST GO. IT'S WAY TOO COLD.
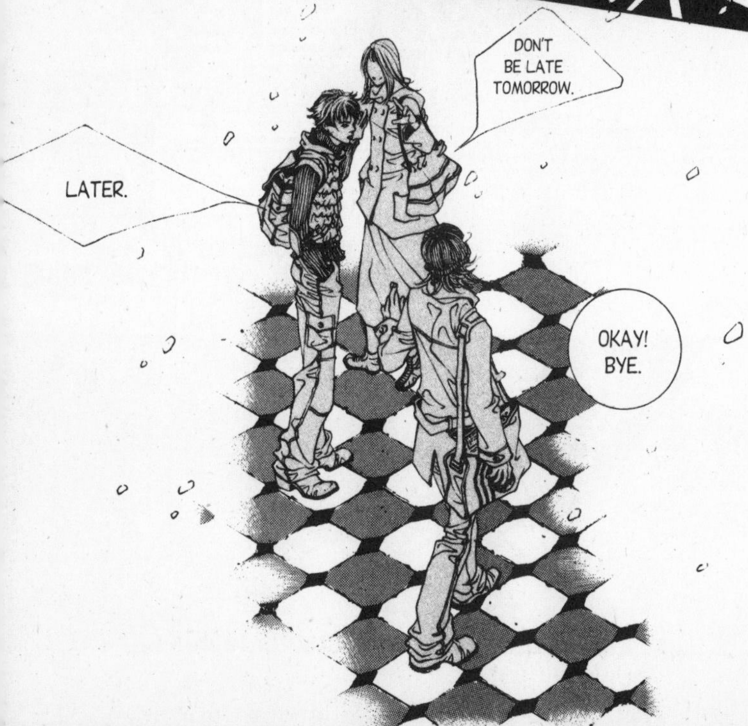
DON'T BE LATE TOMORROW.
LATER.
OKAY! BYE.

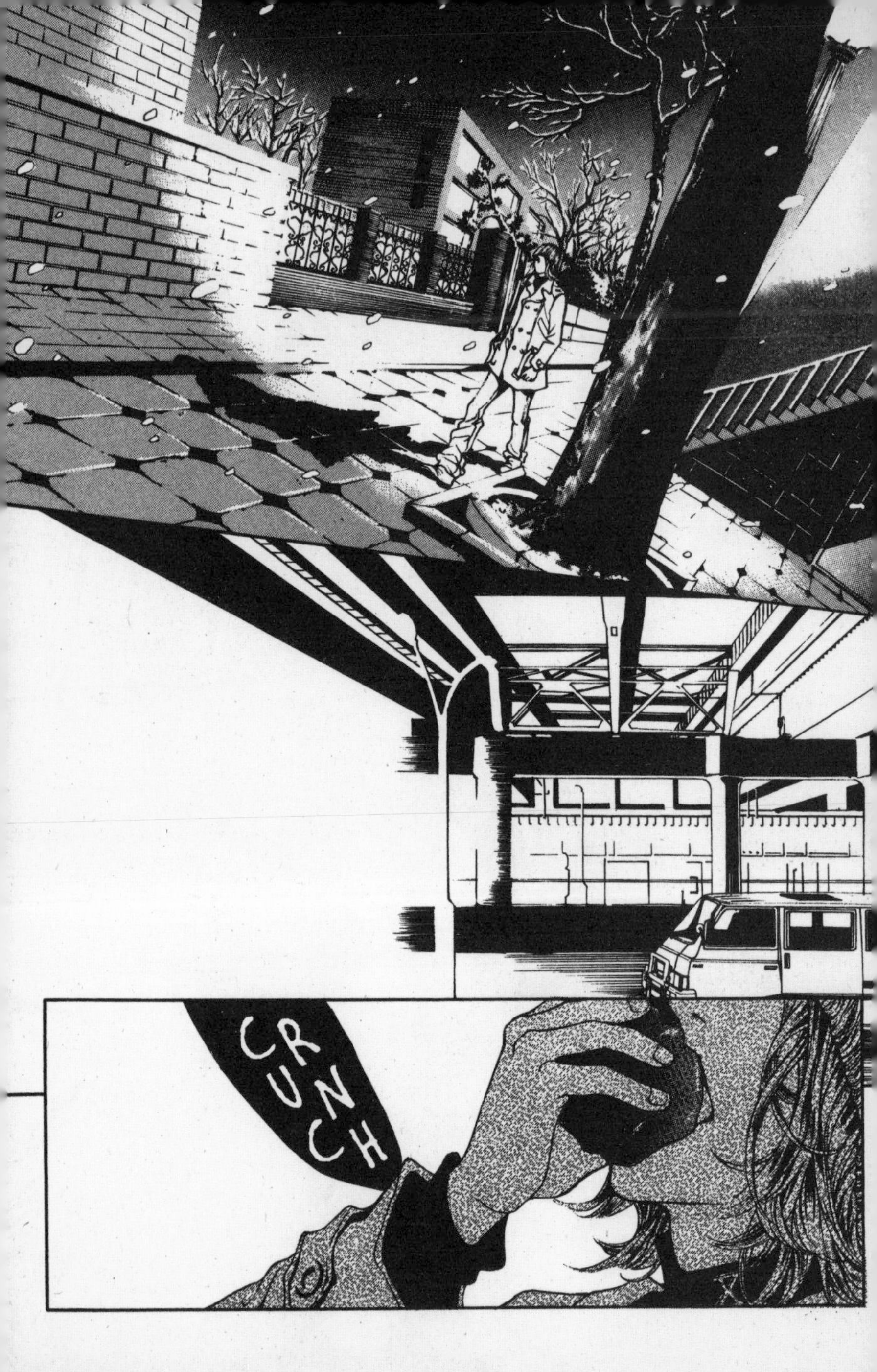
CRUNCH

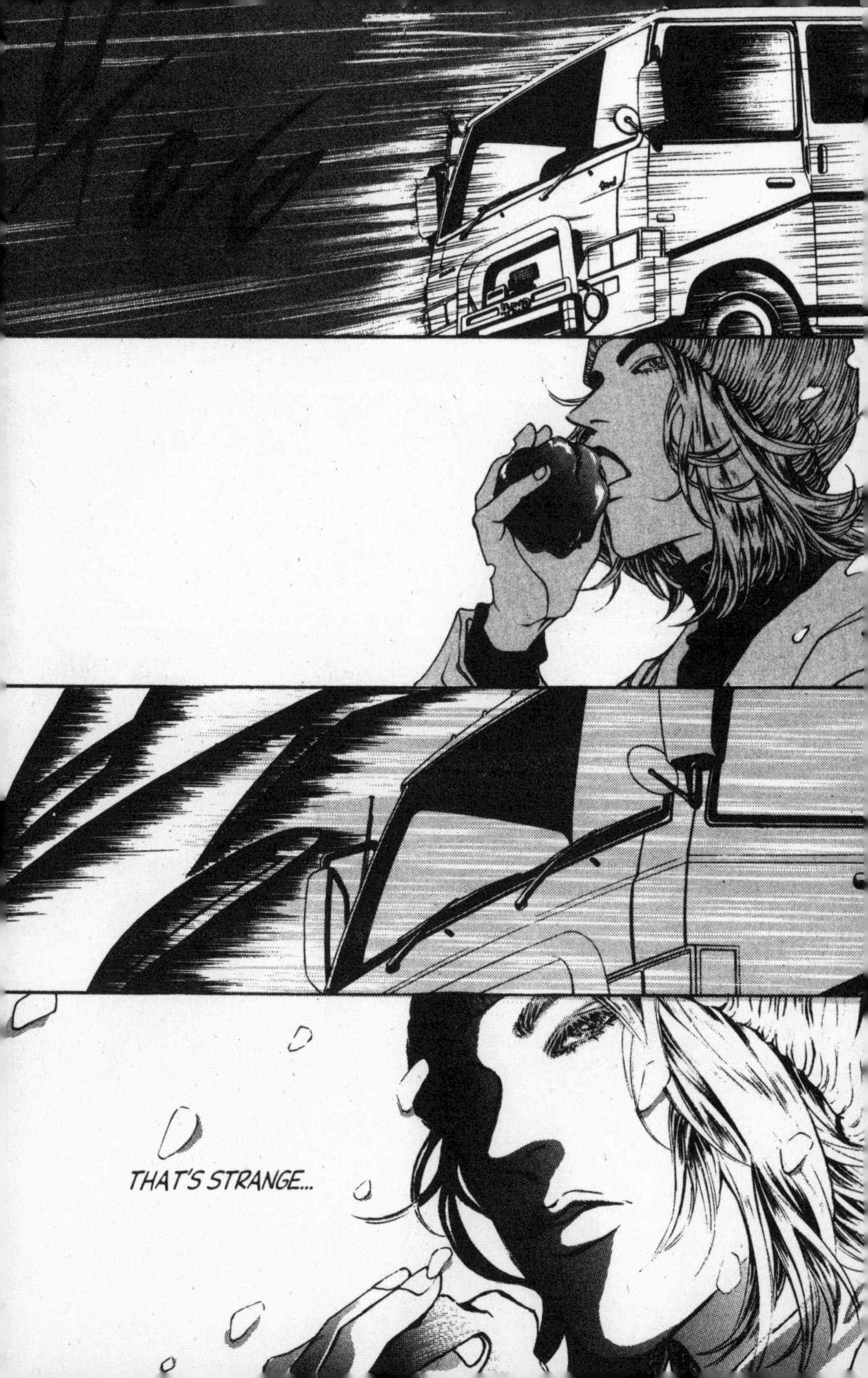
THAT'S STRANGE...

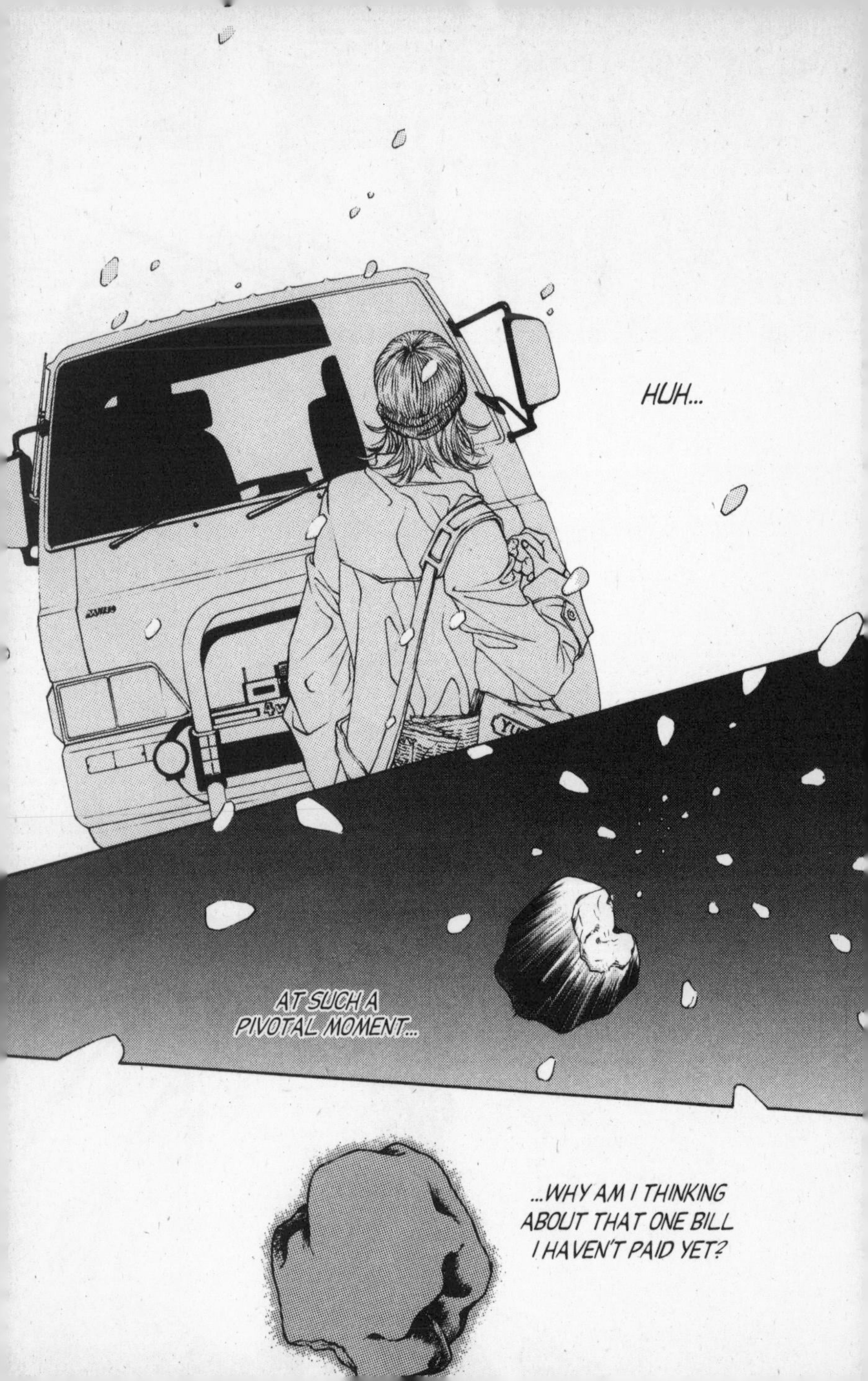
HUH...
AT SUCH A PIVOTAL MOMENT...
...WHY AM I THINKING ABOUT THAT ONE BILL I HAVEN'T PAID YET?

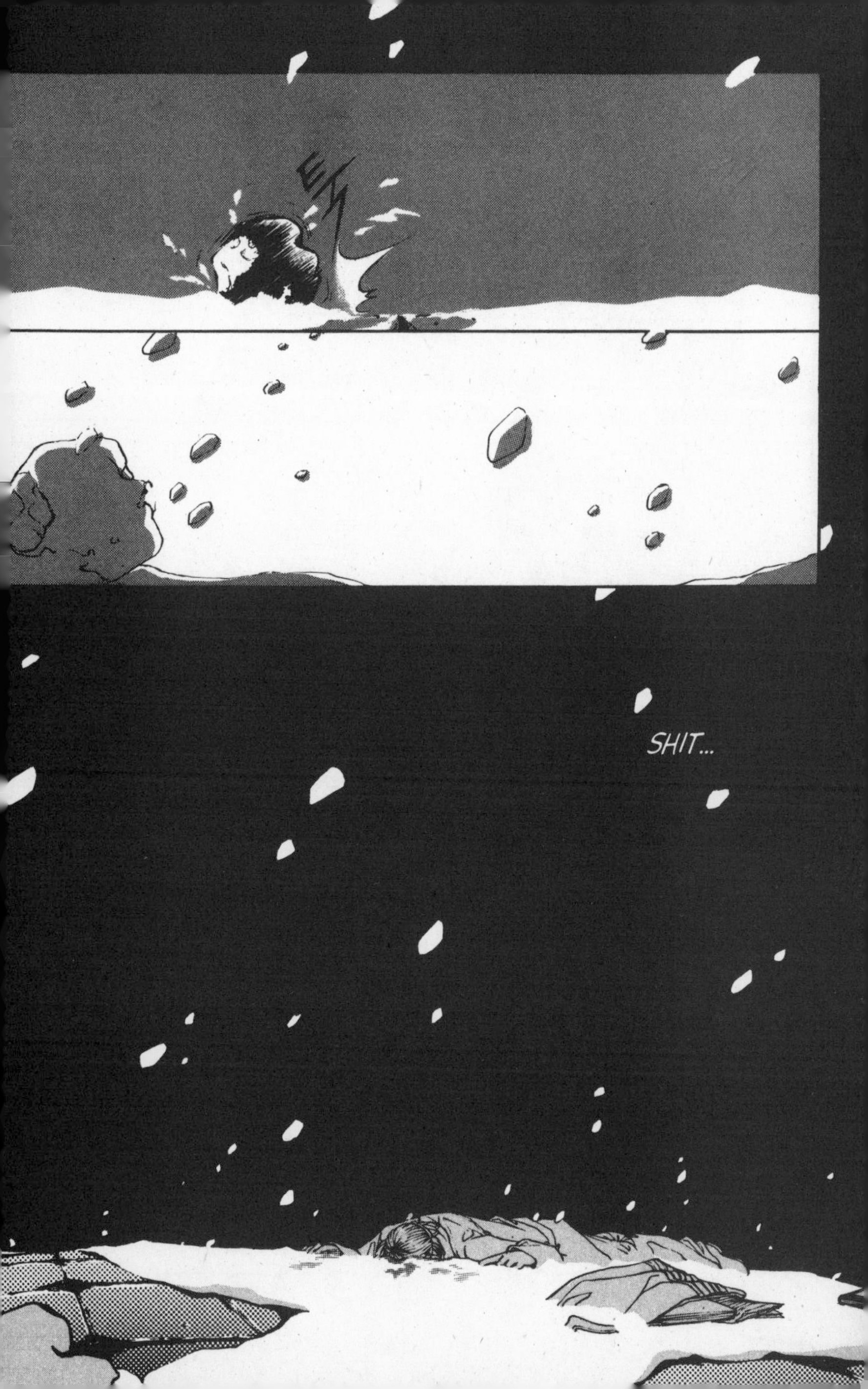
SHIT...

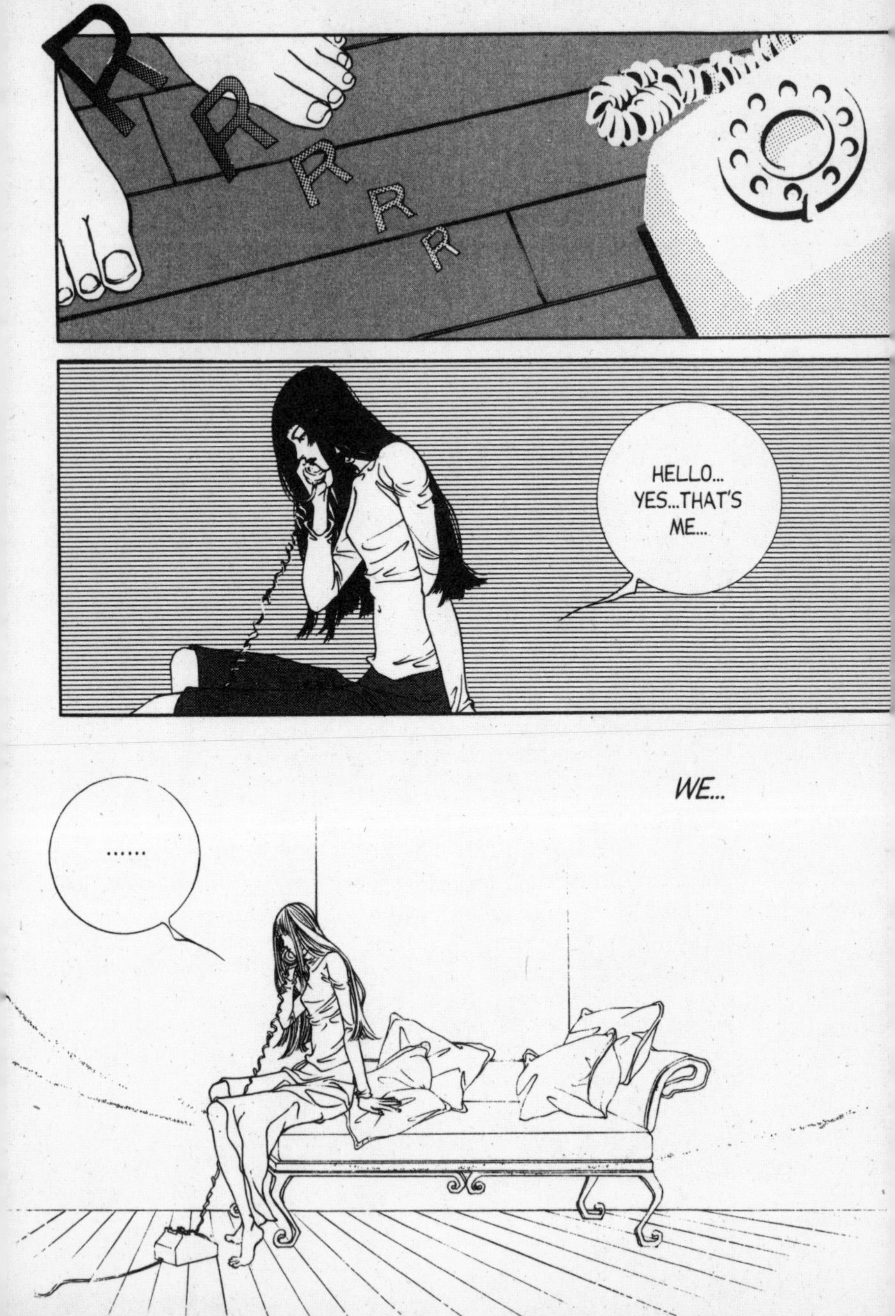
RRRRRR
HELLO... YES...THAT'S ME...
......
WE...

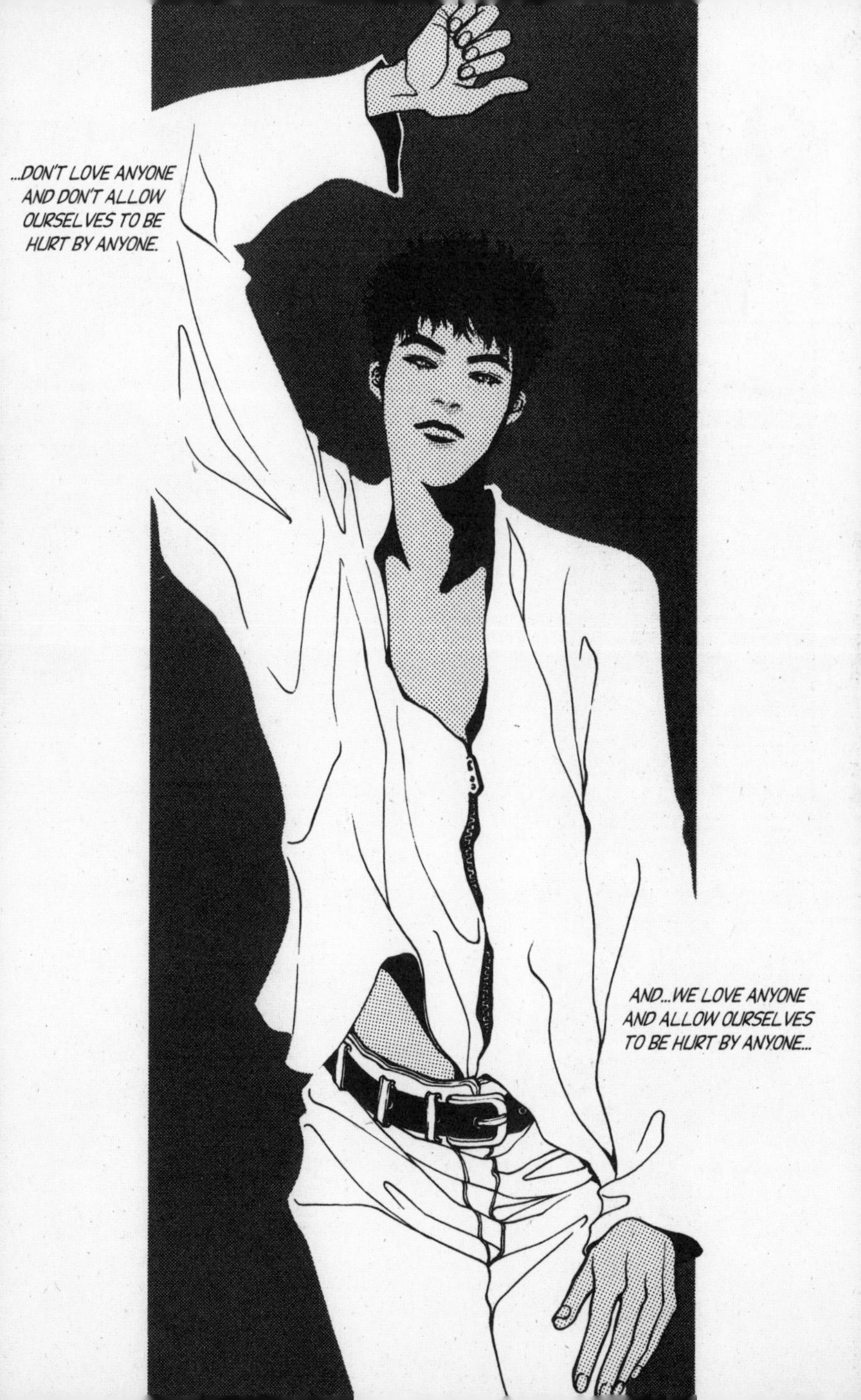
...DON'T LOVE ANYONE AND DON'T ALLOW OURSELVES TO BE HURT BY ANYONE.
AND...WE LOVE ANYONE AND ALLOW OURSELVES TO BE HURT BY ANYONE...

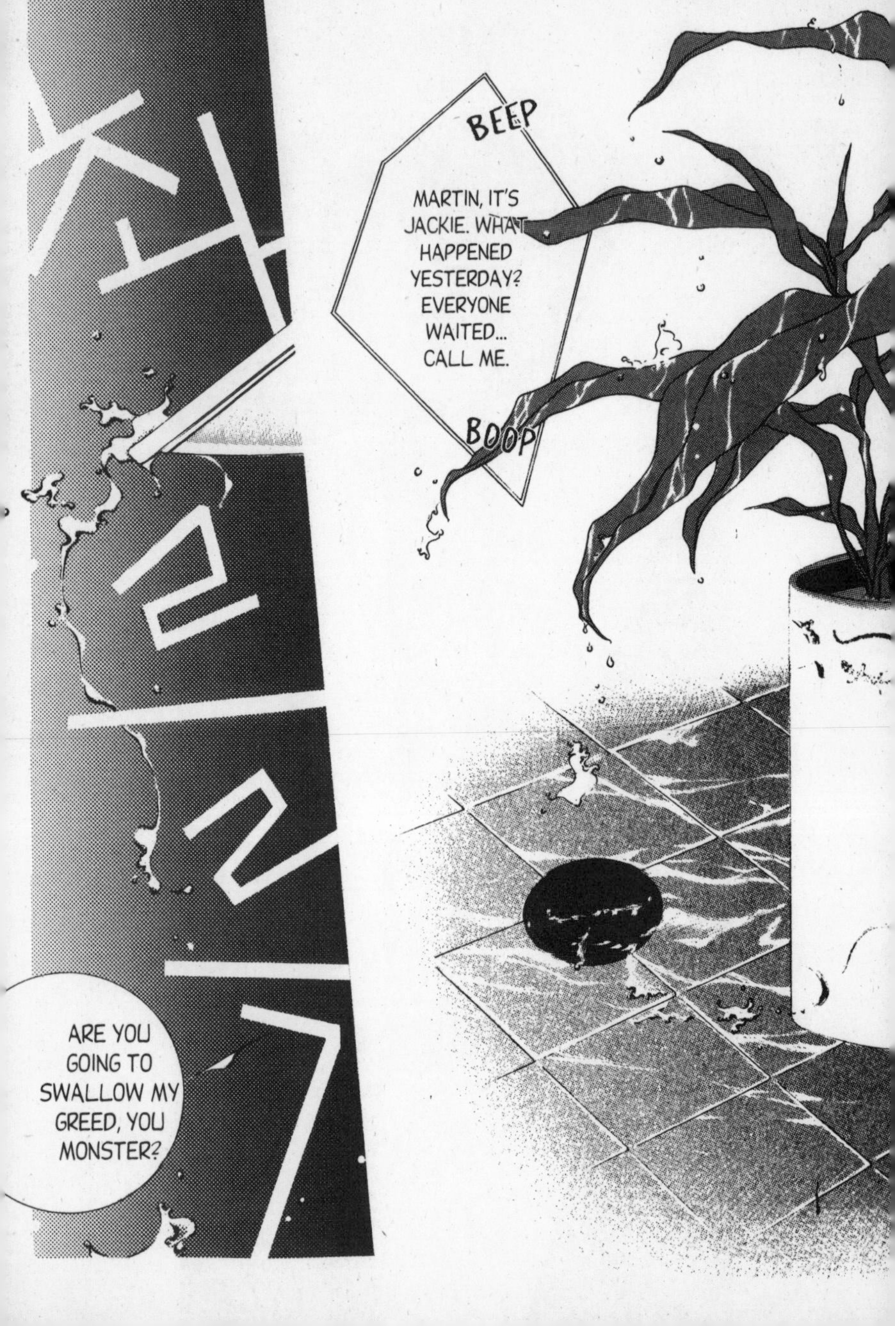
ARE YOU GOING TO SWALLOW MY GREED, YOU MONSTER?
BEEP
MARTIN, IT'S JACKIE. WHAT HAPPENED YESTERDAY? EVERYONE WAITED... CALL ME.
BOOP

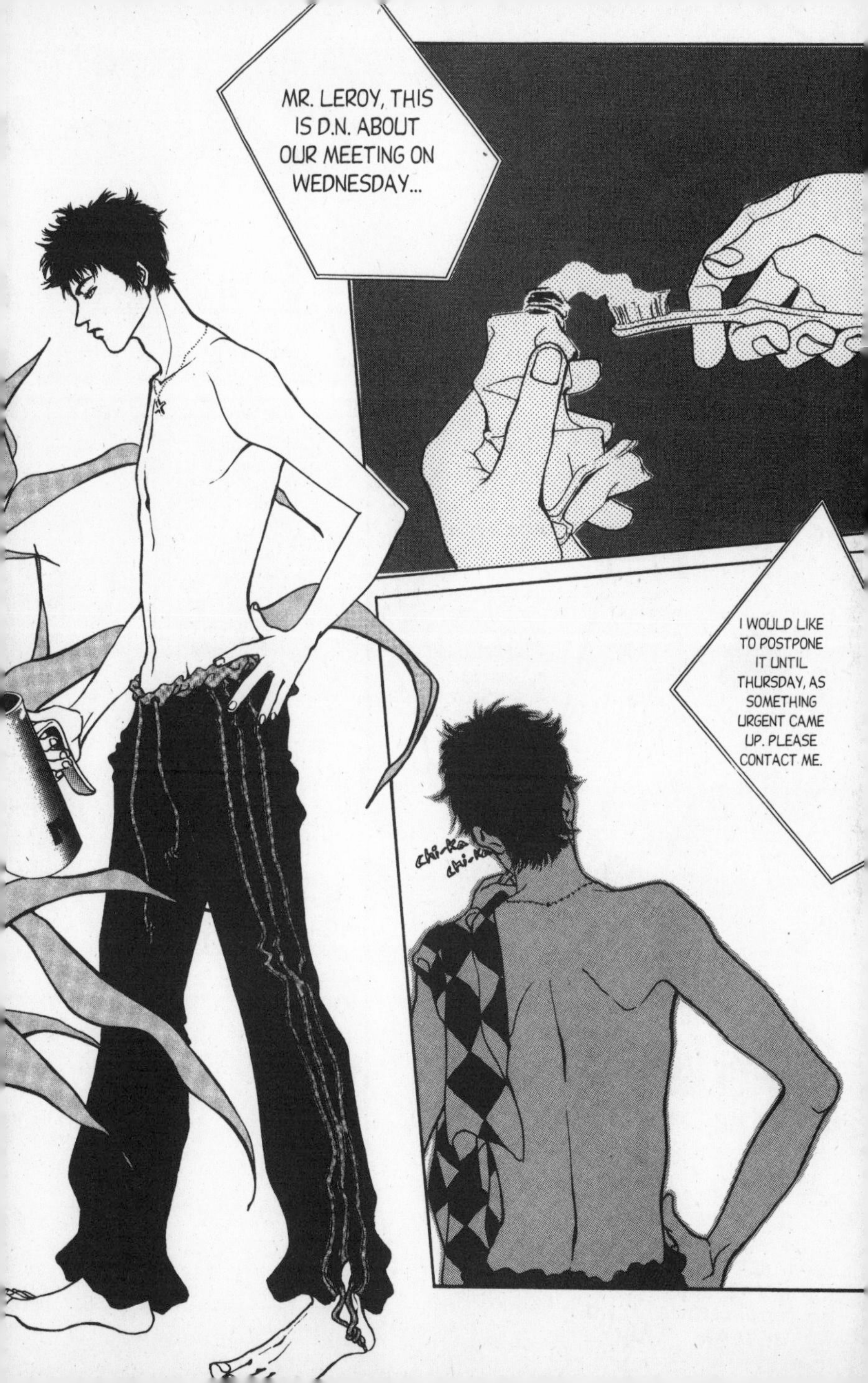
MR. LEROY, THIS IS D.N. ABOUT OUR MEETING ON WEDNESDAY...
I WOULD LIKE TO POSTPONE IT UNTIL THURSDAY, AS SOMETHING URGENT CAME UP. PLEASE CONTACT ME.
chi-ka chi-ka

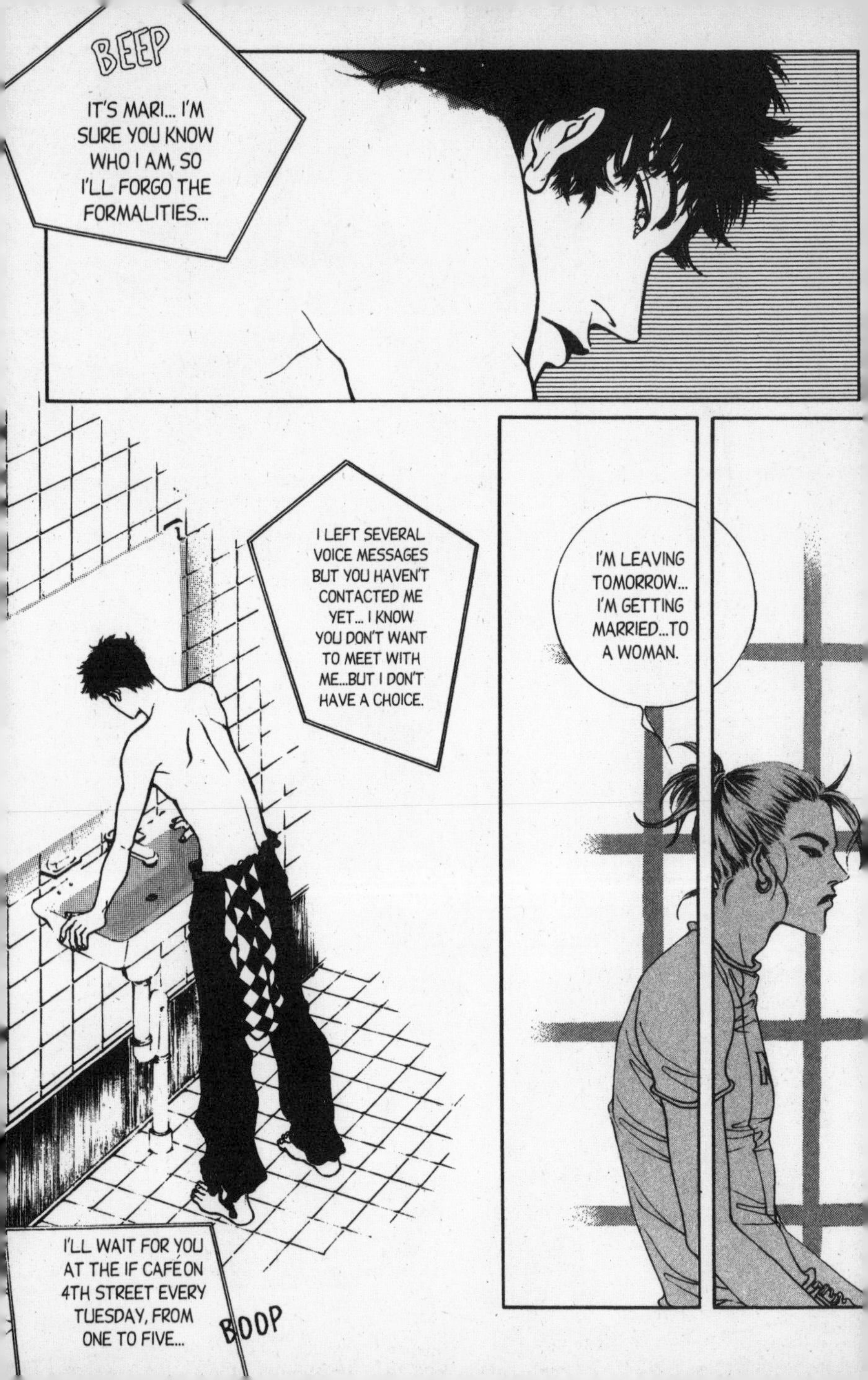
BEEP
IT'S MARI... I'M SURE YOU KNOW WHO I AM, SO I'LL FORGO THE FORMALITIES...
I LEFT SEVERAL VOICE MESSAGES BUT YOU HAVEN'T CONTACTED ME YET... I KNOW YOU DON'T WANT TO MEET WITH ME...BUT I DON'T HAVE A CHOICE.
I'LL WAIT FOR YOU AT THE IF CAFÉ ON 4TH STREET EVERY TUESDAY, FROM ONE TO FIVE...
BOOP
I'M LEAVING TOMORROW... I'M GETTING MARRIED...TO A WOMAN.

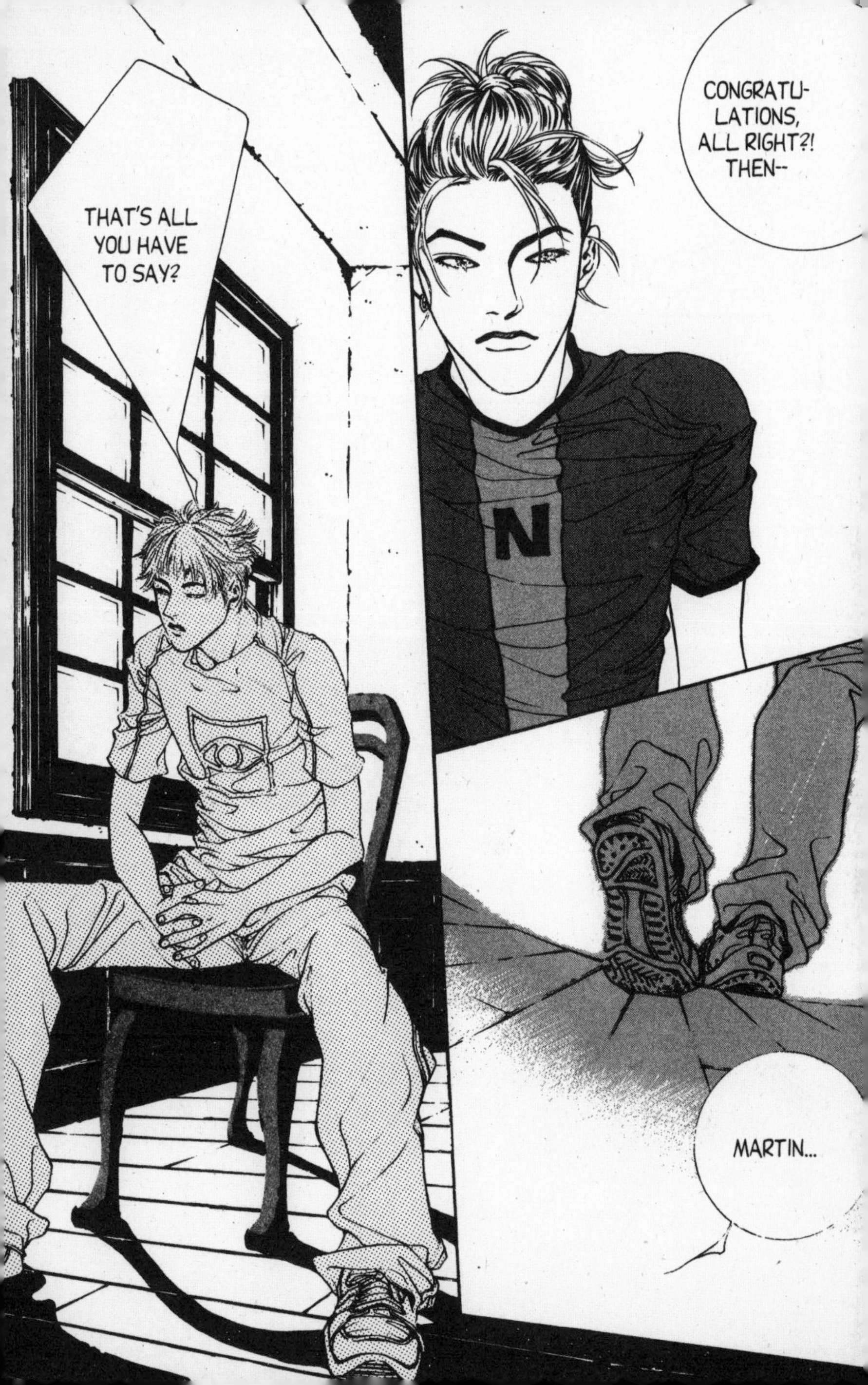
THAT'S ALL YOU HAVE TO SAY?
CONGRATU-LATIONS, ALL RIGHT?! THEN--
N
MARTIN...

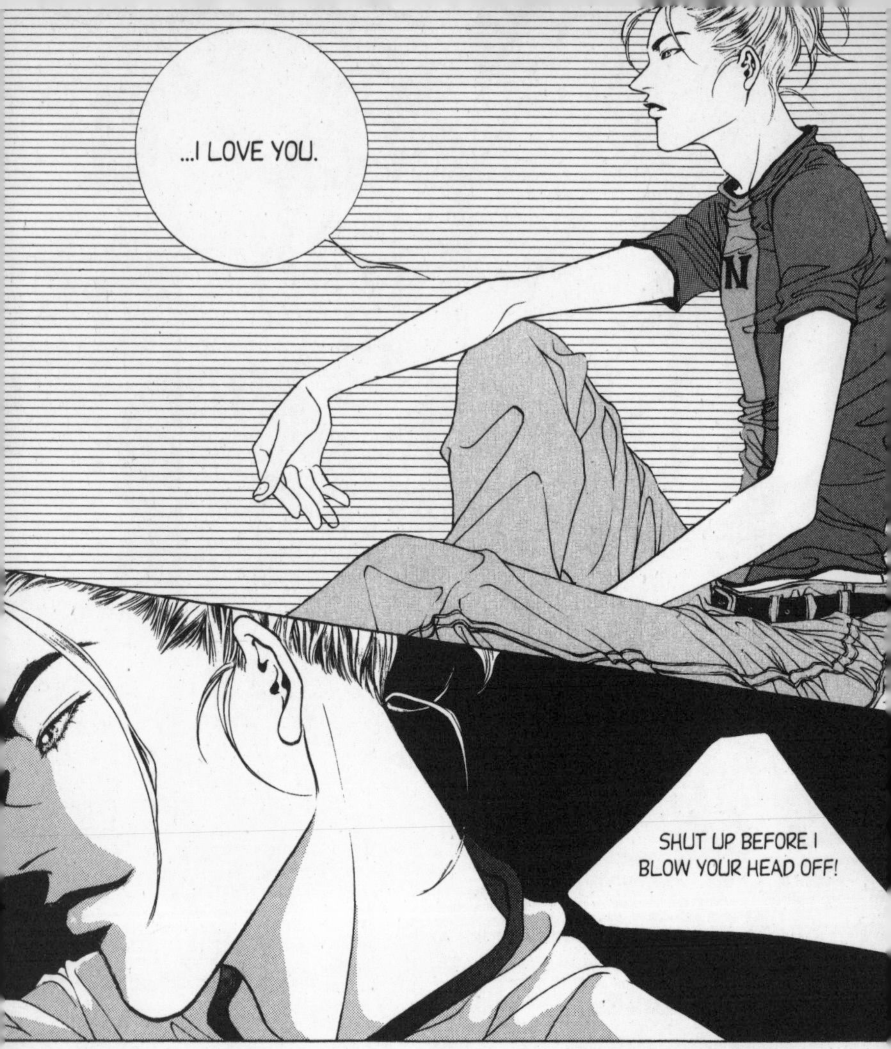
...I LOVE YOU.
SHUT UP BEFORE I BLOW YOUR HEAD OFF!

JOHN LEFT THE DAY AFTER THAT, AND THE LIME SCENT THAT HAD PERVADED THE BATHROOM FOR THREE YEARS ALSO DISAPPEARED.

I HATED THAT SMELL.

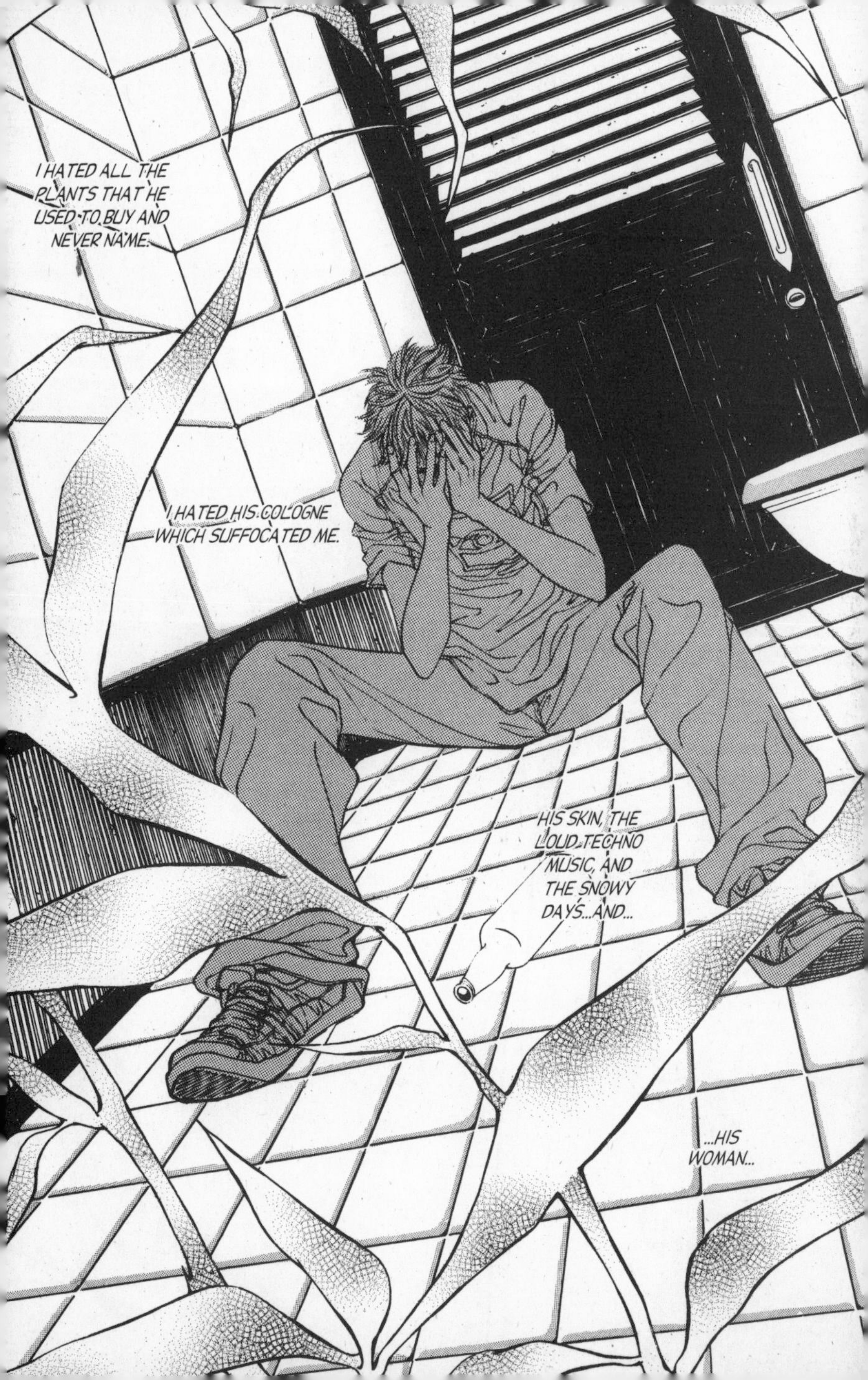
I HATED ALL THE PLANTS THAT HE USED TO BUY AND NEVER NAME.
I HATED HIS COLOGNE WHICH SUFFOCATED ME.
HIS SKIN, THE LOUD TECHNO MUSIC, AND THE SNOWY DAYS...AND...
...HIS WOMAN...

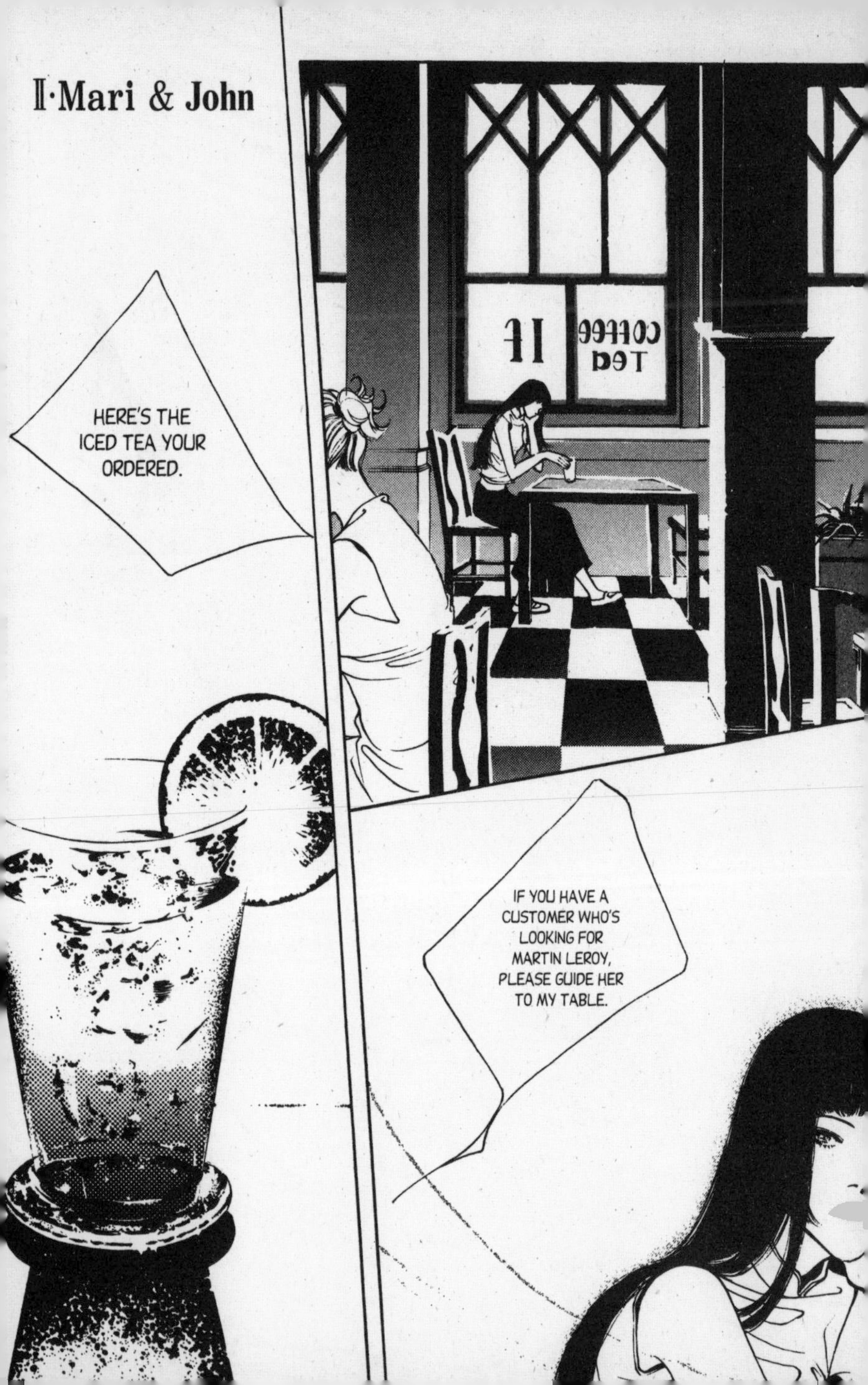
II·Mari & John
HERE'S THE ICED TEA YOUR ORDERED.
IF YOU HAVE A CUSTOMER WHO'S LOOKING FOR MARTIN LEROY, PLEASE GUIDE HER TO MY TABLE.

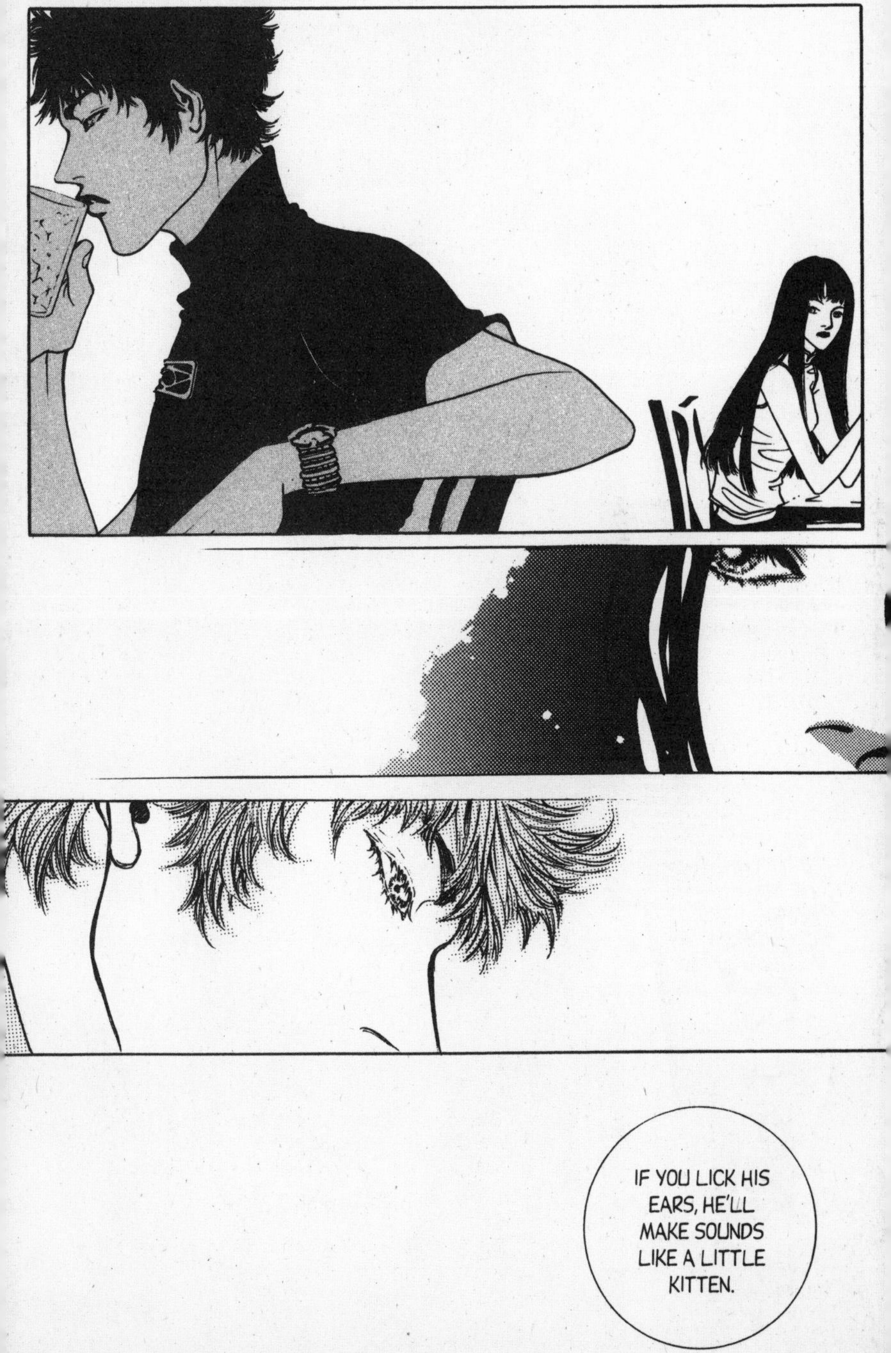
IF YOU LICK HIS EARS, HE'LL MAKE SOUNDS LIKE A LITTLE KITTEN.

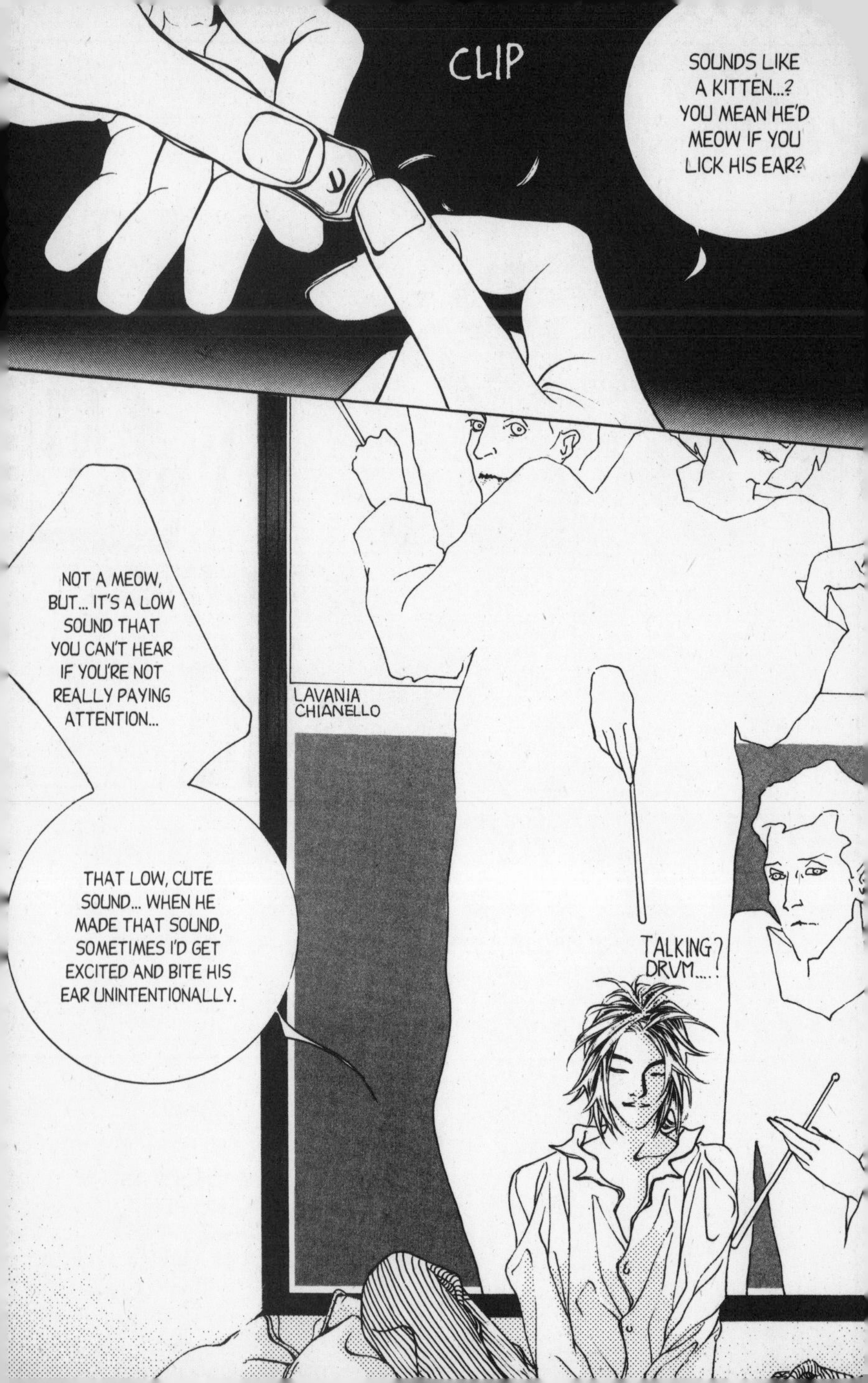
CLIP
SOUNDS LIKE A KITTEN...? YOU MEAN HE'D MEOW IF YOU LICK HIS EAR?
NOT A MEOW, BUT... IT'S A LOW SOUND THAT YOU CAN'T HEAR IF YOU'RE NOT REALLY PAYING ATTENTION...
LAVANIA CHIANELLO
THAT LOW, CUTE SOUND... WHEN HE MADE THAT SOUND, SOMETIMES I'D GET EXCITED AND BITE HIS EAR UNINTENTIONALLY.
TALKING DRUM...?

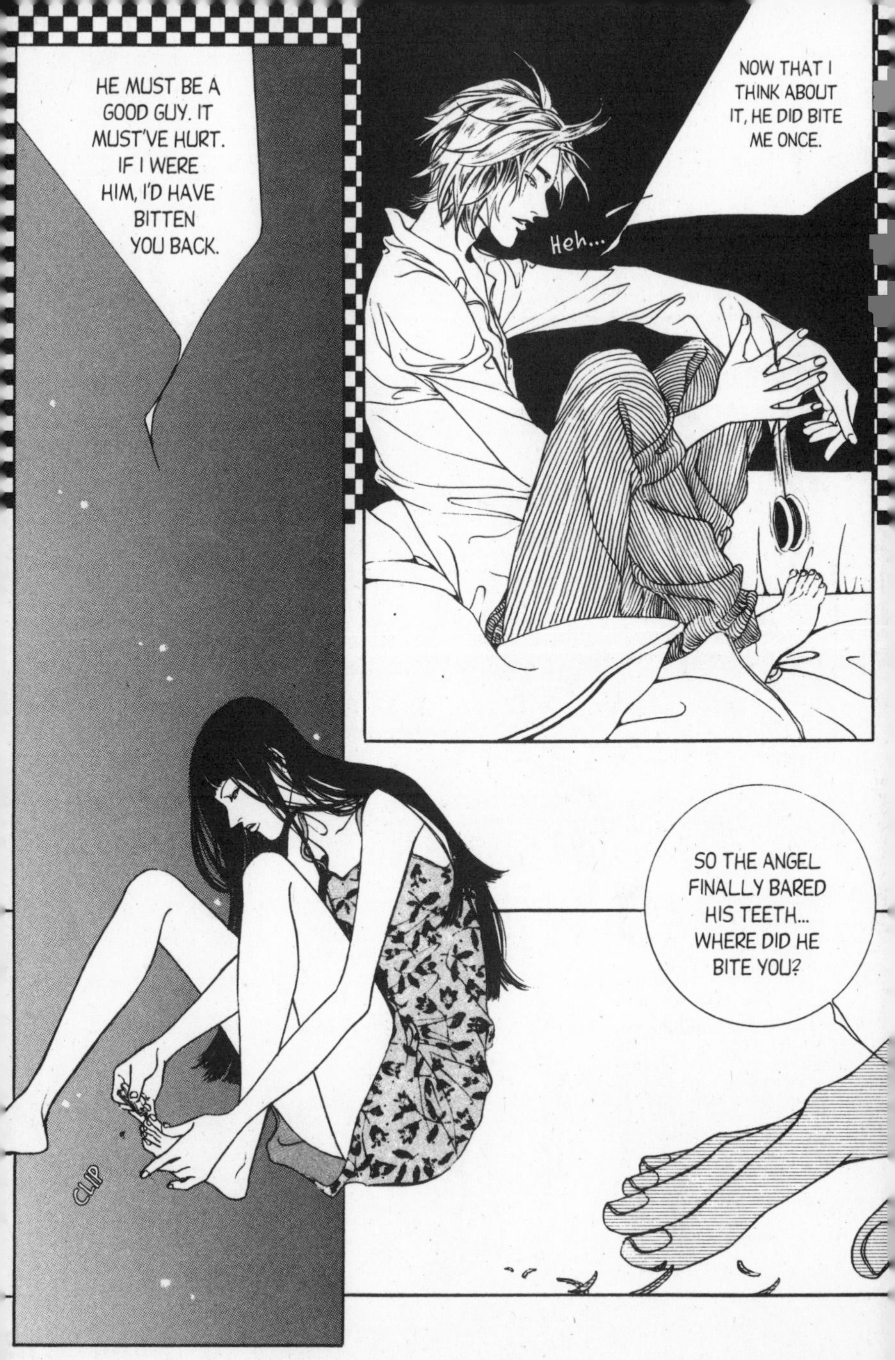
HE MUST BE A GOOD GUY. IT MUST'VE HURT. IF I WERE HIM, I'D HAVE BITTEN YOU BACK.
CLIP
NOW THAT I THINK ABOUT IT, HE DID BITE ME ONCE.
Heh...
SO THE ANGEL FINALLY BARED HIS TEETH... WHERE DID HE BITE YOU?

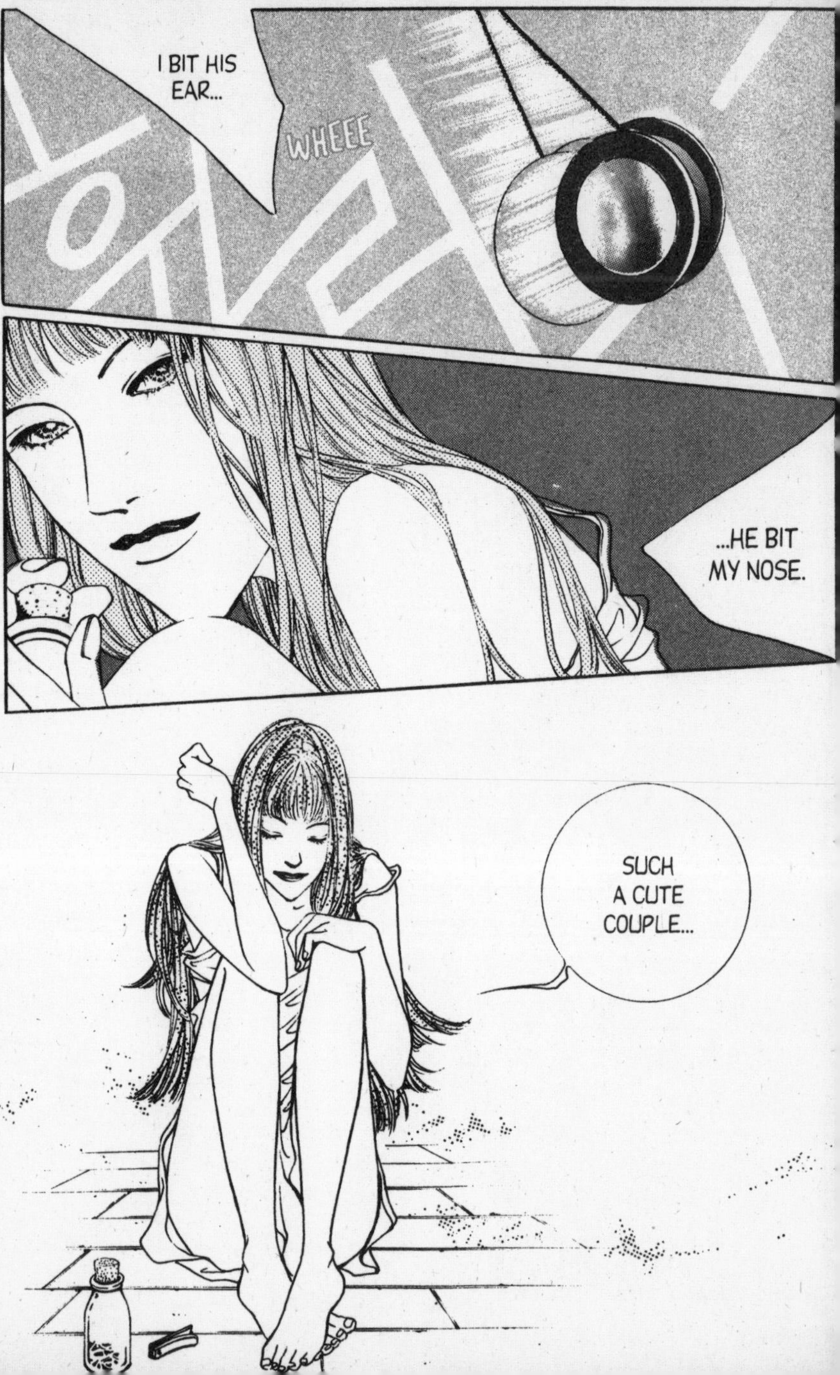
I BIT HIS EAR...
WHEEE
...HE BIT MY NOSE.
SUCH A CUTE COUPLE...

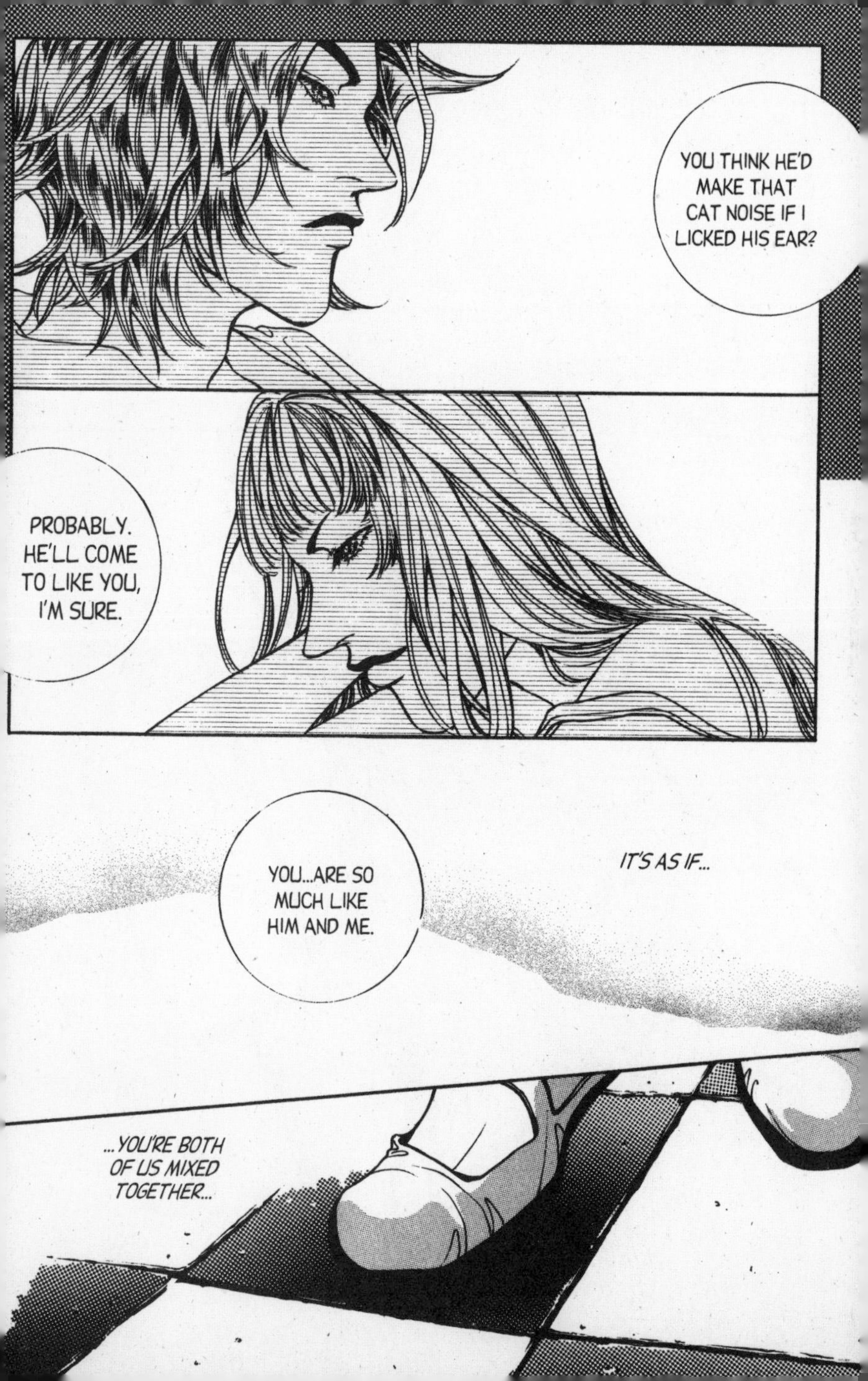
YOU THINK HE'D MAKE THAT CAT NOISE IF I LICKED HIS EAR?
PROBABLY. HE'LL COME TO LIKE YOU, I'M SURE.
YOU...ARE SO MUCH LIKE HIM AND ME.
IT'S AS IF...
...YOU'RE BOTH OF US MIXED TOGETHER...

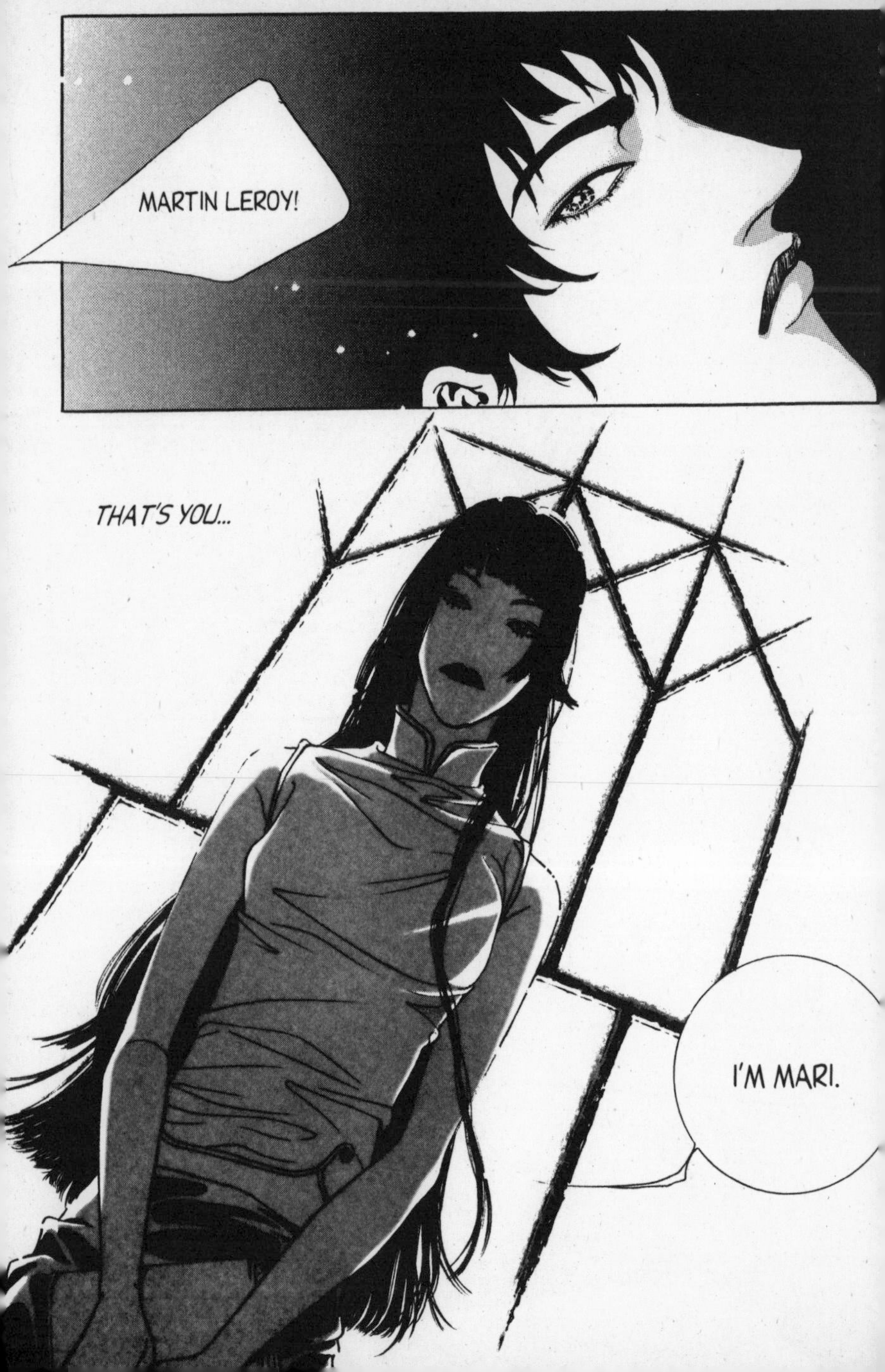
MARTIN LEROY!
THAT'S YOU...
I'M MARI.

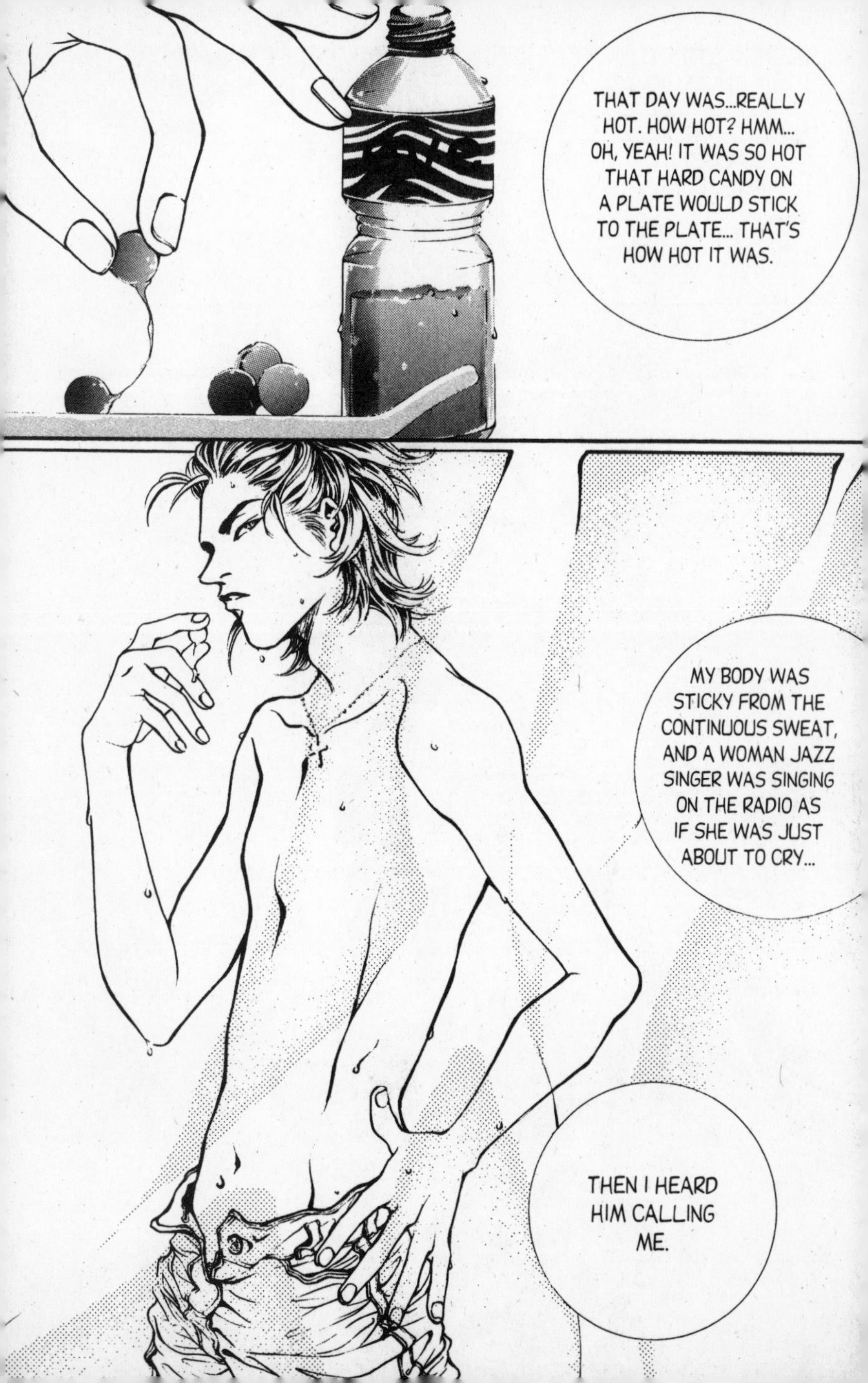
THAT DAY WAS...REALLY HOT. HOW HOT? HMM... OH, YEAH! IT WAS SO HOT THAT HARD CANDY ON A PLATE WOULD STICK TO THE PLATE... THAT'S HOW HOT IT WAS.
MY BODY WAS STICKY FROM THE CONTINUOUS SWEAT, AND A WOMAN JAZZ SINGER WAS SINGING ON THE RADIO AS IF SHE WAS JUST ABOUT TO CRY...
THEN I HEARD HIM CALLING ME.

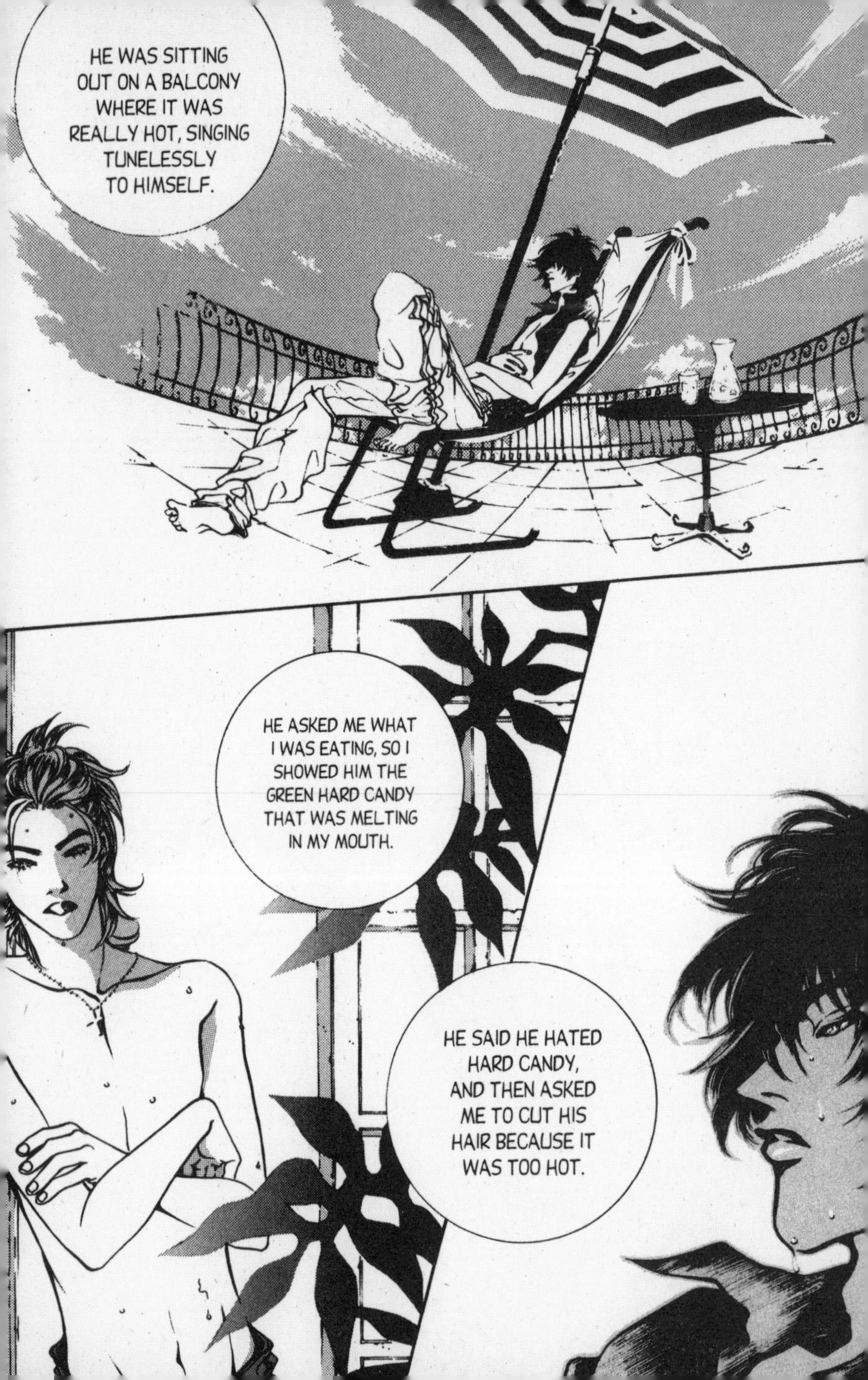
HE WAS SITTING OUT ON A BALCONY WHERE IT WAS REALLY HOT, SINGING TUNELESSLY TO HIMSELF.
HE ASKED ME WHAT I WAS EATING, SO I SHOWED HIM THE GREEN HARD CANDY THAT WAS MELTING IN MY MOUTH.
HE SAID HE HATED HARD CANDY, AND THEN ASKED ME TO CUT HIS HAIR BECAUSE IT WAS TOO HOT.

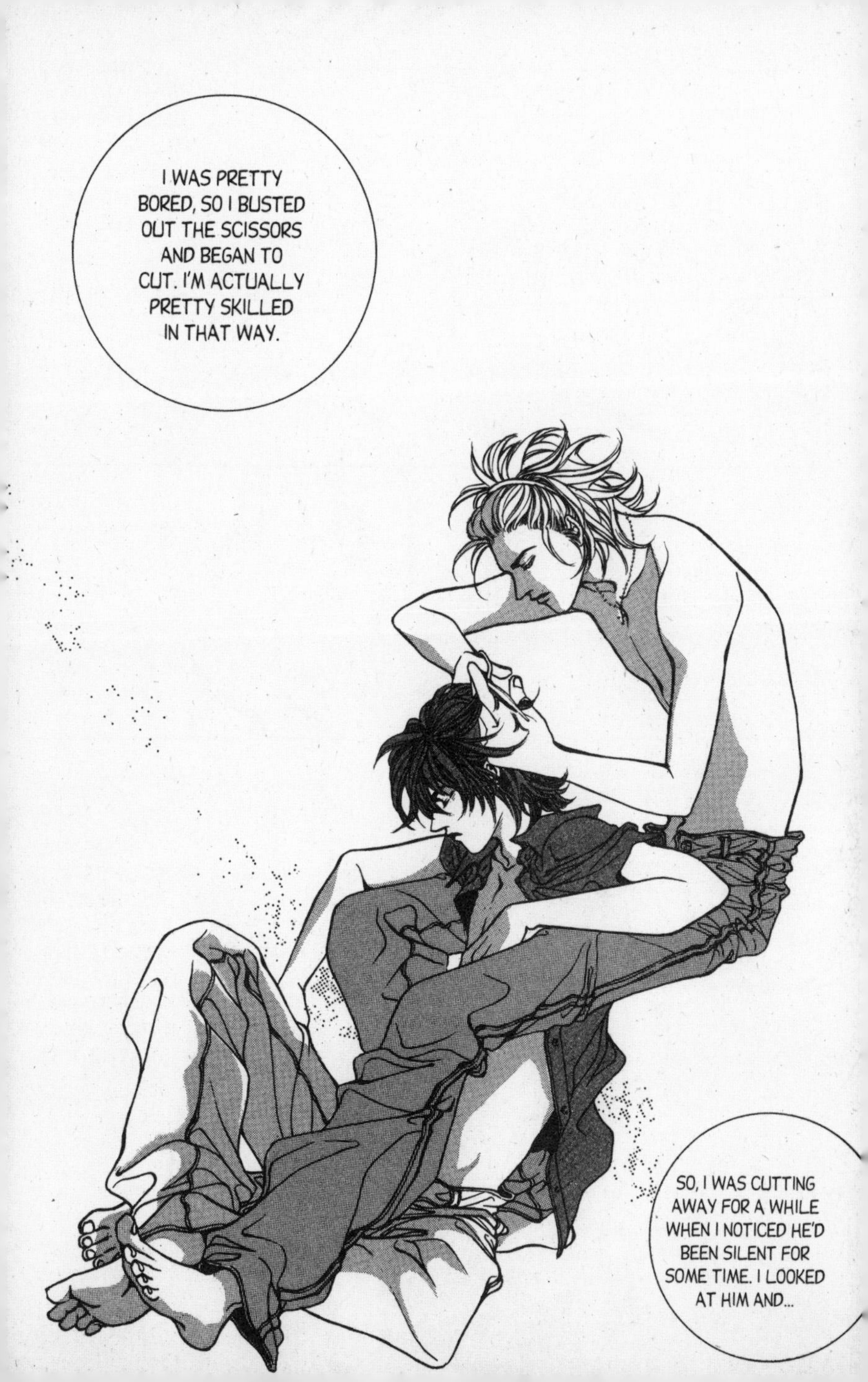
I WAS PRETTY BORED, SO I BUSTED OUT THE SCISSORS AND BEGAN TO CUT. I'M ACTUALLY PRETTY SKILLED IN THAT WAY.
SO, I WAS CUTTING AWAY FOR A WHILE WHEN I NOTICED HE'D BEEN SILENT FOR SOME TIME. I LOOKED AT HIM AND...

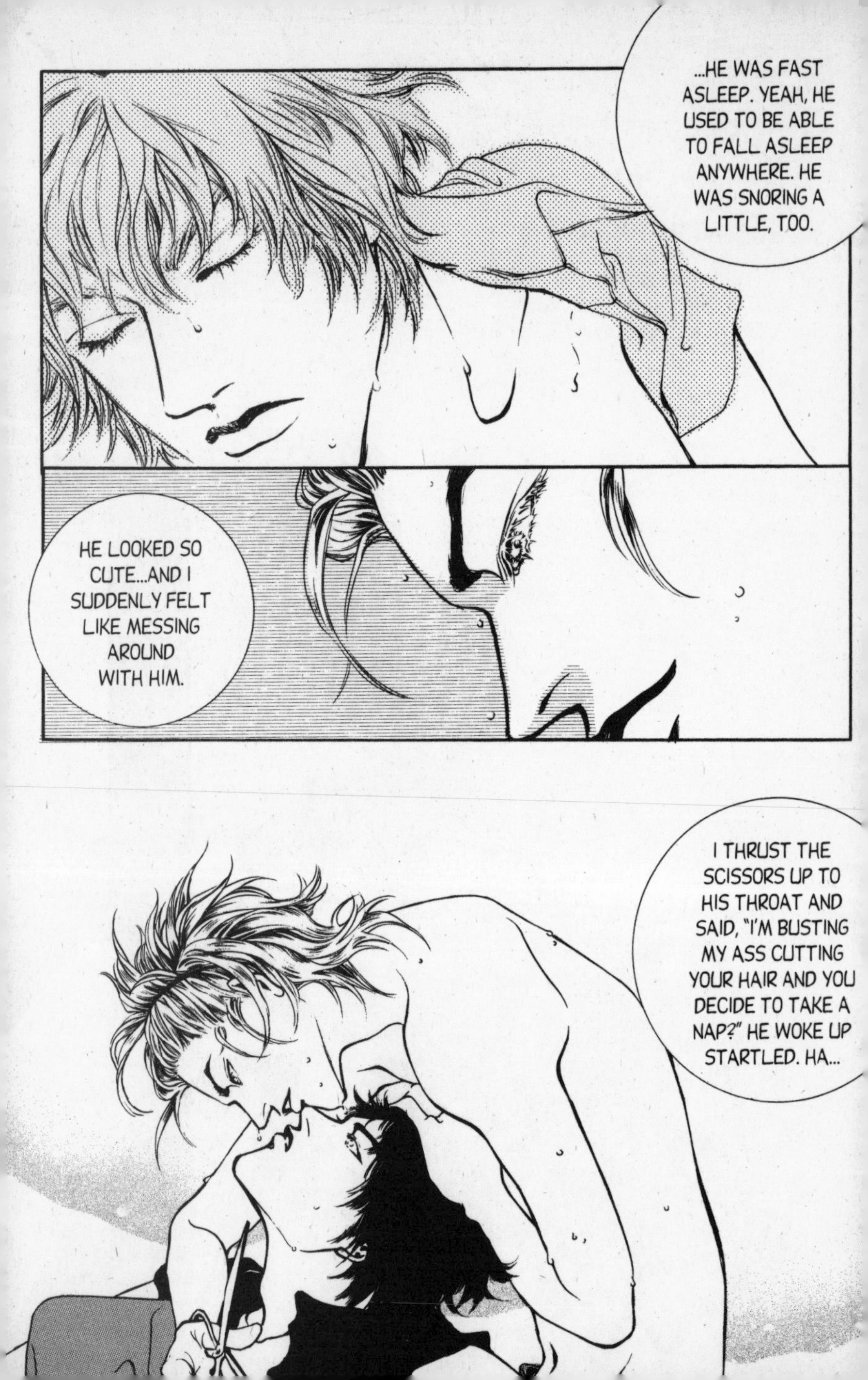
...HE WAS FAST ASLEEP. YEAH, HE USED TO BE ABLE TO FALL ASLEEP ANYWHERE. HE WAS SNORING A LITTLE, TOO.
HE LOOKED SO CUTE...AND I SUDDENLY FELT LIKE MESSING AROUND WITH HIM.
I THRUST THE SCISSORS UP TO HIS THROAT AND SAID, "I'M BUSTING MY ASS CUTTING YOUR HAIR AND YOU DECIDE TO TAKE A NAP?" HE WOKE UP STARTLED. HA...

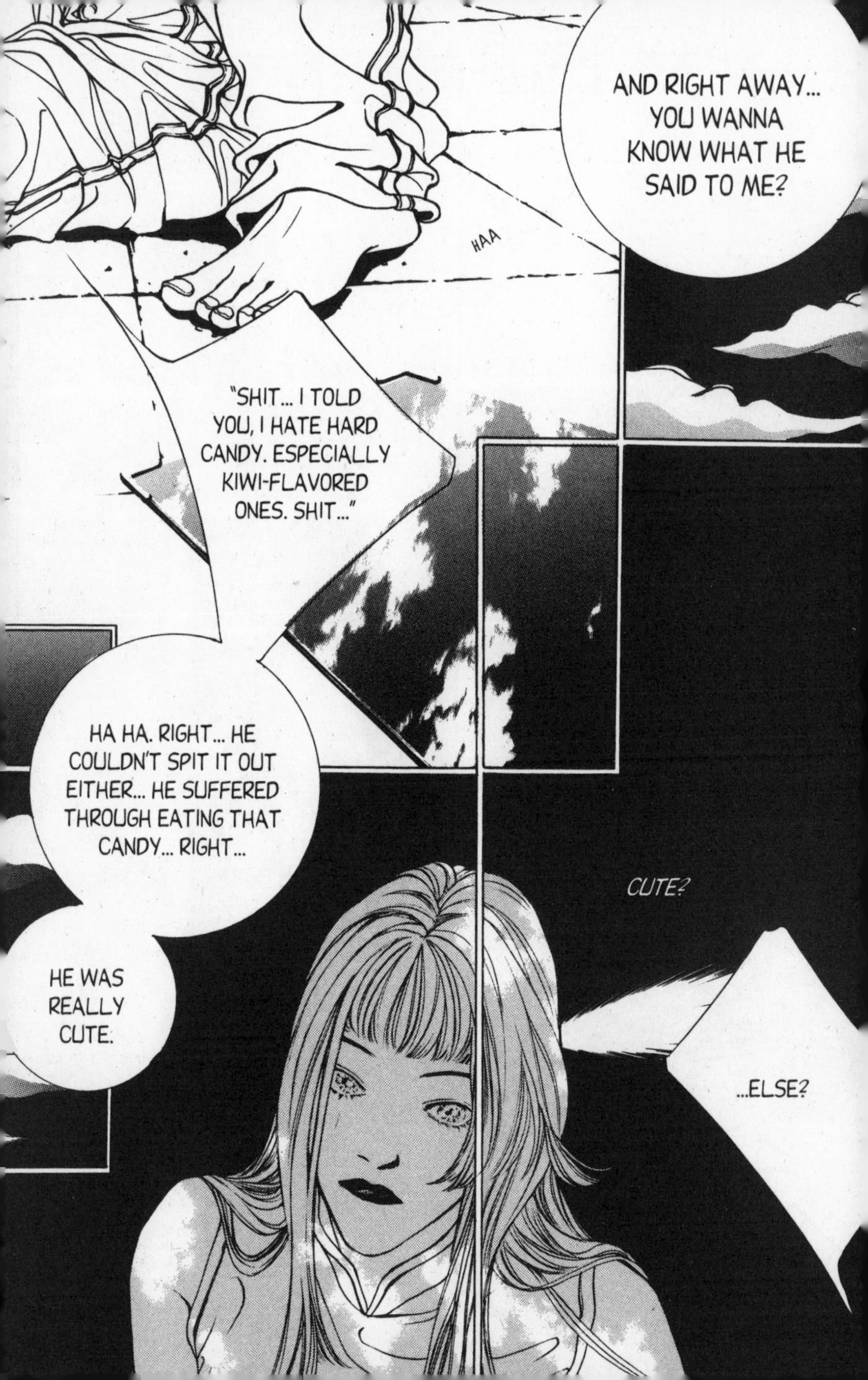
HAA
AND RIGHT AWAY... YOU WANNA KNOW WHAT HE SAID TO ME?
"SHIT... I TOLD YOU, I HATE HARD CANDY. ESPECIALLY KIWI-FLAVORED ONES. SHIT..."
HA HA. RIGHT... HE COULDN'T SPIT IT OUT EITHER... HE SUFFERED THROUGH EATING THAT CANDY... RIGHT...
HE WAS REALLY CUTE.
CUTE?
...ELSE?

Ⅲ · Mari

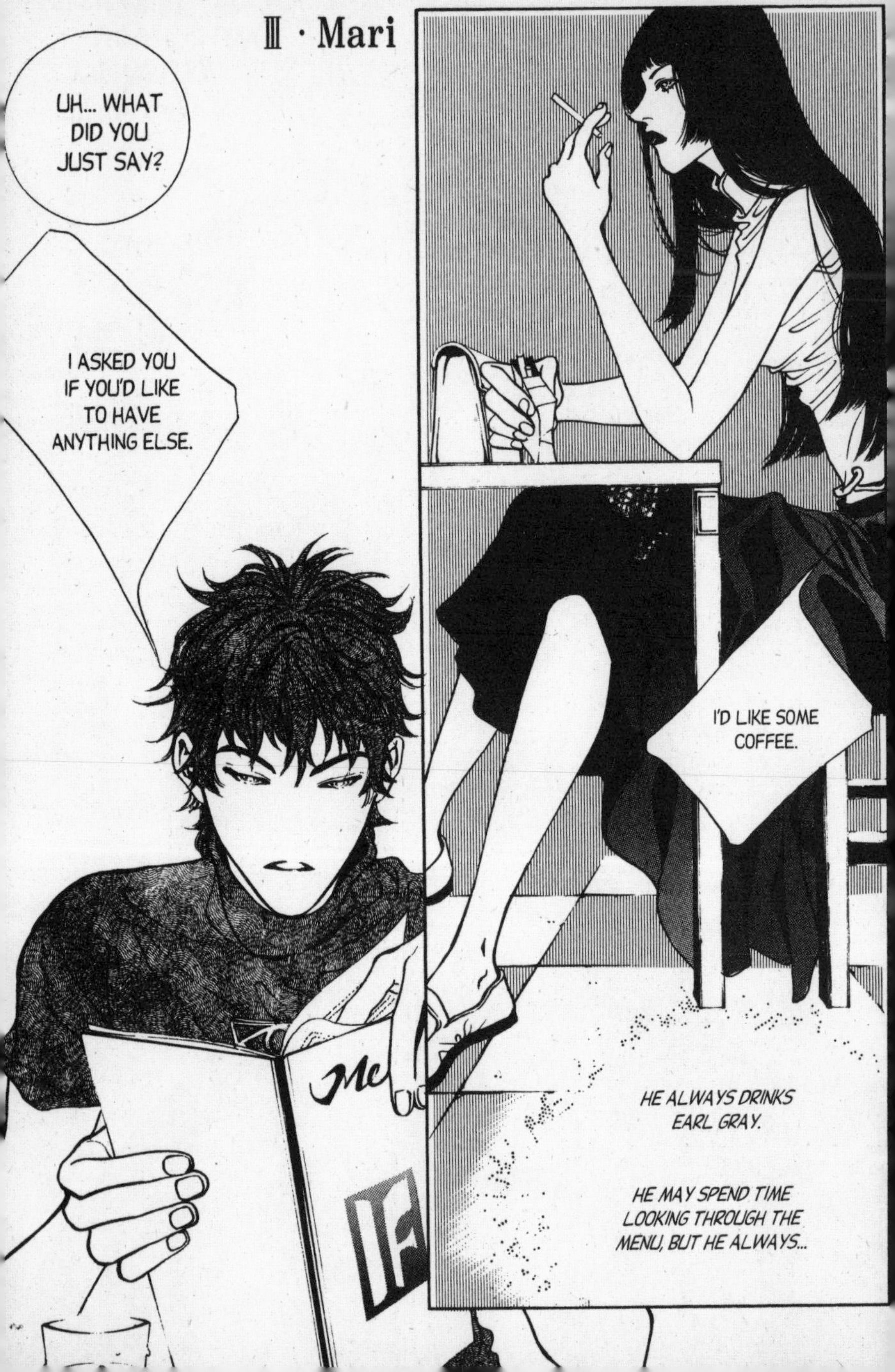
UH... WHAT DID YOU JUST SAY?
I ASKED YOU IF YOU'D LIKE TO HAVE ANYTHING ELSE.
I'D LIKE SOME COFFEE.
HE ALWAYS DRINKS EARL GRAY.
HE MAY SPEND TIME LOOKING THROUGH THE MENU, BUT HE ALWAYS...

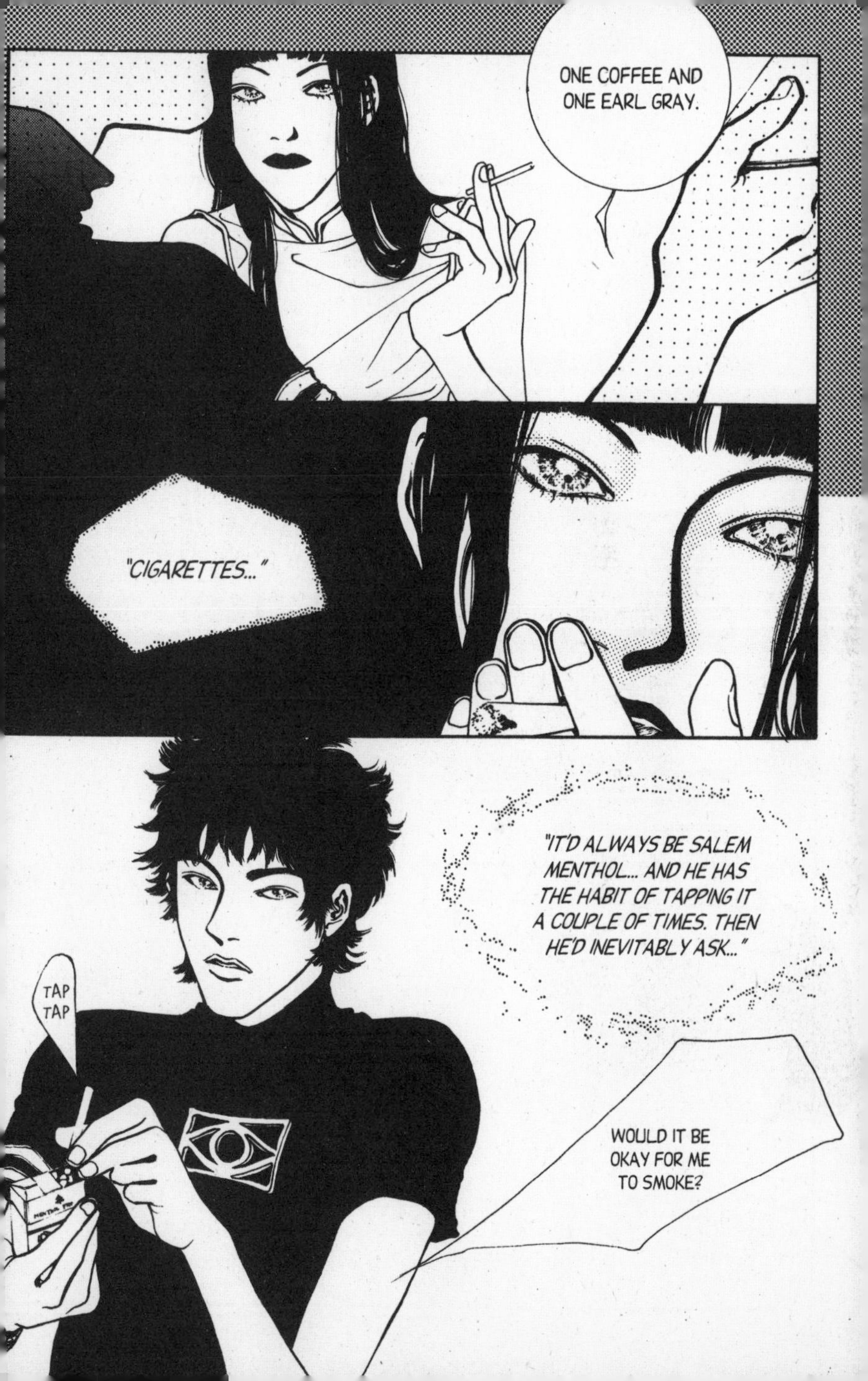
ONE COFFEE AND ONE EARL GRAY.
"CIGARETTES..."
TAP TAP
"IT'D ALWAYS BE SALEM MENTHOL... AND HE HAS THE HABIT OF TAPPING IT A COUPLE OF TIMES. THEN HE'D INEVITABLY ASK..."
WOULD IT BE OKAY FOR ME TO SMOKE?

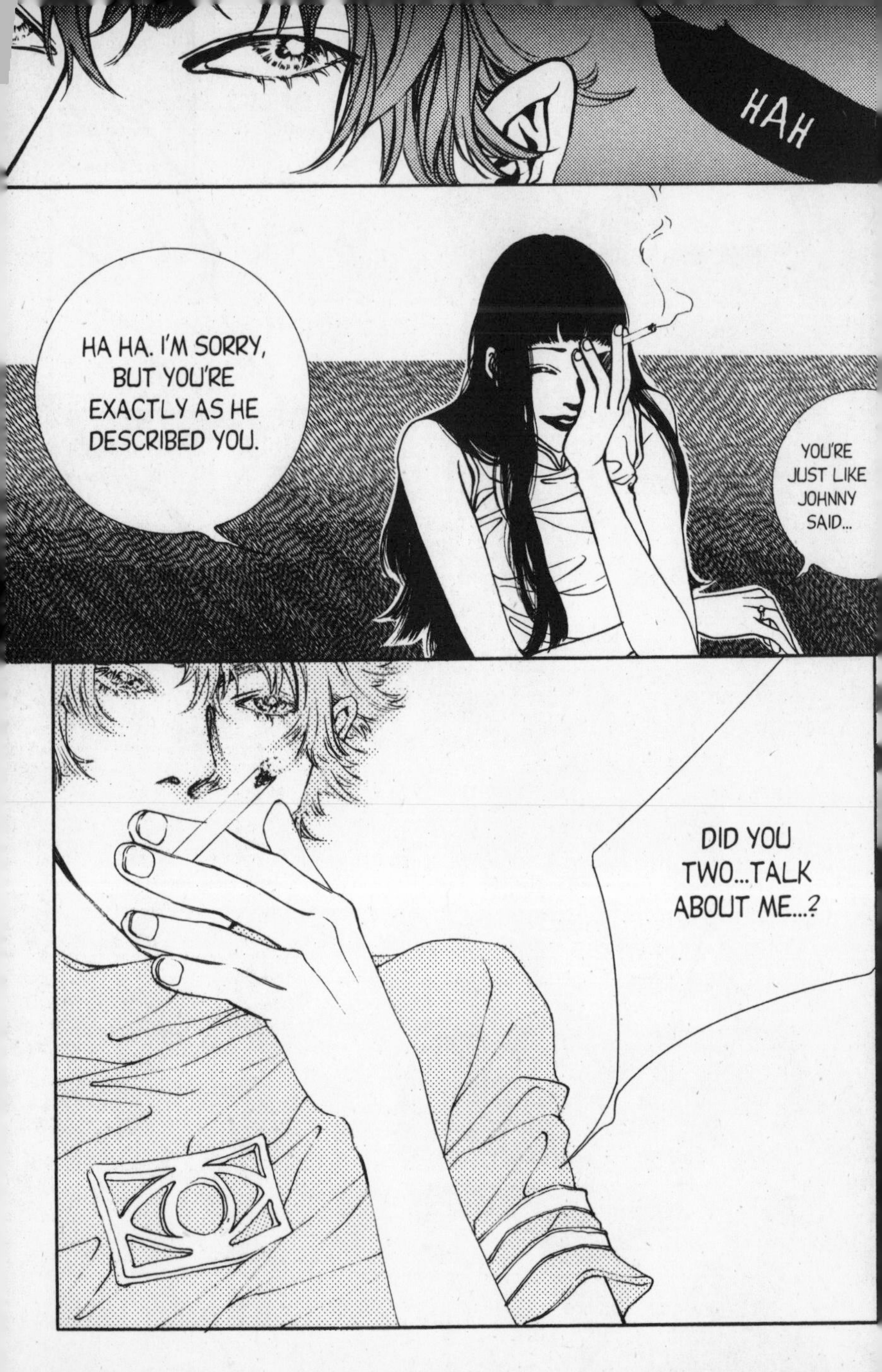
HAH
HA HA. I'M SORRY, BUT YOU'RE EXACTLY AS HE DESCRIBED YOU.
YOU'RE JUST LIKE JOHNNY SAID...
DID YOU TWO...TALK ABOUT ME...?

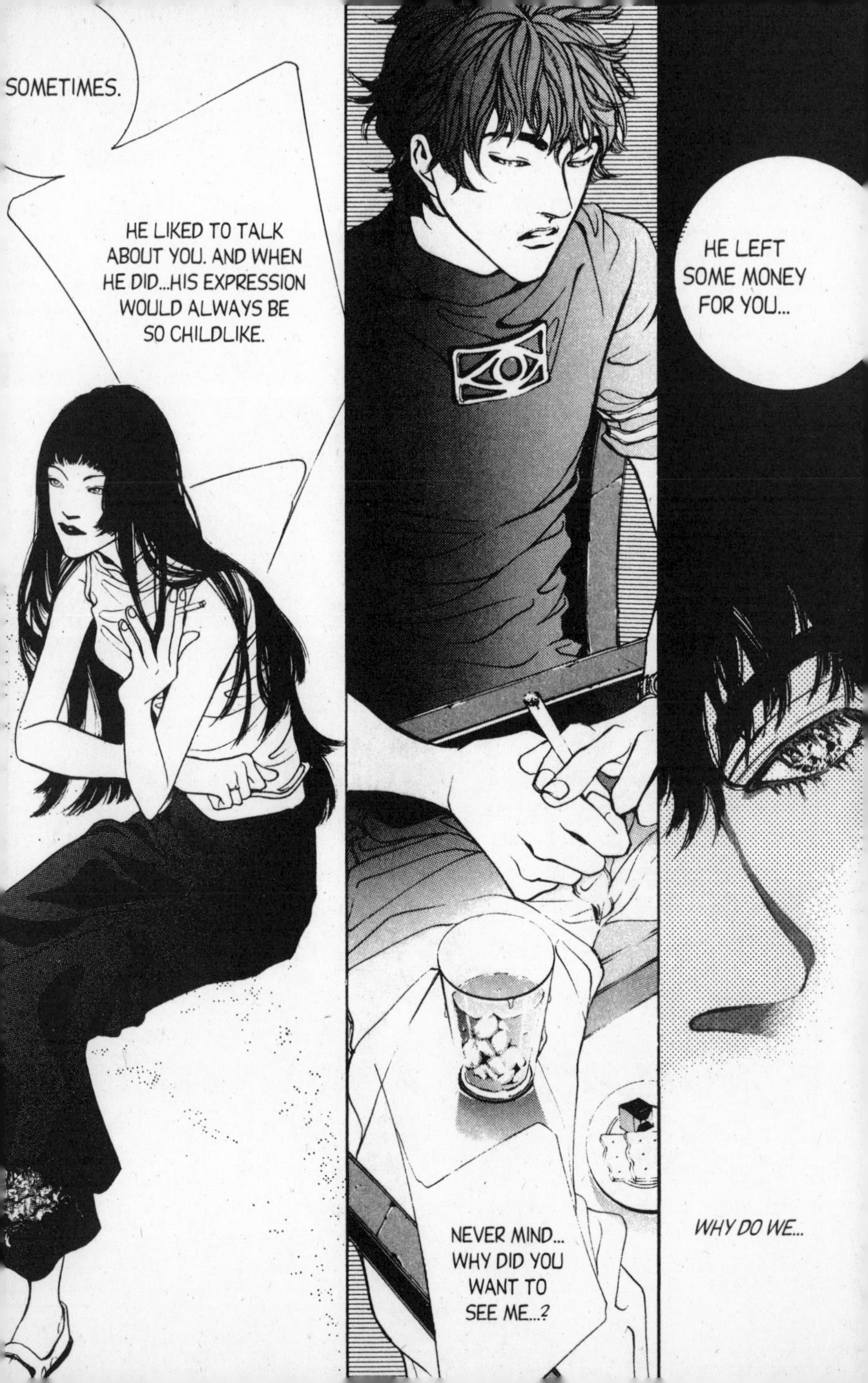
SOMETIMES.
HE LIKED TO TALK ABOUT YOU. AND WHEN HE DID...HIS EXPRESSION WOULD ALWAYS BE SO CHILDLIKE.
NEVER MIND... WHY DID YOU WANT TO SEE ME...?
HE LEFT SOME MONEY FOR YOU...
WHY DO WE...

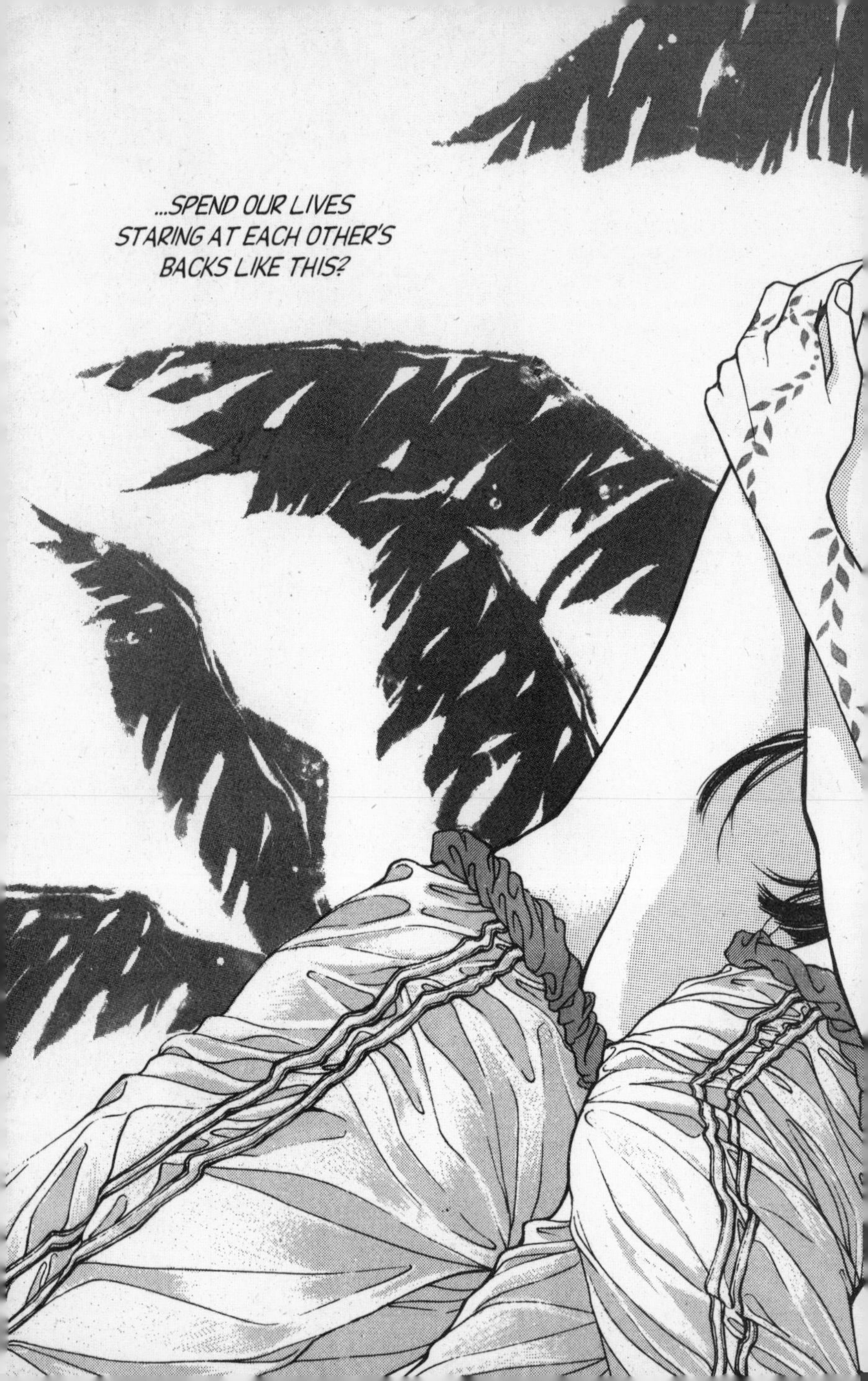
...SPEND OUR LIVES STARING AT EACH OTHER'S BACKS LIKE THIS?

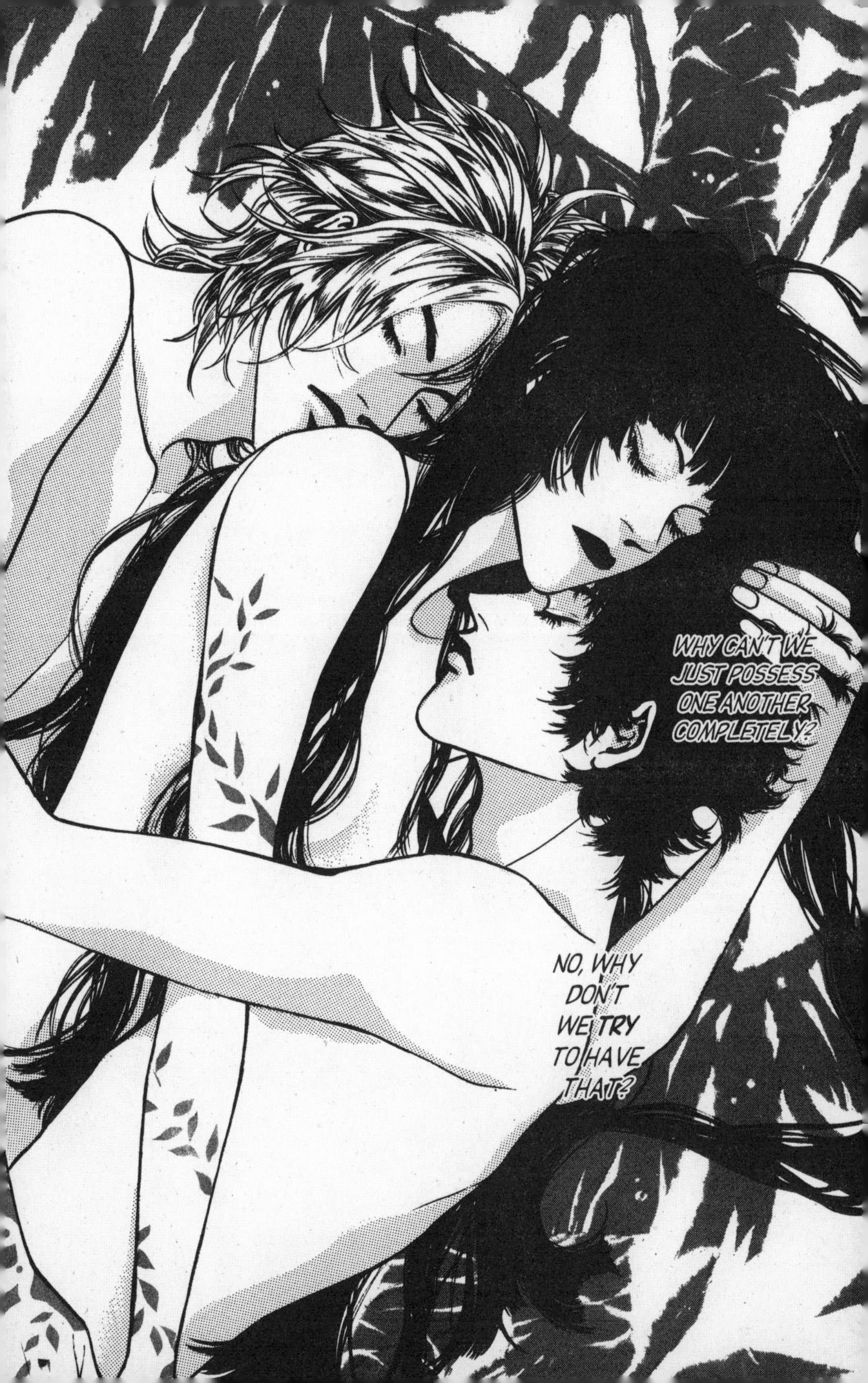
WHY CAN'T WE JUST POSSESS ONE ANOTHER COMPLETELY?
NO, WHY DON'T WE TRY TO HAVE THAT?

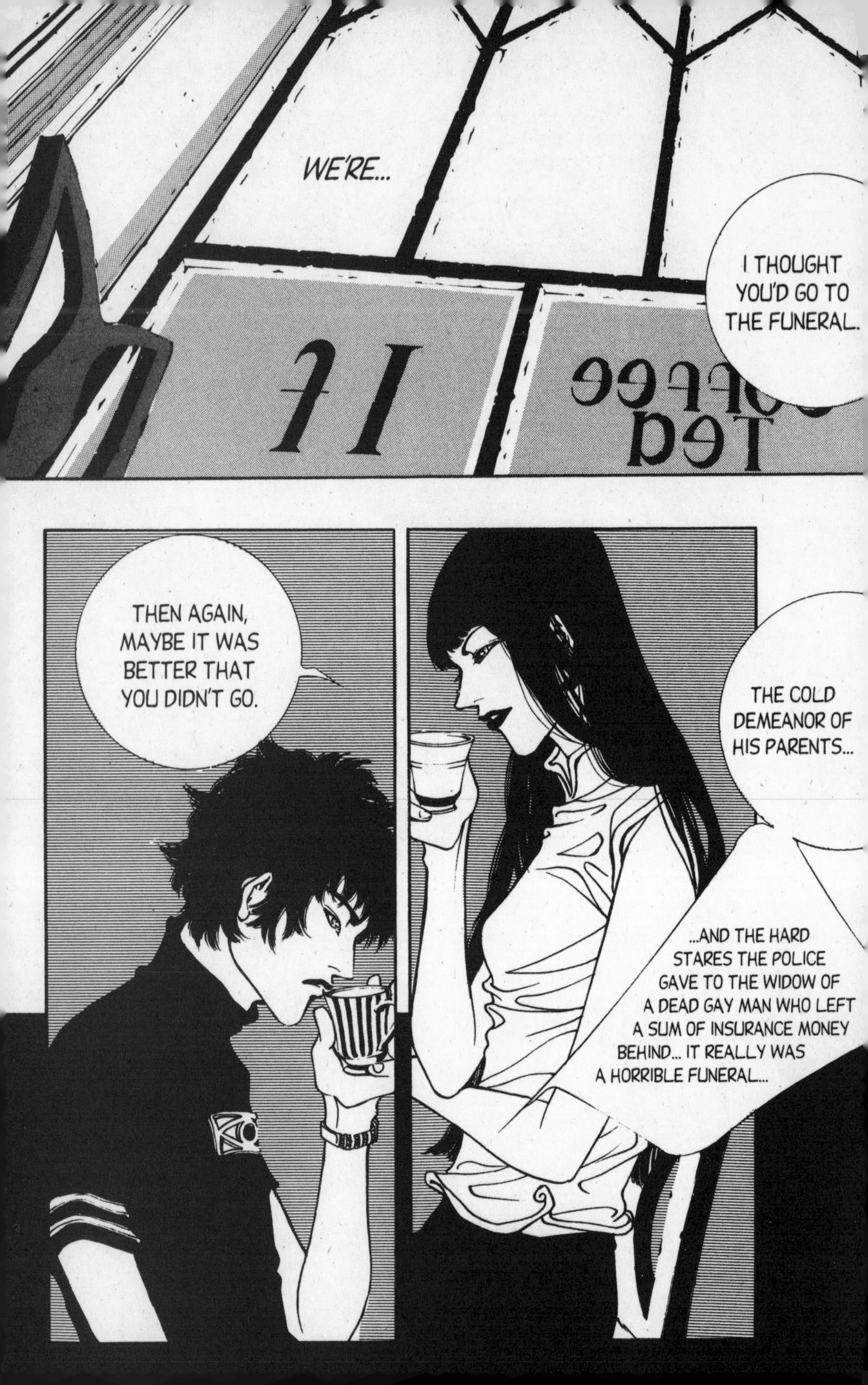
WE'RE...
I THOUGHT YOU'D GO TO THE FUNERAL.
THEN AGAIN, MAYBE IT WAS BETTER THAT YOU DIDN'T GO.
THE COLD DEMEANOR OF HIS PARENTS...
...AND THE HARD STARES THE POLICE GAVE TO THE WIDOW OF A DEAD GAY MAN WHO LEFT A SUM OF INSURANCE MONEY BEHIND... IT REALLY WAS A HORRIBLE FUNERAL...

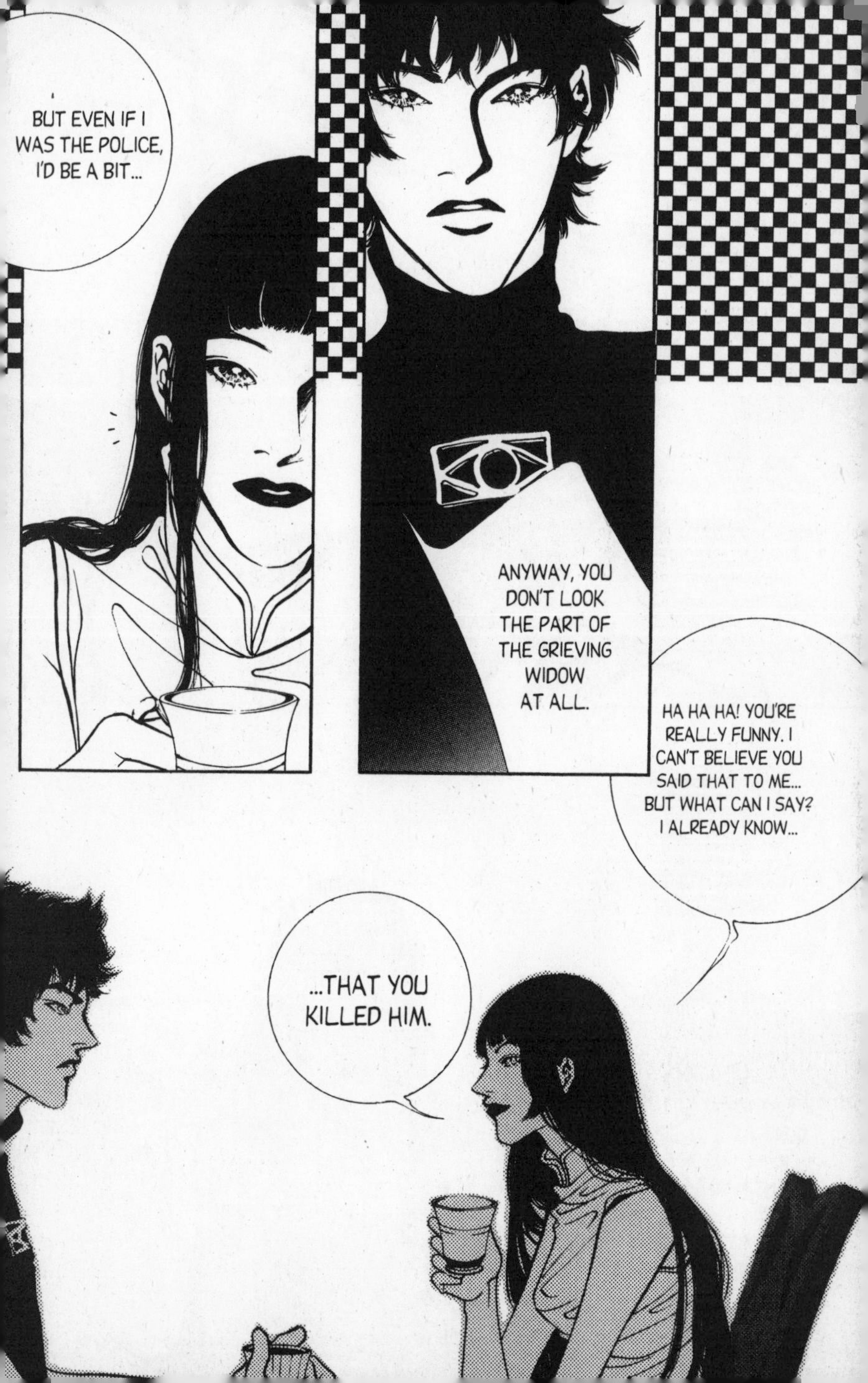
BUT EVEN IF I WAS THE POLICE, I'D BE A BIT...
ANYWAY, YOU DON'T LOOK THE PART OF THE GRIEVING WIDOW AT ALL.
HA HA HA! YOU'RE REALLY FUNNY. I CAN'T BELIEVE YOU SAID THAT TO ME... BUT WHAT CAN I SAY? I ALREADY KNOW...
...THAT YOU KILLED HIM.

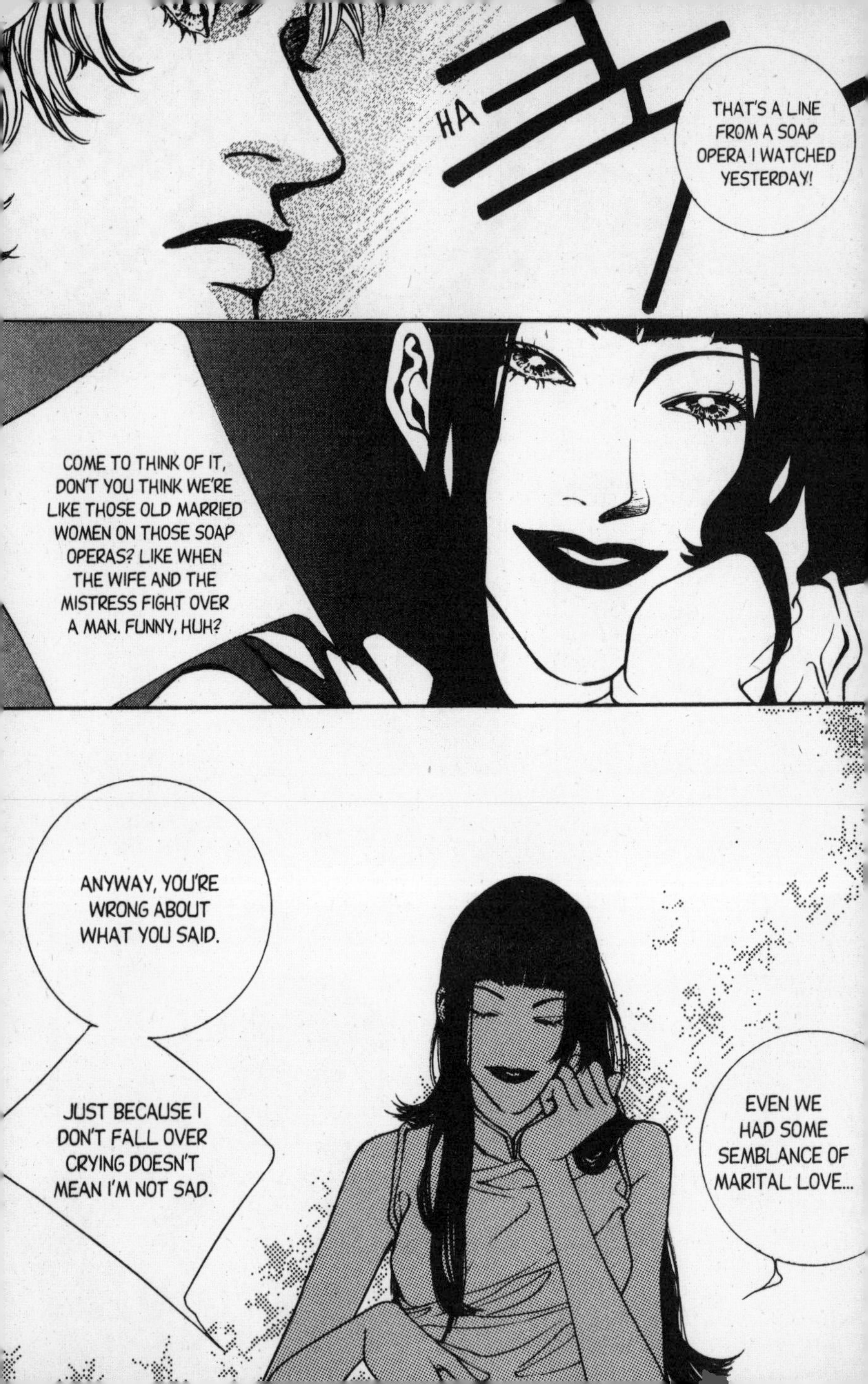
HA
THAT'S A LINE FROM A SOAP OPERA I WATCHED YESTERDAY!
COME TO THINK OF IT, DON'T YOU THINK WE'RE LIKE THOSE OLD MARRIED WOMEN ON THOSE SOAP OPERAS? LIKE WHEN THE WIFE AND THE MISTRESS FIGHT OVER A MAN. FUNNY, HUH?
ANYWAY, YOU'RE WRONG ABOUT WHAT YOU SAID.
JUST BECAUSE I DON'T FALL OVER CRYING DOESN'T MEAN I'M NOT SAD.
EVEN WE HAD SOME SEMBLANCE OF MARITAL LOVE...

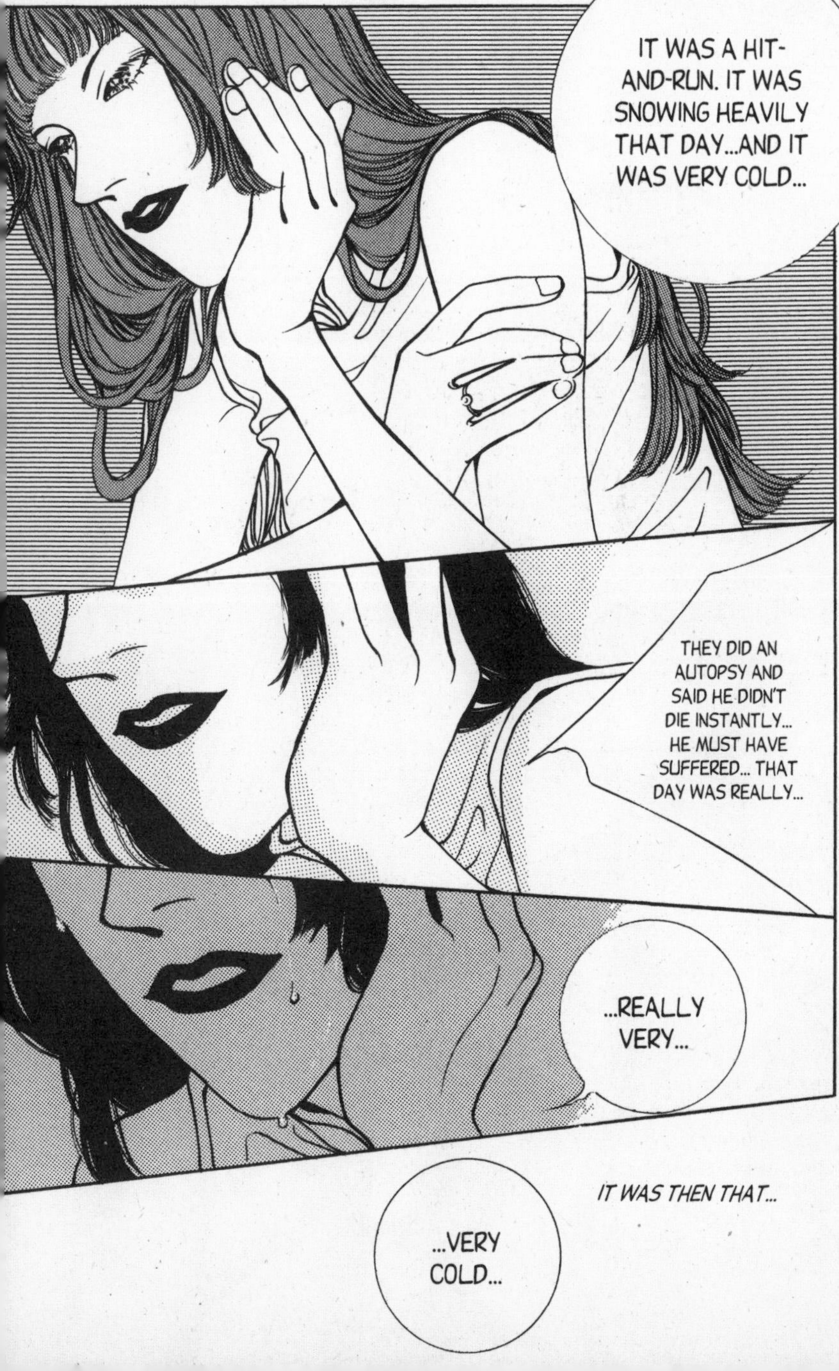
IT WAS A HIT-AND-RUN. IT WAS SNOWING HEAVILY THAT DAY...AND IT WAS VERY COLD...
THEY DID AN AUTOPSY AND SAID HE DIDN'T DIE INSTANTLY... HE MUST HAVE SUFFERED... THAT DAY WAS REALLY...
...REALLY VERY...
...VERY COLD...
IT WAS THEN THAT...

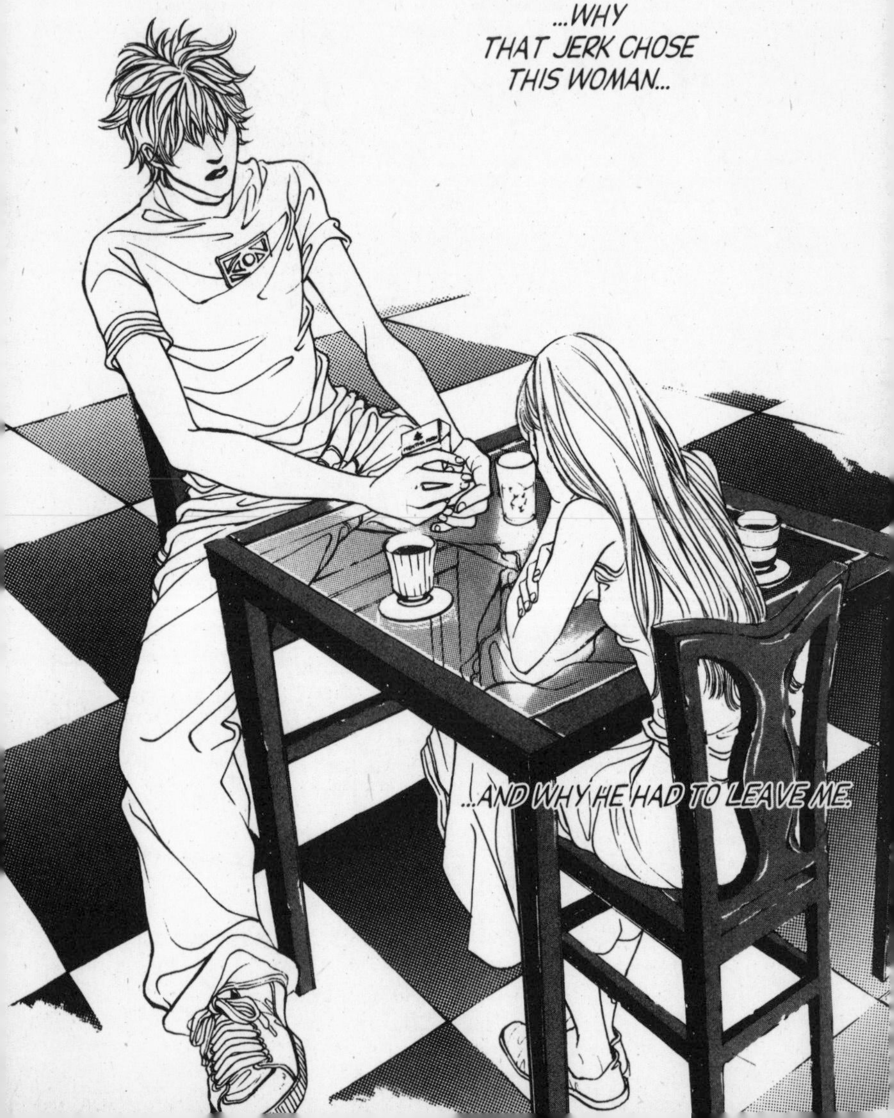
...I BEGAN TO UNDERSTAND...
...WHY THAT JERK CHOSE THIS WOMAN...
...AND WHY HE HAD TO LEAVE ME.

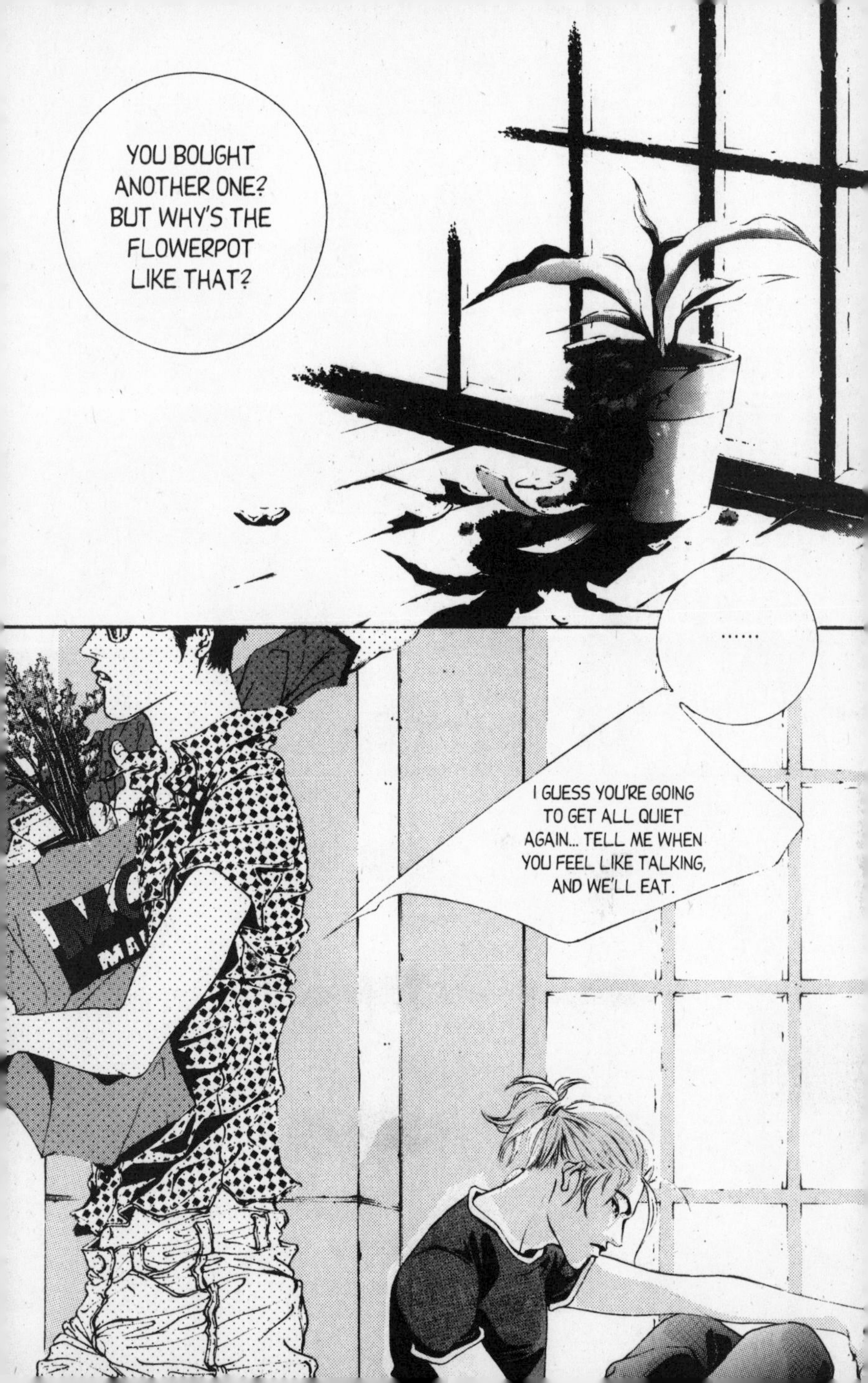
YOU BOUGHT ANOTHER ONE? BUT WHY'S THE FLOWERPOT LIKE THAT?
......
I GUESS YOU'RE GOING TO GET ALL QUIET AGAIN... TELL ME WHEN YOU FEEL LIKE TALKING, AND WE'LL EAT.

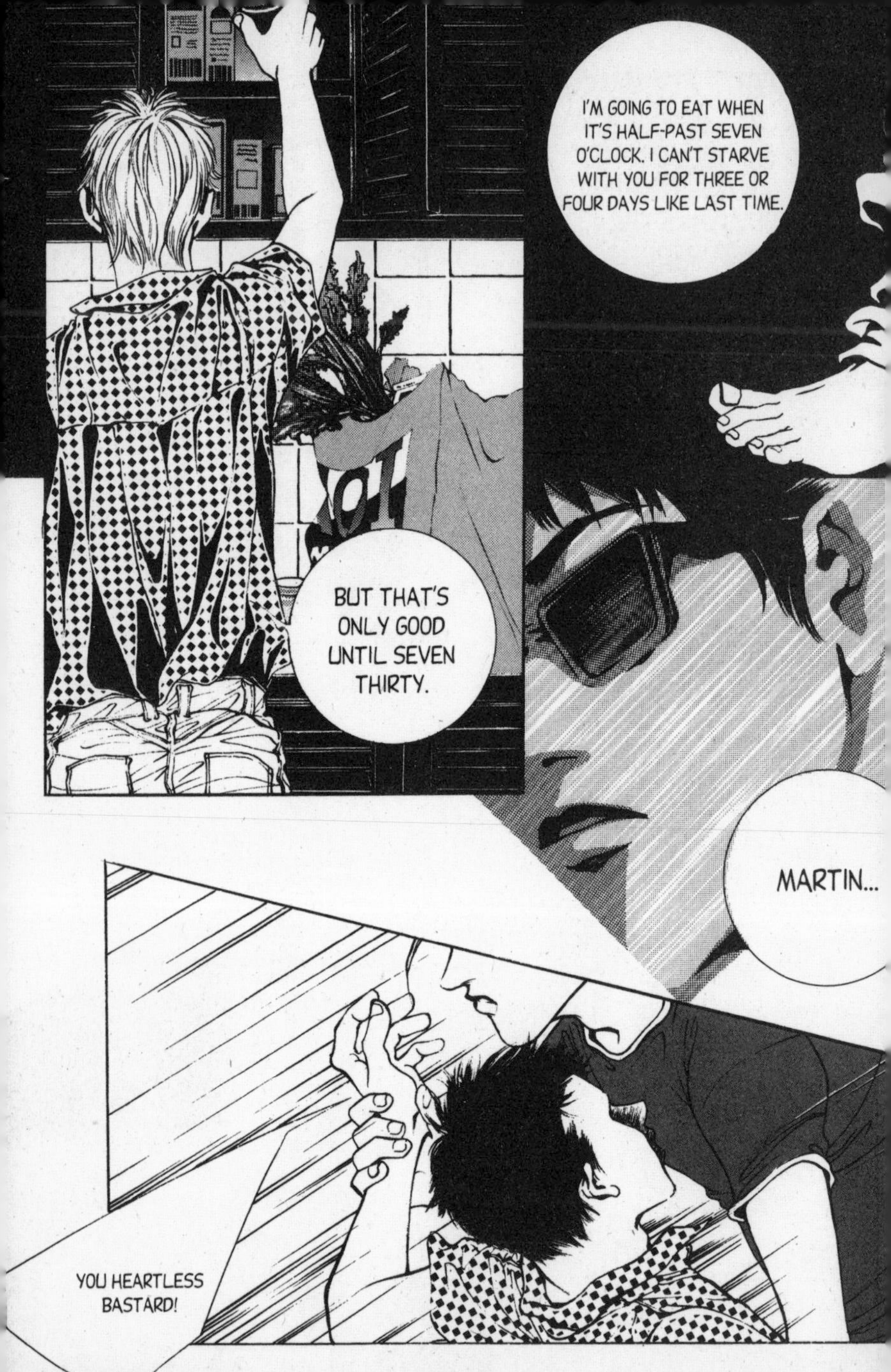
BUT THAT'S ONLY GOOD UNTIL SEVEN THIRTY.
I'M GOING TO EAT WHEN IT'S HALF-PAST SEVEN O'CLOCK. I CAN'T STARVE WITH YOU FOR THREE OR FOUR DAYS LIKE LAST TIME.
MARTIN...
YOU HEARTLESS BASTARD!

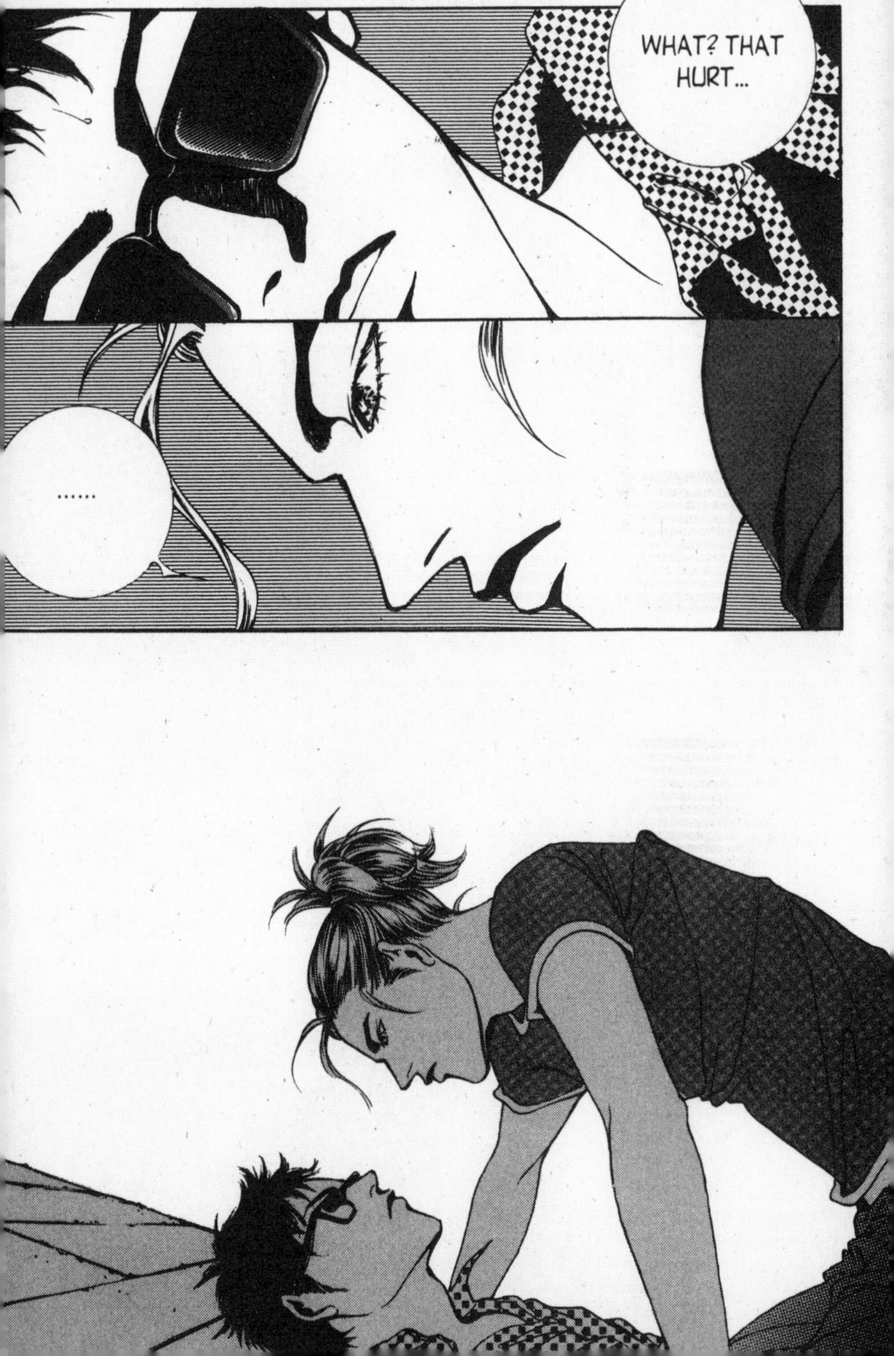
WHAT? THAT HURT...
......

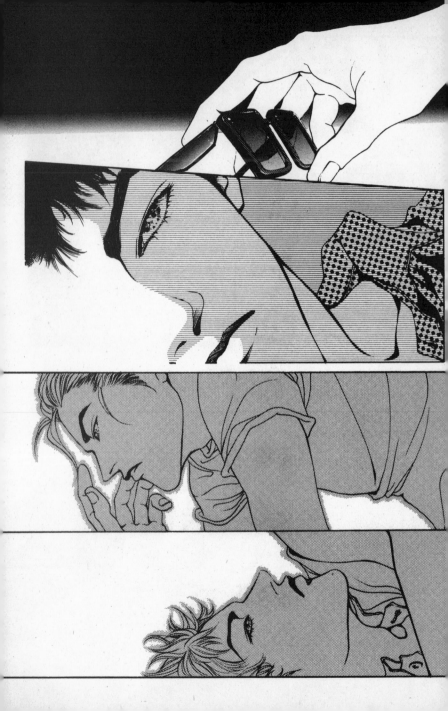

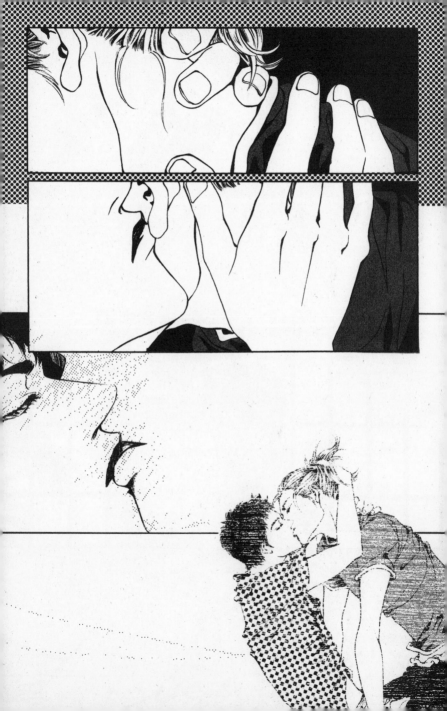

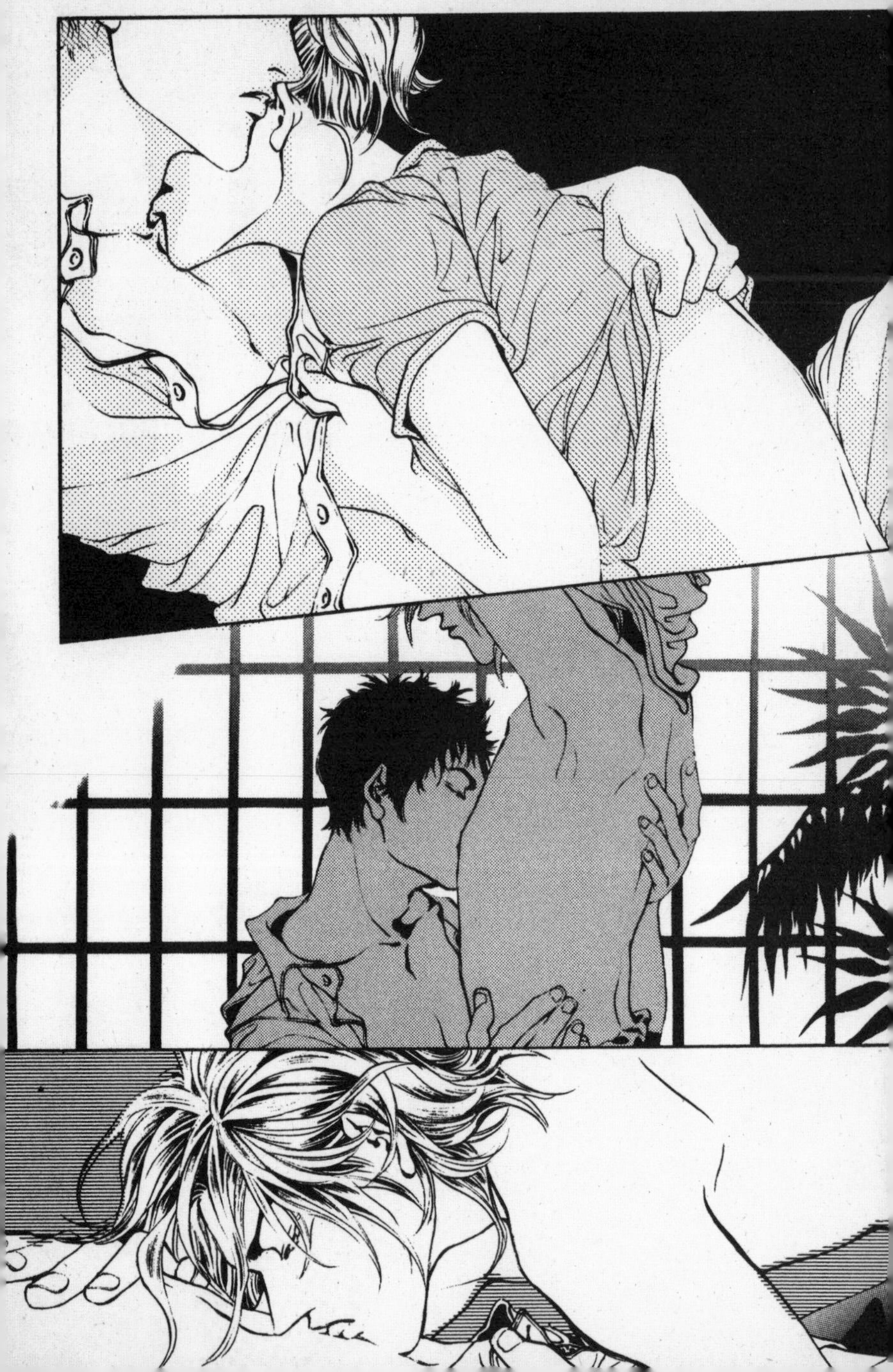

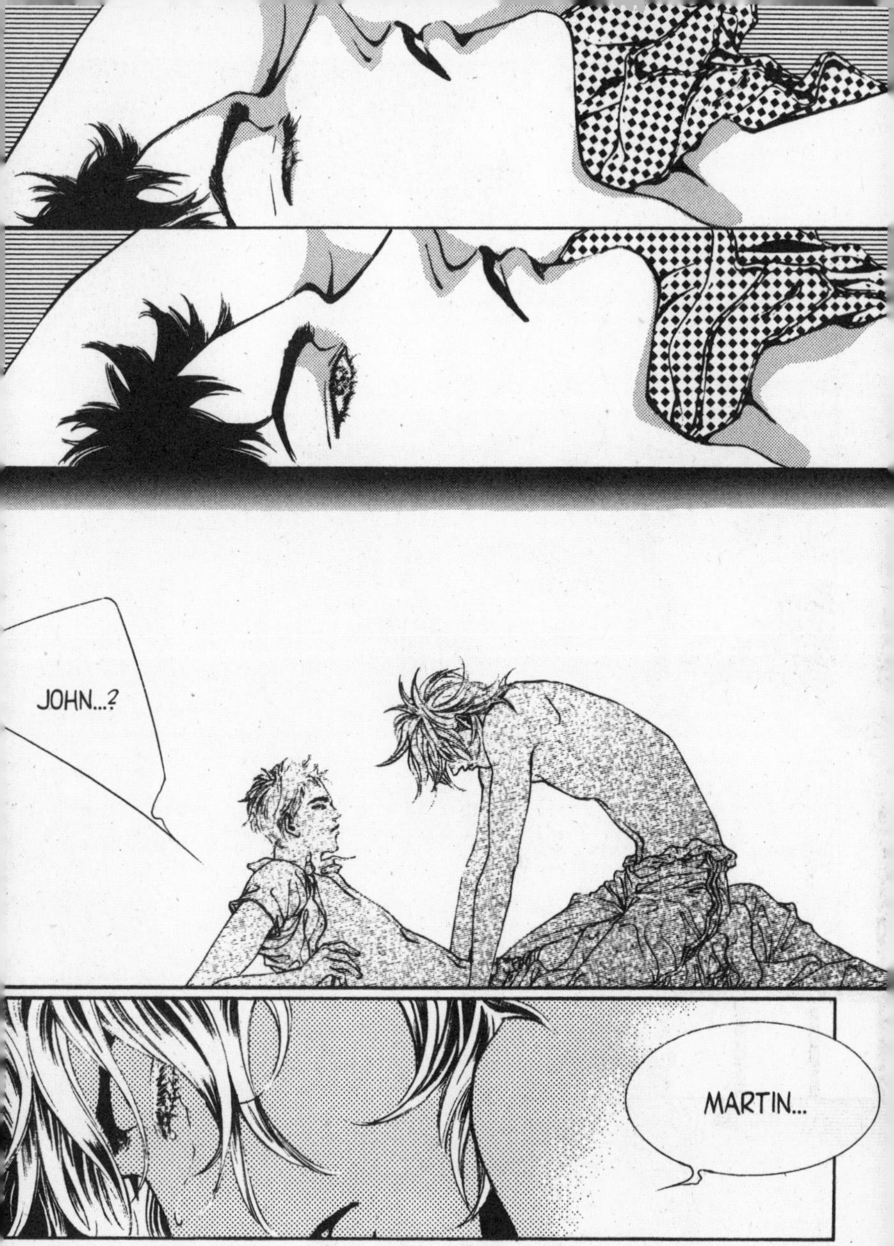
JOHN...?
MARTIN...

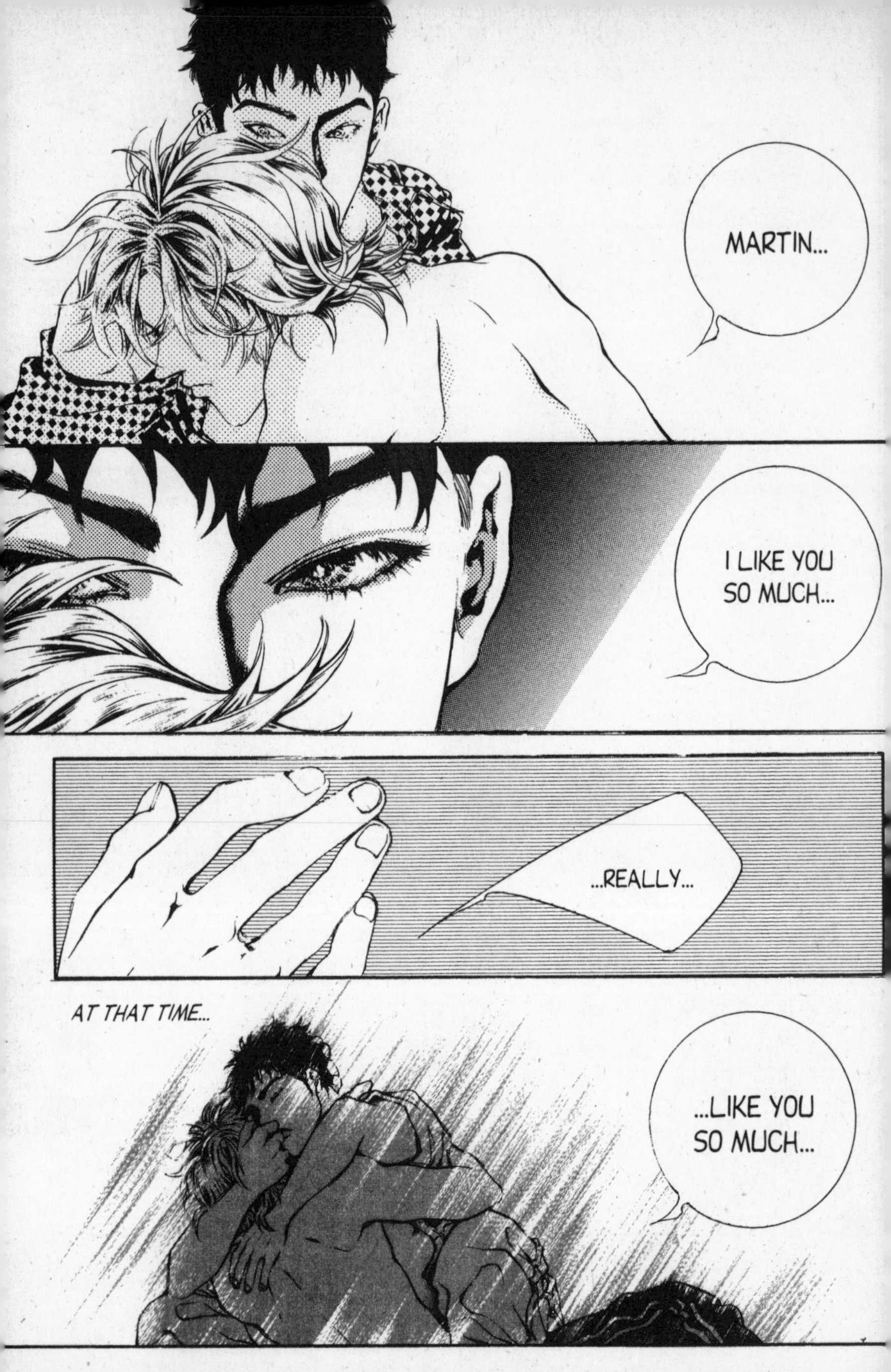
MARTIN...
I LIKE YOU SO MUCH...
...REALLY...
AT THAT TIME...
...LIKE YOU SO MUCH...

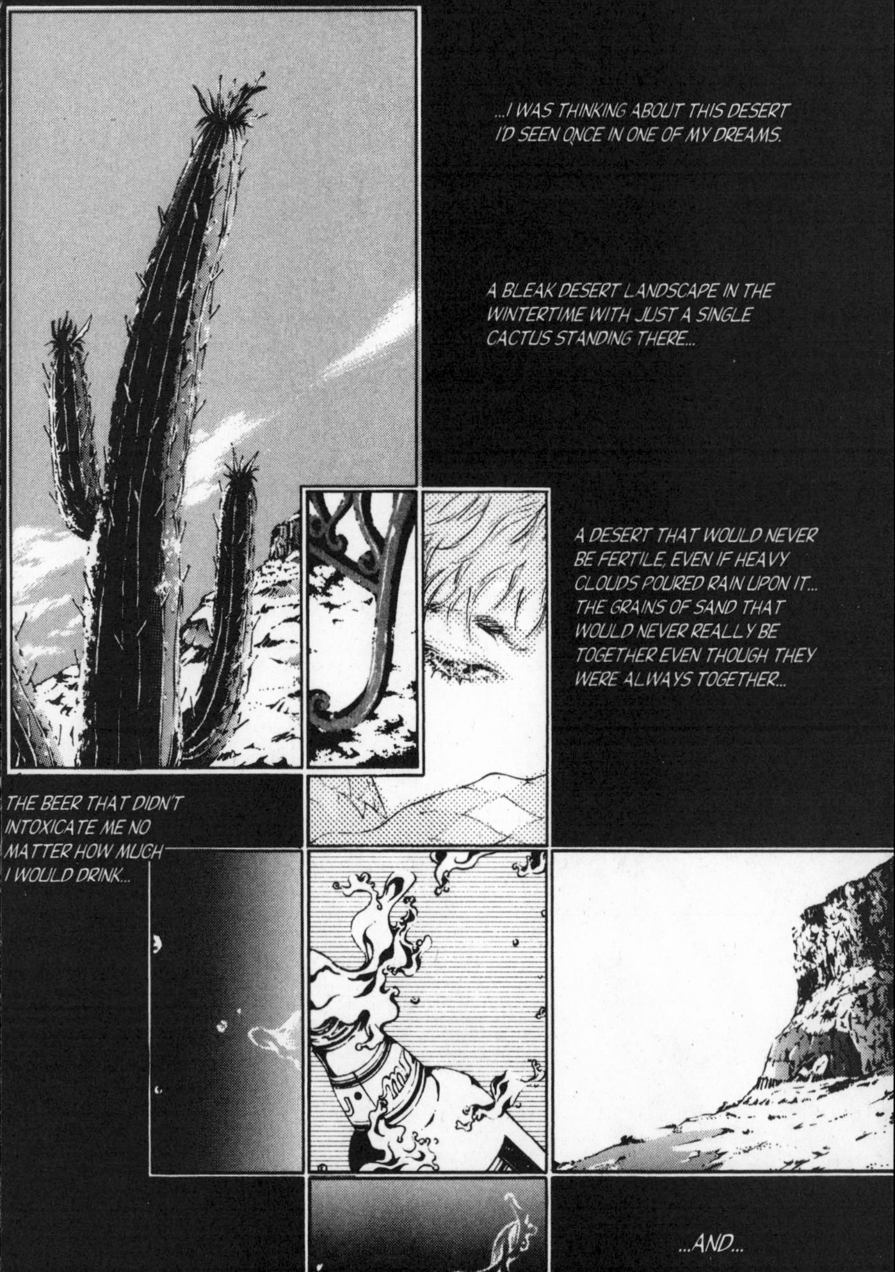
...I WAS THINKING ABOUT THIS DESERT I'D SEEN ONCE IN ONE OF MY DREAMS.
A BLEAK DESERT LANDSCAPE IN THE WINTERTIME WITH JUST A SINGLE CACTUS STANDING THERE...
A DESERT THAT WOULD NEVER BE FERTILE, EVEN IF HEAVY CLOUDS POURED RAIN UPON IT... THE GRAINS OF SAND THAT WOULD NEVER REALLY BE TOGETHER EVEN THOUGH THEY WERE ALWAYS TOGETHER...
THE BEER THAT DIDN'T INTOXICATE ME NO MATTER HOW MUCH I WOULD DRINK...
...AND...

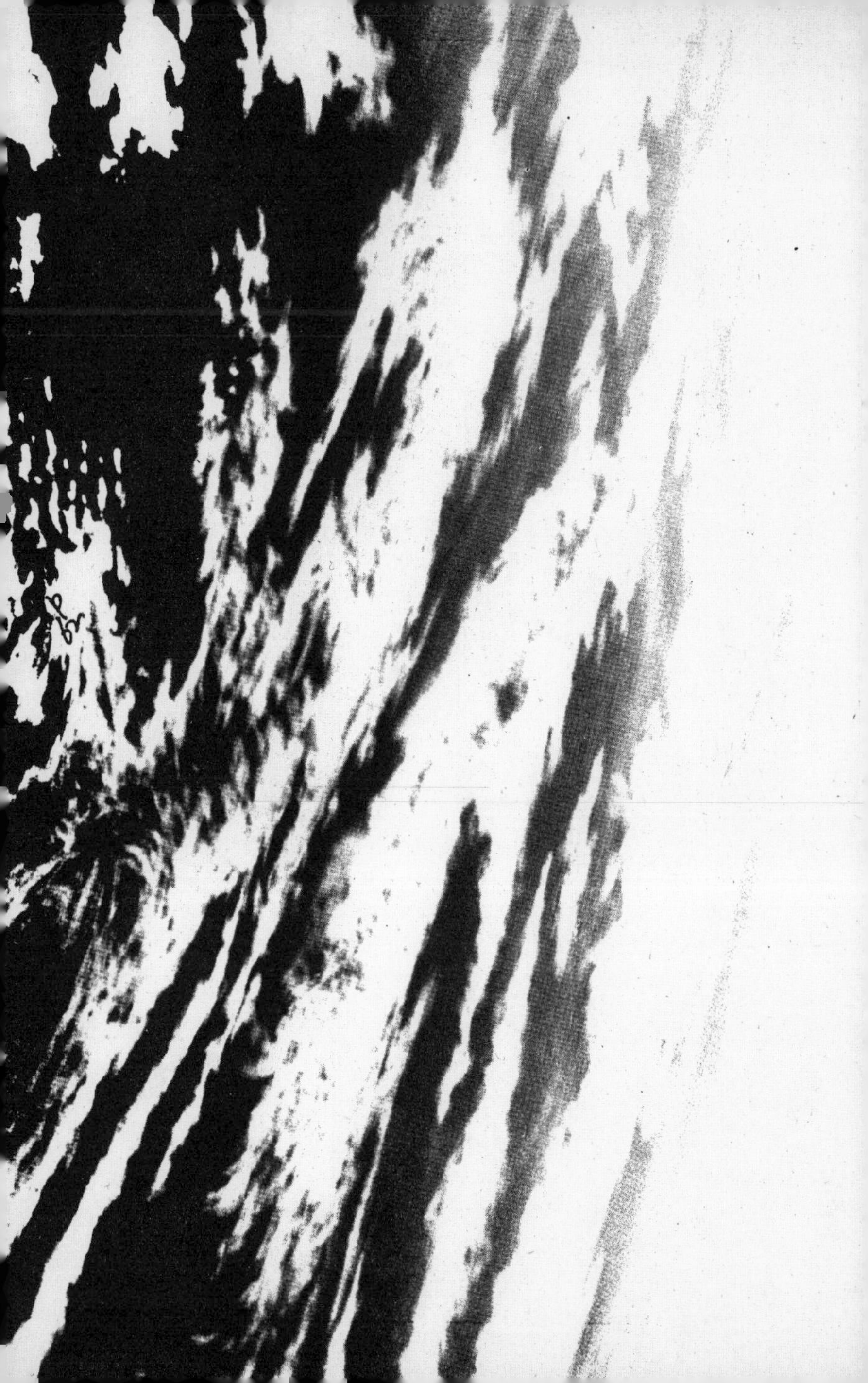

IV · John

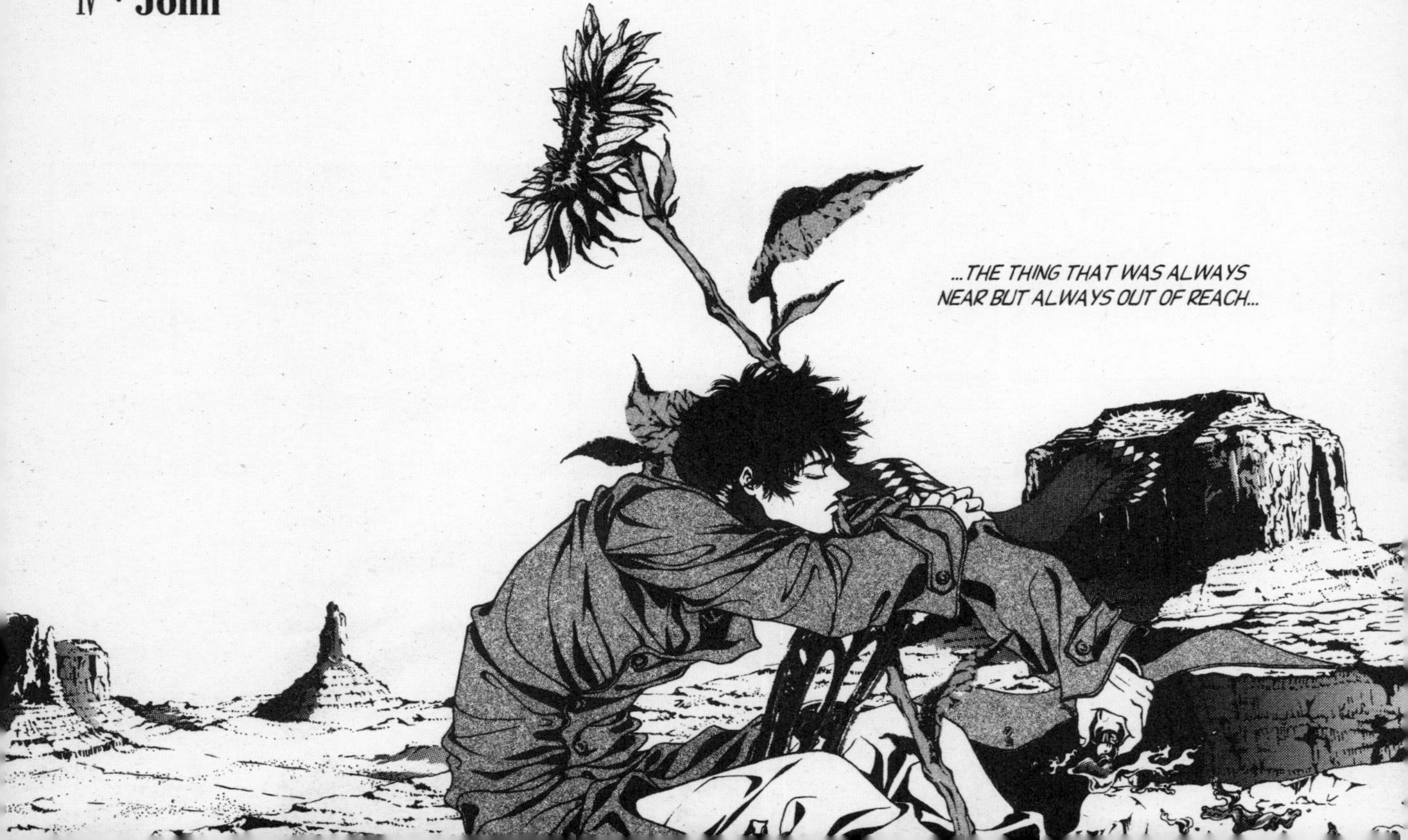
...THE THING THAT WAS ALWAYS NEAR BUT ALWAYS OUT OF REACH...

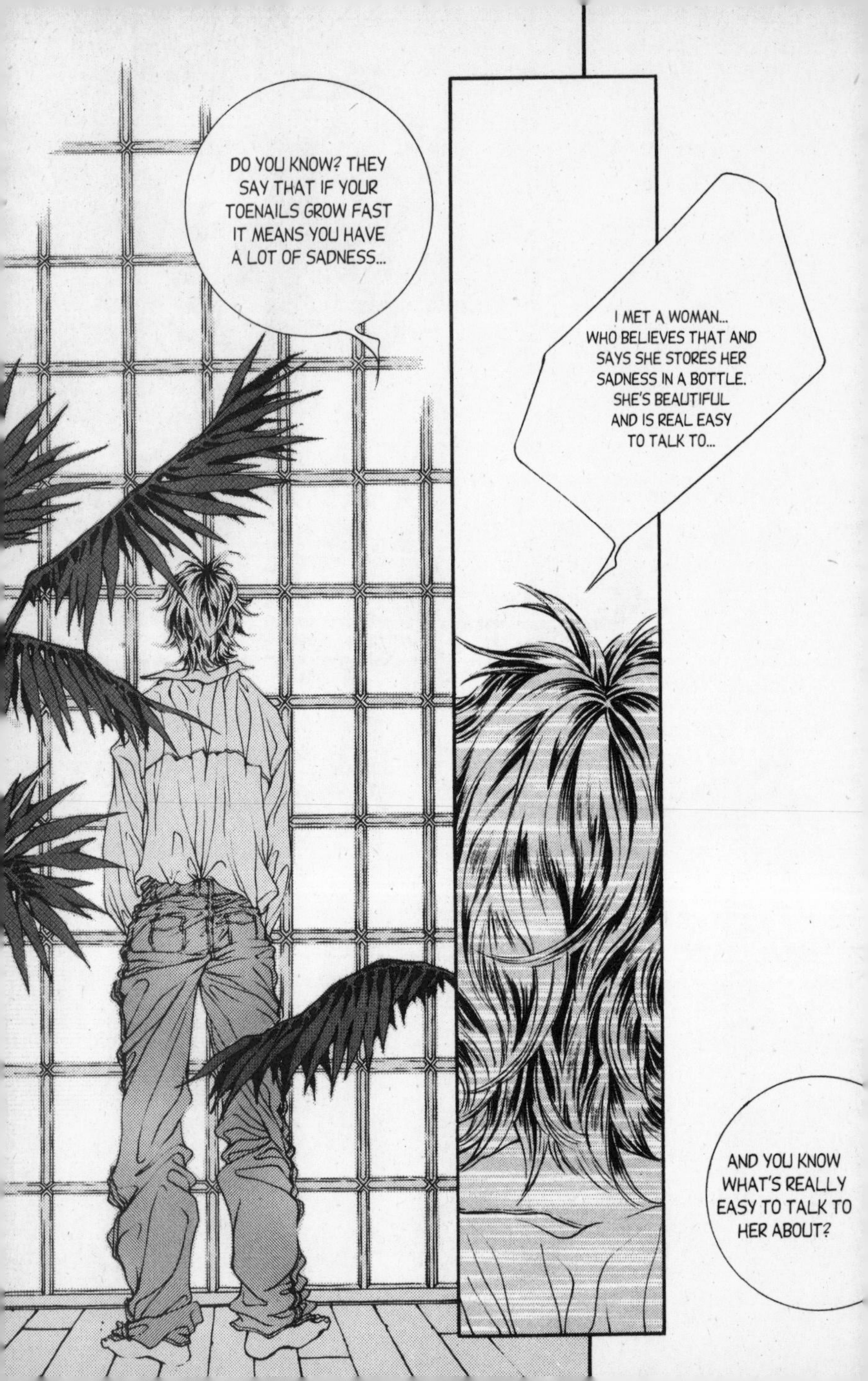
DO YOU KNOW? THEY SAY THAT IF YOUR TOENAILS GROW FAST IT MEANS YOU HAVE A LOT OF SADNESS...
I MET A WOMAN... WHO BELIEVES THAT AND SAYS SHE STORES HER SADNESS IN A BOTTLE. SHE'S BEAUTIFUL AND IS REAL EASY TO TALK TO...
AND YOU KNOW WHAT'S REALLY EASY TO TALK TO HER ABOUT?

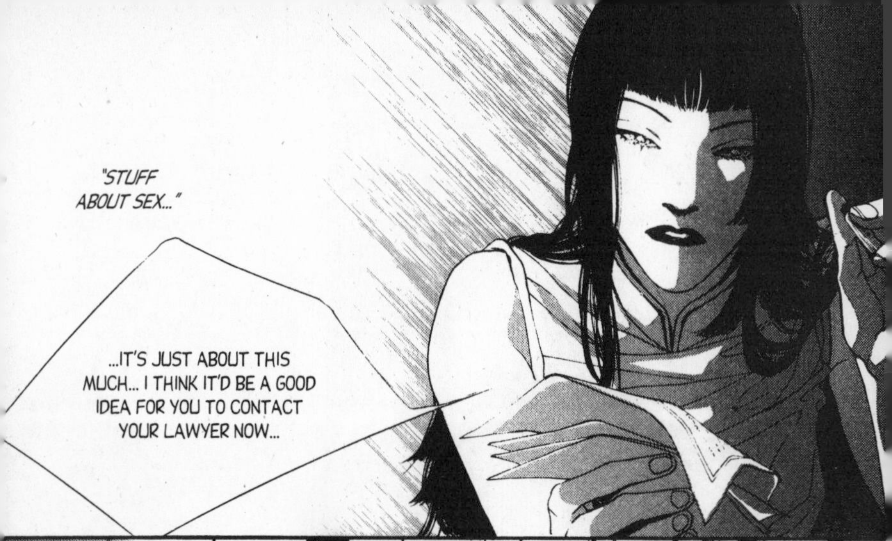
"STUFF ABOUT SEX..."
...IT'S JUST ABOUT THIS MUCH... I THINK IT'D BE A GOOD IDEA FOR YOU TO CONTACT YOUR LAWYER NOW...

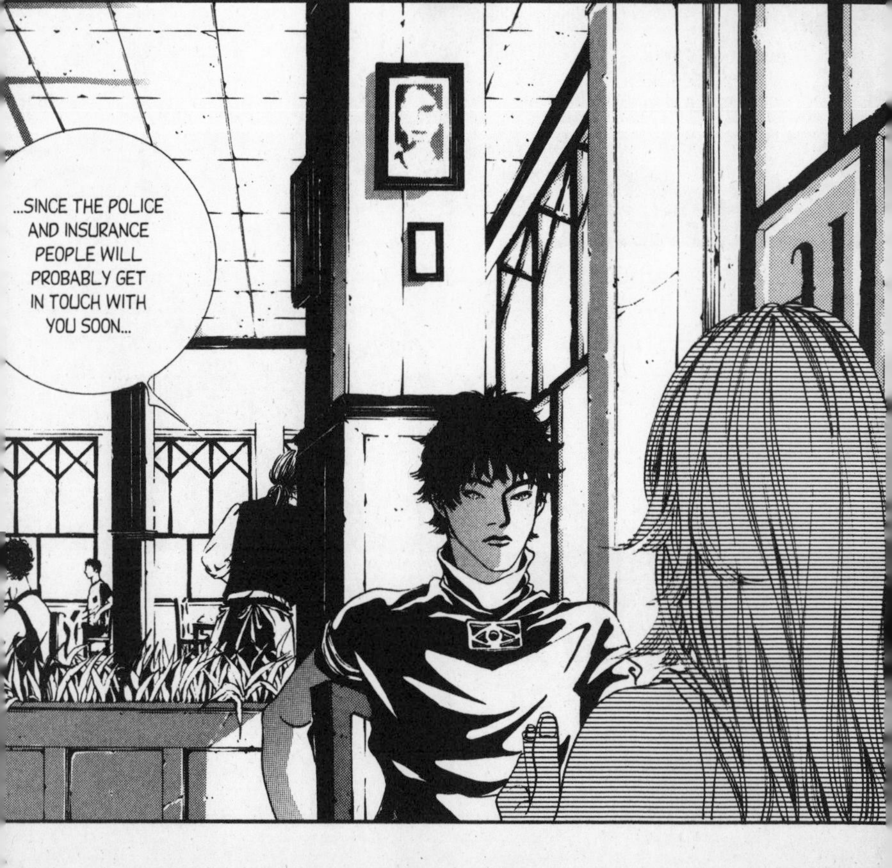
...SINCE THE POLICE AND INSURANCE PEOPLE WILL PROBABLY GET IN TOUCH WITH YOU SOON...

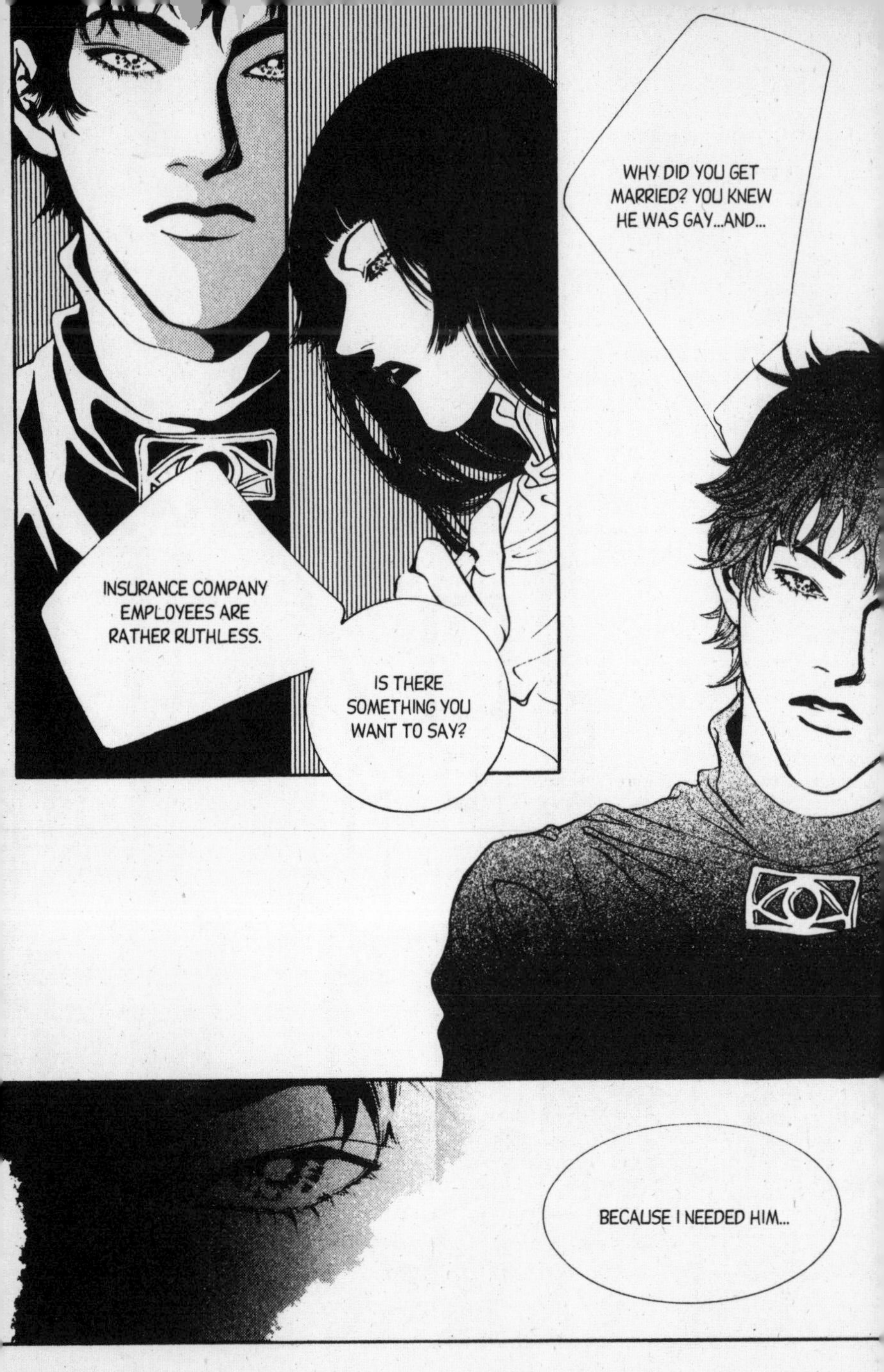
INSURANCE COMPANY EMPLOYEES ARE RATHER RUTHLESS.
IS THERE SOMETHING YOU WANT TO SAY?
WHY DID YOU GET MARRIED? YOU KNEW HE WAS GAY...AND...
BECAUSE I NEEDED HIM...

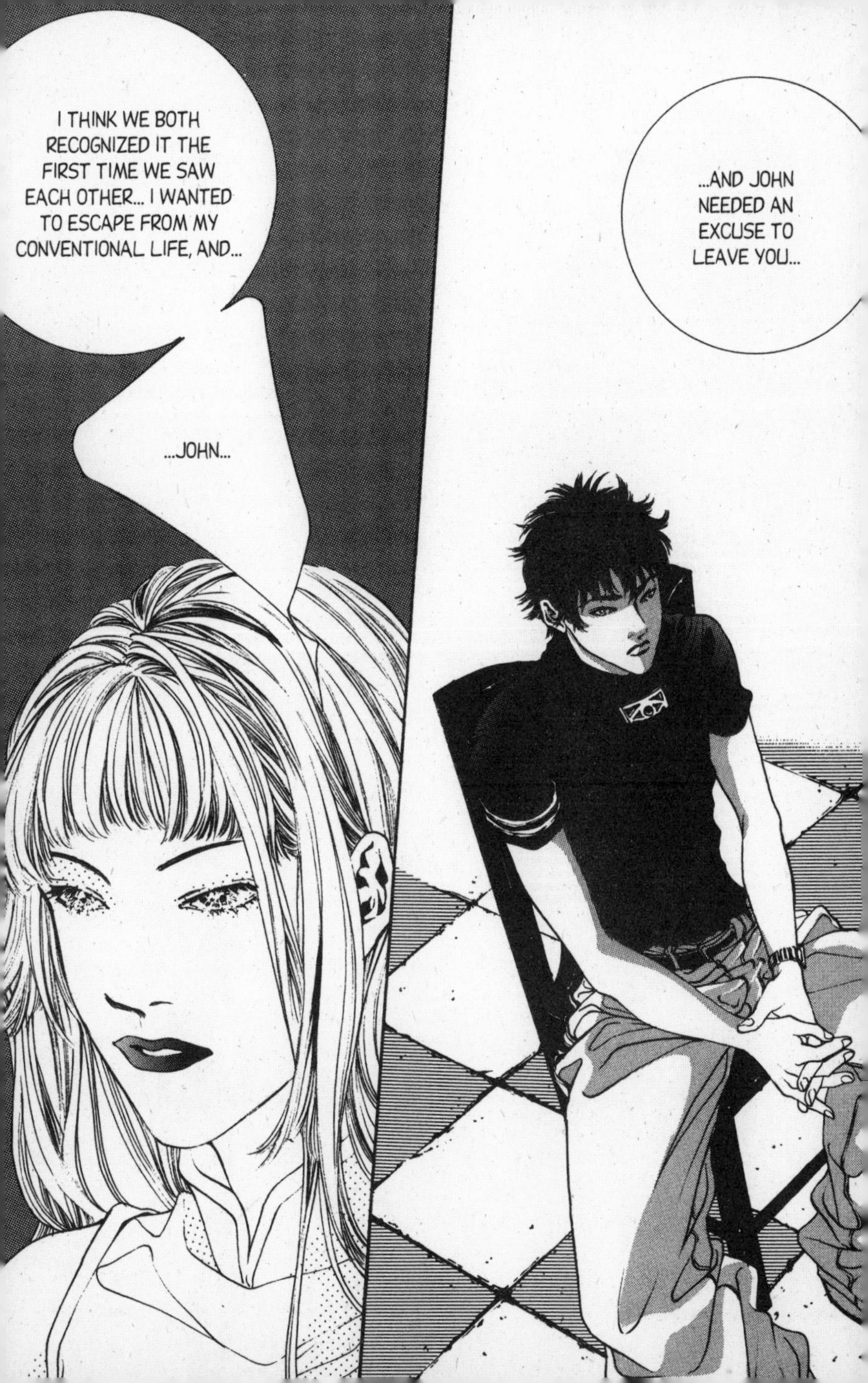
I THINK WE BOTH RECOGNIZED IT THE FIRST TIME WE SAW EACH OTHER... I WANTED TO ESCAPE FROM MY CONVENTIONAL LIFE, AND...
...JOHN...
...AND JOHN NEEDED AN EXCUSE TO LEAVE YOU...

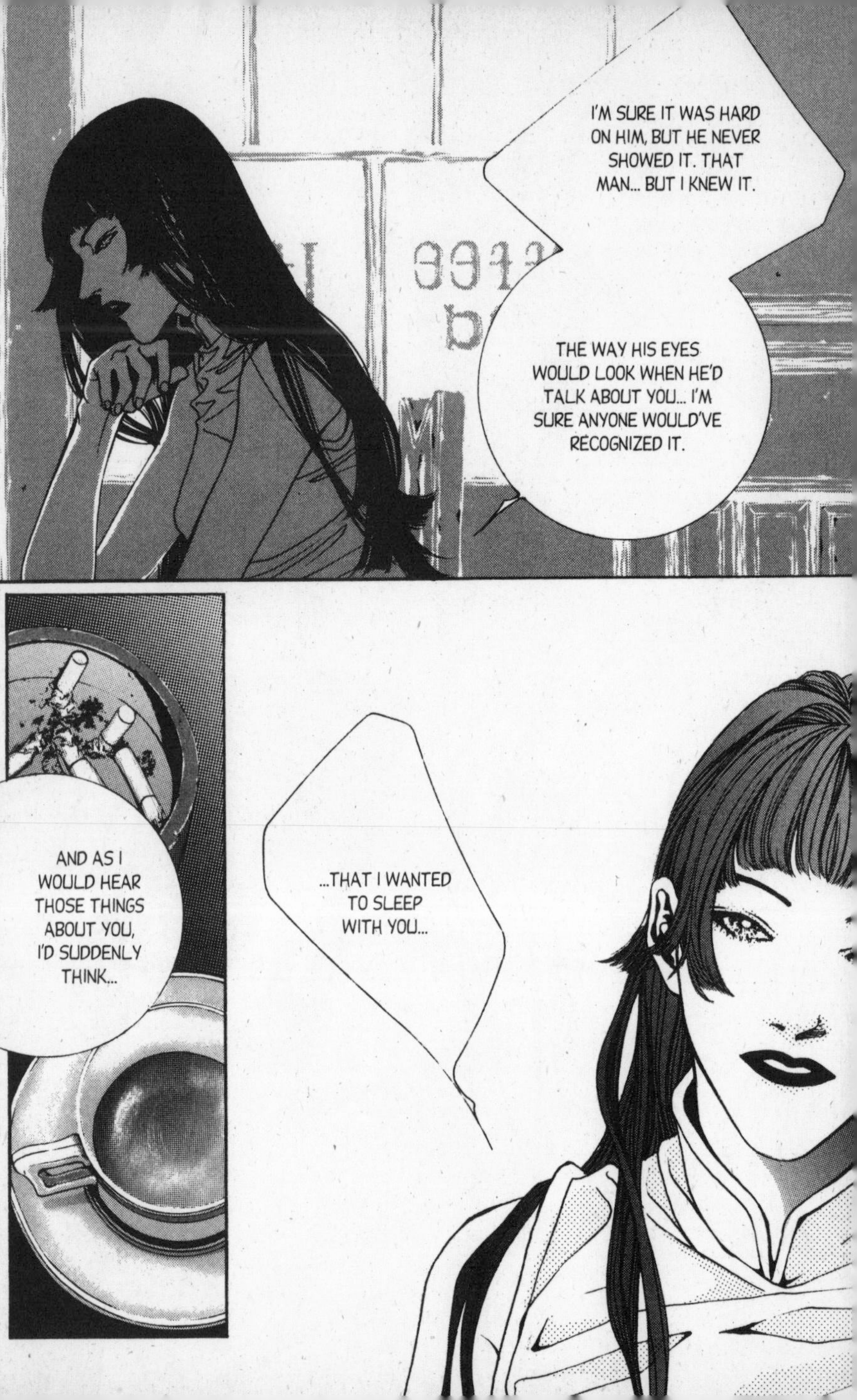
I'M SURE IT WAS HARD ON HIM, BUT HE NEVER SHOWED IT. THAT MAN... BUT I KNEW IT.
THE WAY HIS EYES WOULD LOOK WHEN HE'D TALK ABOUT YOU... I'M SURE ANYONE WOULD'VE RECOGNIZED IT.
AND AS I WOULD HEAR THOSE THINGS ABOUT YOU, I'D SUDDENLY THINK...
...THAT I WANTED TO SLEEP WITH YOU...

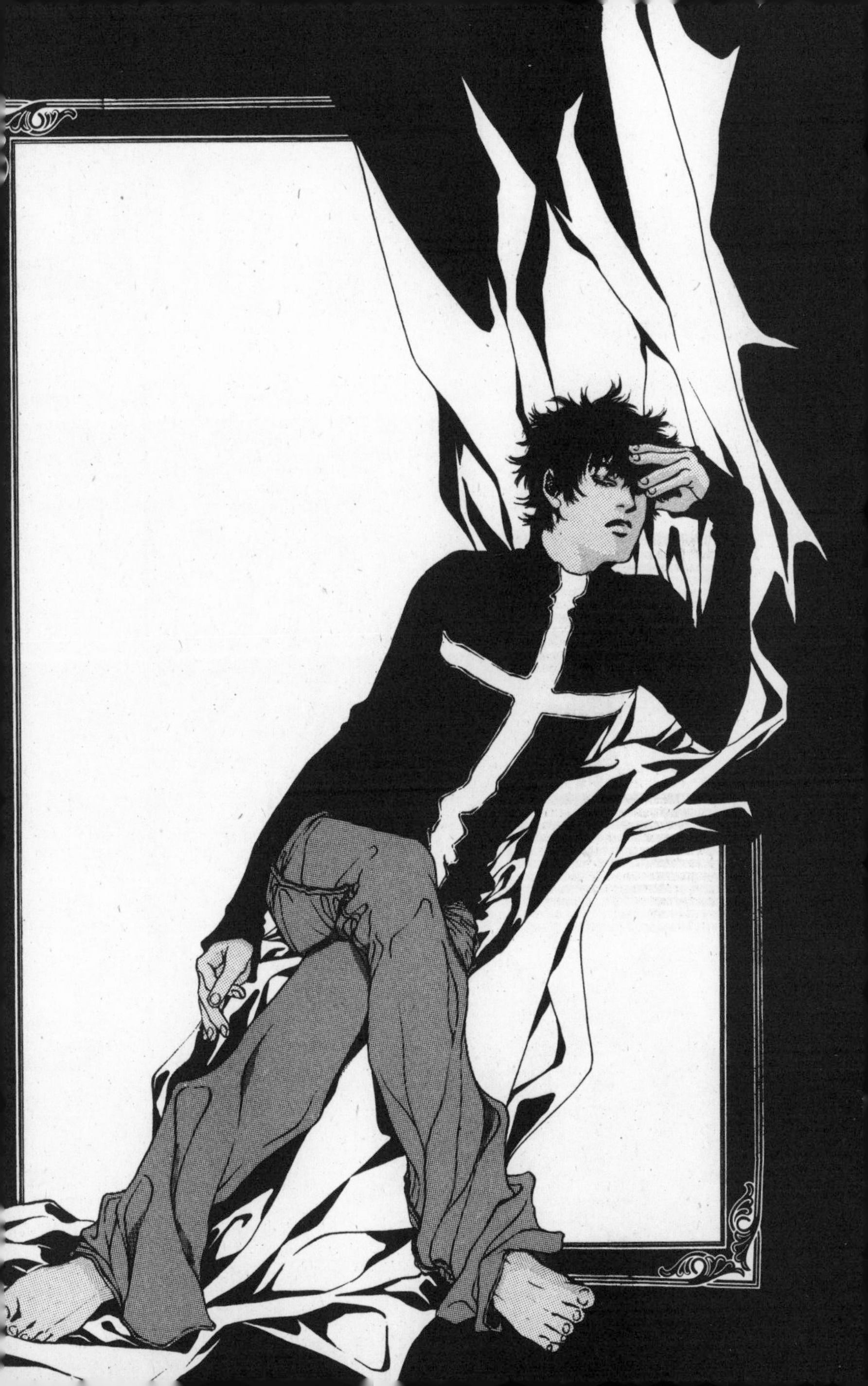

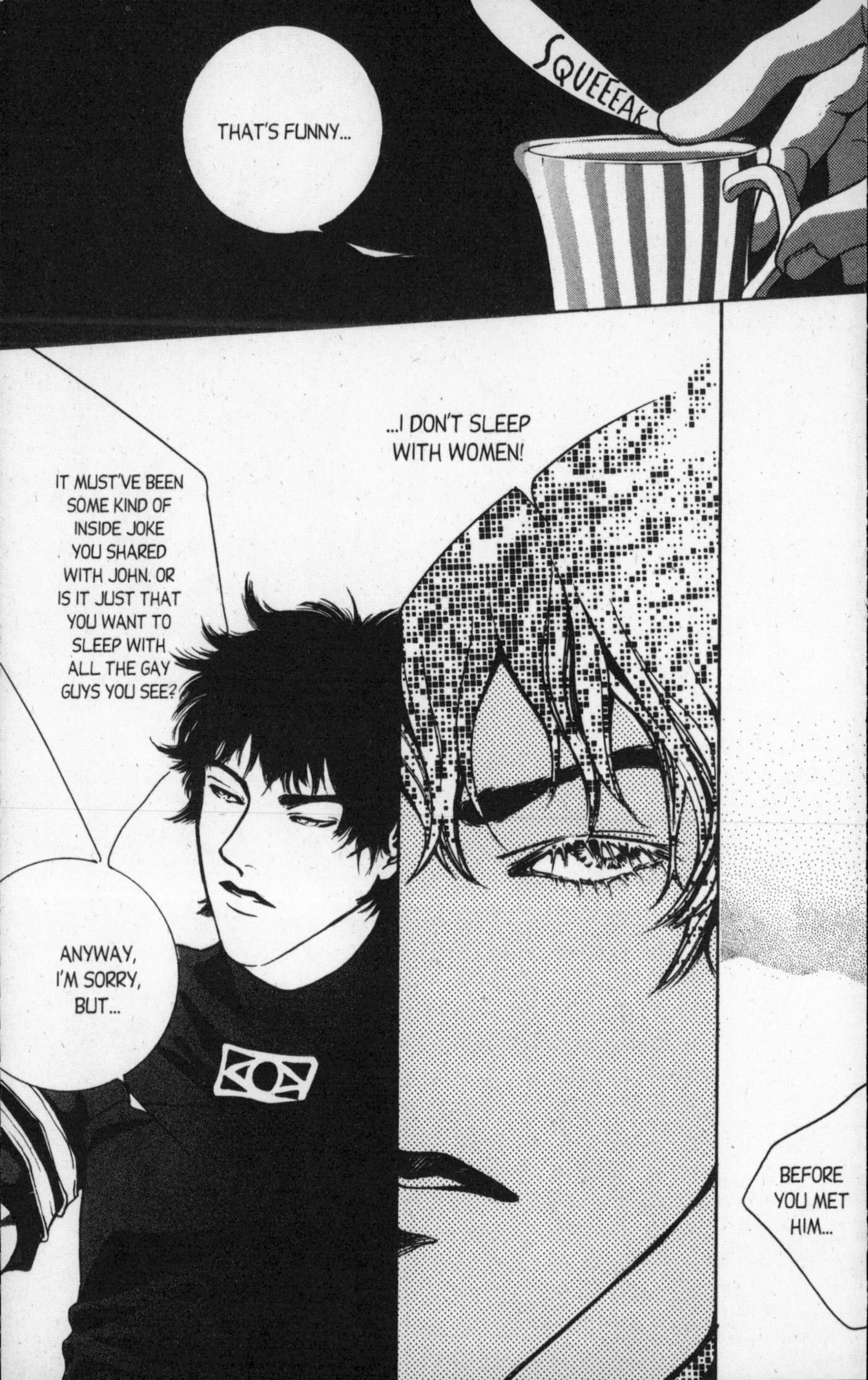
THAT'S FUNNY...
SQUEEEAK
IT MUST'VE BEEN SOME KIND OF INSIDE JOKE YOU SHARED WITH JOHN. OR IS IT JUST THAT YOU WANT TO SLEEP WITH ALL THE GAY GUYS YOU SEE?
...I DON'T SLEEP WITH WOMEN!
ANYWAY, I'M SORRY, BUT...
BEFORE YOU MET HIM...

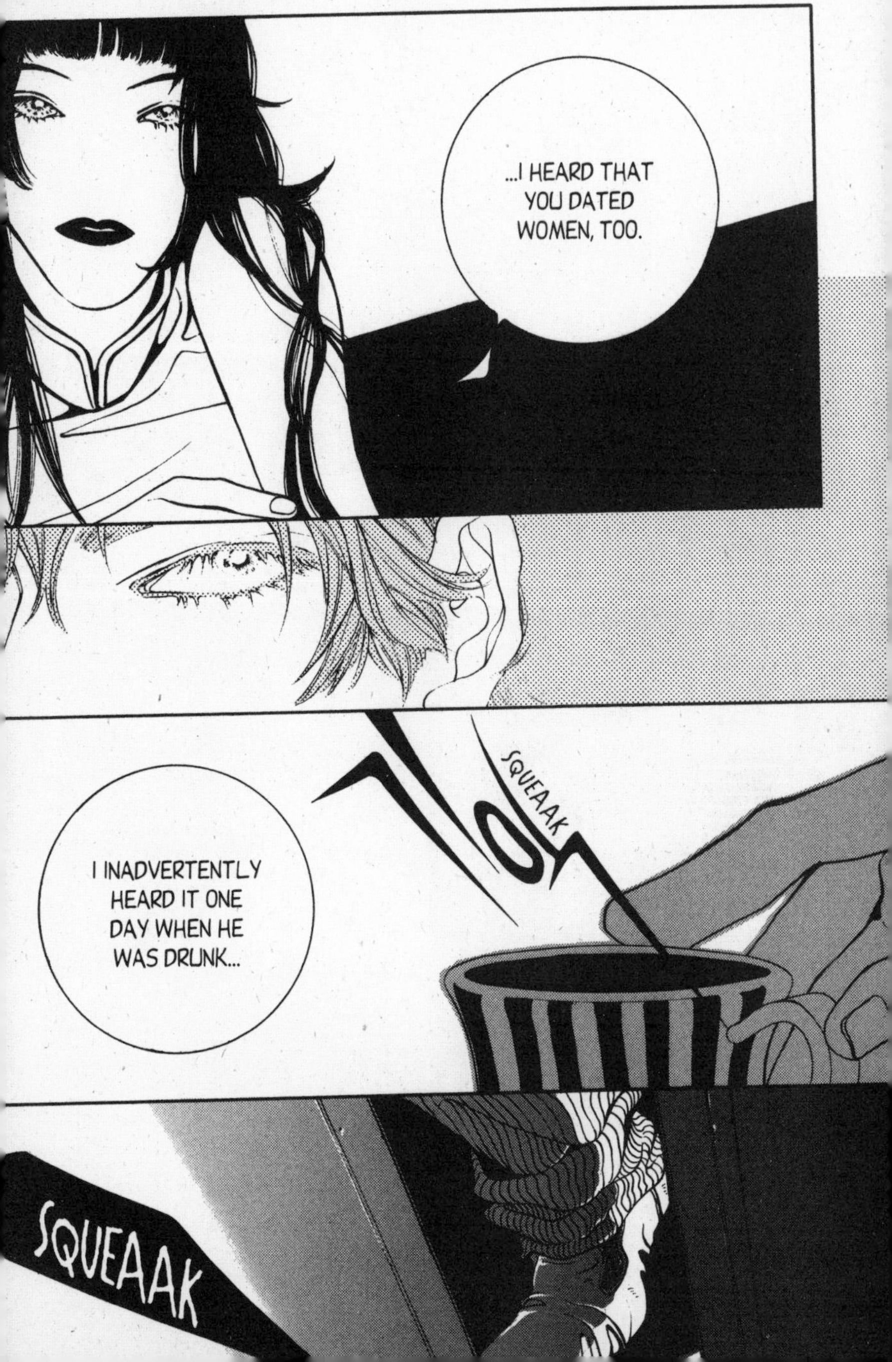
...I HEARD THAT YOU DATED WOMEN, TOO.
I INADVERTENTLY HEARD IT ONE DAY WHEN HE WAS DRUNK...
SQUEAAK
SQUEAAK

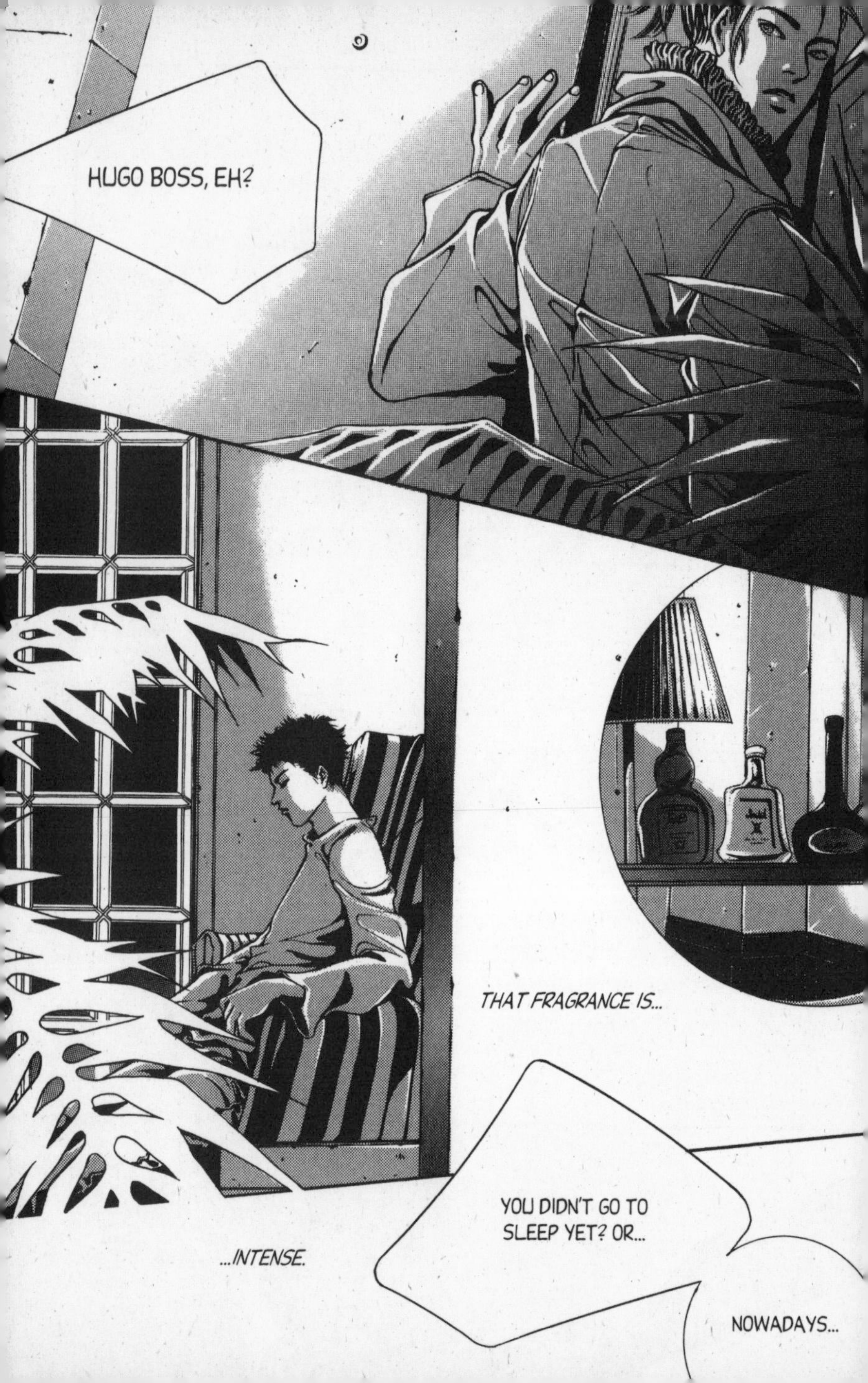
HUGO BOSS, EH?
THAT FRAGRANCE IS...
...INTENSE.
YOU DIDN'T GO TO SLEEP YET? OR...
NOWADAYS...

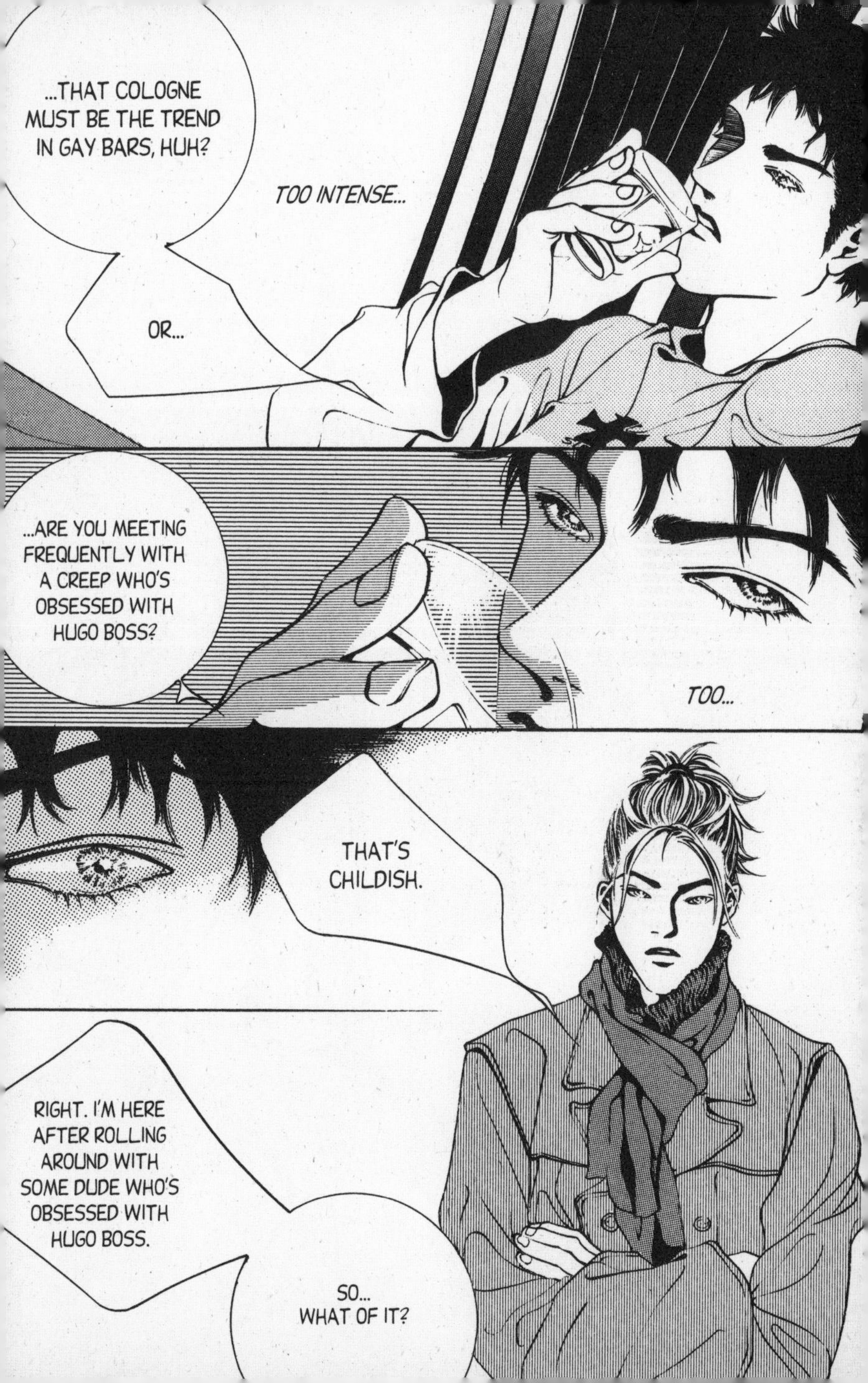
...THAT COLOGNE MUST BE THE TREND IN GAY BARS, HUH?
TOO INTENSE...
OR...
...ARE YOU MEETING FREQUENTLY WITH A CREEP WHO'S OBSESSED WITH HUGO BOSS?
TOO...
THAT'S CHILDISH.
RIGHT. I'M HERE AFTER ROLLING AROUND WITH SOME DUDE WHO'S OBSESSED WITH HUGO BOSS.
SO... WHAT OF IT?

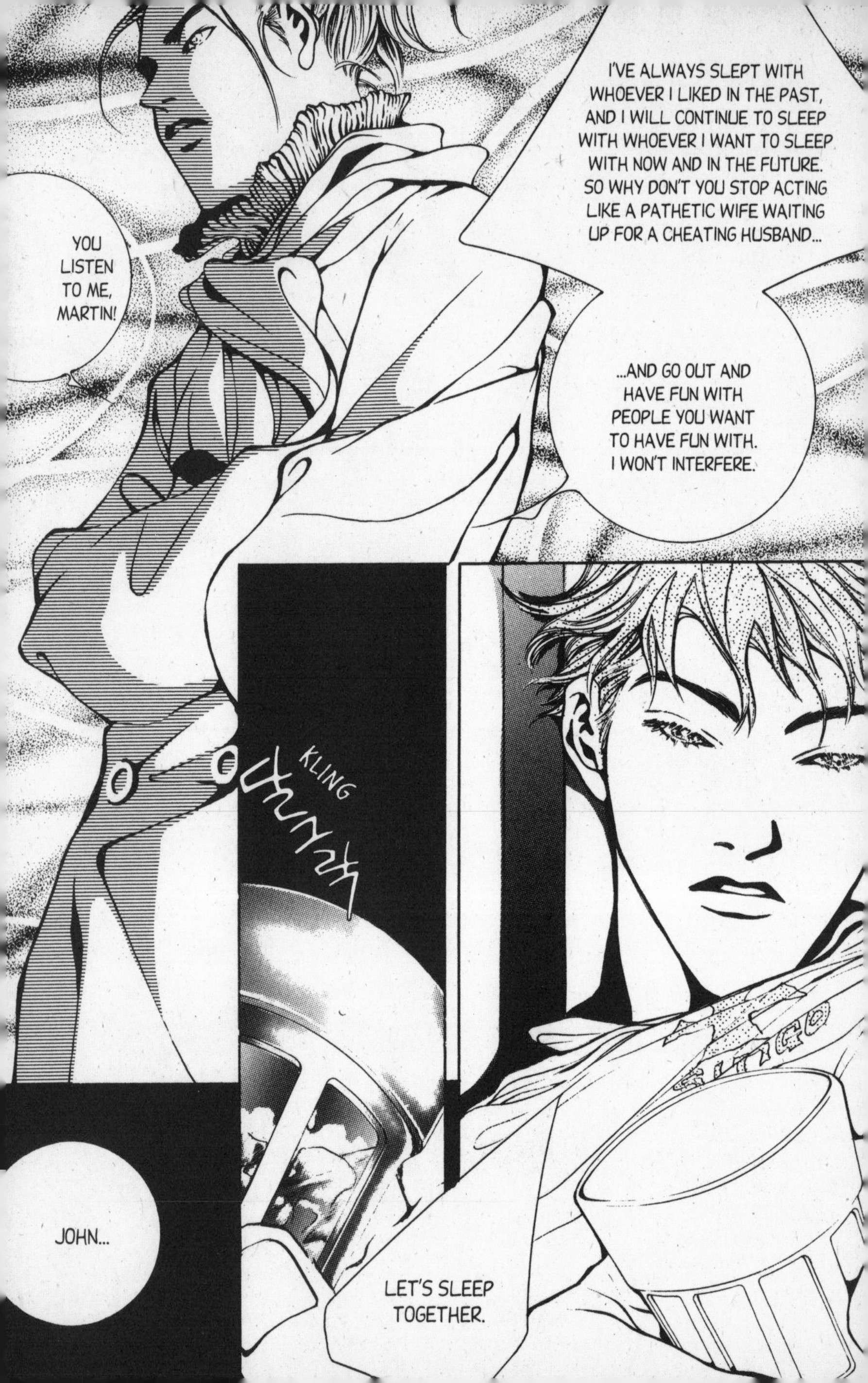
YOU LISTEN TO ME, MARTIN!
I'VE ALWAYS SLEPT WITH WHOEVER I LIKED IN THE PAST, AND I WILL CONTINUE TO SLEEP WITH WHOEVER I WANT TO SLEEP WITH NOW AND IN THE FUTURE. SO WHY DON'T YOU STOP ACTING LIKE A PATHETIC WIFE WAITING UP FOR A CHEATING HUSBAND...
...AND GO OUT AND HAVE FUN WITH PEOPLE YOU WANT TO HAVE FUN WITH. I WON'T INTERFERE.
JOHN...
KLING
LET'S SLEEP TOGETHER.

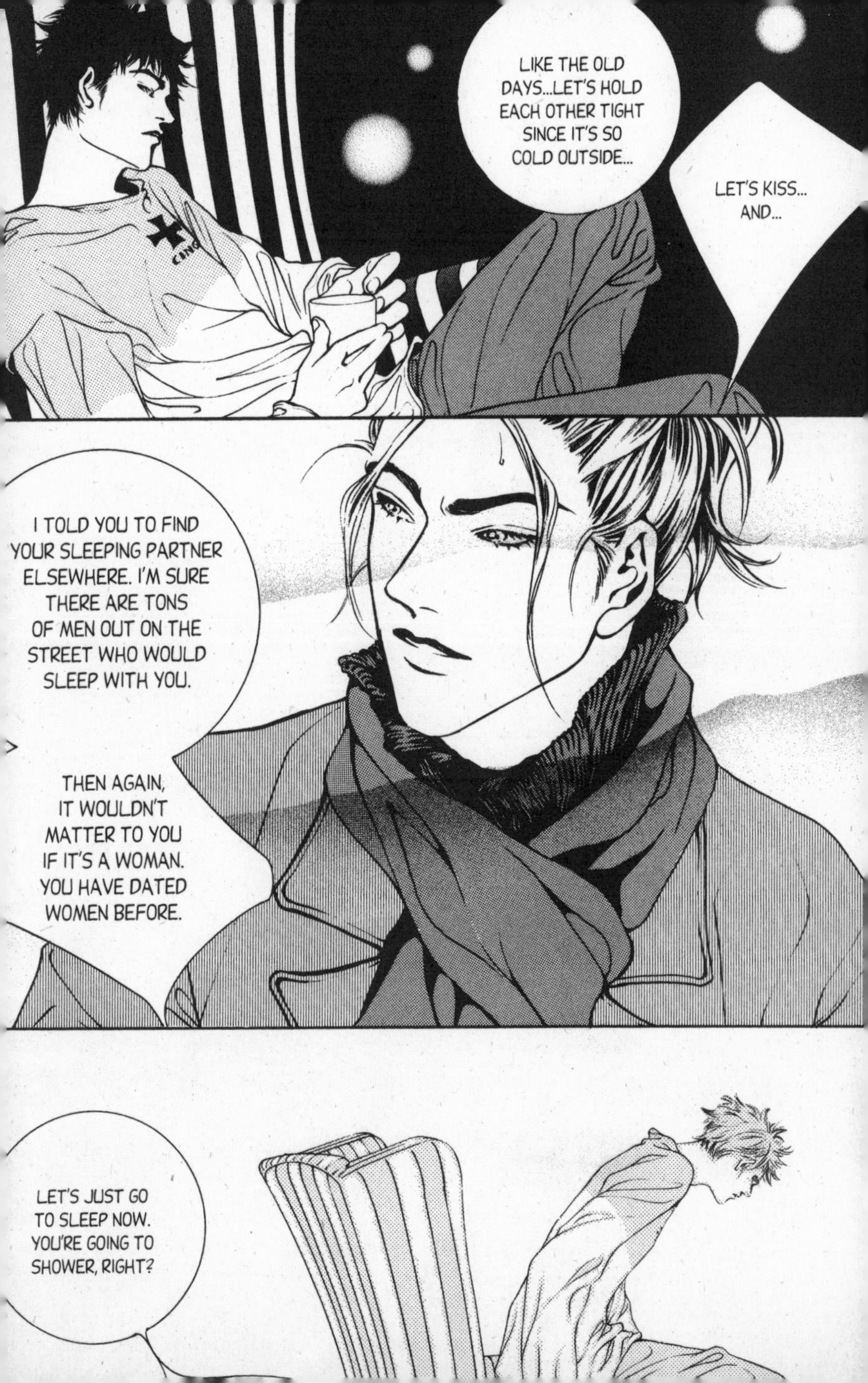
LIKE THE OLD DAYS...LET'S HOLD EACH OTHER TIGHT SINCE IT'S SO COLD OUTSIDE...
LET'S KISS... AND...
I TOLD YOU TO FIND YOUR SLEEPING PARTNER ELSEWHERE. I'M SURE THERE ARE TONS OF MEN OUT ON THE STREET WHO WOULD SLEEP WITH YOU.
THEN AGAIN, IT WOULDN'T MATTER TO YOU IF IT'S A WOMAN. YOU HAVE DATED WOMEN BEFORE.
LET'S JUST GO TO SLEEP NOW. YOU'RE GOING TO SHOWER, RIGHT?

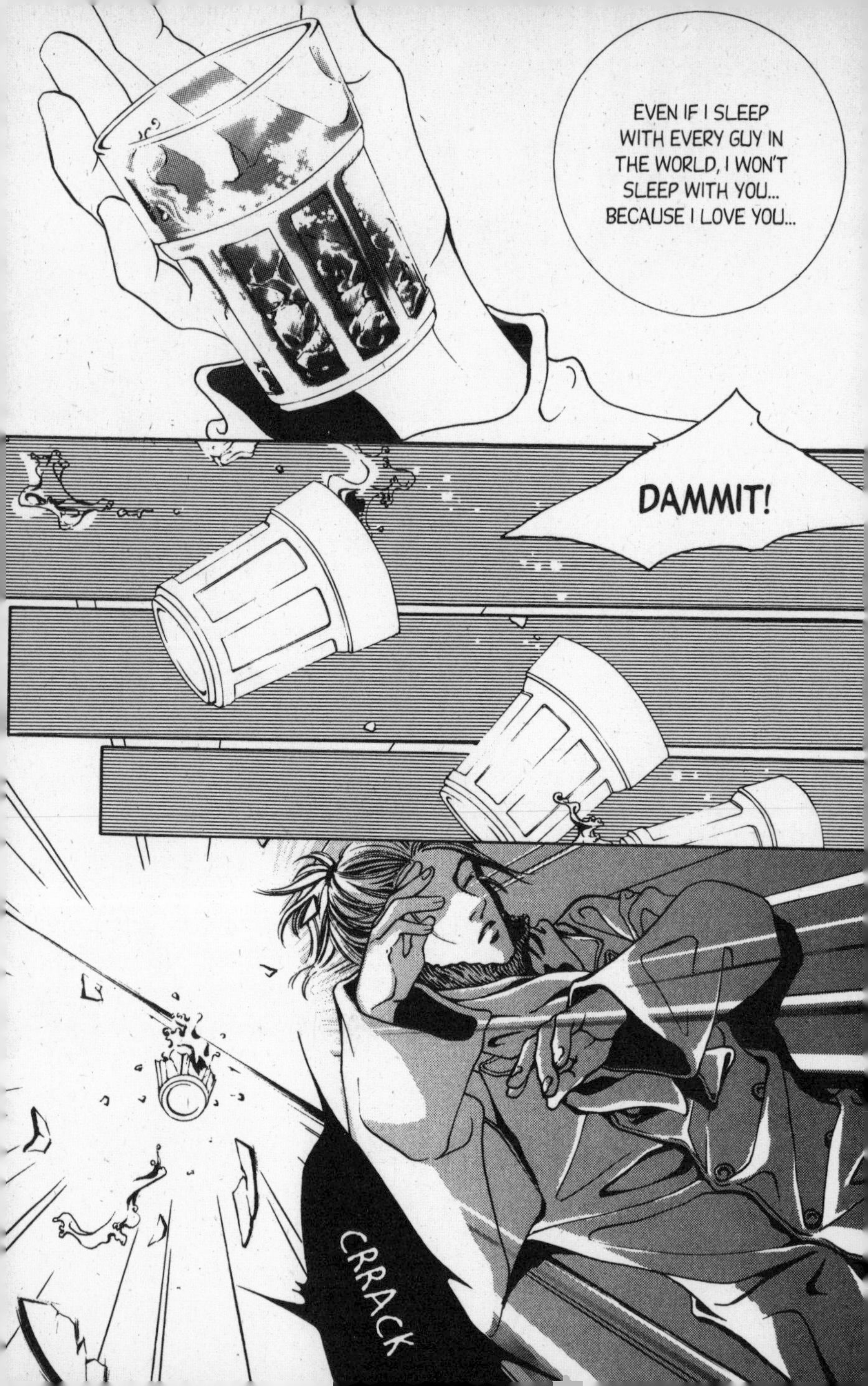
EVEN IF I SLEEP WITH EVERY GUY IN THE WORLD, I WON'T SLEEP WITH YOU... BECAUSE I LOVE YOU...
DAMMIT!
CRRACK

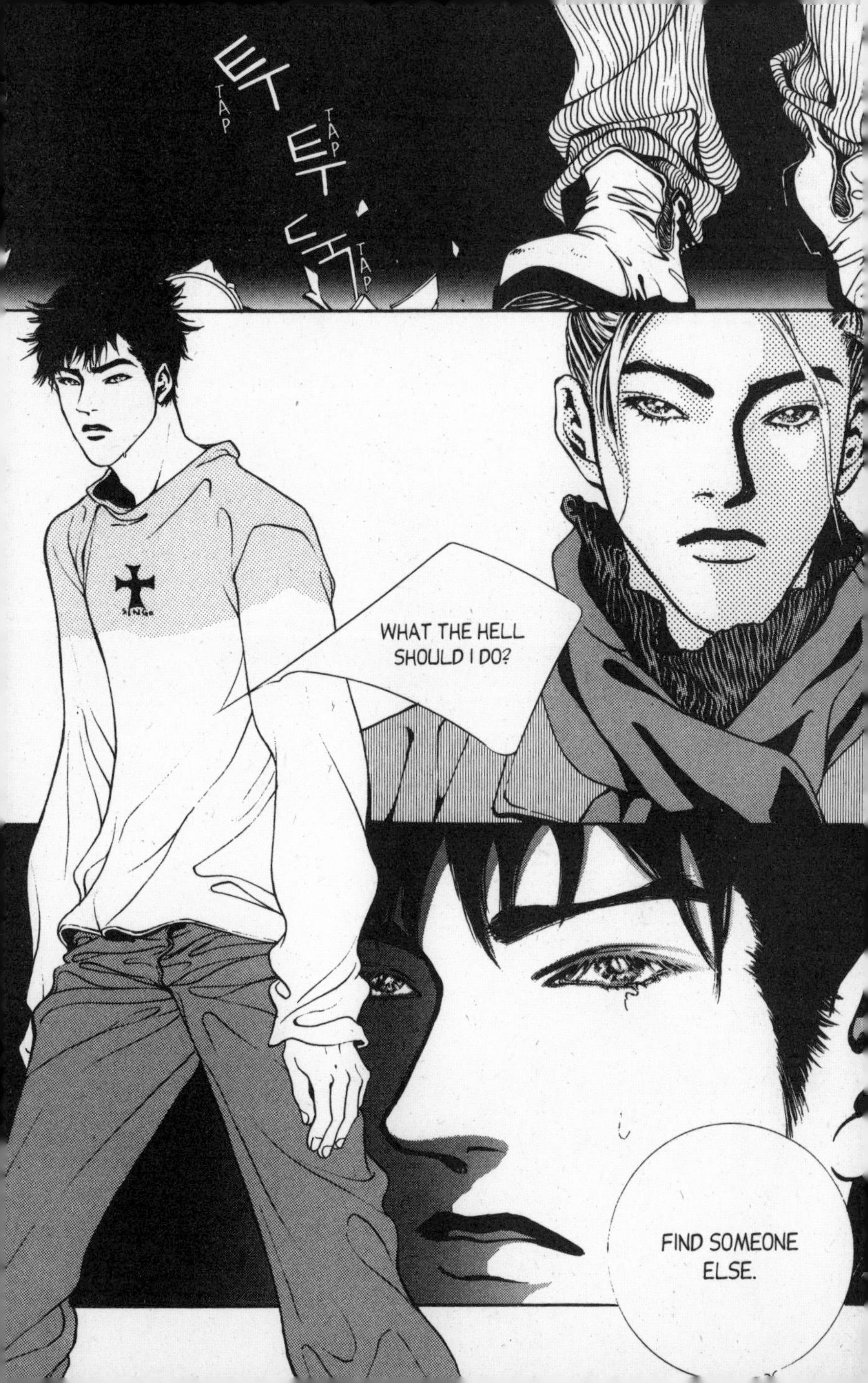

탁 탁 탁
TAP TAP TAP
WHAT THE HELL SHOULD I DO?
FIND SOMEONE ELSE.

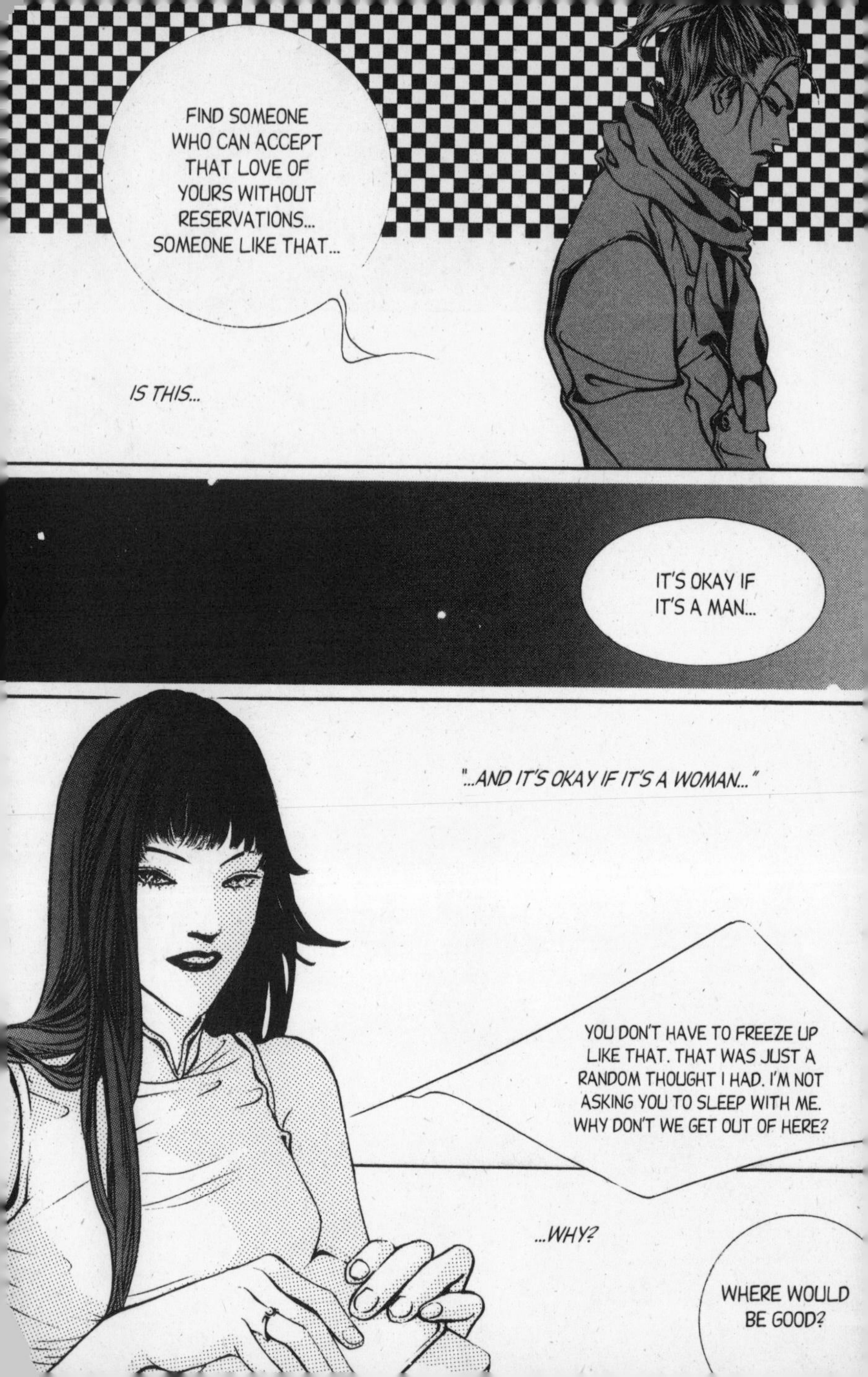
FIND SOMEONE WHO CAN ACCEPT THAT LOVE OF YOURS WITHOUT RESERVATIONS... SOMEONE LIKE THAT...
IS THIS...
IT'S OKAY IF IT'S A MAN...
"...AND IT'S OKAY IF IT'S A WOMAN..."
YOU DON'T HAVE TO FREEZE UP LIKE THAT. THAT WAS JUST A RANDOM THOUGHT I HAD. I'M NOT ASKING YOU TO SLEEP WITH ME. WHY DON'T WE GET OUT OF HERE?
...WHY?
WHERE WOULD BE GOOD?

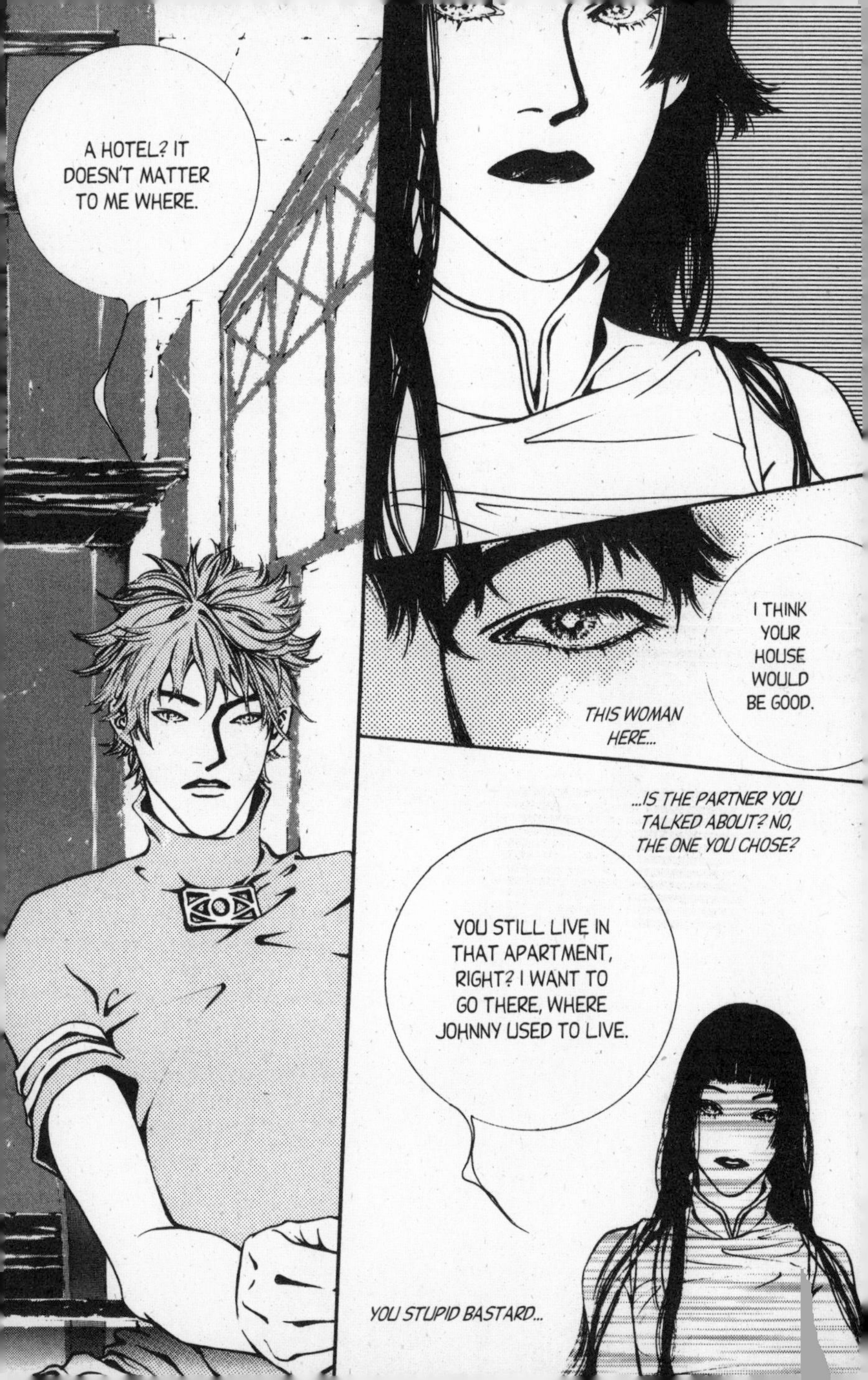
A HOTEL? IT DOESN'T MATTER TO ME WHERE.
I THINK YOUR HOUSE WOULD BE GOOD.
THIS WOMAN HERE...
...IS THE PARTNER YOU TALKED ABOUT? NO, THE ONE YOU CHOSE?
YOU STILL LIVE IN THAT APARTMENT, RIGHT? I WANT TO GO THERE, WHERE JOHNNY USED TO LIVE.
YOU STUPID BASTARD...

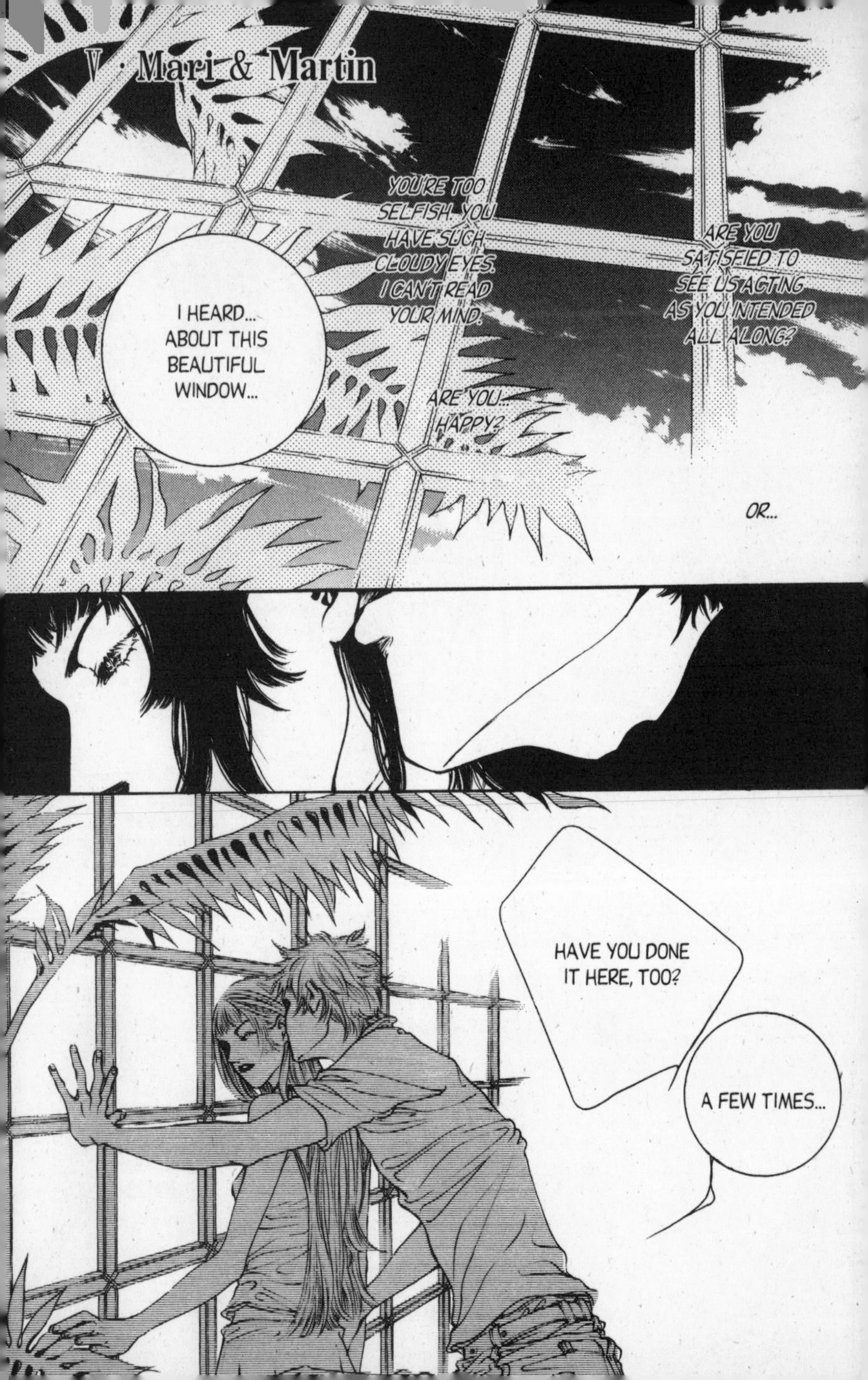
V · Mari & Martin
I HEARD... ABOUT THIS BEAUTIFUL WINDOW...
YOU'RE TOO SELFISH. YOU HAVE SUCH CLOUDY EYES. I CAN'T READ YOUR MIND.
ARE YOU... HAPPY?
ARE YOU SATISFIED TO SEE US ACTING AS YOU INTENDED ALL ALONG?
OR...
HAVE YOU DONE IT HERE, TOO?
A FEW TIMES...

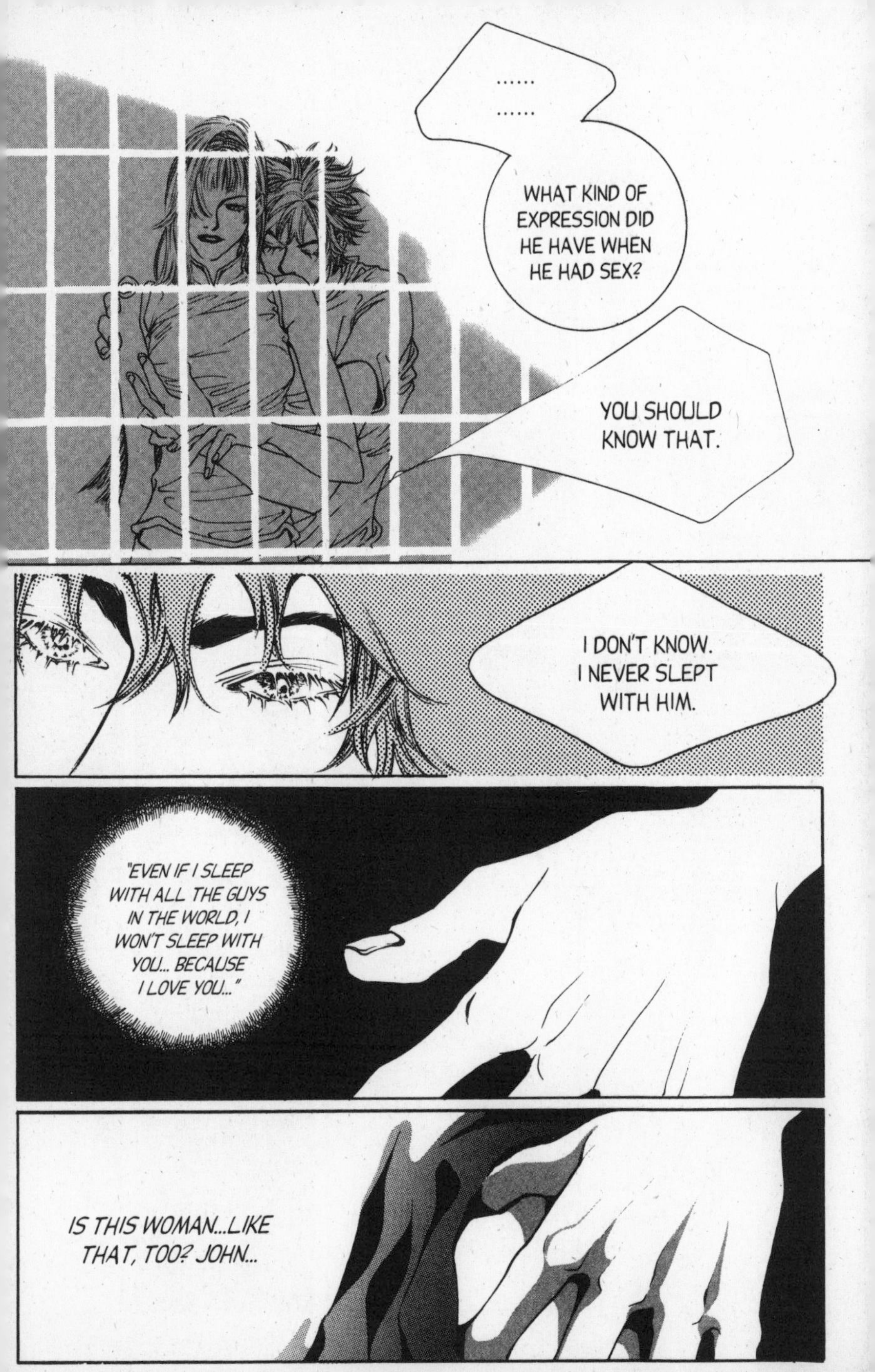

......
......
WHAT KIND OF EXPRESSION DID HE HAVE WHEN HE HAD SEX?
YOU SHOULD KNOW THAT.
I DON'T KNOW. I NEVER SLEPT WITH HIM.
"EVEN IF I SLEEP WITH ALL THE GUYS IN THE WORLD, I WON'T SLEEP WITH YOU... BECAUSE I LOVE YOU..."
IS THIS WOMAN...LIKE THAT, TOO? JOHN...

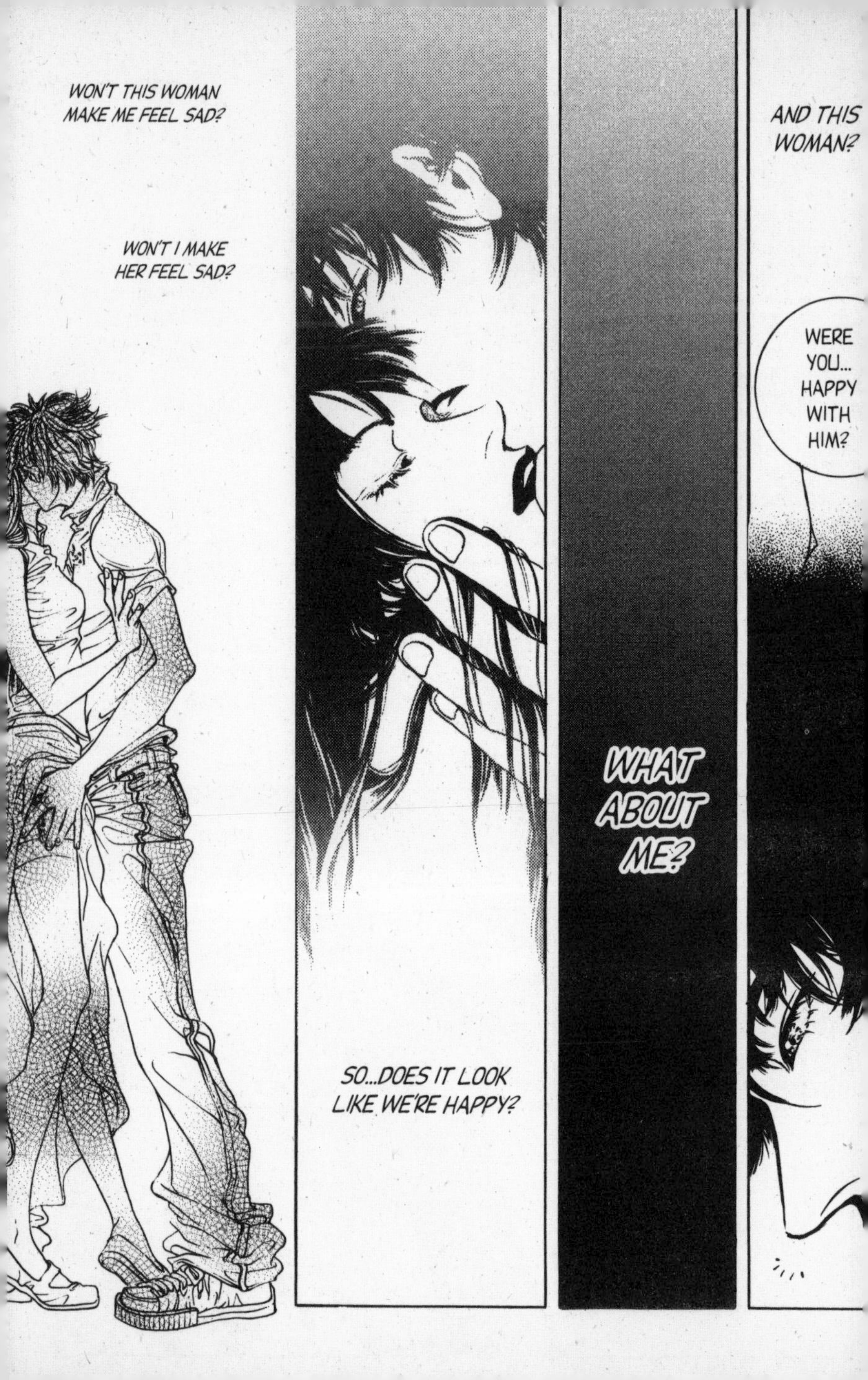
WON'T THIS WOMAN MAKE ME FEEL SAD?
WON'T I MAKE HER FEEL SAD?
SO...DOES IT LOOK LIKE WE'RE HAPPY?
WHAT ABOUT ME?
AND THIS WOMAN?
WERE YOU... HAPPY WITH HIM?

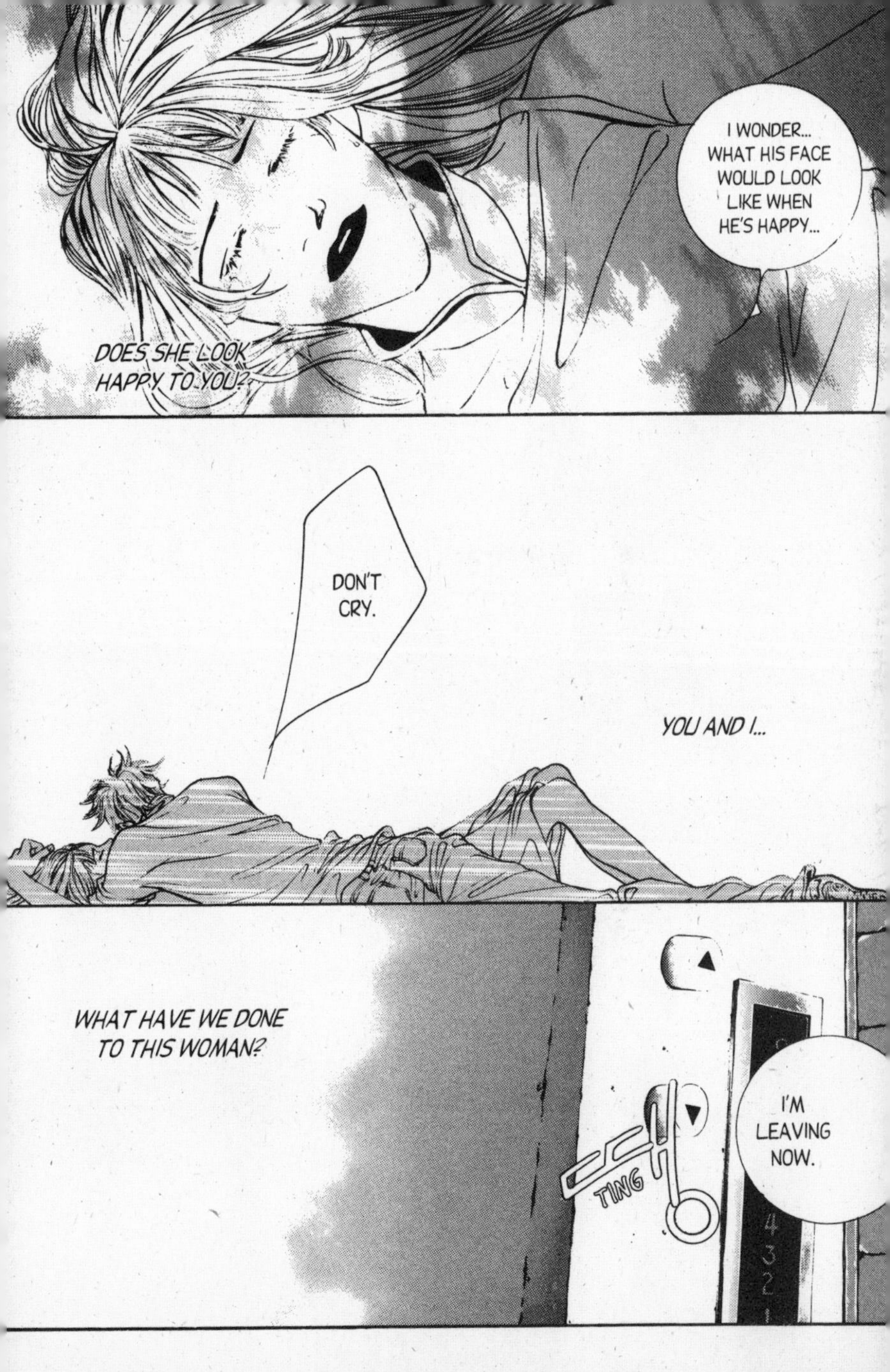
I WONDER... WHAT HIS FACE WOULD LOOK LIKE WHEN HE'S HAPPY...
DOES SHE LOOK HAPPY TO YOU?
DON'T CRY.
YOU AND I...
WHAT HAVE WE DONE TO THIS WOMAN?
TING
I'M LEAVING NOW.

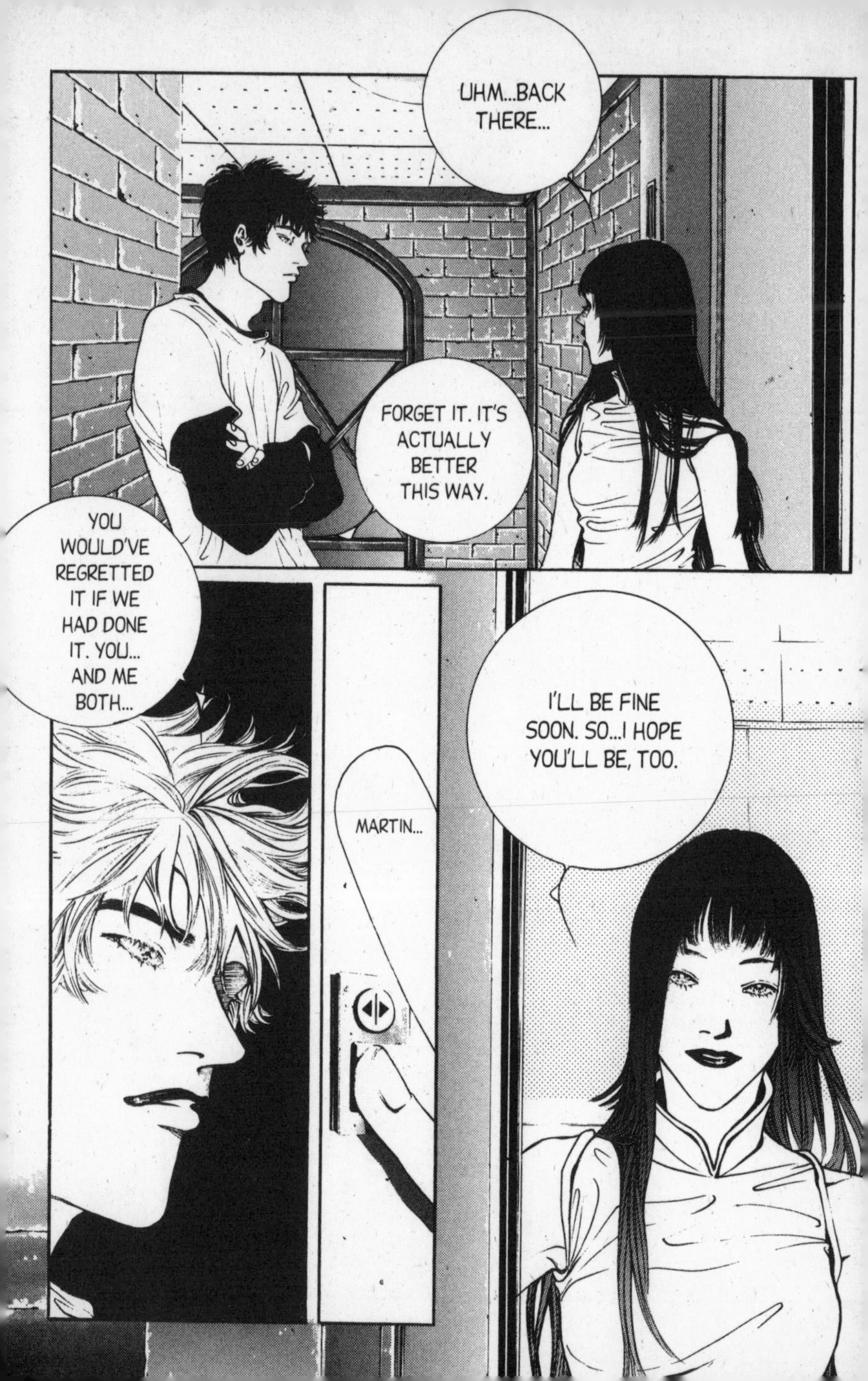
UHM...BACK THERE...
FORGET IT. IT'S ACTUALLY BETTER THIS WAY.
YOU WOULD'VE REGRETTED IT IF WE HAD DONE IT. YOU... AND ME BOTH...
MARTIN...
I'LL BE FINE SOON. SO...I HOPE YOU'LL BE, TOO.

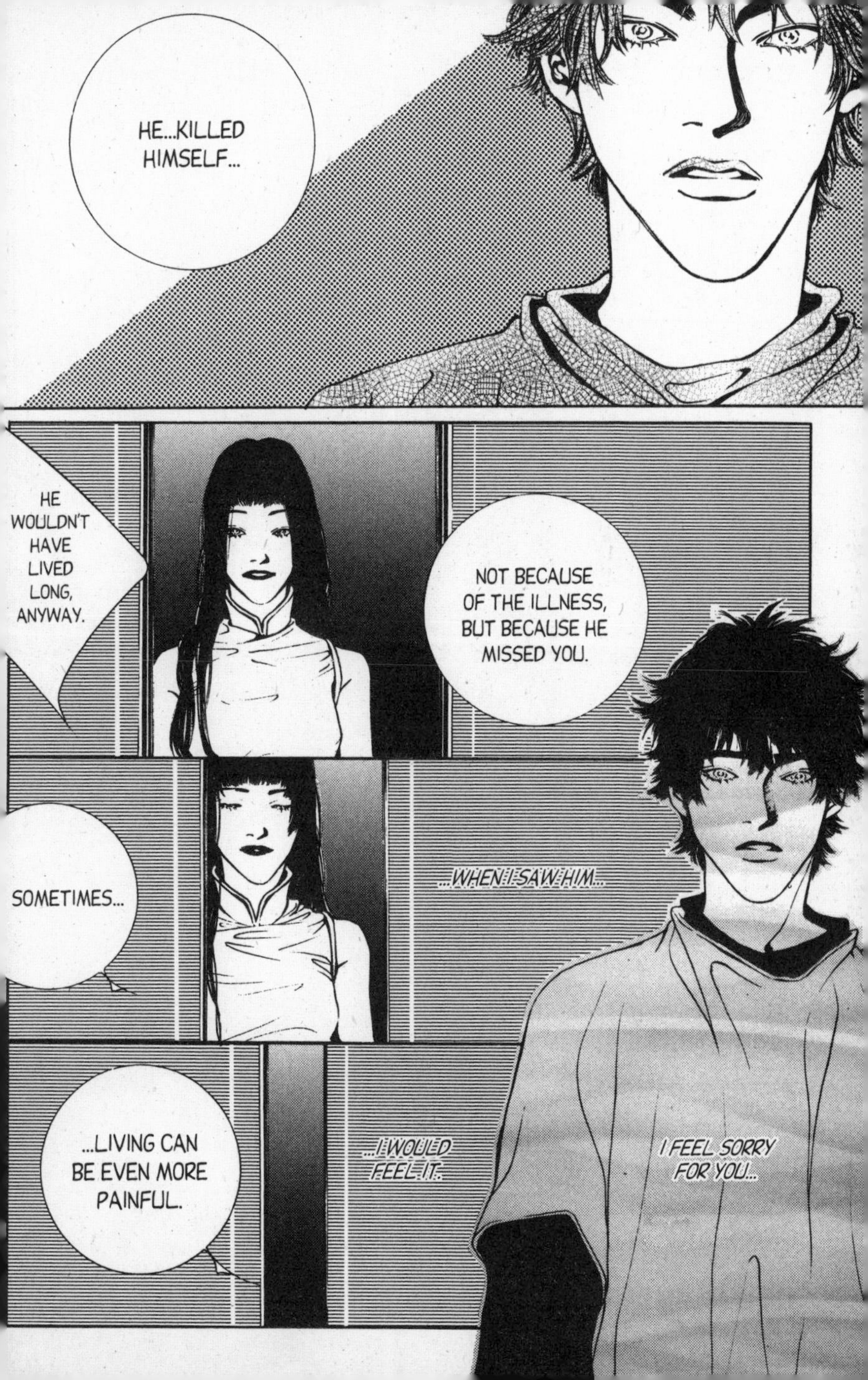
HE...KILLED HIMSELF...
HE WOULDN'T HAVE LIVED LONG, ANYWAY.
NOT BECAUSE OF THE ILLNESS, BUT BECAUSE HE MISSED YOU.
SOMETIMES...
...WHEN I SAW HIM...
...LIVING CAN BE EVEN MORE PAINFUL.
...I WOULD FEEL IT.
I FEEL SORRY FOR YOU...

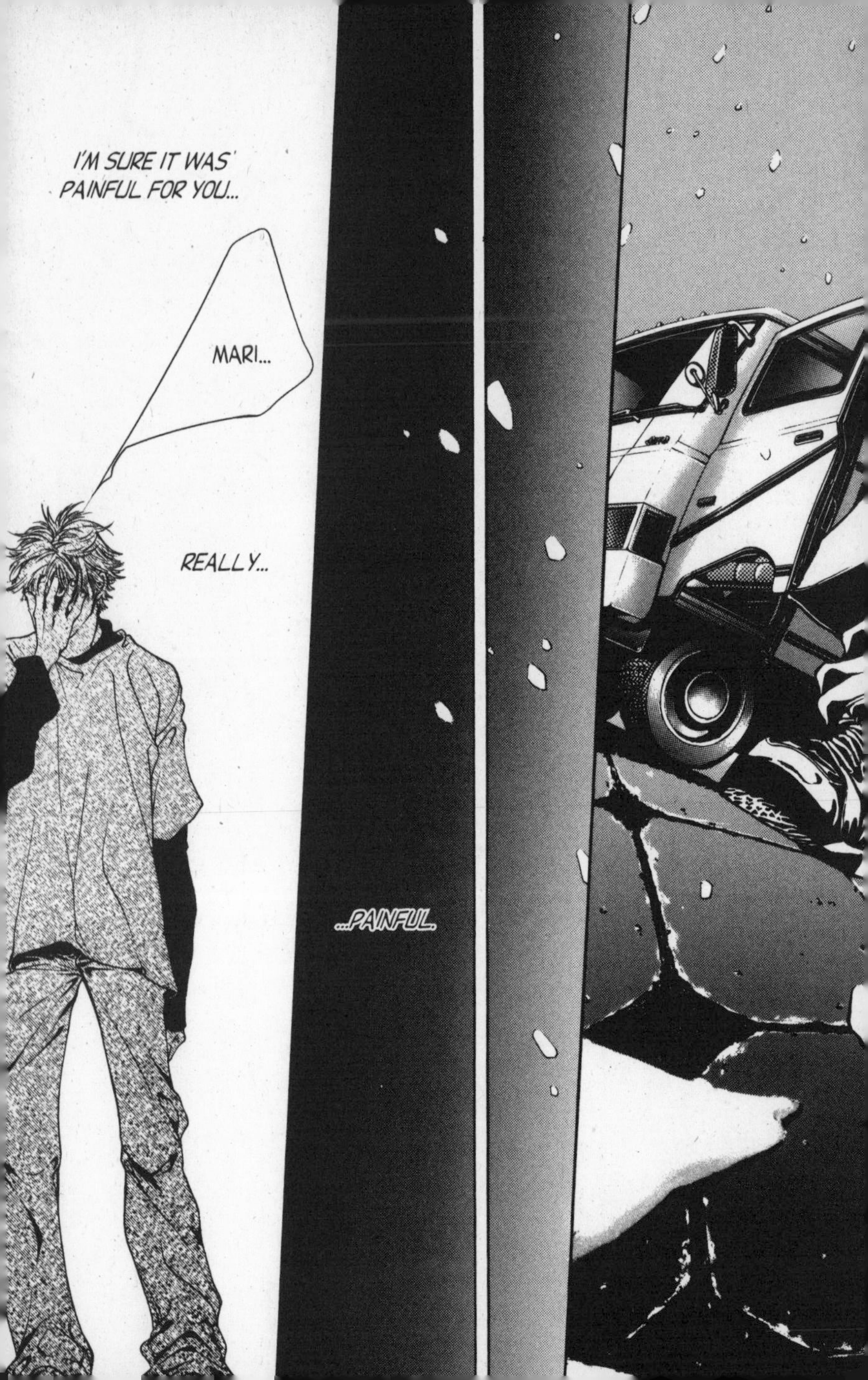
I'M SURE IT WAS PAINFUL FOR YOU...
MARI...
REALLY...
...PAINFUL.

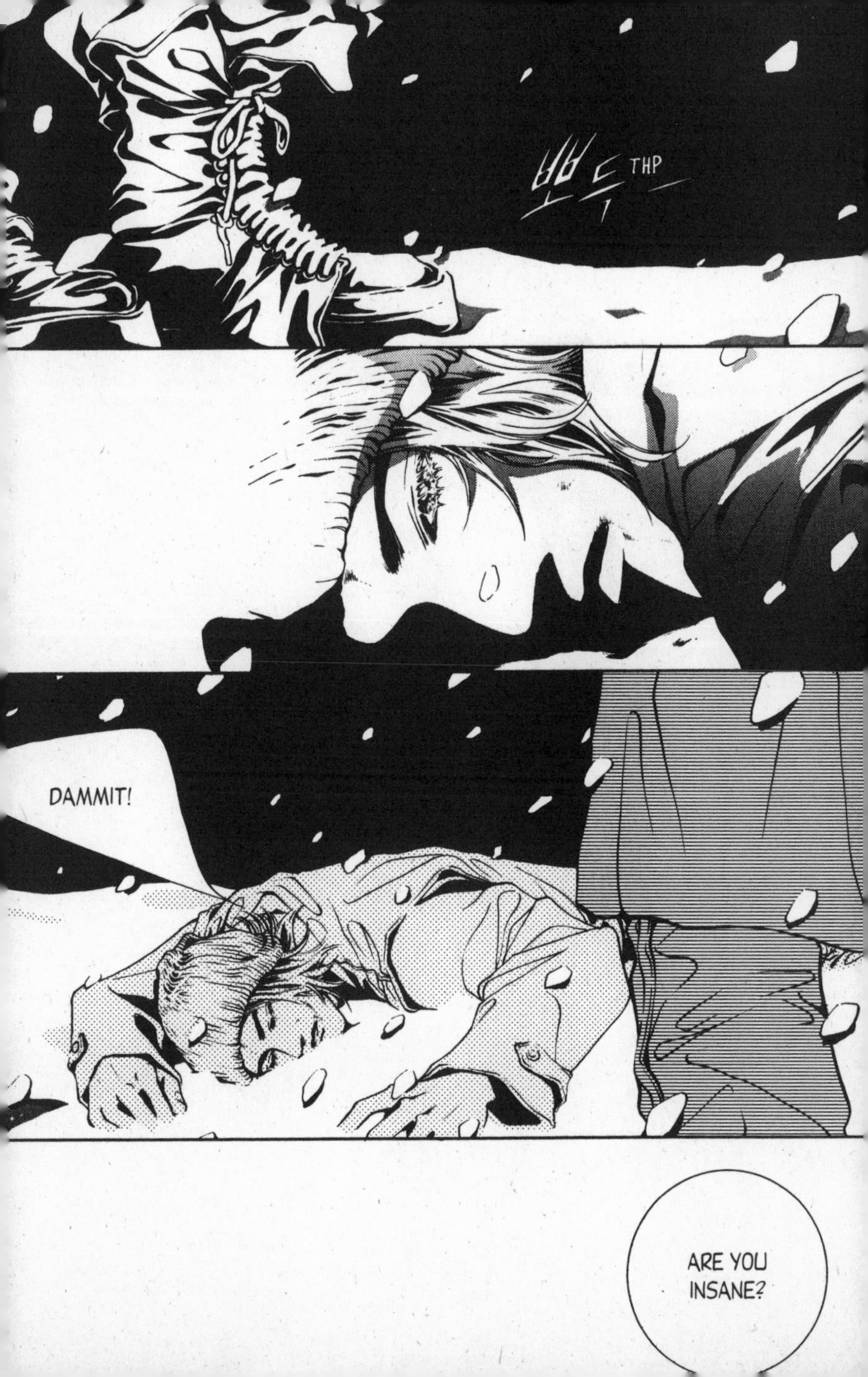
뽀득
THP
DAMMIT!
ARE YOU INSANE?

VI · Martin & John
WHAT'S WITH THE CLOTHES? DON'T YOU KNOW IT'S REALLY COLD TODAY?

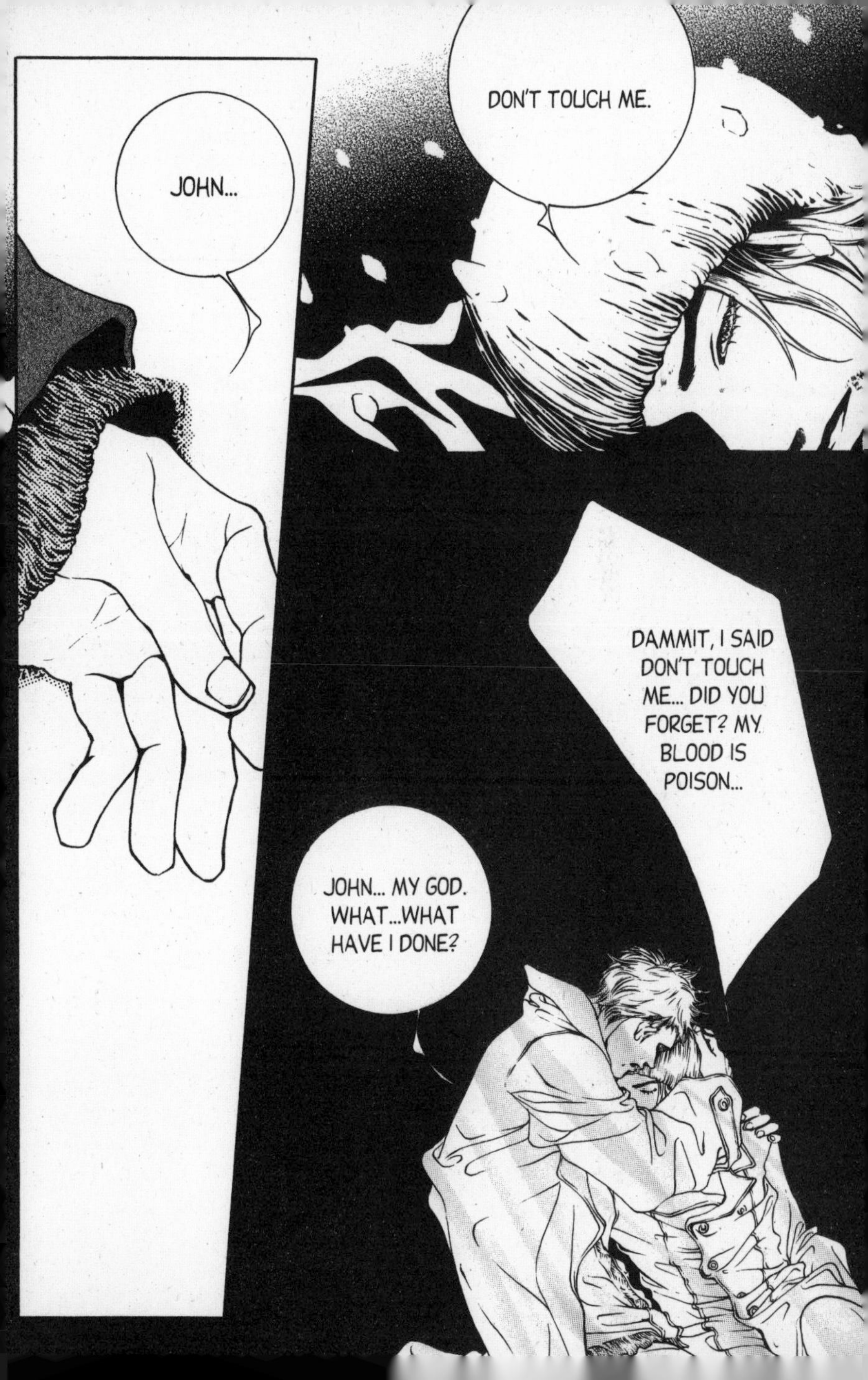
JOHN...
DON'T TOUCH ME.
DAMMIT, I SAID DON'T TOUCH ME... DID YOU FORGET? MY BLOOD IS POISON...
JOHN... MY GOD. WHAT...WHAT HAVE I DONE?

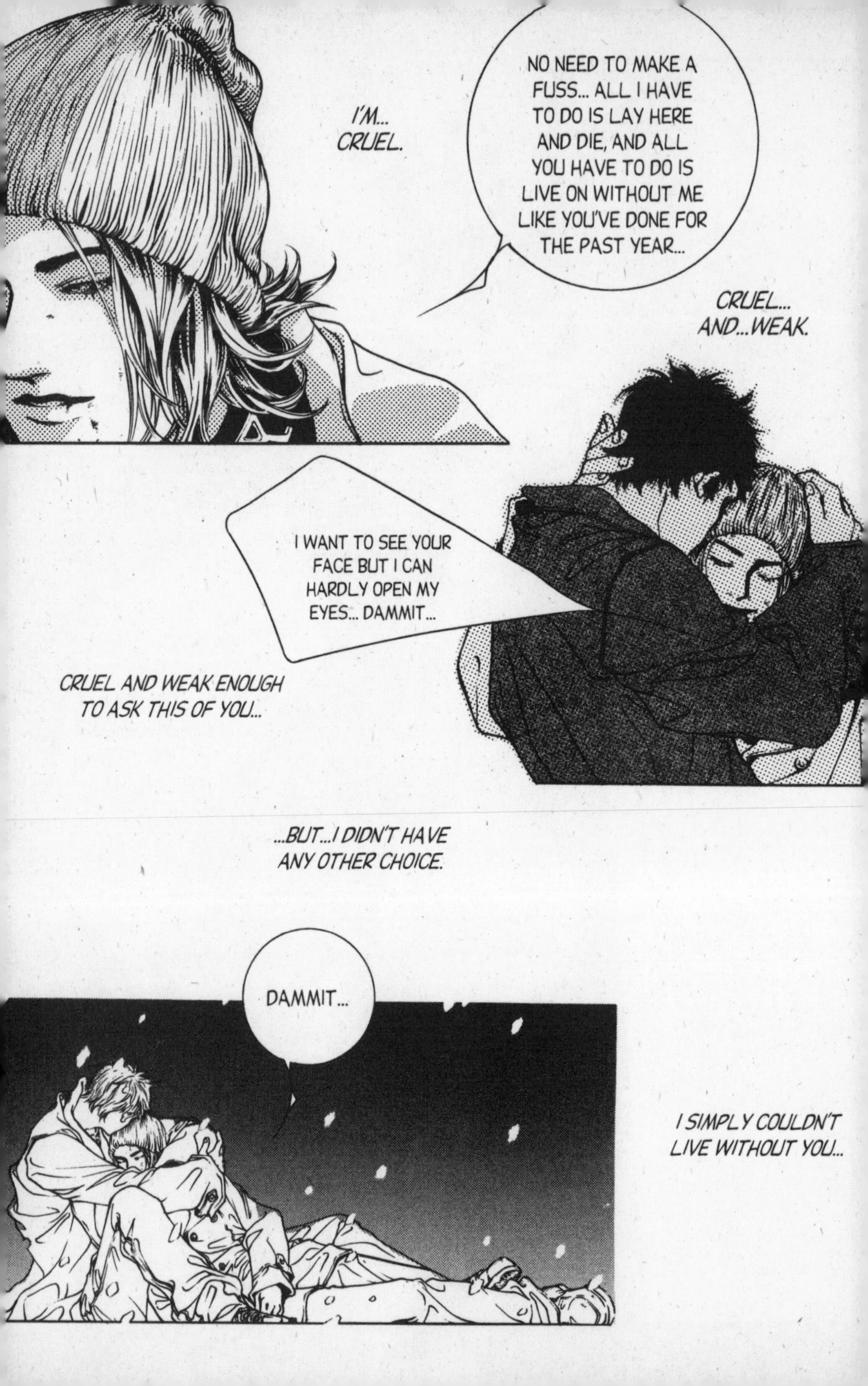
I'M... CRUEL.
NO NEED TO MAKE A FUSS... ALL I HAVE TO DO IS LAY HERE AND DIE, AND ALL YOU HAVE TO DO IS LIVE ON WITHOUT ME LIKE YOU'VE DONE FOR THE PAST YEAR...
CRUEL... AND...WEAK.
I WANT TO SEE YOUR FACE BUT I CAN HARDLY OPEN MY EYES... DAMMIT...
CRUEL AND WEAK ENOUGH TO ASK THIS OF YOU...
...BUT...I DIDN'T HAVE ANY OTHER CHOICE.
DAMMIT...
I SIMPLY COULDN'T LIVE WITHOUT YOU...

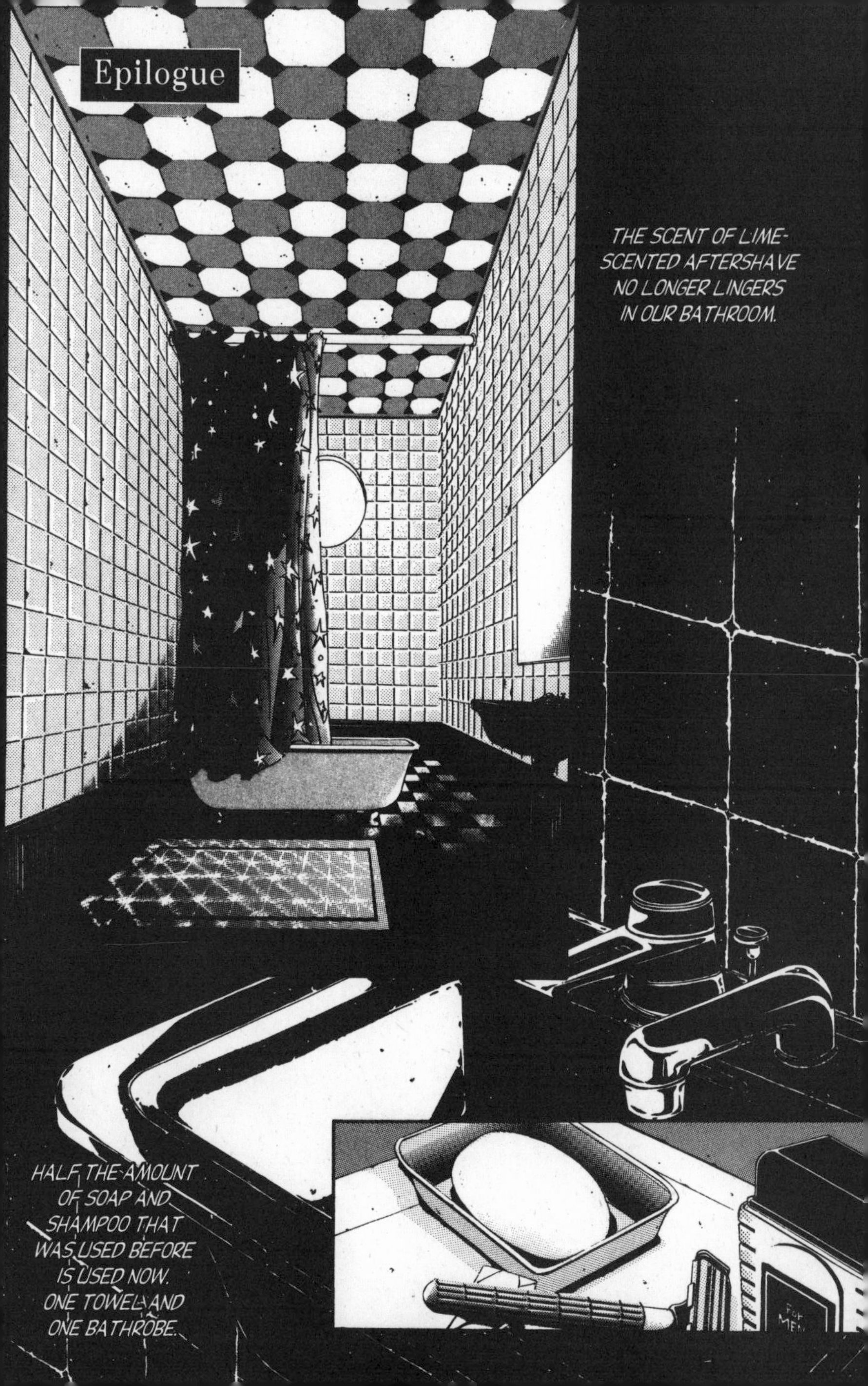
Epilogue
THE SCENT OF LIME-SCENTED AFTERSHAVE NO LONGER LINGERS IN OUR BATHROOM.
HALF THE AMOUNT OF SOAP AND SHAMPOO THAT WAS USED BEFORE IS USED NOW. ONE TOWEL AND ONE BATHROBE.

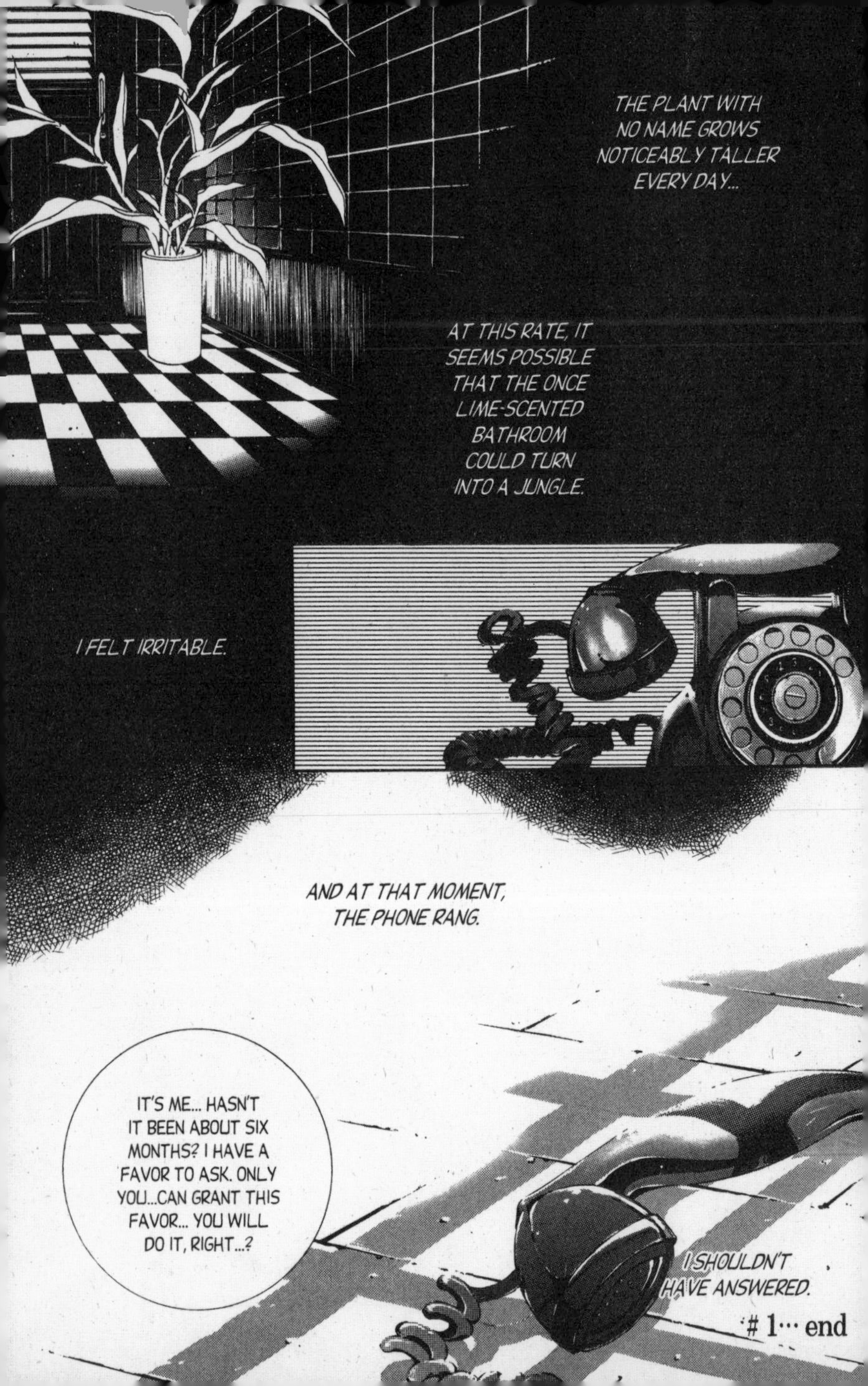
THE PLANT WITH NO NAME GROWS NOTICEABLY TALLER EVERY DAY...
AT THIS RATE, IT SEEMS POSSIBLE THAT THE ONCE LIME-SCENTED BATHROOM COULD TURN INTO A JUNGLE.
I FELT IRRITABLE.
AND AT THAT MOMENT, THE PHONE RANG.
IT'S ME... HASN'T IT BEEN ABOUT SIX MONTHS? I HAVE A FAVOR TO ASK. ONLY YOU...CAN GRANT THIS FAVOR... YOU WILL DO IT, RIGHT...?
I SHOULDN'T HAVE ANSWERED.
1··· end

#2

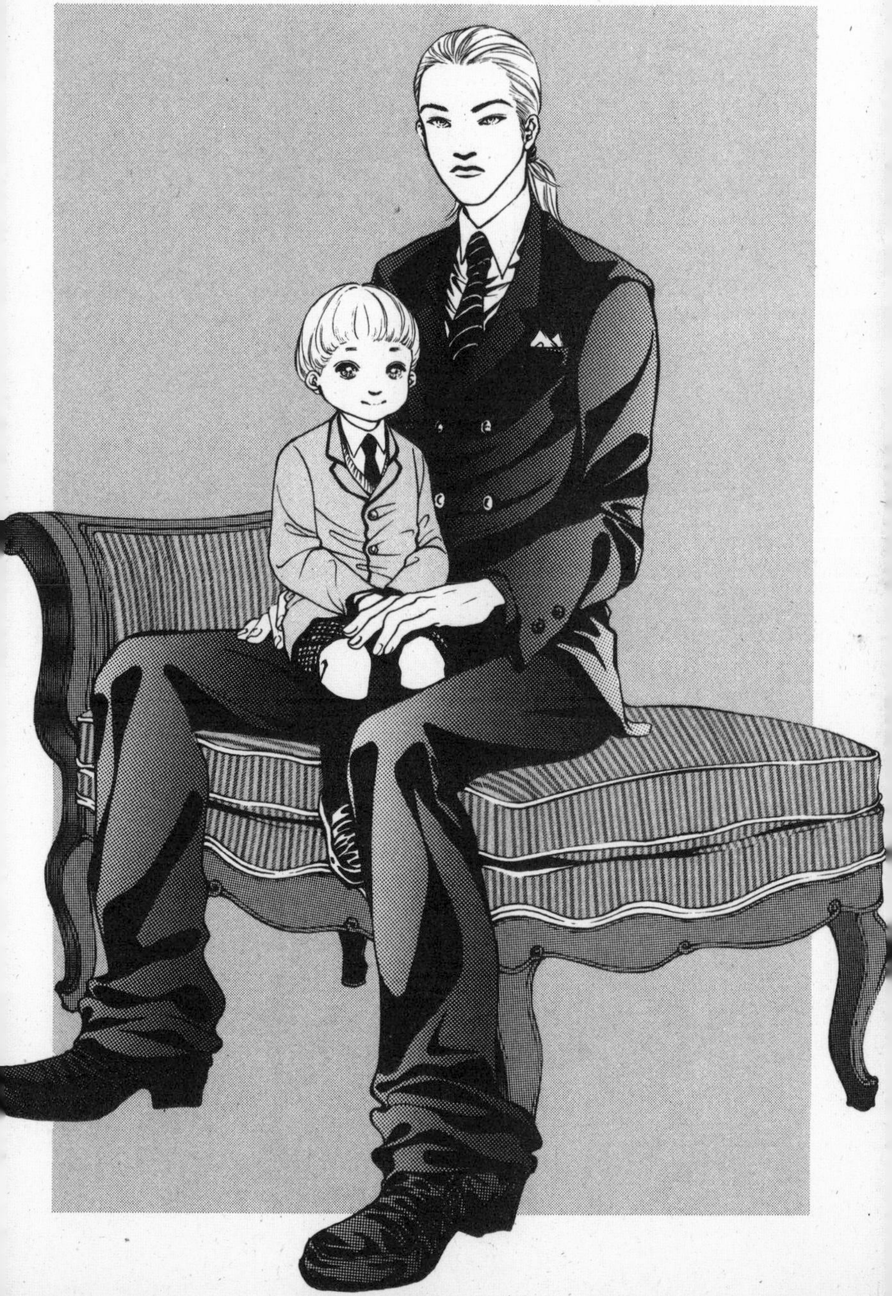

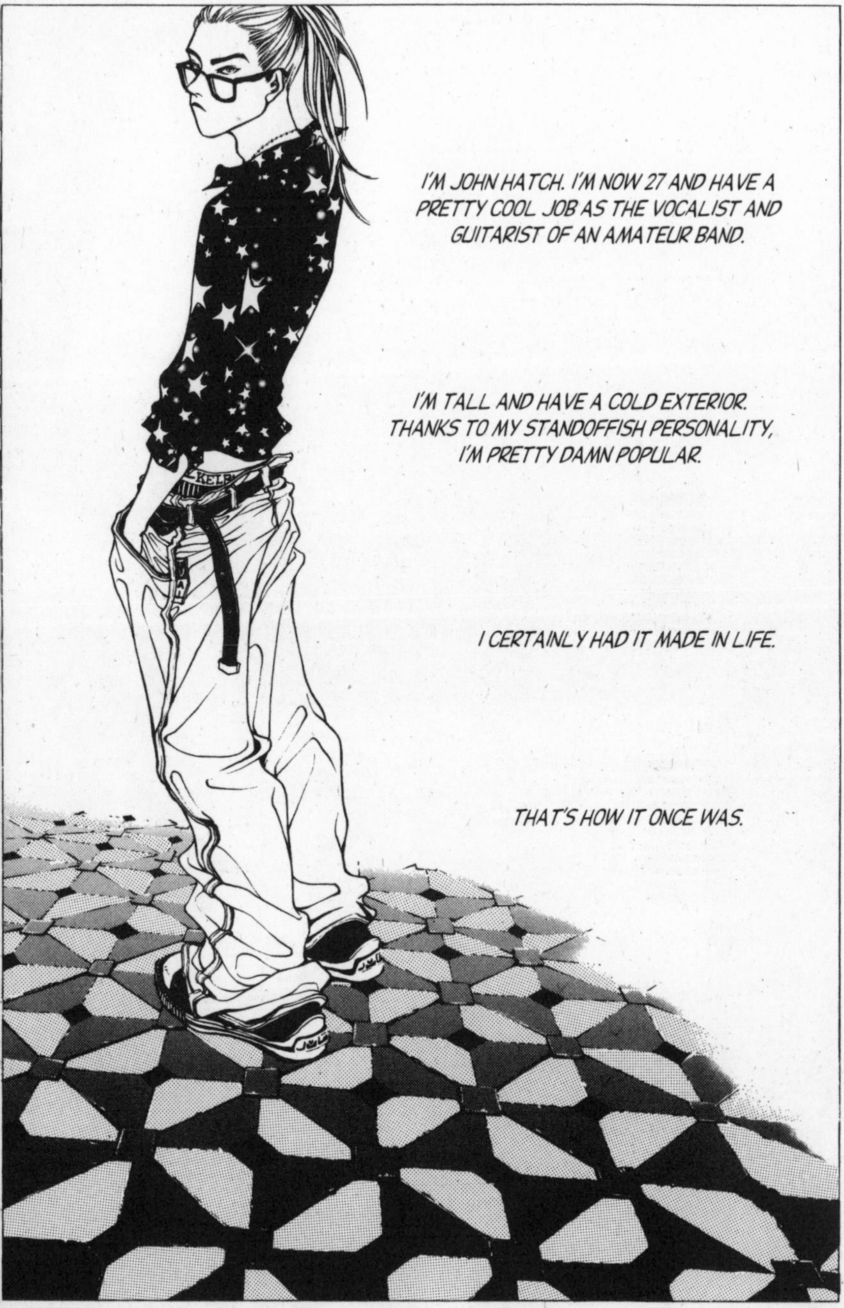
I'M JOHN HATCH. I'M NOW 27 AND HAVE A PRETTY COOL JOB AS THE VOCALIST AND GUITARIST OF AN AMATEUR BAND.
I'M TALL AND HAVE A COLD EXTERIOR. THANKS TO MY STANDOFFISH PERSONALITY, I'M PRETTY DAMN POPULAR.
I CERTAINLY HAD IT MADE IN LIFE.
THAT'S HOW IT ONCE WAS.

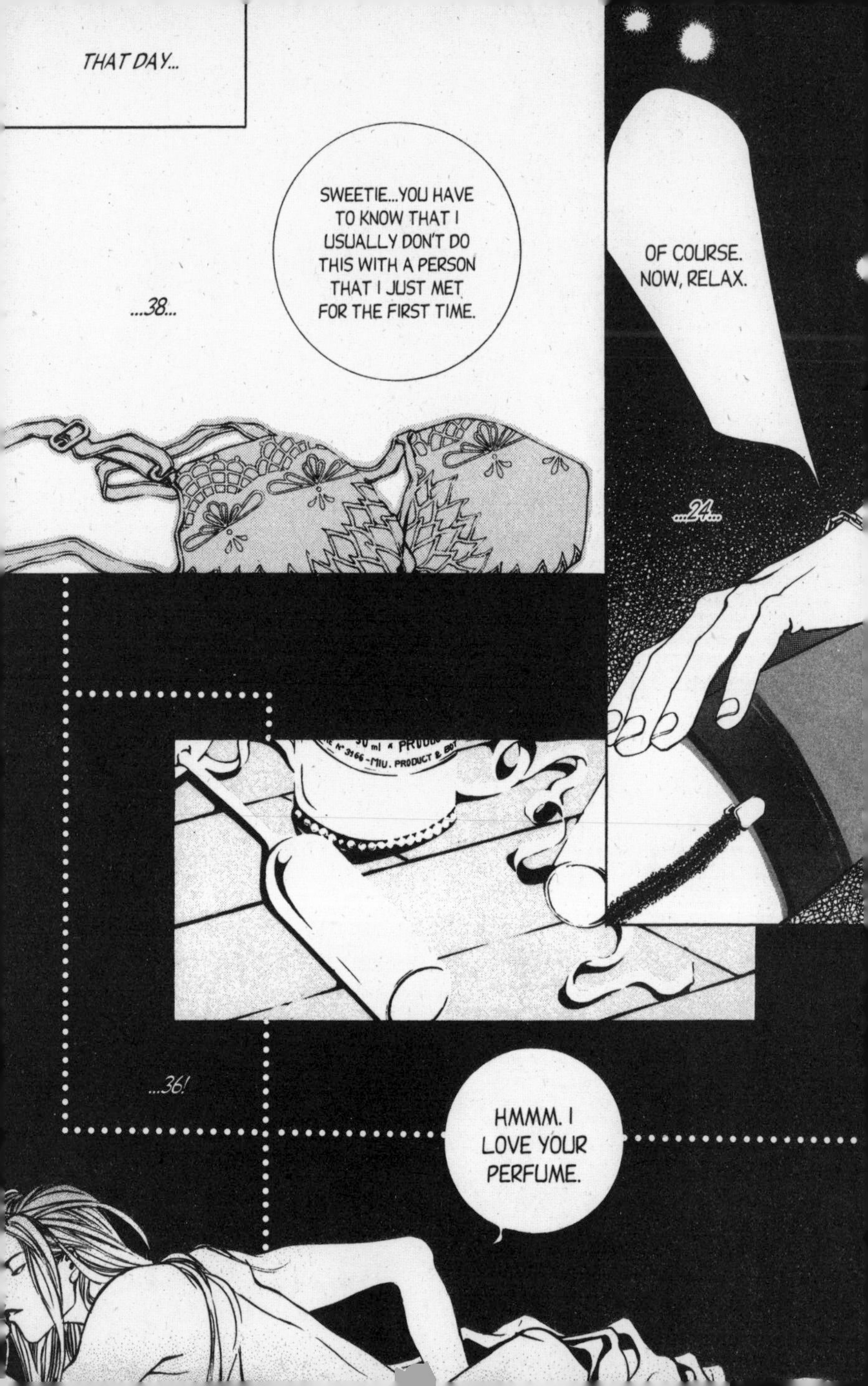
THAT DAY...
...38...
SWEETIE...YOU HAVE TO KNOW THAT I USUALLY DON'T DO THIS WITH A PERSON THAT I JUST MET FOR THE FIRST TIME.
OF COURSE. NOW, RELAX.
...24...
...36!
HMMM. I LOVE YOUR PERFUME.

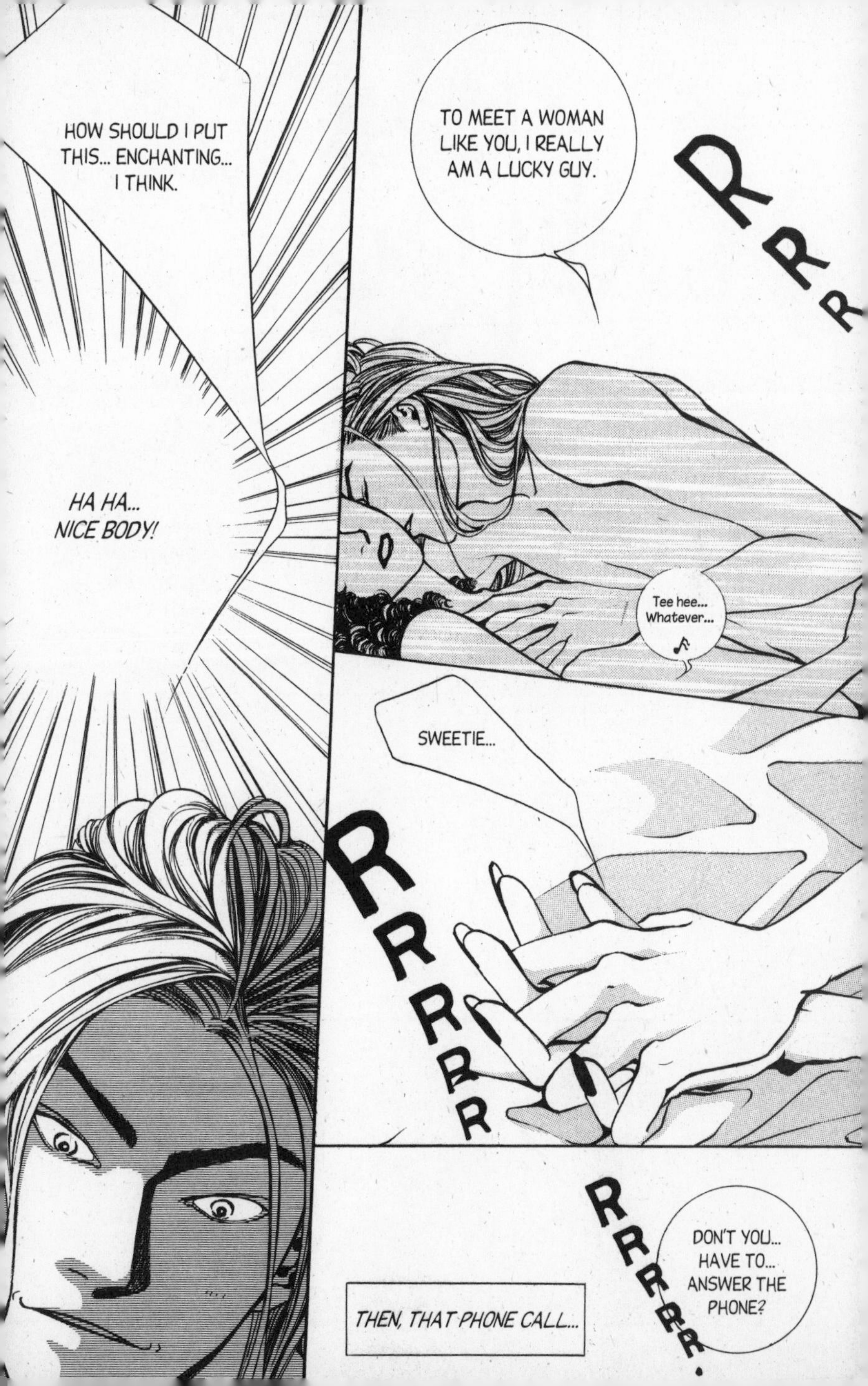

HOW SHOULD I PUT THIS... ENCHANTING... I THINK.
HA HA... NICE BODY!
TO MEET A WOMAN LIKE YOU, I REALLY AM A LUCKY GUY.
RRR
Tee hee... Whatever...
SWEETIE...
RRRRR
THEN, THAT PHONE CALL...
RRRRR.
DON'T YOU... HAVE TO... ANSWER THE PHONE?

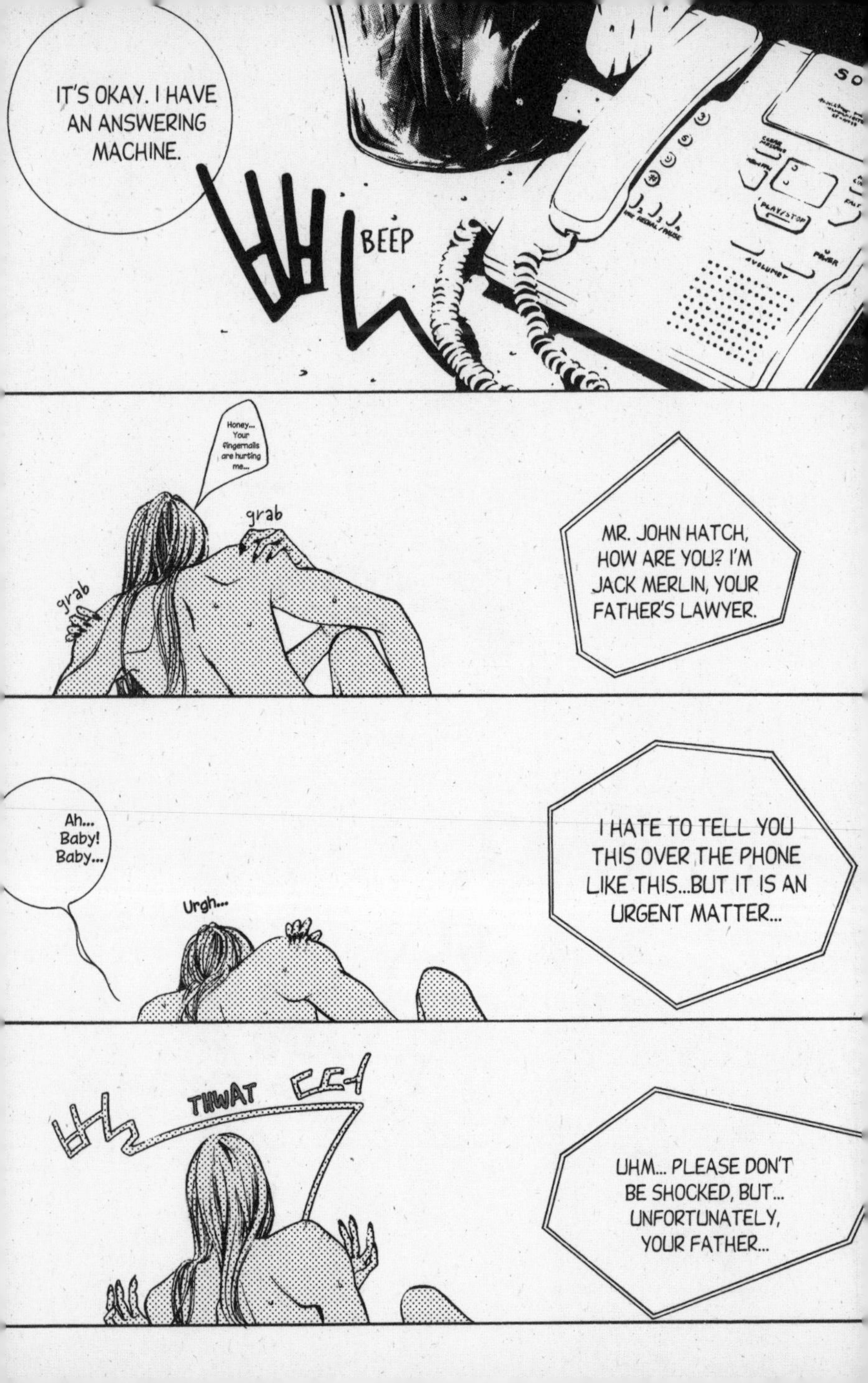
IT'S OKAY. I HAVE AN ANSWERING MACHINE.
BEEP
Honey... Your fingernails are hurting me...
grab
grab
MR. JOHN HATCH, HOW ARE YOU? I'M JACK MERLIN, YOUR FATHER'S LAWYER.
Ah... Baby! Baby...
Urgh...
I HATE TO TELL YOU THIS OVER THE PHONE LIKE THIS...BUT IT IS AN URGENT MATTER...
THWAT
UHM... PLEASE DON'T BE SHOCKED, BUT... UNFORTUNATELY, YOUR FATHER...

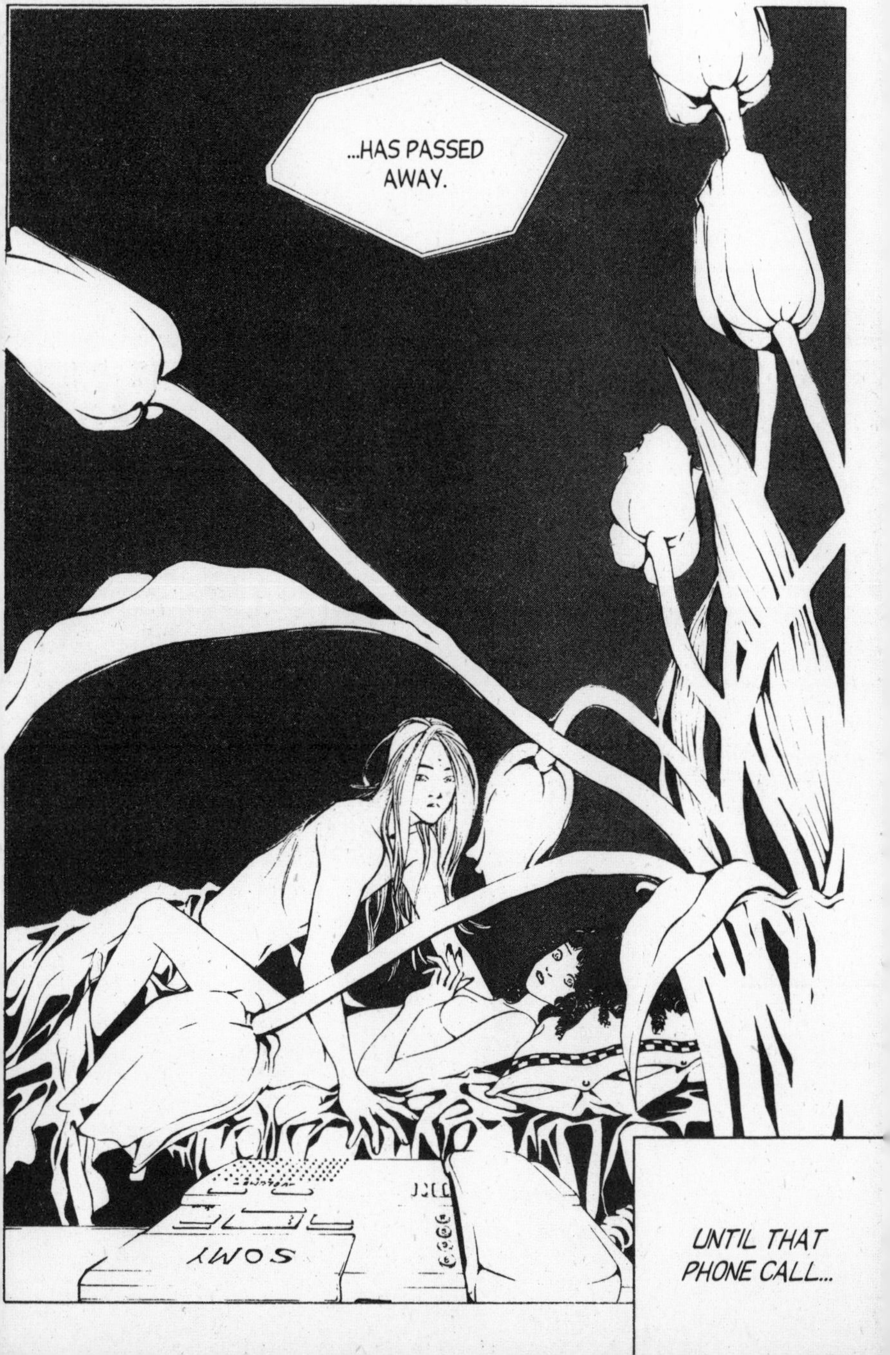
...HAS PASSED AWAY.
UNTIL THAT PHONE CALL...

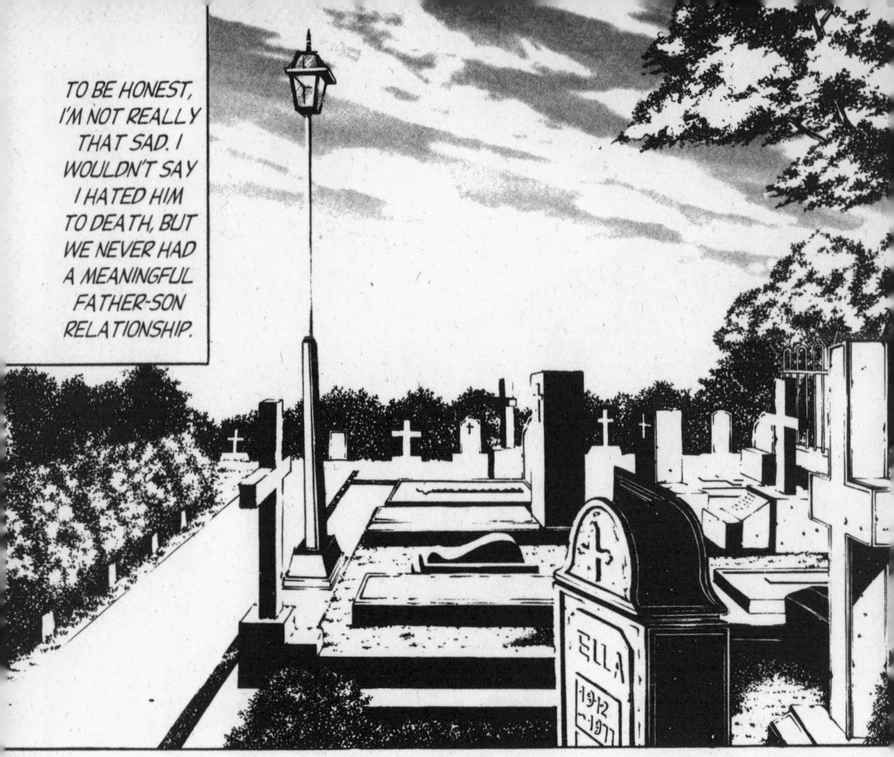
TO BE HONEST, I'M NOT REALLY THAT SAD. I WOULDN'T SAY I HATED HIM TO DEATH, BUT WE NEVER HAD A MEANINGFUL FATHER-SON RELATIONSHIP.
ELLA

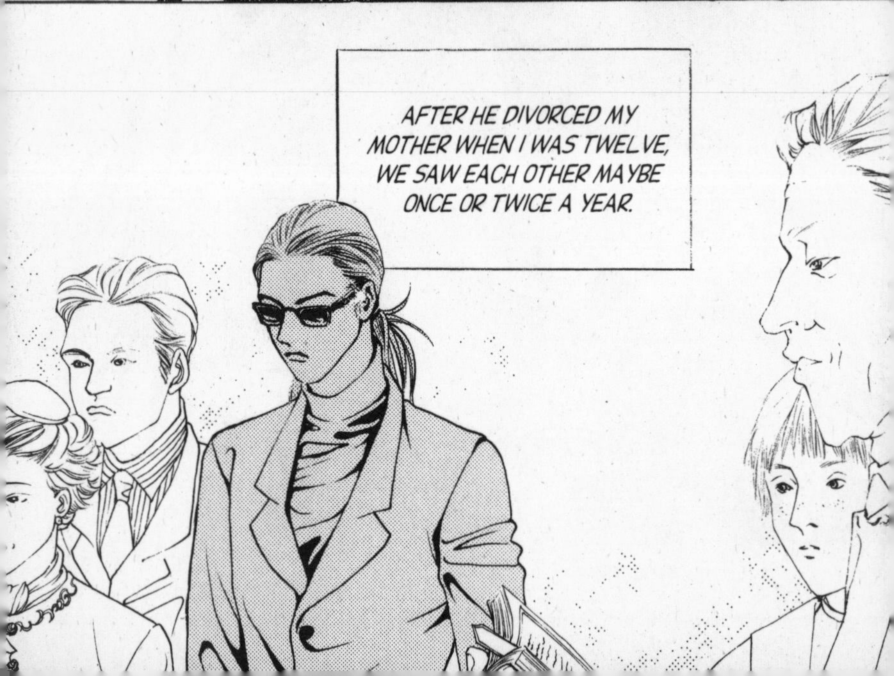
AFTER HE DIVORCED MY MOTHER WHEN I WAS TWELVE, WE SAW EACH OTHER MAYBE ONCE OR TWICE A YEAR.

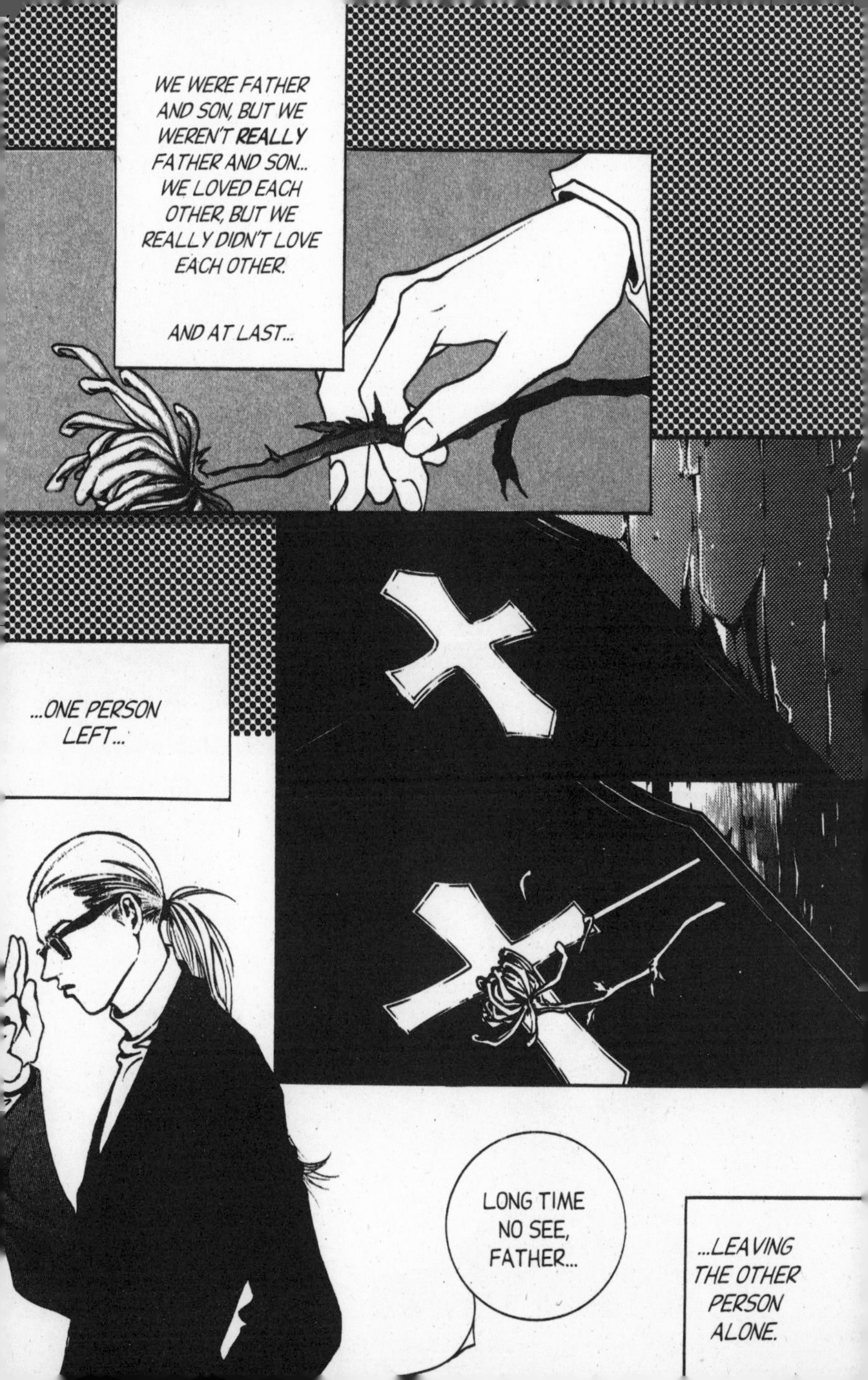

WE WERE FATHER AND SON, BUT WE WEREN'T REALLY FATHER AND SON... WE LOVED EACH OTHER, BUT WE REALLY DIDN'T LOVE EACH OTHER.
AND AT LAST...
...ONE PERSON LEFT...
LONG TIME NO SEE, FATHER...
...LEAVING THE OTHER PERSON ALONE.

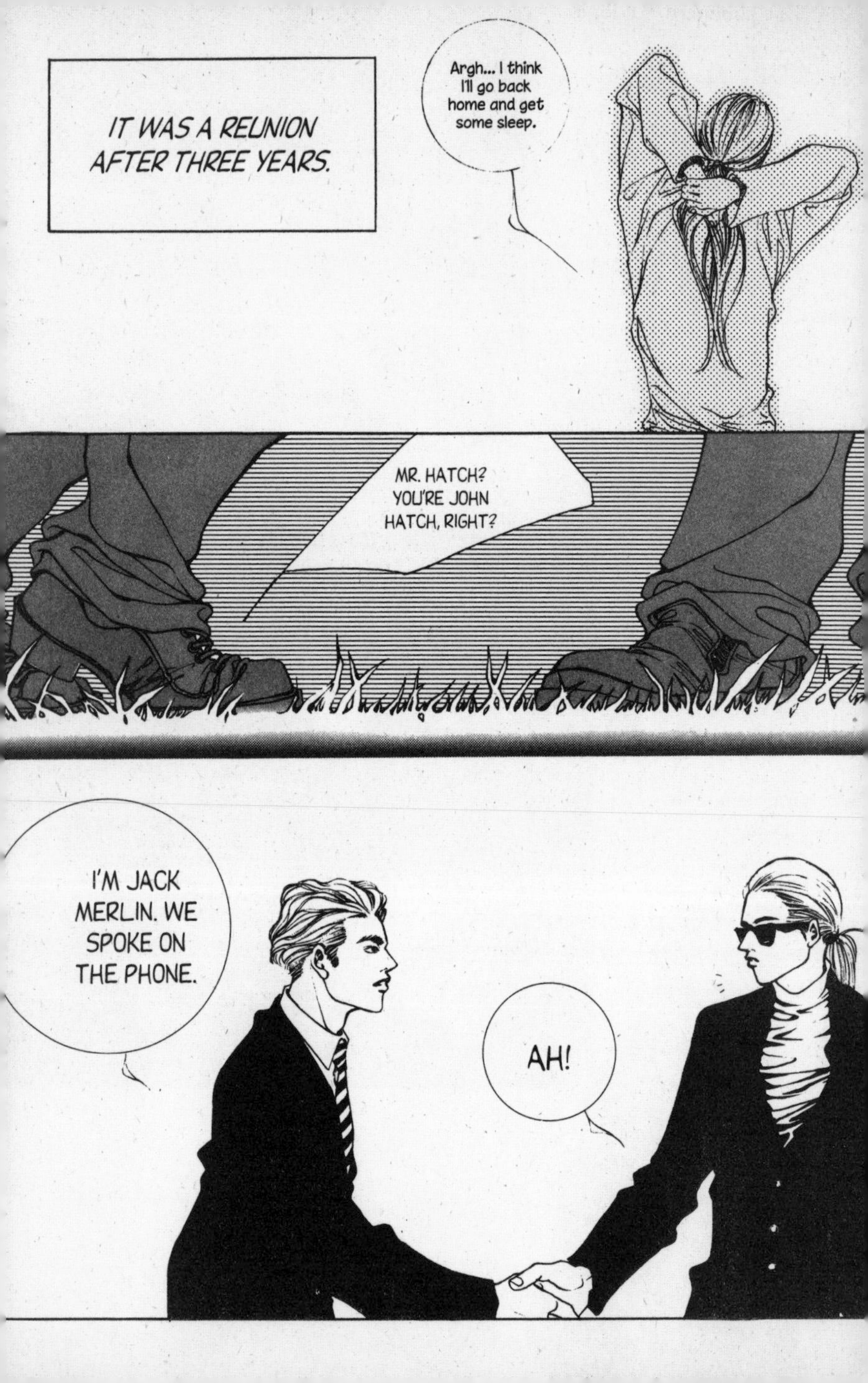
IT WAS A REUNION AFTER THREE YEARS.
Argh... I think I'll go back home and get some sleep.
MR. HATCH? YOU'RE JOHN HATCH, RIGHT?
I'M JACK MERLIN. WE SPOKE ON THE PHONE.
AH!

IT'S A SHAME, ISN'T IT? HE WAS A GOOD MAN... SUCH A KINDHEARTED, RIGHTEOUS...
IF I JUST LEFT HIM ALONE, HOW LONG COULD HE GO ON BLABBERING ABOUT MY FATHER? TEN MINUTES? TWENTY MINUTES?
I, MYSELF...HMM...ONLY KNOW A COUPLE OF THINGS ABOUT HIM... ANYWAY, THE ONE THING THAT'S CERTAIN HERE IS THAT THIS GUY KNOWS A WHOLE LOT MORE ABOUT MY FATHER THAN I DO.
BUT...WHAT IS HE SAYING?

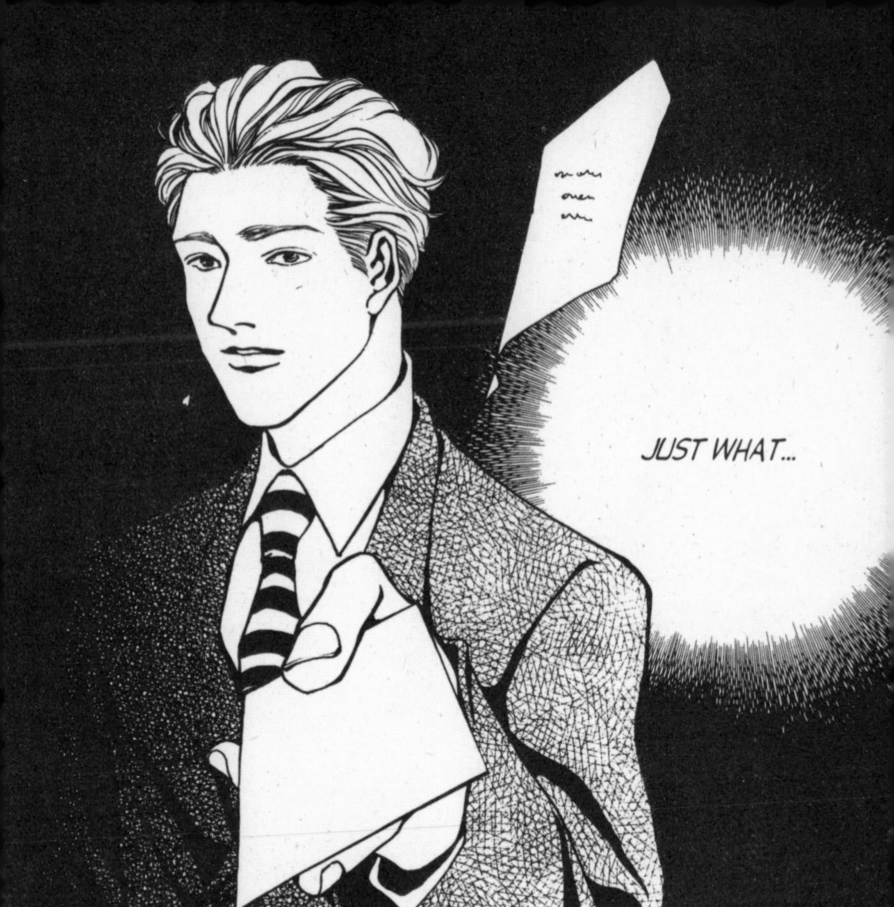
JUST WHAT...
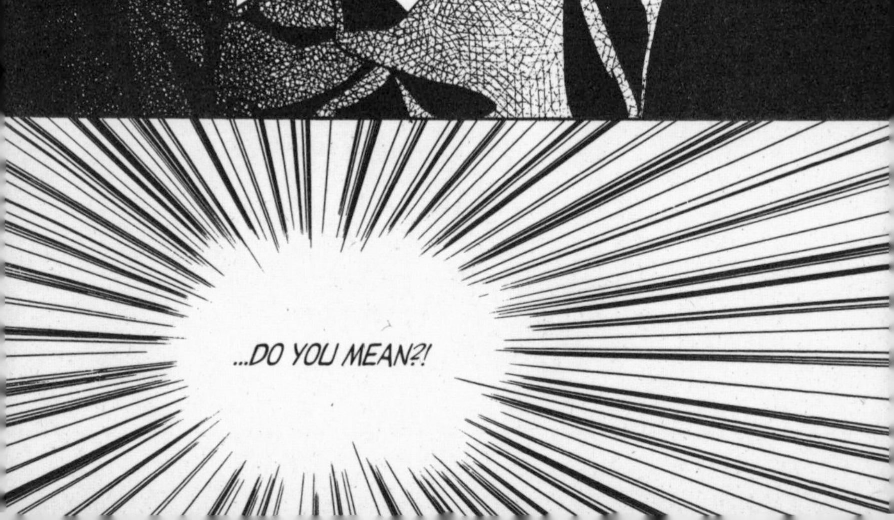
...DO YOU MEAN?!

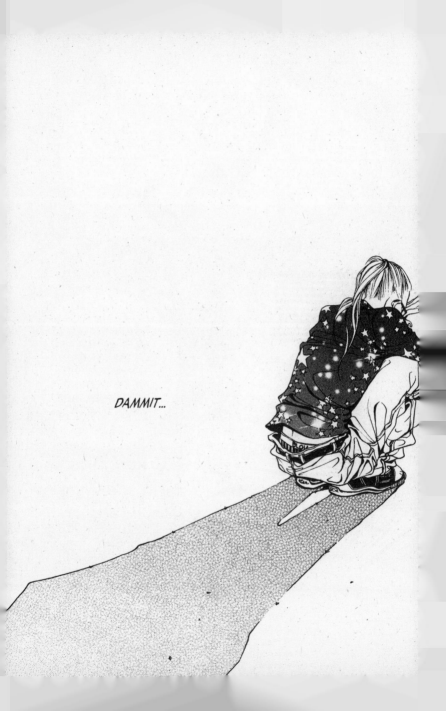

DAMMIT...

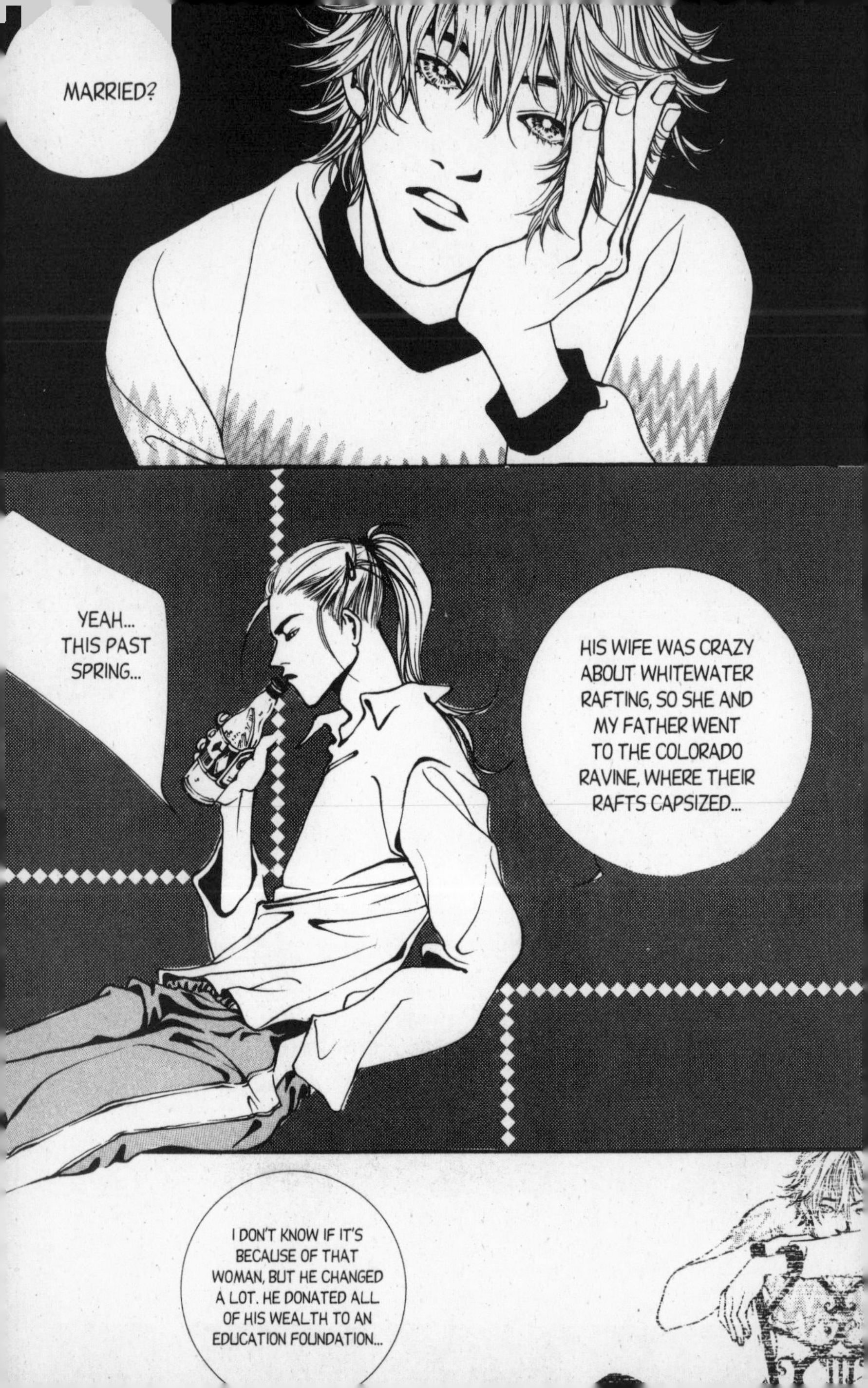
MARRIED?
YEAH... THIS PAST SPRING...
HIS WIFE WAS CRAZY ABOUT WHITEWATER RAFTING, SO SHE AND MY FATHER WENT TO THE COLORADO RAVINE, WHERE THEIR RAFTS CAPSIZED...
I DON'T KNOW IF IT'S BECAUSE OF THAT WOMAN, BUT HE CHANGED A LOT. HE DONATED ALL OF HIS WEALTH TO AN EDUCATION FOUNDATION...

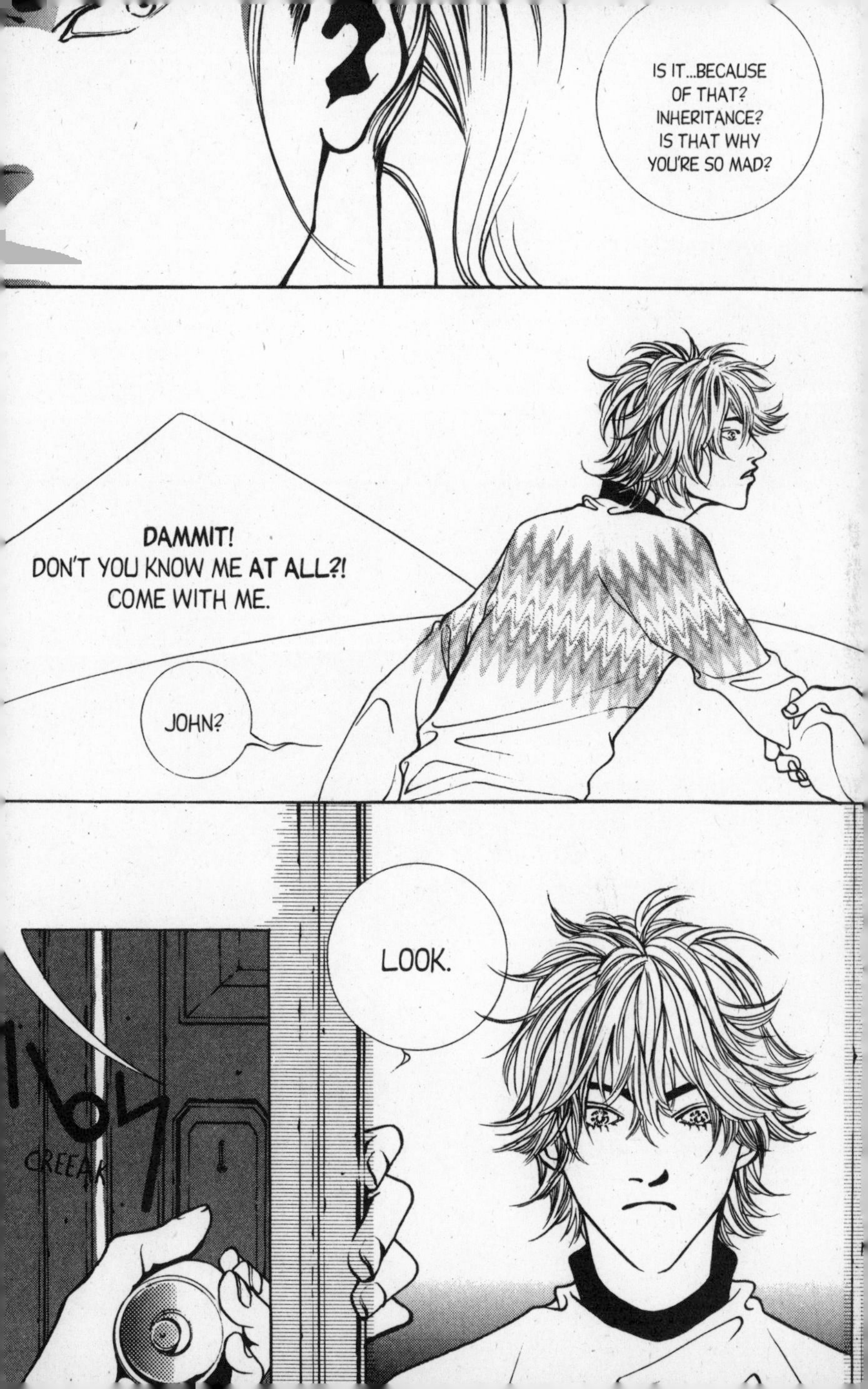
IS IT...BECAUSE OF THAT? INHERITANCE? IS THAT WHY YOU'RE SO MAD?
DAMMIT! DON'T YOU KNOW ME AT ALL?! COME WITH ME.
JOHN?
CREEAK
LOOK.

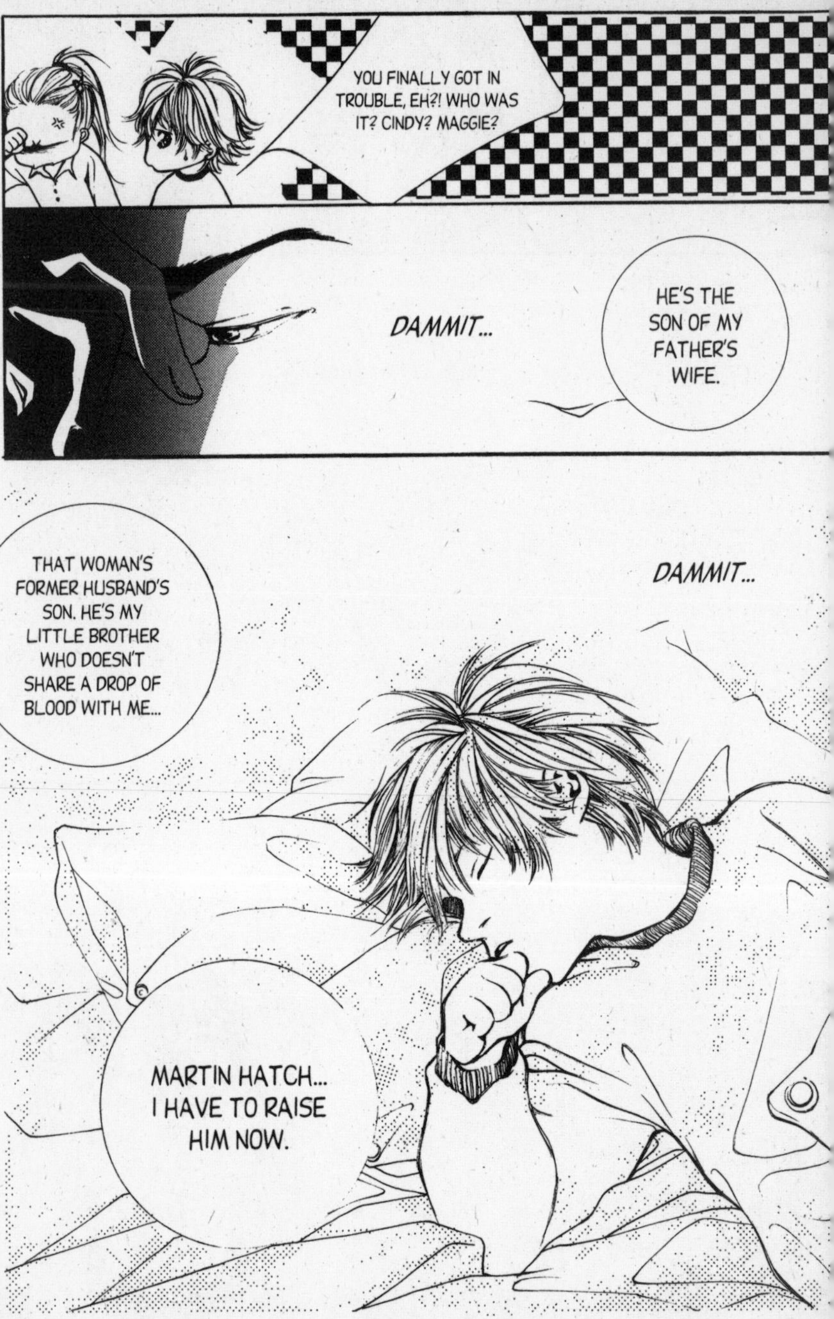
YOU FINALLY GOT IN TROUBLE, EH?! WHO WAS IT? CINDY? MAGGIE?
DAMMIT...
HE'S THE SON OF MY FATHER'S WIFE.
THAT WOMAN'S FORMER HUSBAND'S SON. HE'S MY LITTLE BROTHER WHO DOESN'T SHARE A DROP OF BLOOD WITH ME...
DAMMIT...
MARTIN HATCH... I HAVE TO RAISE HIM NOW.

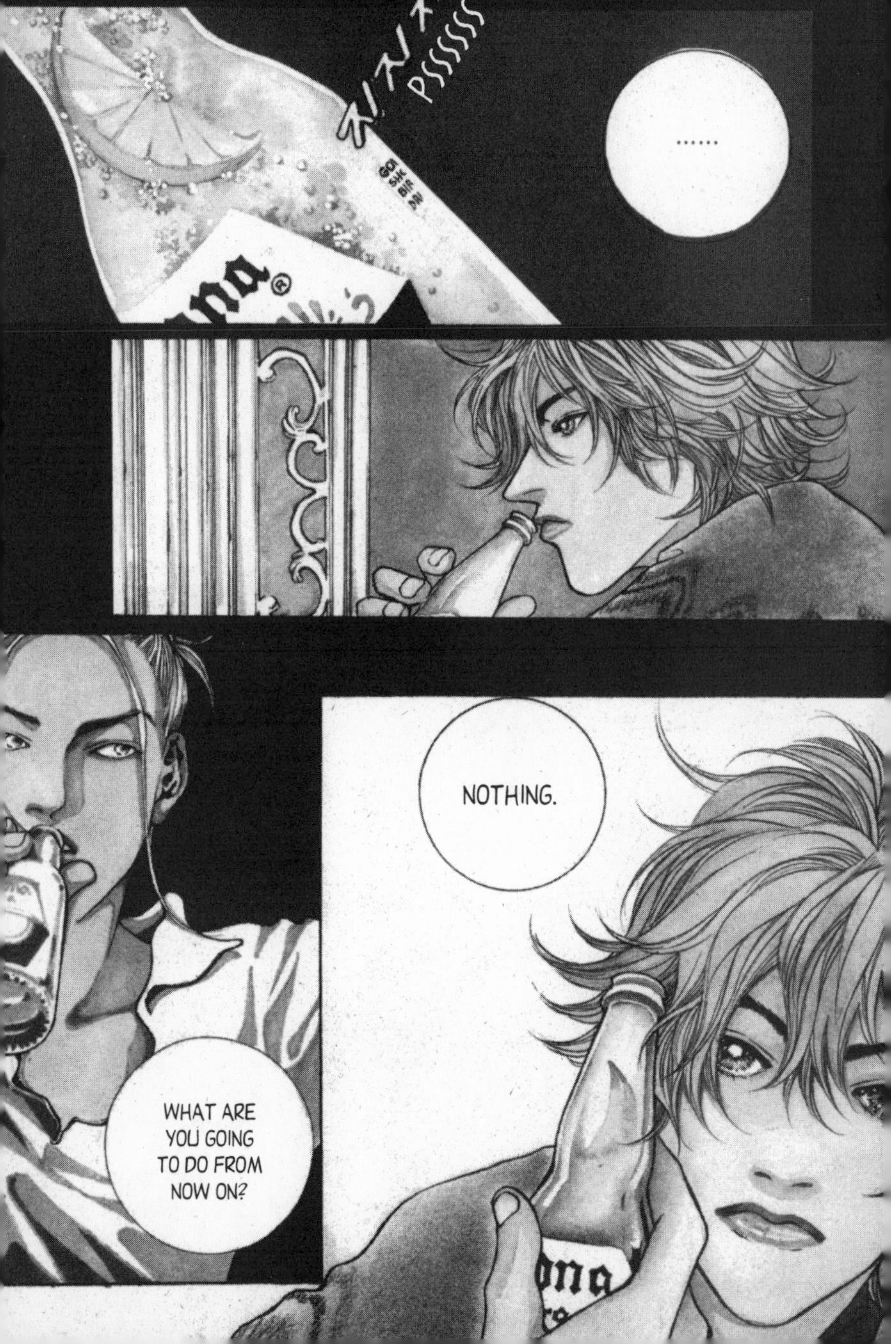
PSSSSSS
......
WHAT ARE YOU GOING TO DO FROM NOW ON?
NOTHING.

NOTHING WILL CHANGE.
THAT KID WILL DO HIS THING; I'LL DO MY THING... WE'LL BE ROOMMATES WHO HAVE NO MEANING TO EACH OTHER.
THERE'S NO NEED FOR EITHER OF US TO LOVE OR RECEIVE LOVE...
IT MAY SOUND FUNNY, BUT PEOPLE CAN LIVE LIKE THAT, YOU KNOW... LIKE WHEN I WAS YOUNGER...

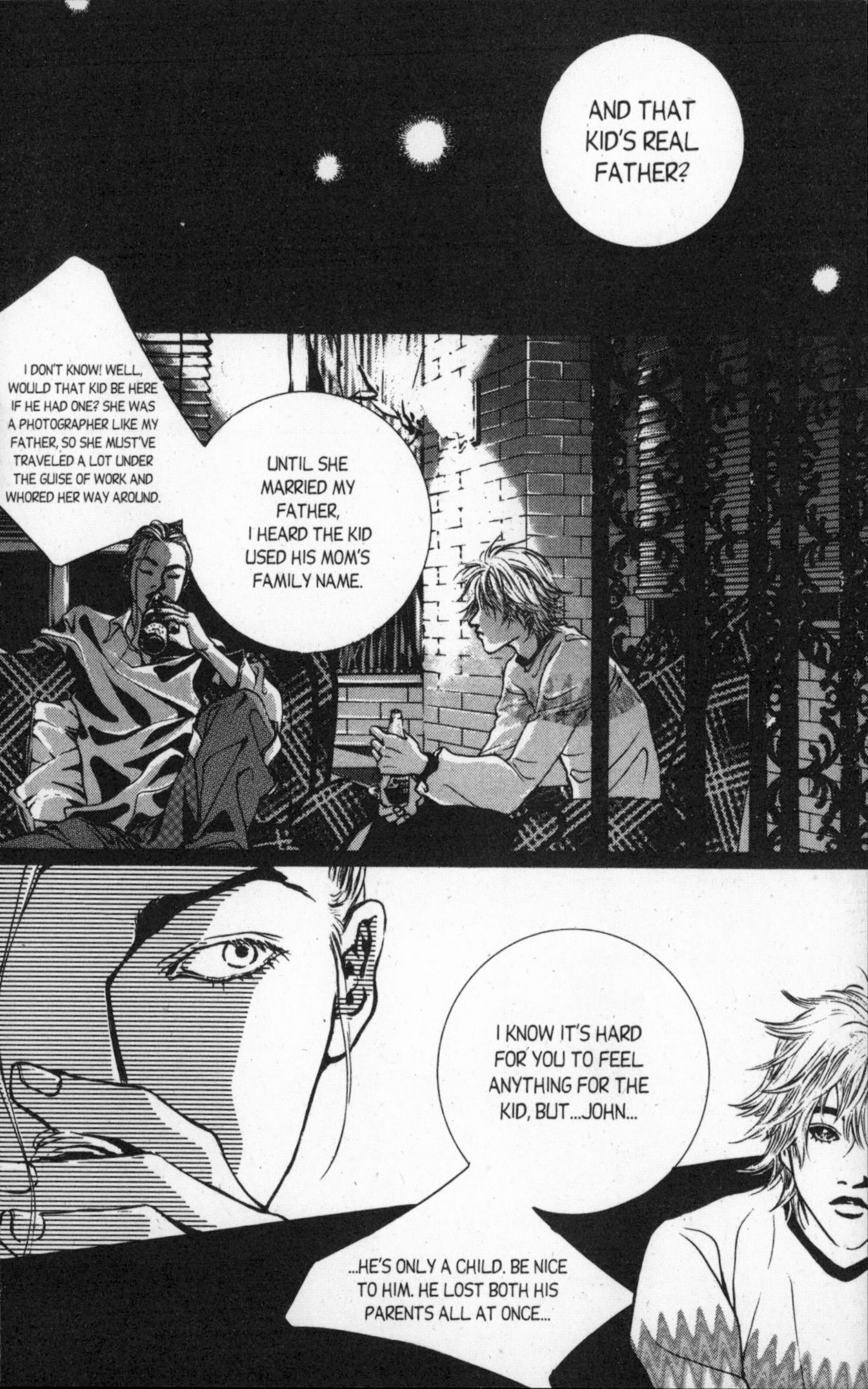
AND THAT KID'S REAL FATHER?
I DON'T KNOW! WELL, WOULD THAT KID BE HERE IF HE HAD ONE? SHE WAS A PHOTOGRAPHER LIKE MY FATHER, SO SHE MUST'VE TRAVELED A LOT UNDER THE GUISE OF WORK AND WHORED HER WAY AROUND.
UNTIL SHE MARRIED MY FATHER, I HEARD THE KID USED HIS MOM'S FAMILY NAME.
I KNOW IT'S HARD FOR YOU TO FEEL ANYTHING FOR THE KID, BUT...JOHN...
...HE'S ONLY A CHILD. BE NICE TO HIM. HE LOST BOTH HIS PARENTS ALL AT ONCE...

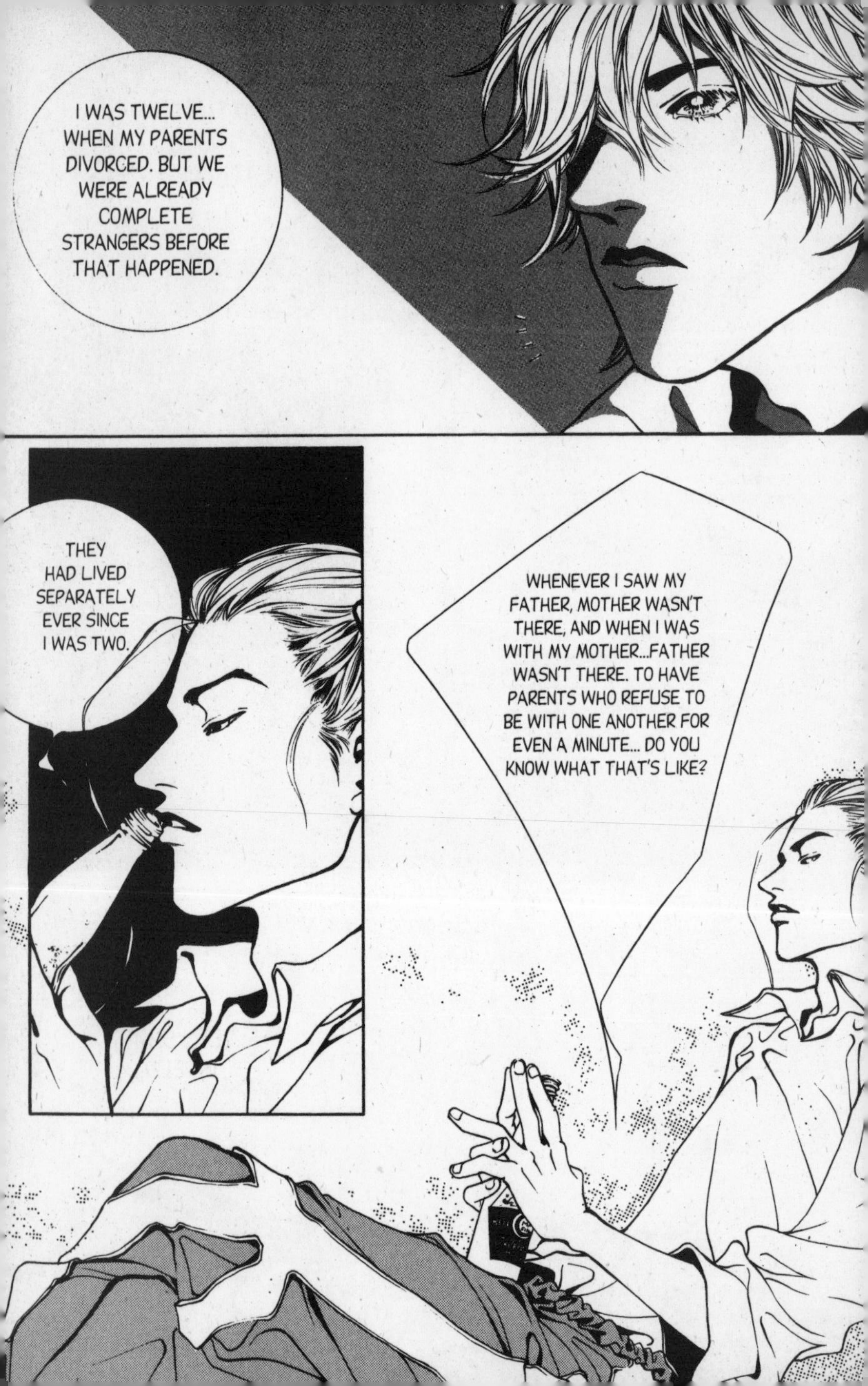
I WAS TWELVE... WHEN MY PARENTS DIVORCED. BUT WE WERE ALREADY COMPLETE STRANGERS BEFORE THAT HAPPENED.
THEY HAD LIVED SEPARATELY EVER SINCE I WAS TWO.
WHENEVER I SAW MY FATHER, MOTHER WASN'T THERE, AND WHEN I WAS WITH MY MOTHER...FATHER WASN'T THERE. TO HAVE PARENTS WHO REFUSE TO BE WITH ONE ANOTHER FOR EVEN A MINUTE... DO YOU KNOW WHAT THAT'S LIKE?

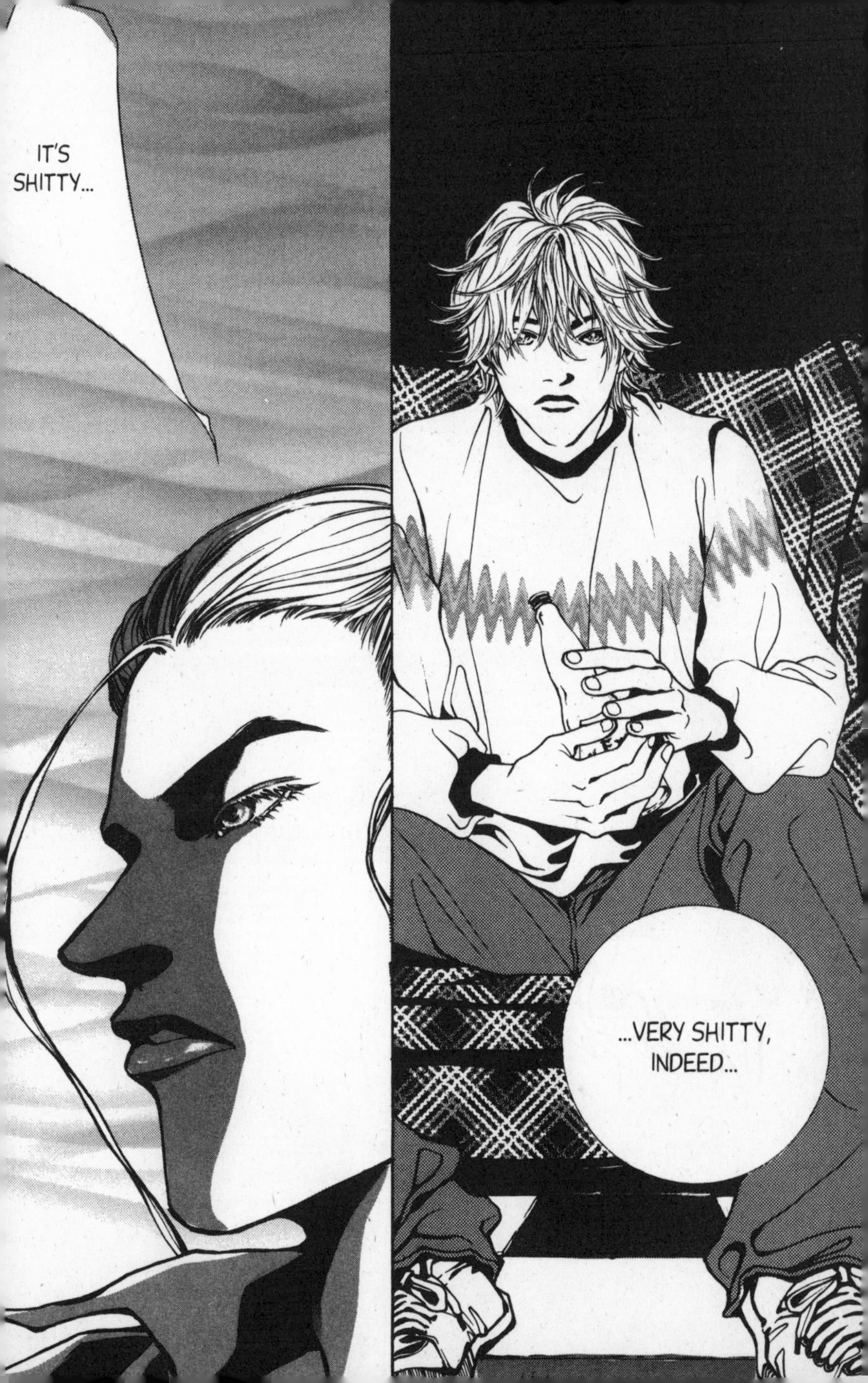
IT'S SHITTY...
...VERY SHITTY, INDEED...

I WAS YOUNG THEN, TOO... DEATH ISN'T THE ONLY WAY YOU CAN LOSE YOUR PARENTS...
IF YOU...
...HAVE SUCH NEGATIVE FEELINGS TOWARD HIM, WHY DID YOU BRING HIM HERE?

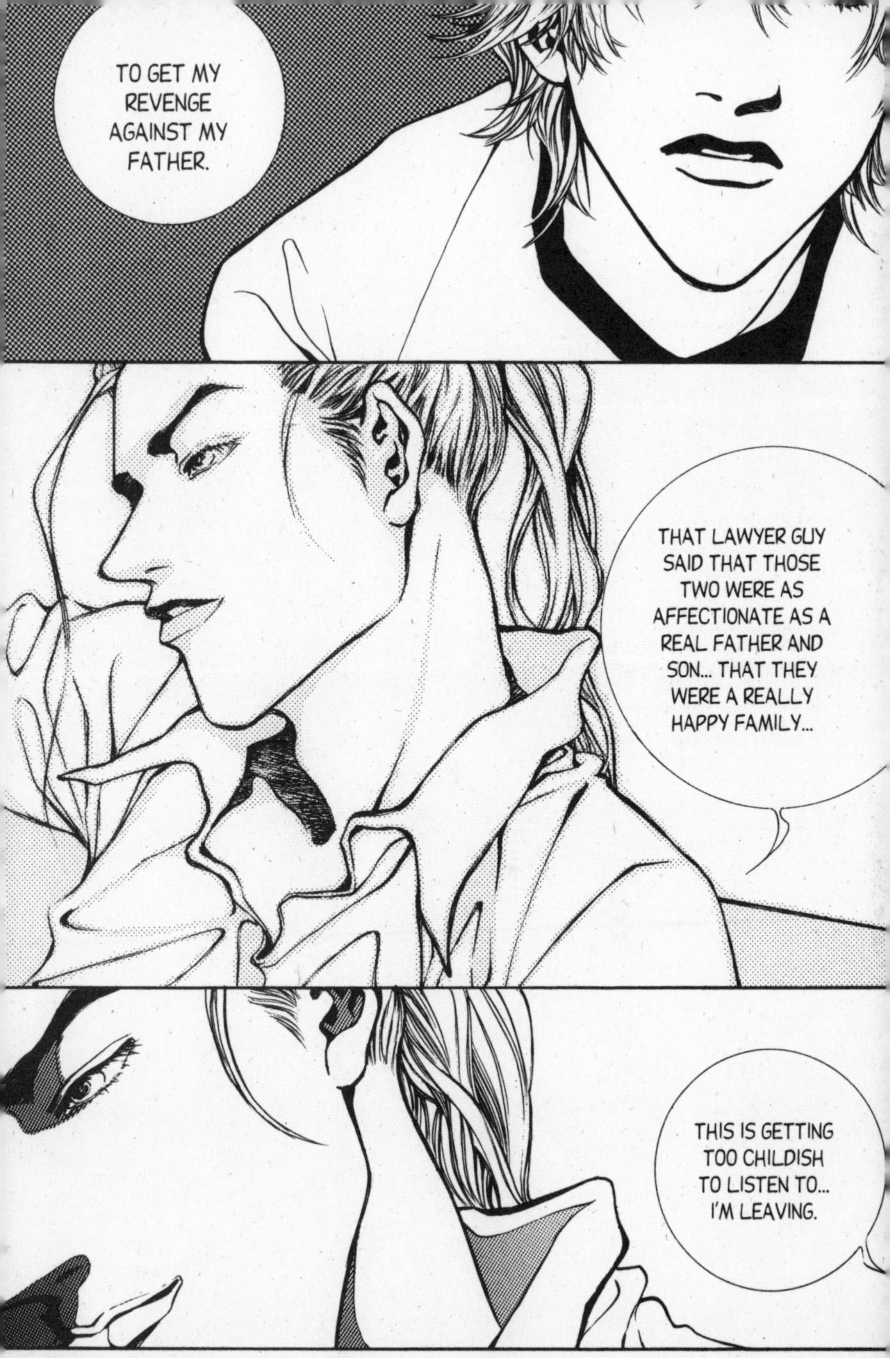
TO GET MY REVENGE AGAINST MY FATHER.
THAT LAWYER GUY SAID THAT THOSE TWO WERE AS AFFECTIONATE AS A REAL FATHER AND SON... THAT THEY WERE A REALLY HAPPY FAMILY...
THIS IS GETTING TOO CHILDISH TO LISTEN TO... I'M LEAVING.

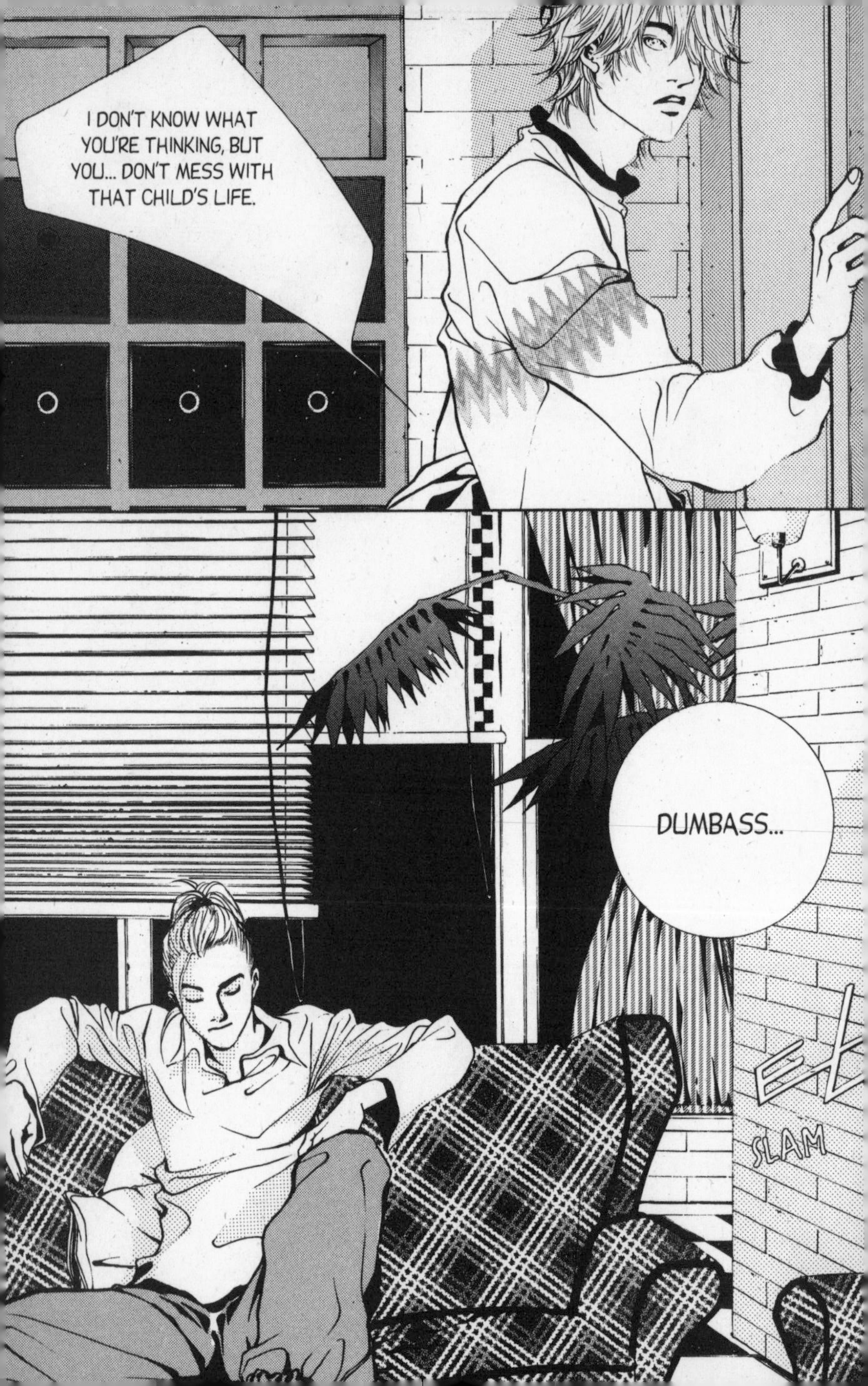
I DON'T KNOW WHAT YOU'RE THINKING, BUT YOU... DON'T MESS WITH THAT CHILD'S LIFE.
DUMBASS...
SLAM

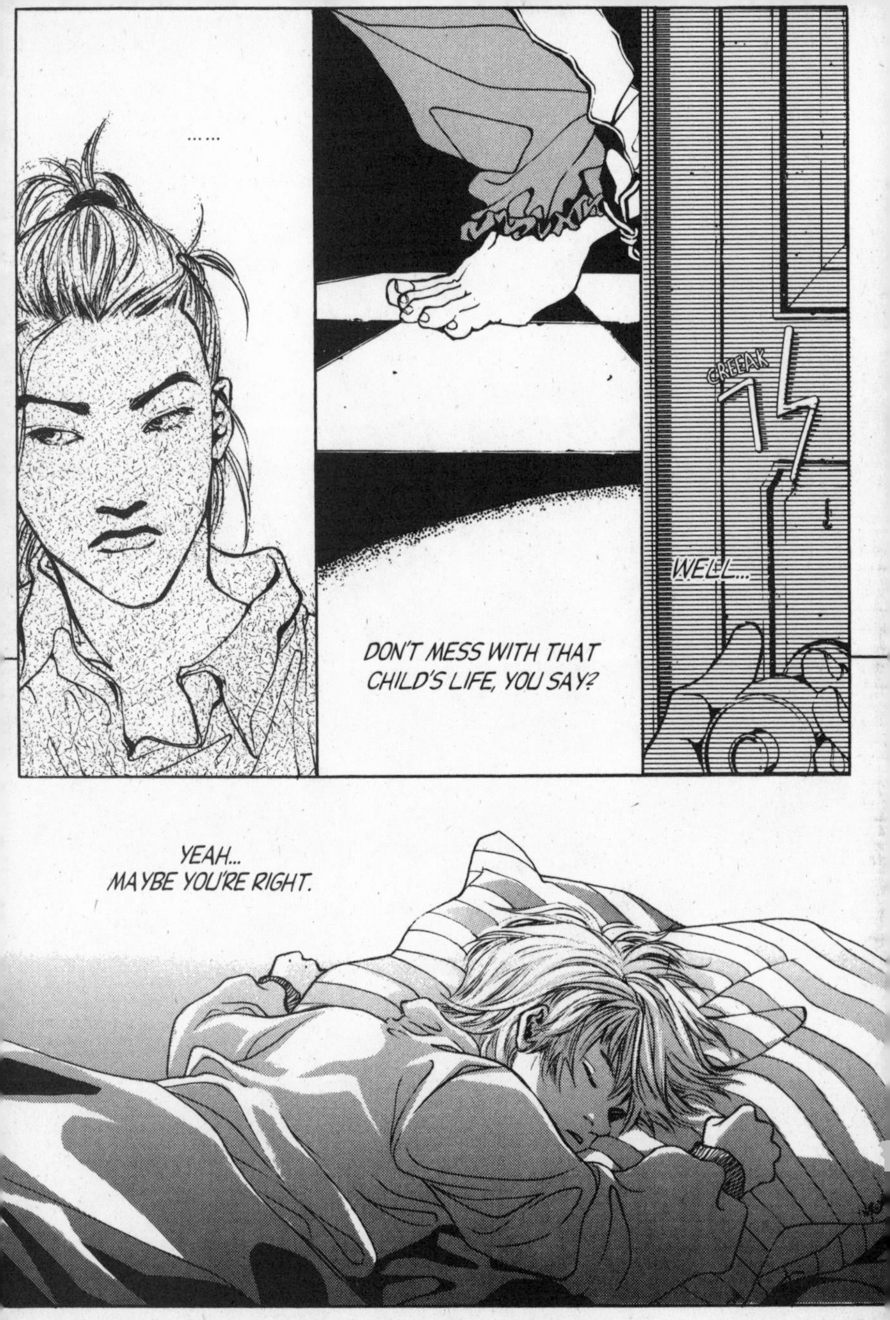
……
CREEAK
WELL…
DON'T MESS WITH THAT CHILD'S LIFE, YOU SAY?
YEAH… MAYBE YOU'RE RIGHT.

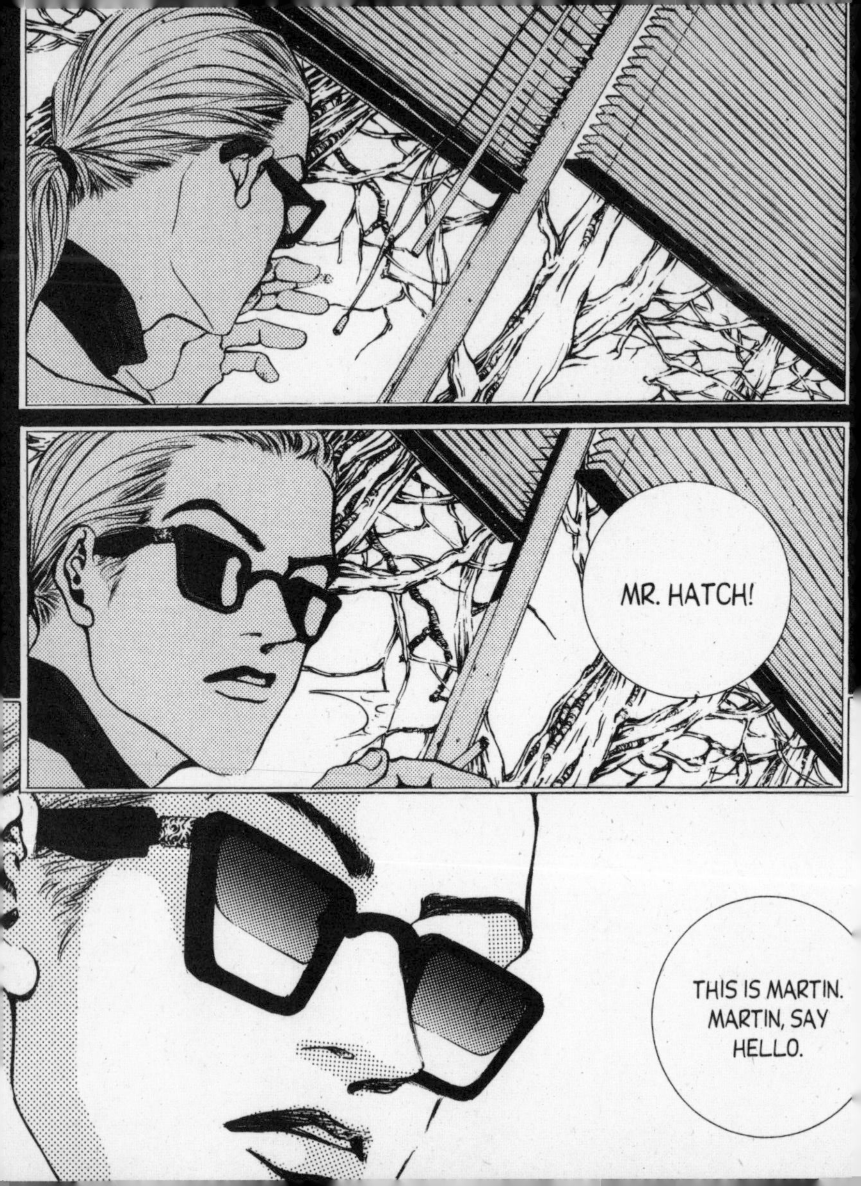

MR. HATCH!
THIS IS MARTIN. MARTIN, SAY HELLO.

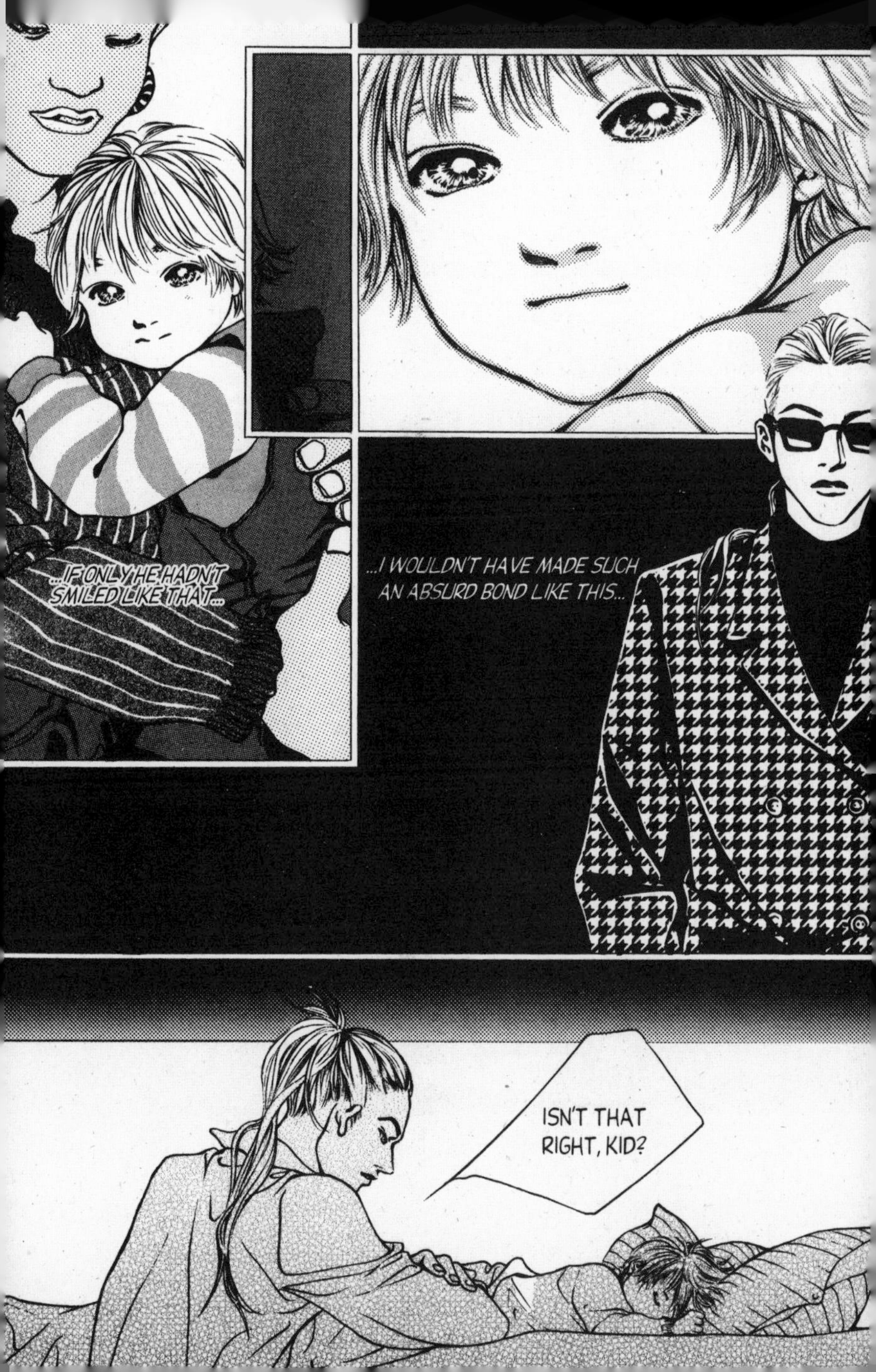
...IF ONLY HE HADN'T SMILED LIKE THAT...
...I WOULDN'T HAVE MADE SUCH AN ABSURD BOND LIKE THIS...
ISN'T THAT RIGHT, KID?

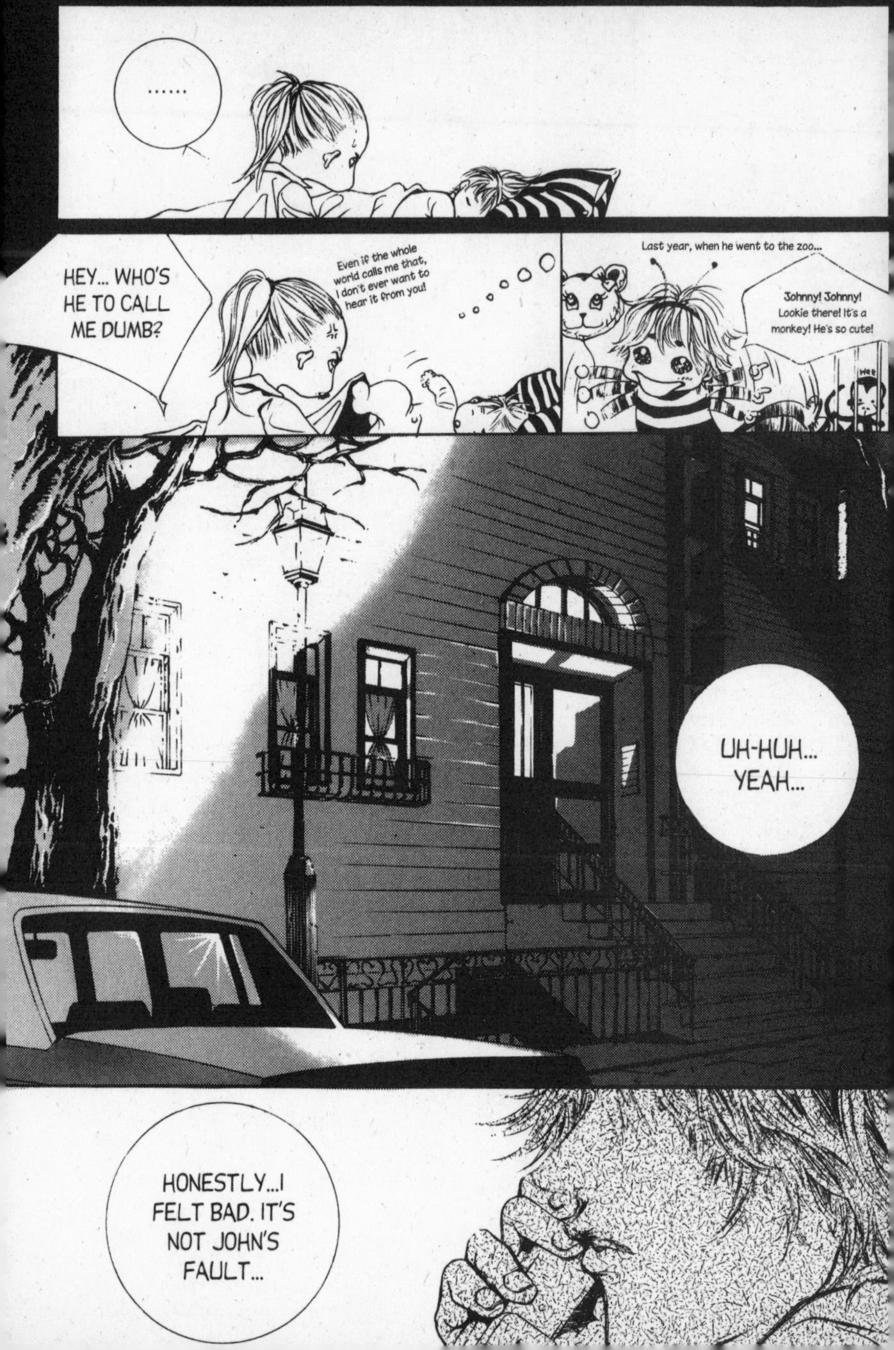
......
HEY... WHO'S HE TO CALL ME DUMB?
Even if the whole world calls me that, I don't ever want to hear it from you!
Last year, when he went to the zoo...
Johnny! Johnny! Lookie there! It's a monkey! He's so cute!
UH-HUH... YEAH...
HONESTLY...I FELT BAD. IT'S NOT JOHN'S FAULT...

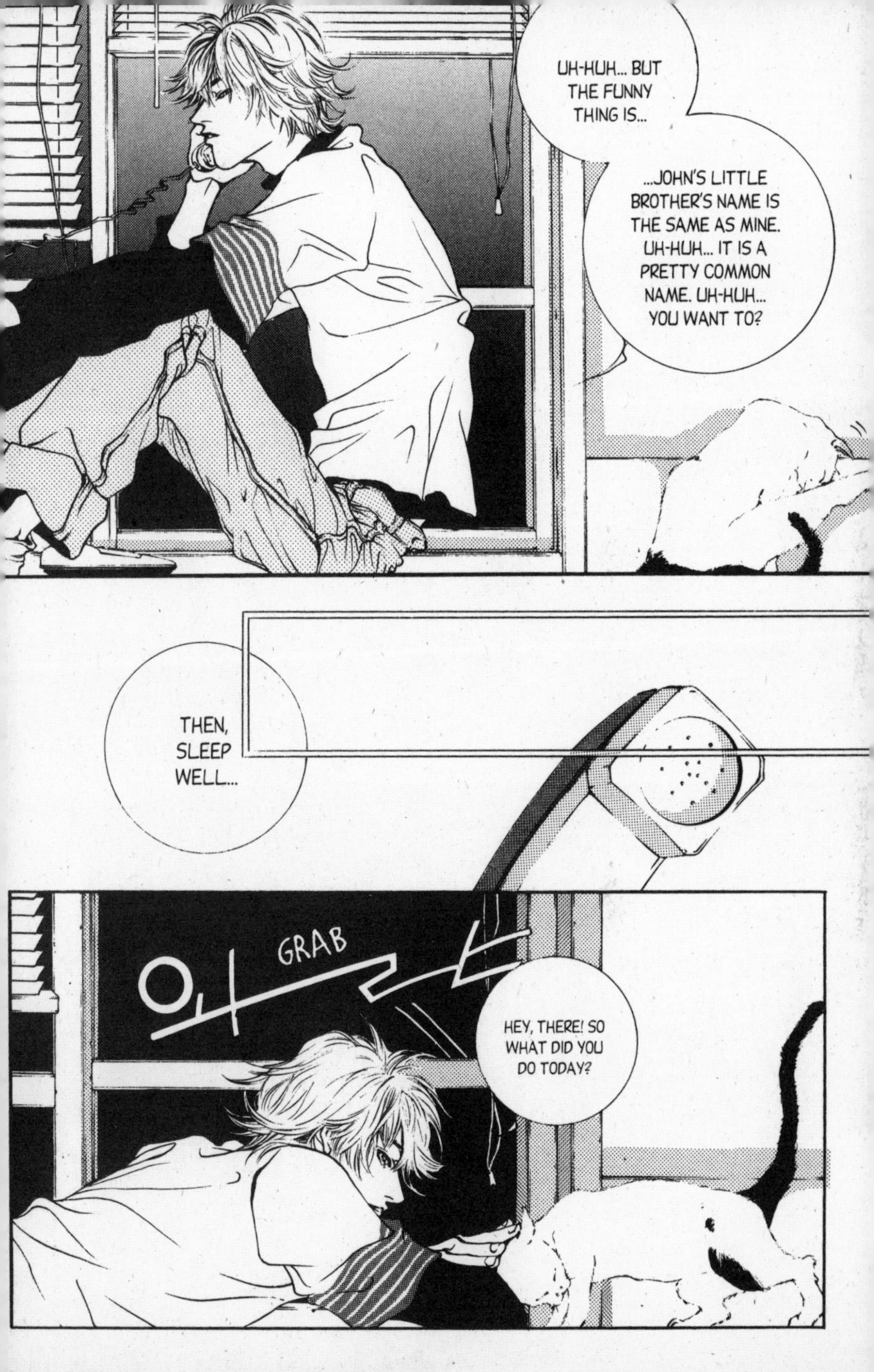
UH-HUH... BUT THE FUNNY THING IS...
...JOHN'S LITTLE BROTHER'S NAME IS THE SAME AS MINE. UH-HUH... IT IS A PRETTY COMMON NAME. UH-HUH... YOU WANT TO?
THEN, SLEEP WELL...
GRAB
HEY, THERE! SO WHAT DID YOU DO TODAY?

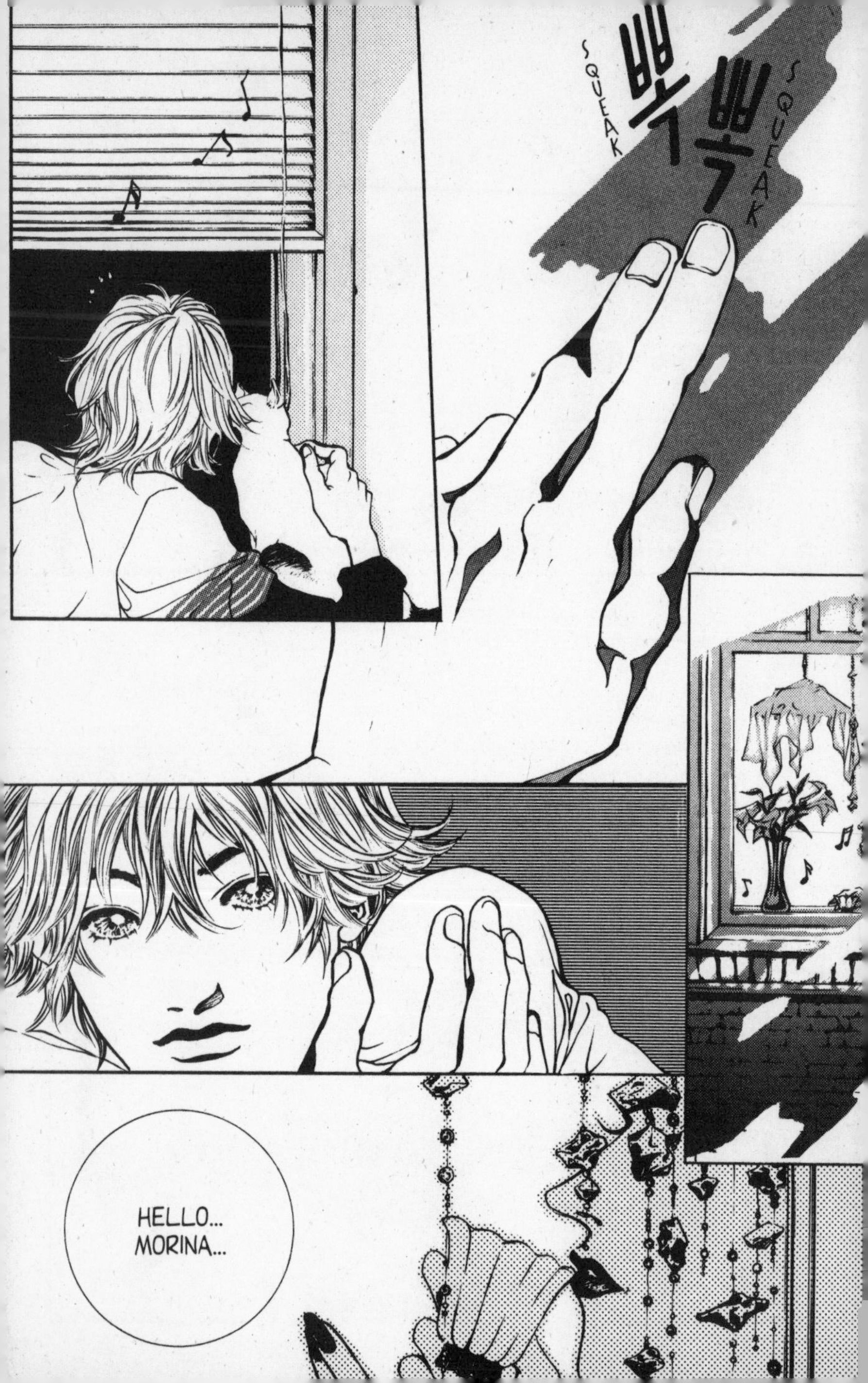
SQUEAK
SQUEAK
HELLO... MORINA...

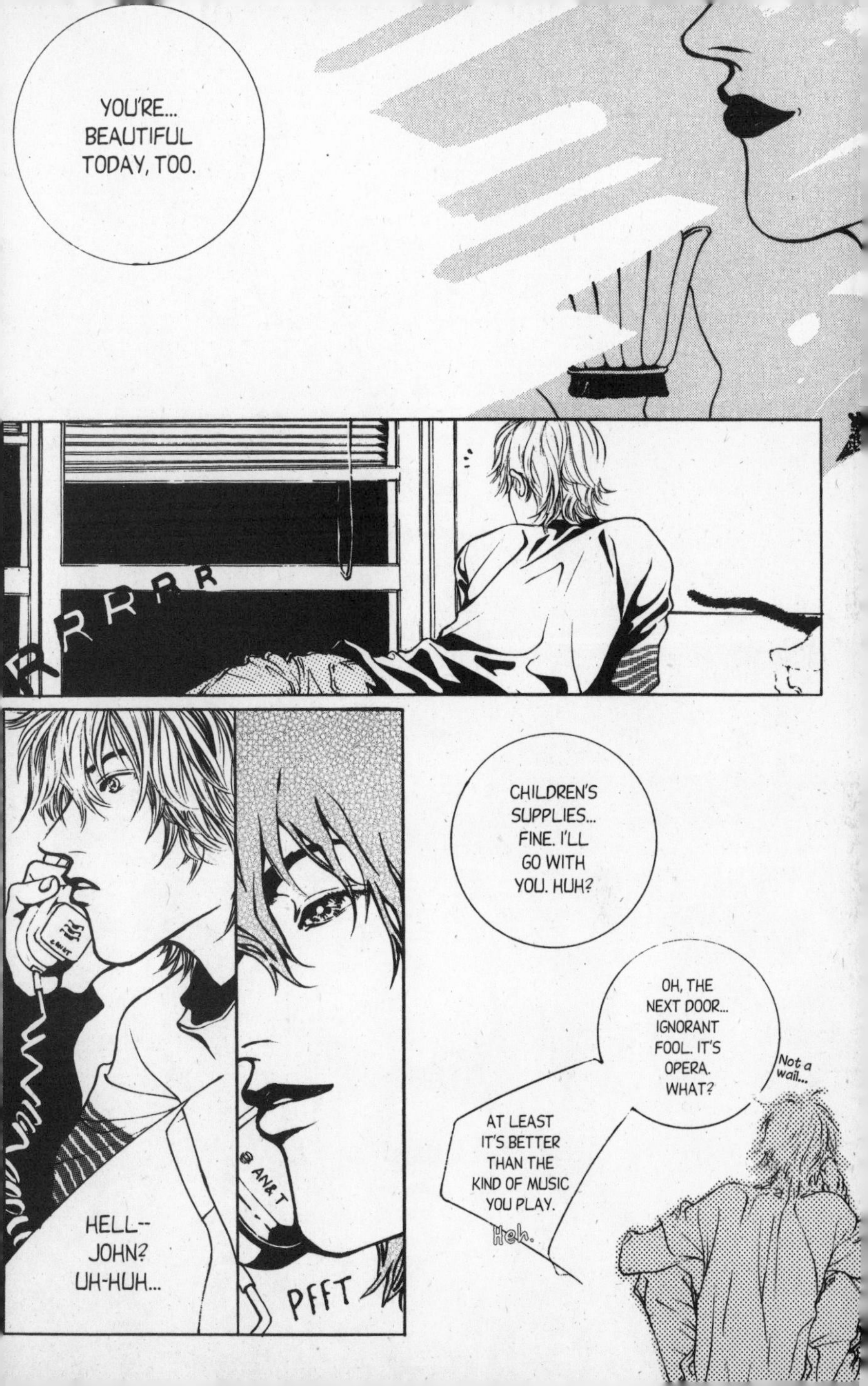
YOU'RE... BEAUTIFUL TODAY, TOO.
RRRRRR
HELL-- JOHN? UH-HUH...
PFFT
CHILDREN'S SUPPLIES... FINE. I'LL GO WITH YOU. HUH?
OH, THE NEXT DOOR... IGNORANT FOOL. IT'S OPERA. WHAT?
Not a wail...
AT LEAST IT'S BETTER THAN THE KIND OF MUSIC YOU PLAY.
Heh.

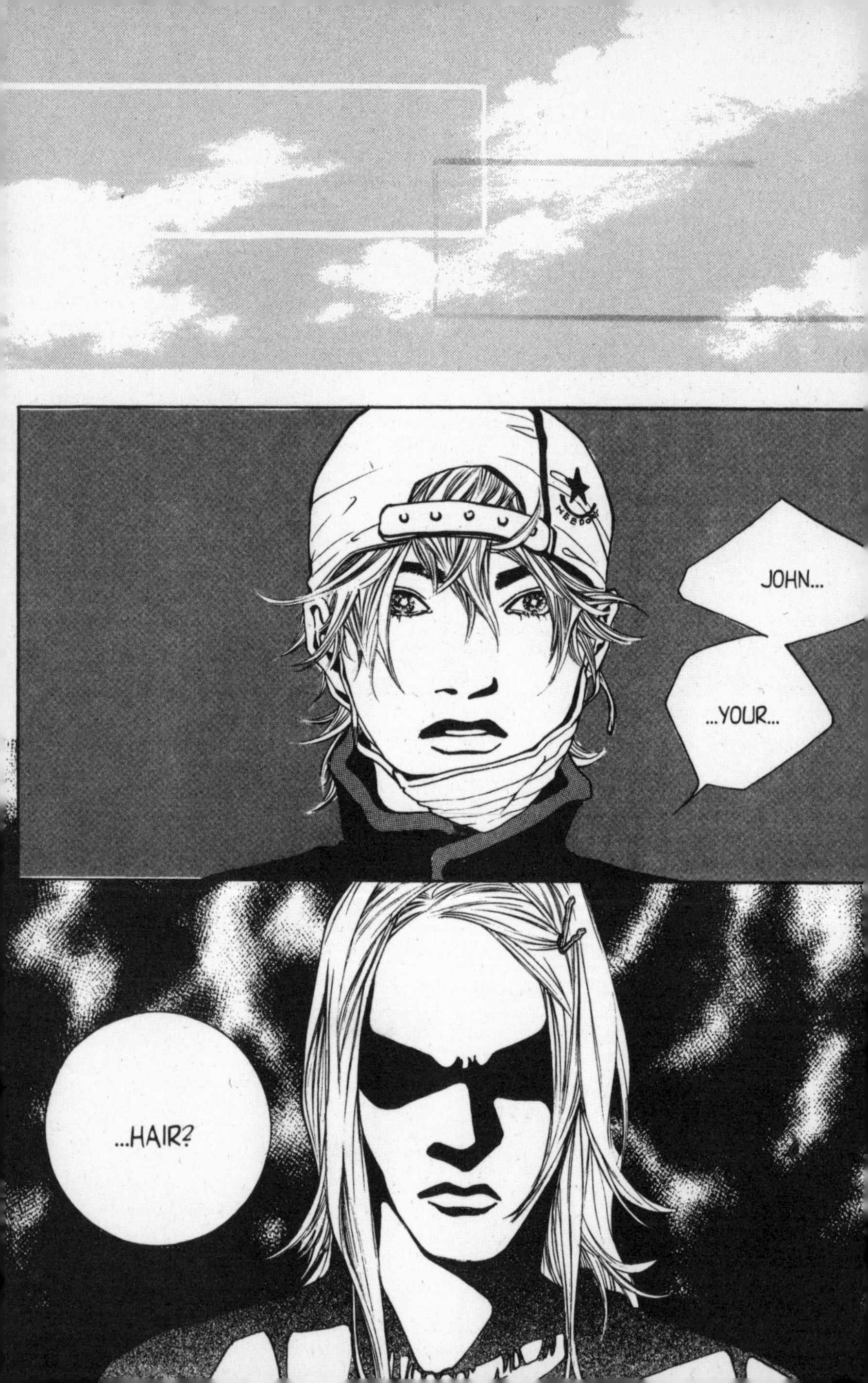
JOHN...
...YOUR...
...HAIR?

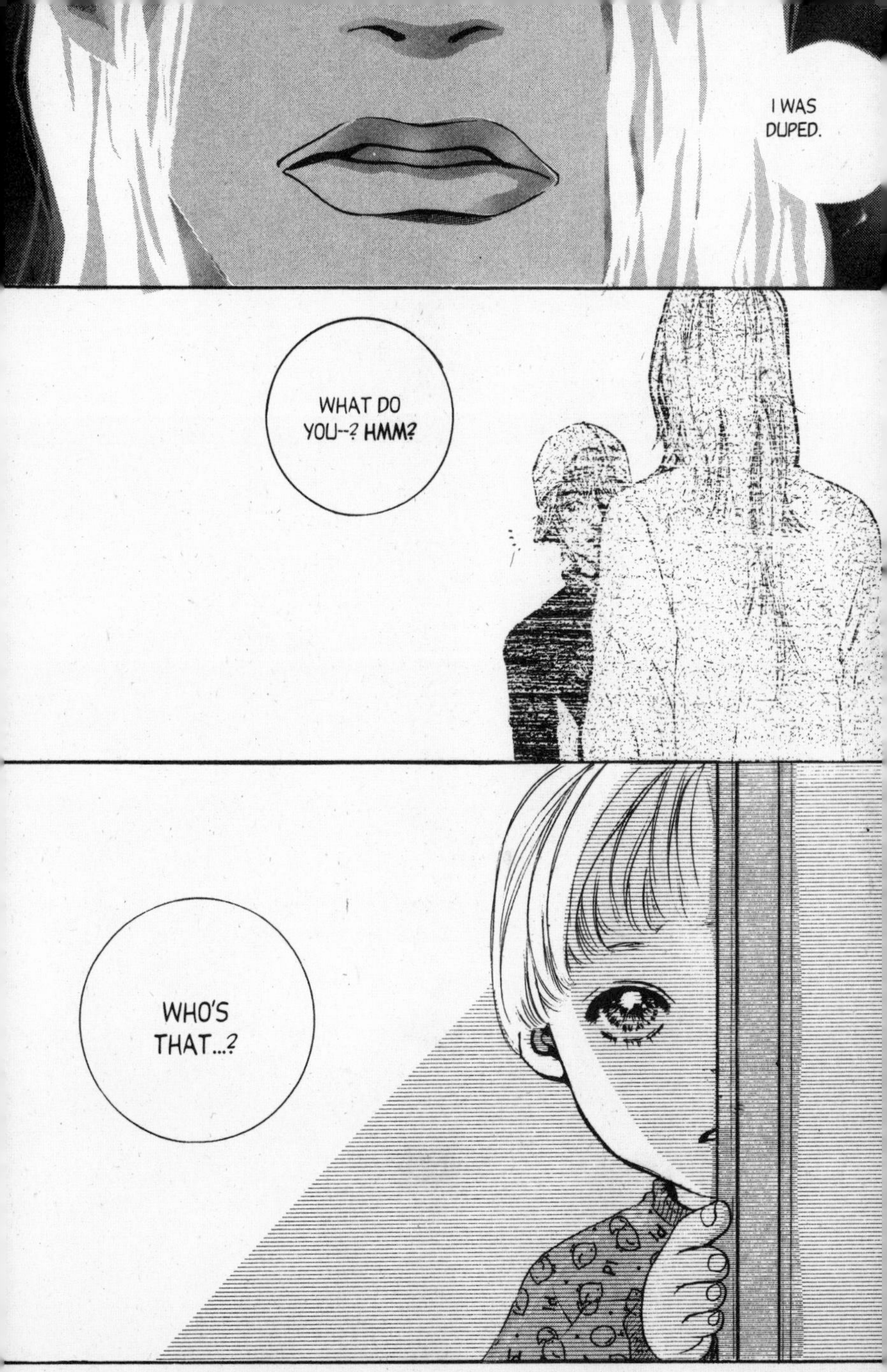
I WAS DUPED.
WHAT DO YOU--? HMM?
WHO'S THAT...?

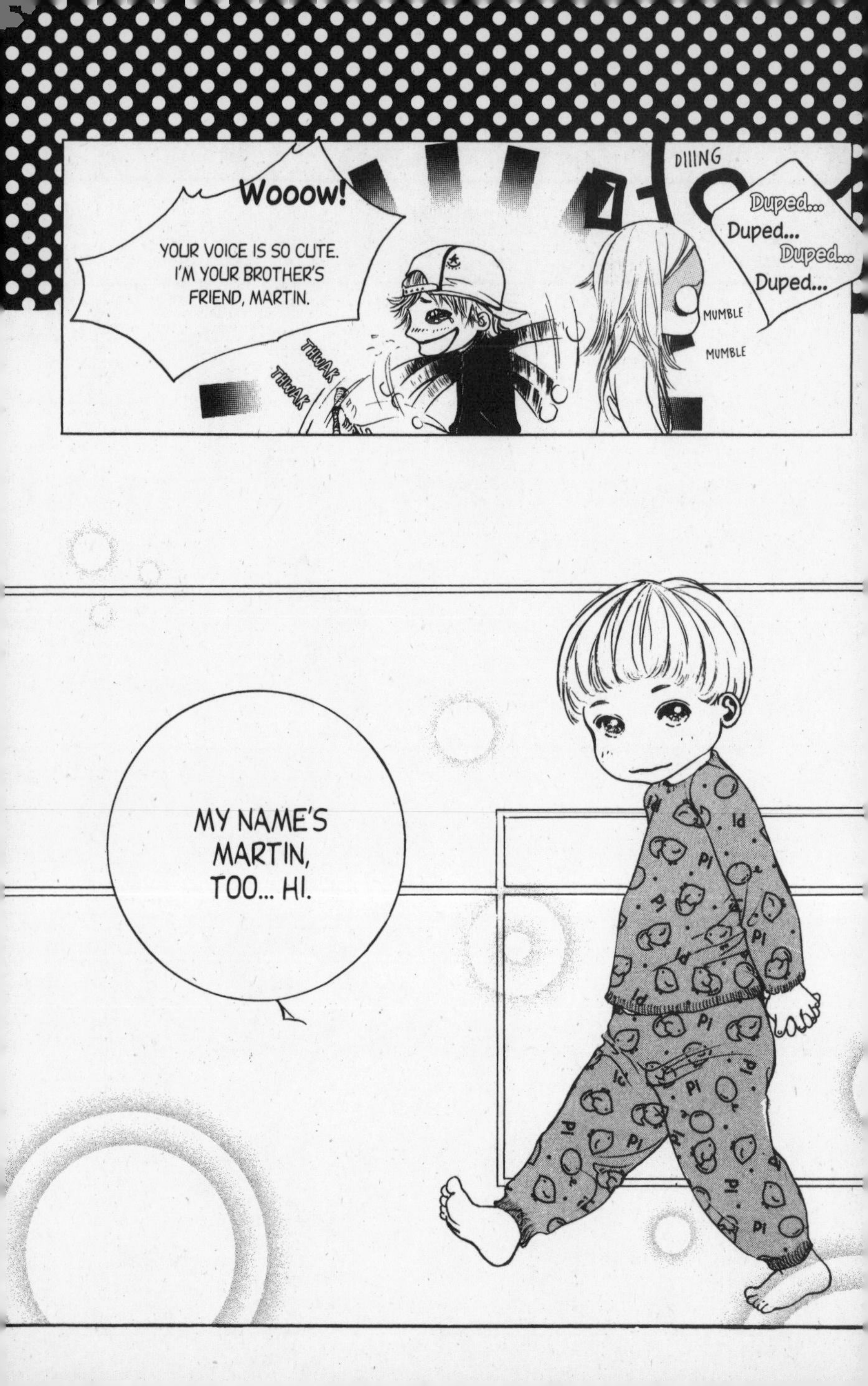
Wooow!
YOUR VOICE IS SO CUTE. I'M YOUR BROTHER'S FRIEND, MARTIN.
THWAK
THWAK
DIIING
MUMBLE
MUMBLE
Duped...
Duped...
Duped...
Duped...
MY NAME'S MARTIN, TOO... HI.

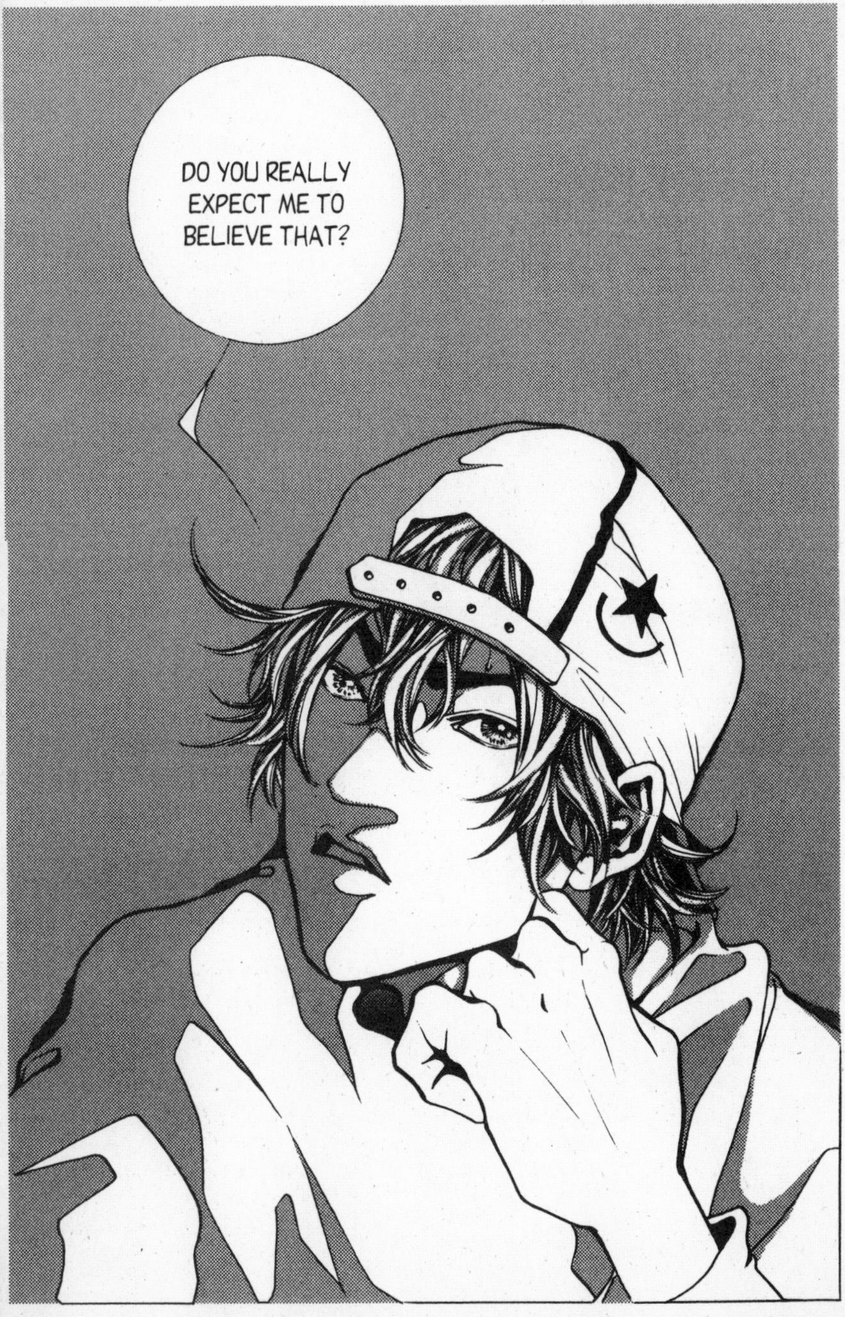
DO YOU REALLY EXPECT ME TO BELIEVE THAT?

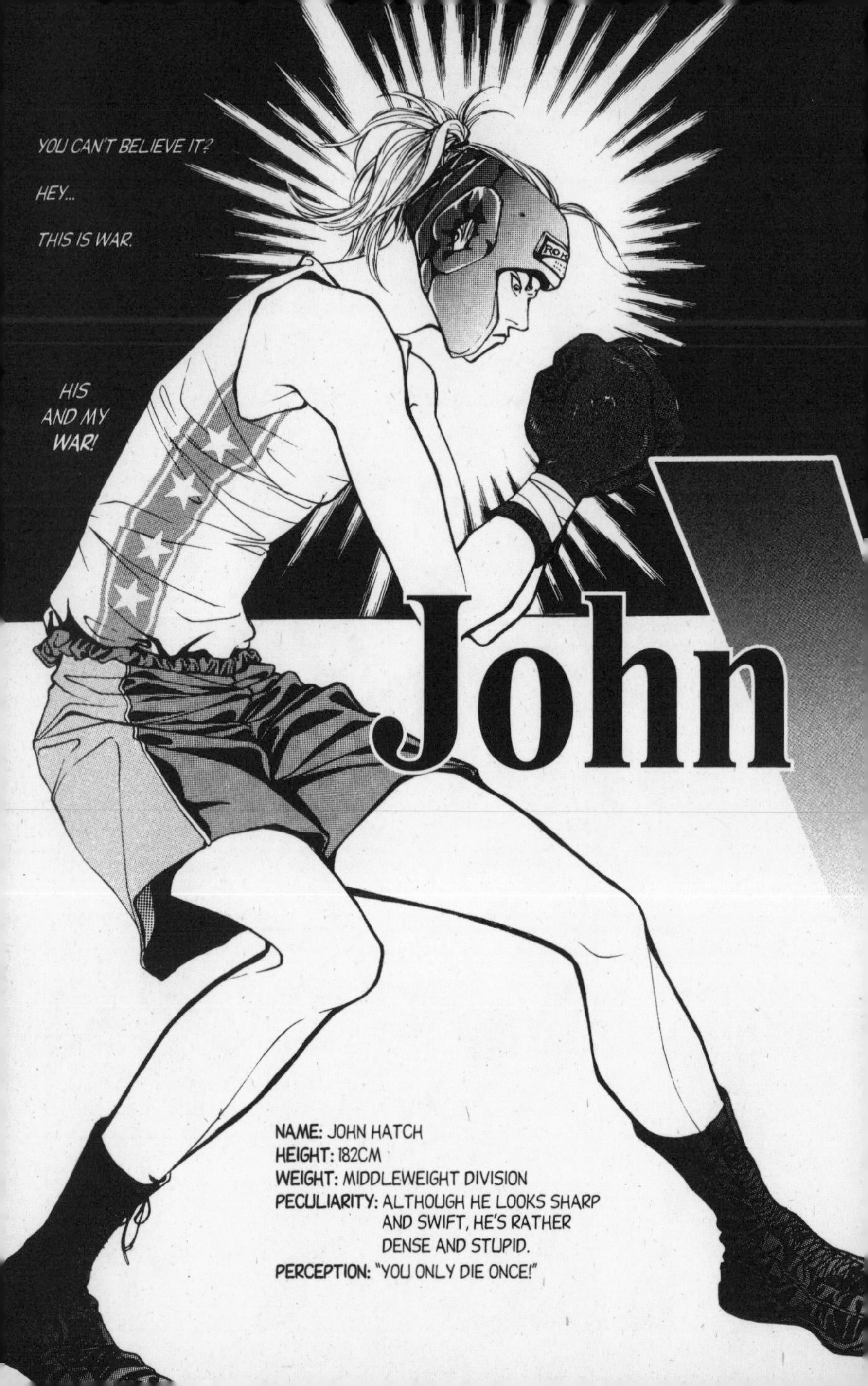
YOU CAN'T BELIEVE IT?
HEY...
THIS IS WAR.
HIS AND MY WAR!
John
NAME: JOHN HATCH
HEIGHT: 182CM
WEIGHT: MIDDLEWEIGHT DIVISION
PECULIARITY: ALTHOUGH HE LOOKS SHARP AND SWIFT, HE'S RATHER DENSE AND STUPID.
PERCEPTION: "YOU ONLY DIE ONCE!"

NAME: MARTIN HATCH
HEIGHT: 125CM
WEIGHT: LIGHTWEIGHT DIVISION
PECULIARITY: BEWILDERING HIS OPPONENT WITH HIS POKER FACE.
PERCEPTION: "YOU CAN DIE TWICE. TASTE MY FURY!"

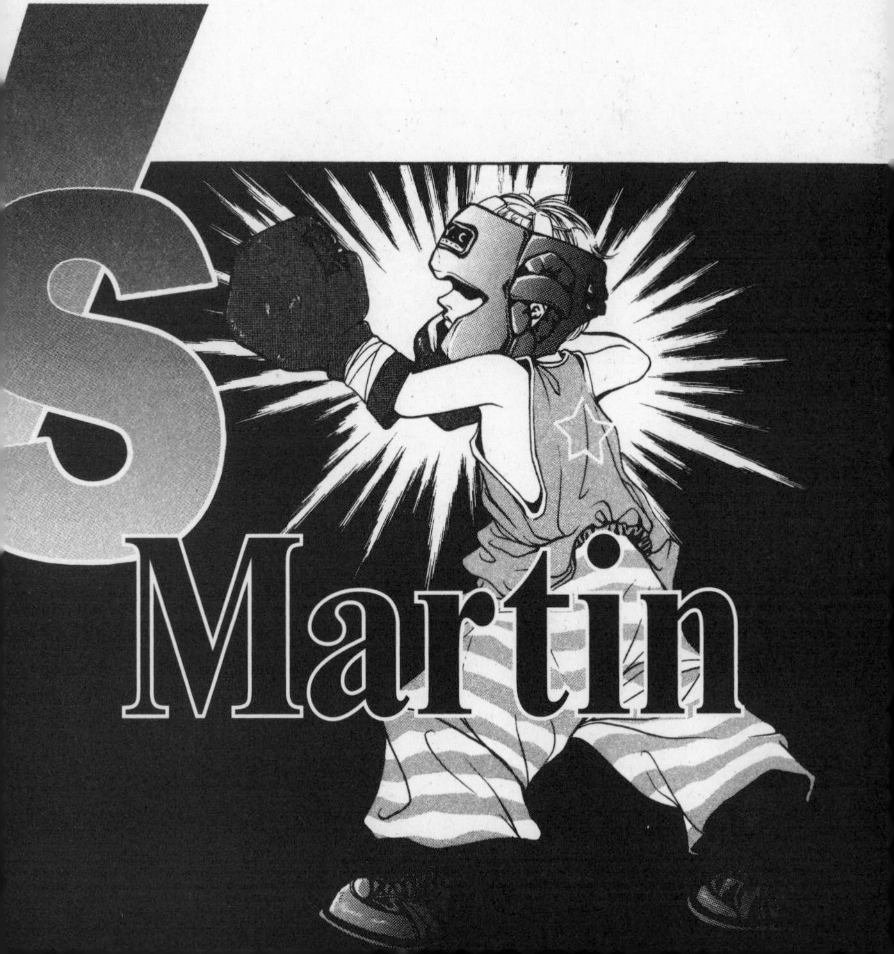
Martin

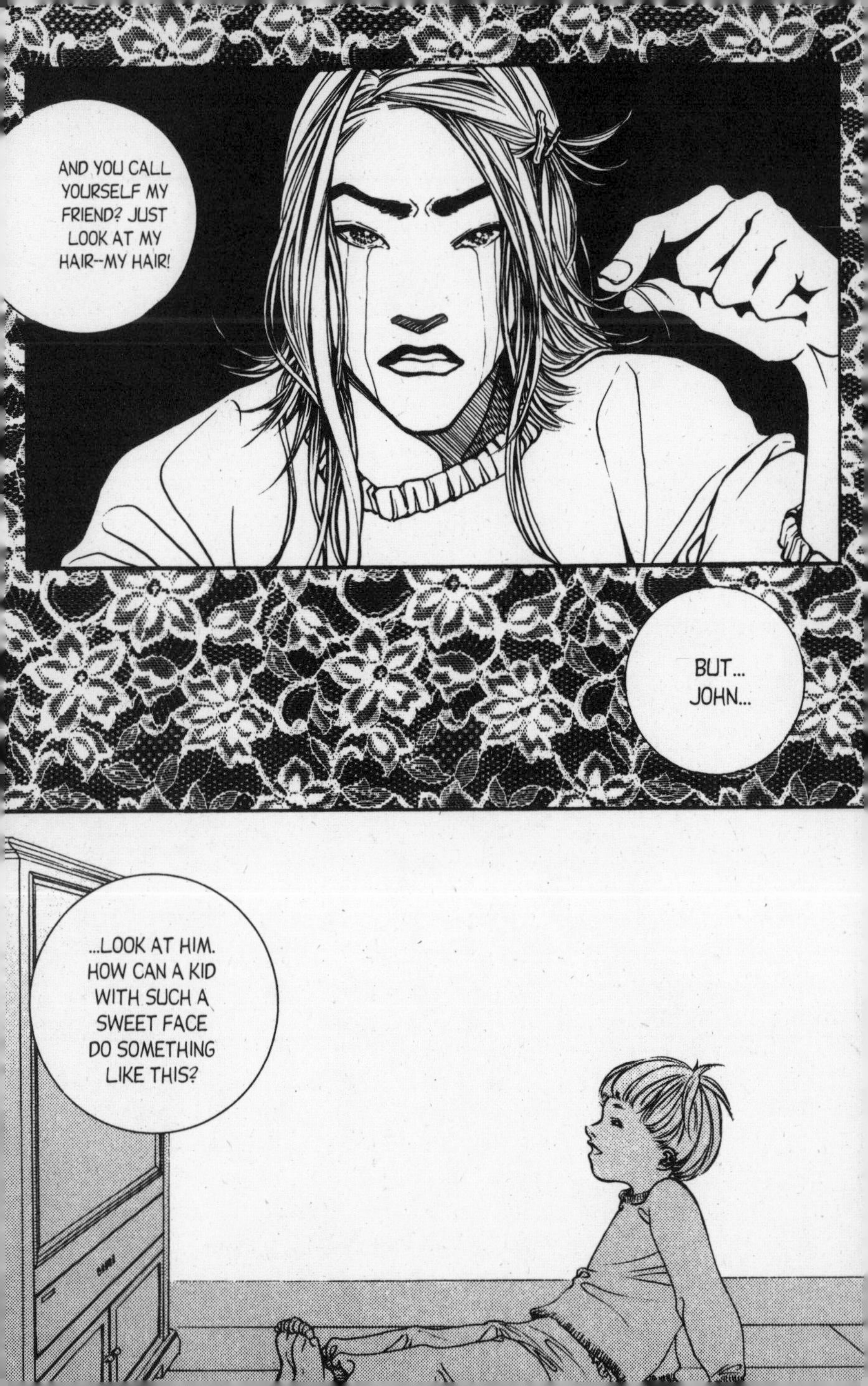
AND YOU CALL YOURSELF MY FRIEND? JUST LOOK AT MY HAIR--MY HAIR!
BUT... JOHN...
...LOOK AT HIM. HOW CAN A KID WITH SUCH A SWEET FACE DO SOMETHING LIKE THIS?

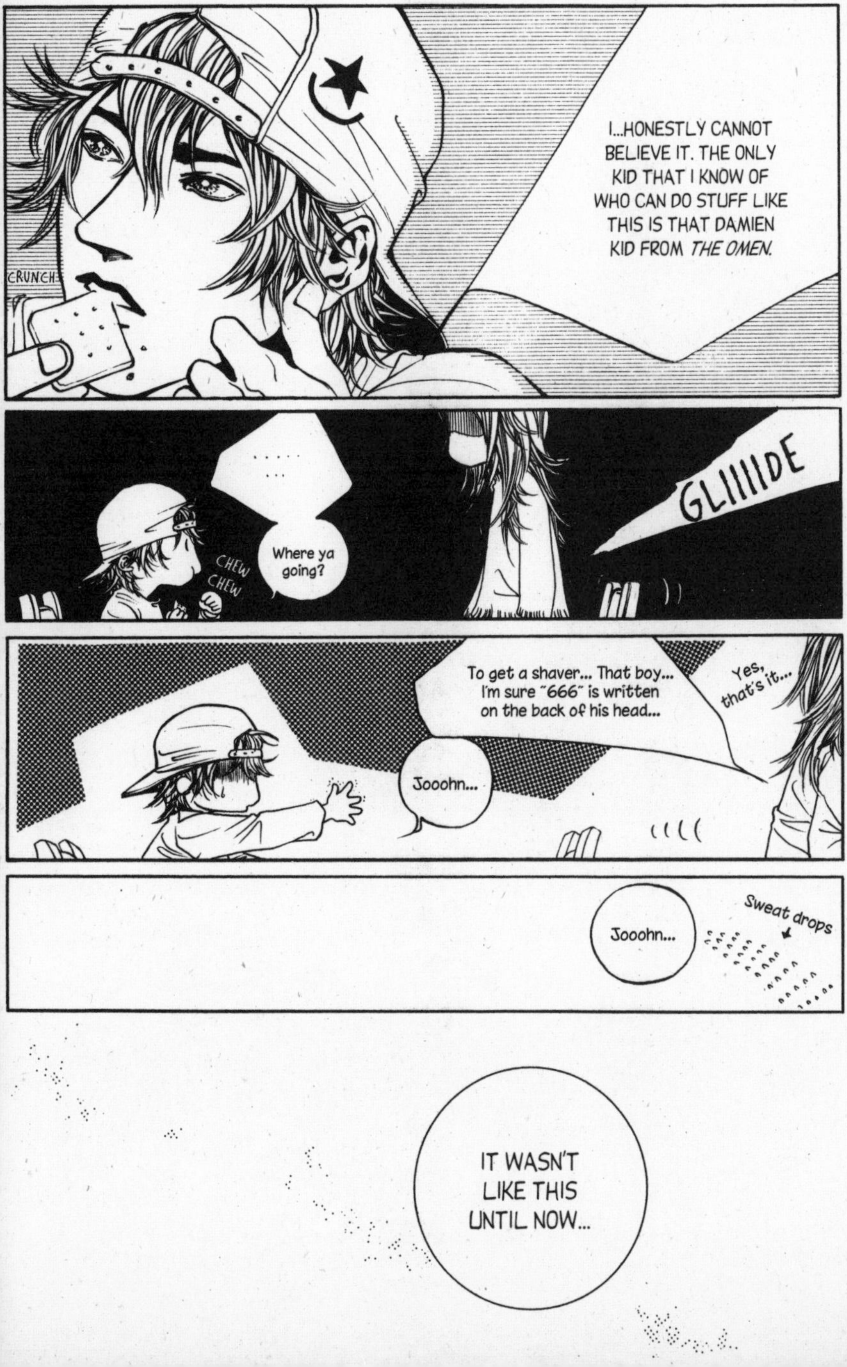
CRUNCH
I...HONESTLY CANNOT BELIEVE IT. THE ONLY KID THAT I KNOW OF WHO CAN DO STUFF LIKE THIS IS THAT DAMIEN KID FROM *THE OMEN.*
......
Where ya going?
CHEW CHEW
GLIIIIDE
To get a shaver... That boy... I'm sure "666" is written on the back of his head...
Yes, that's it...
Jooohn...
Jooohn...
Sweat drops
IT WASN'T LIKE THIS UNTIL NOW...

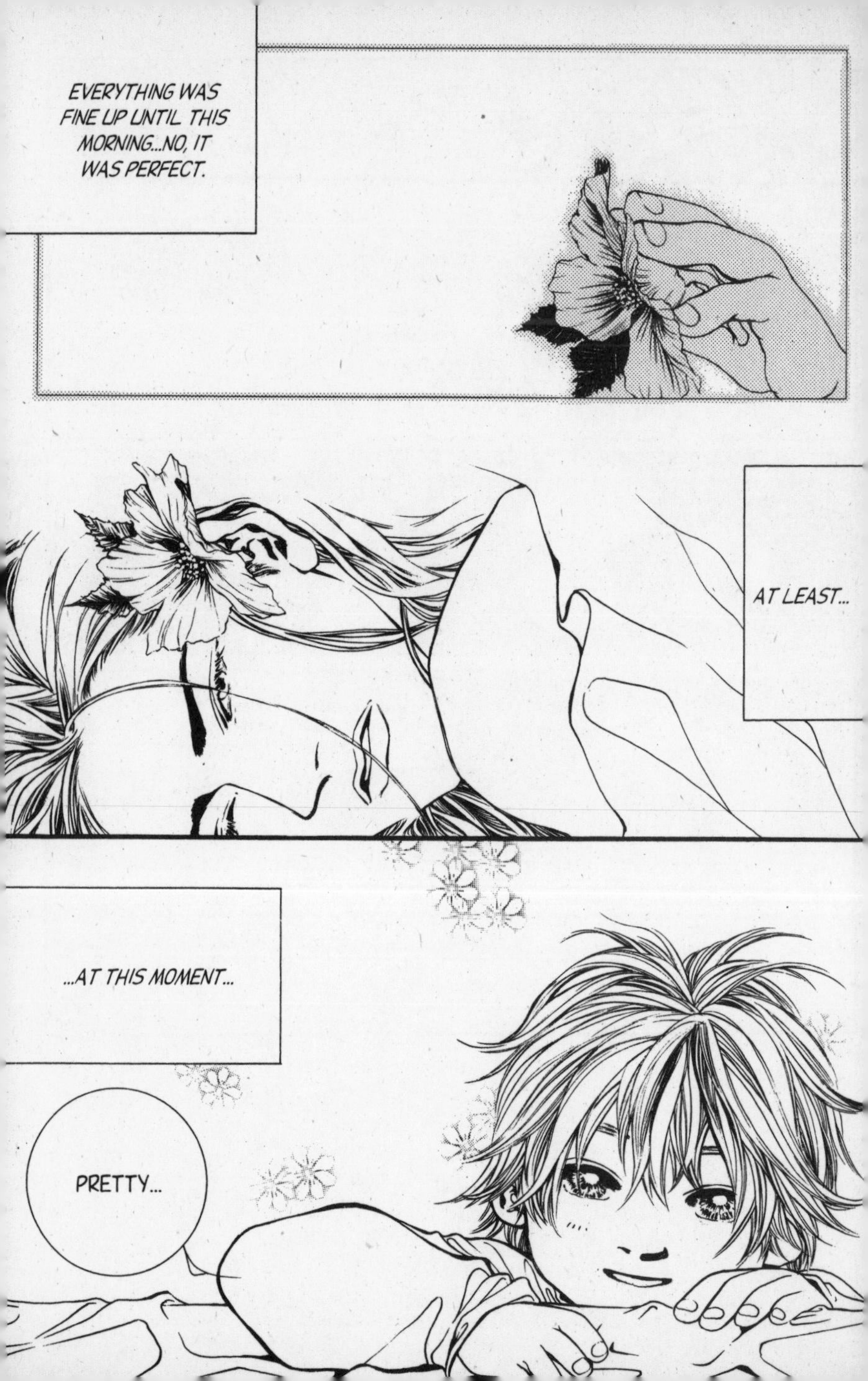
EVERYTHING WAS FINE UP UNTIL THIS MORNING...NO, IT WAS PERFECT.
AT LEAST...
...AT THIS MOMENT...
PRETTY...

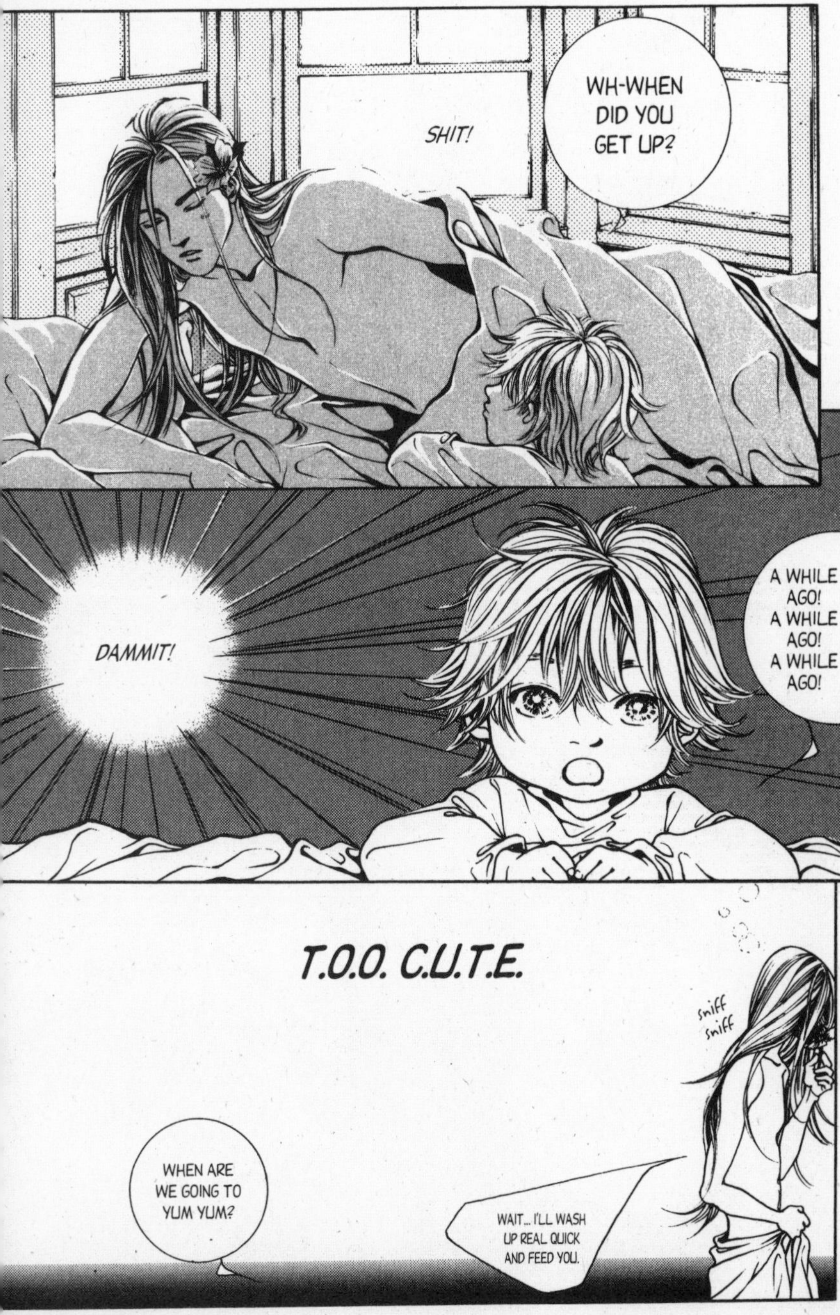
SHIT!
WH-WHEN DID YOU GET UP?
DAMMIT!
A WHILE AGO! A WHILE AGO! A WHILE AGO!
T.O.O. C.U.T.E.
sniff sniff
WHEN ARE WE GOING TO YUM YUM?
WAIT... I'LL WASH UP REAL QUICK AND FEED YOU.

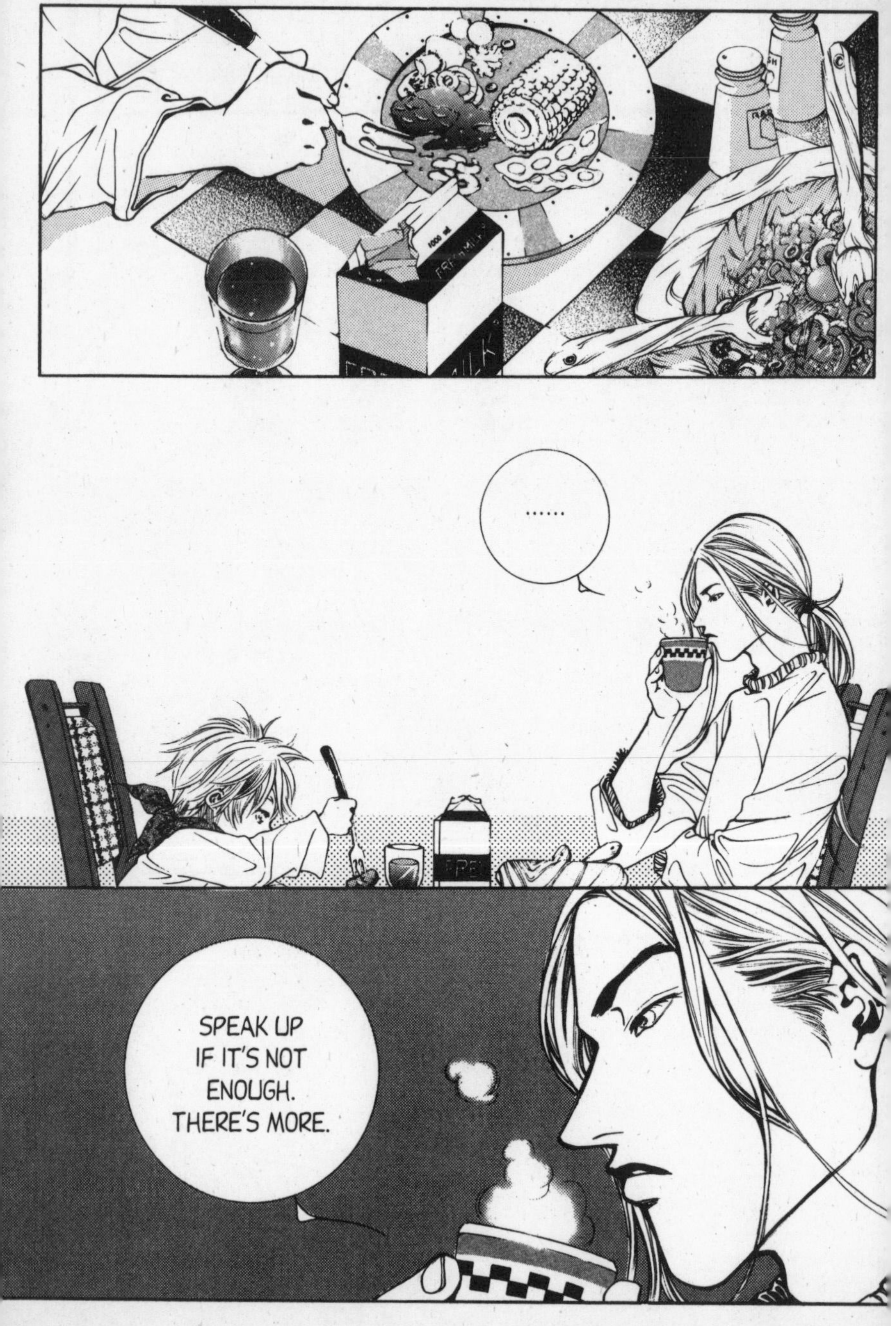
......
SPEAK UP IF IT'S NOT ENOUGH. THERE'S MORE.

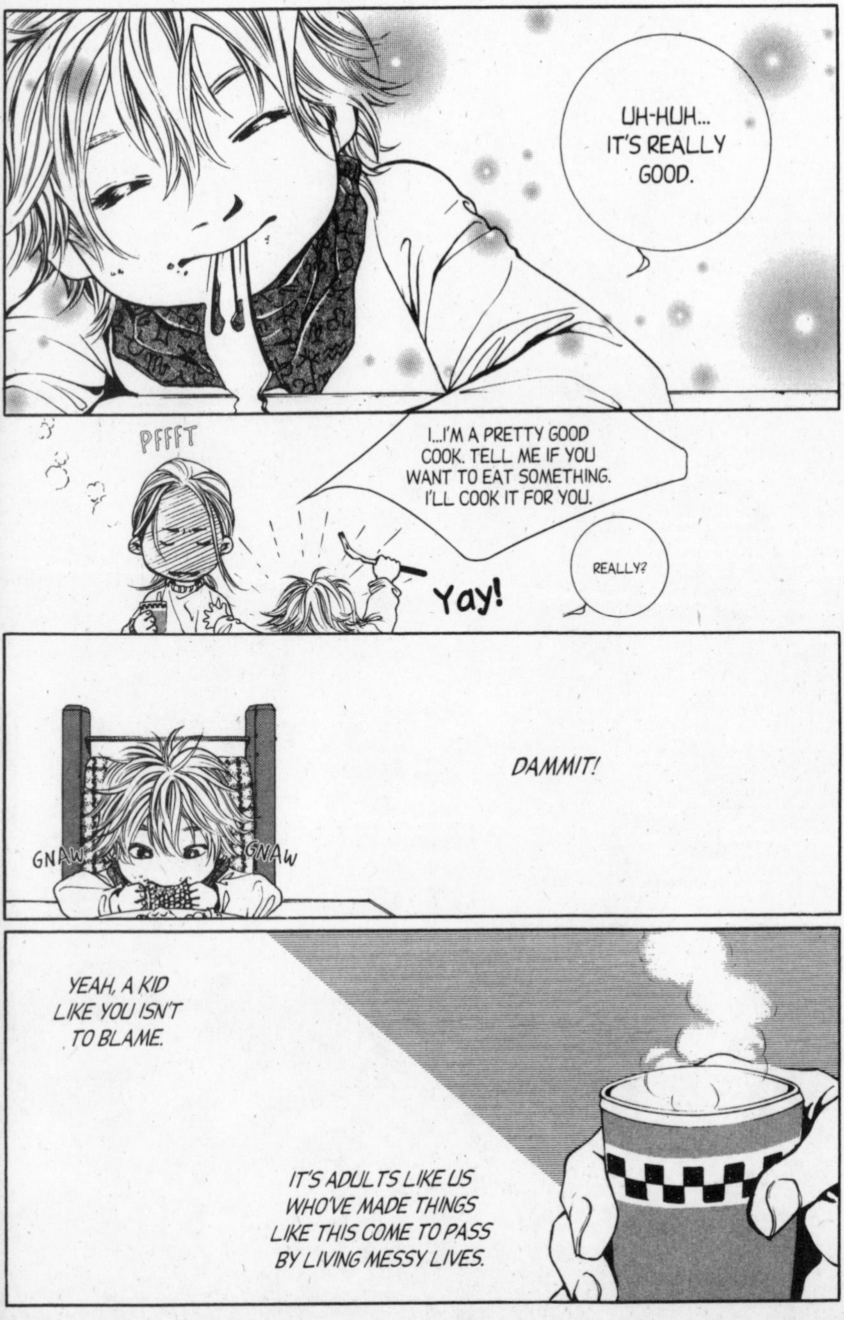
UH-HUH... IT'S REALLY GOOD.
PFFFT
I...I'M A PRETTY GOOD COOK. TELL ME IF YOU WANT TO EAT SOMETHING. I'LL COOK IT FOR YOU.
REALLY?
Yay!
GNAW
GNAW
DAMMIT!
YEAH, A KID LIKE YOU ISN'T TO BLAME.
IT'S ADULTS LIKE US WHO'VE MADE THINGS LIKE THIS COME TO PASS BY LIVING MESSY LIVES.

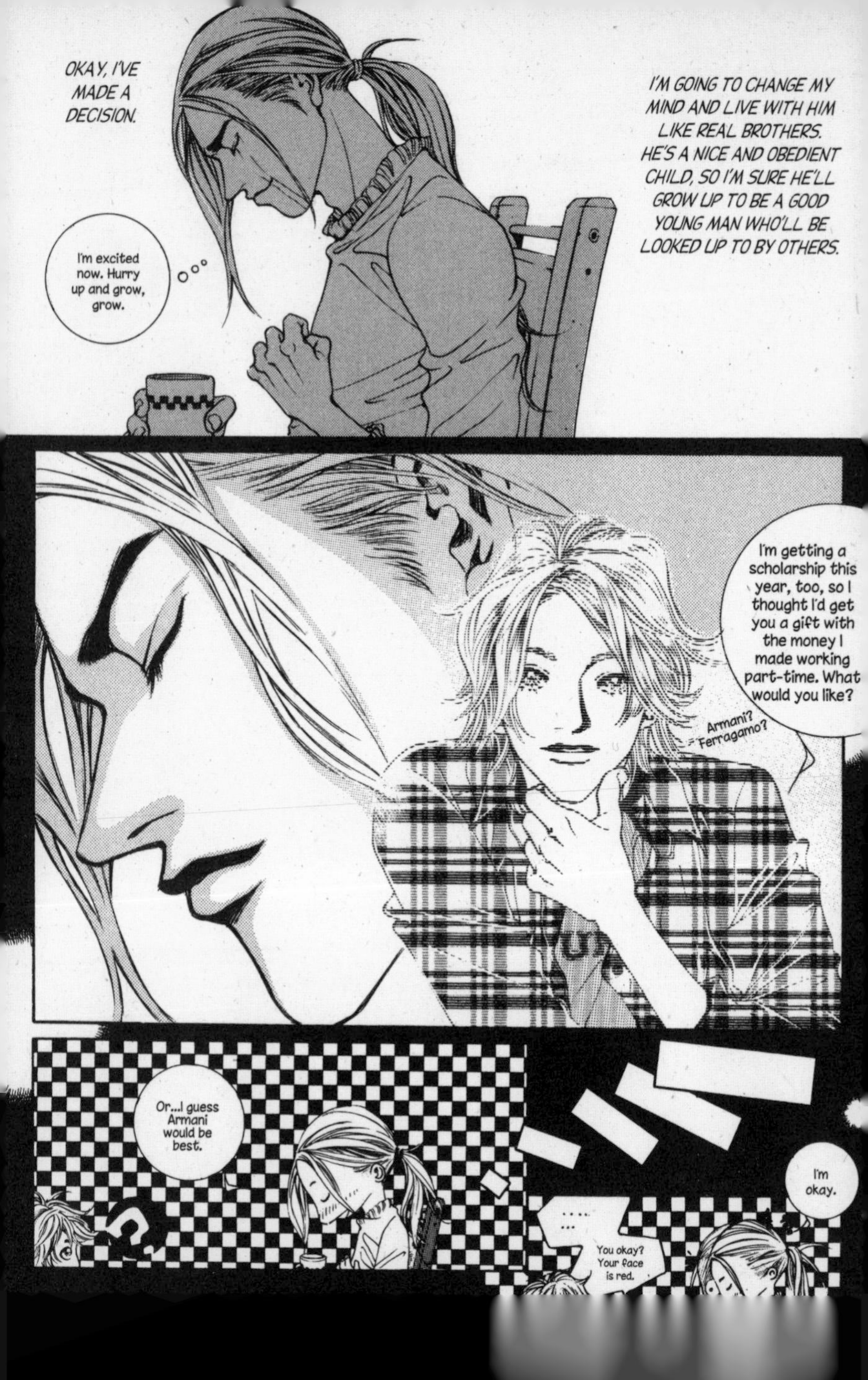
OKAY, I'VE MADE A DECISION.
I'M GOING TO CHANGE MY MIND AND LIVE WITH HIM LIKE REAL BROTHERS. HE'S A NICE AND OBEDIENT CHILD, SO I'M SURE HE'LL GROW UP TO BE A GOOD YOUNG MAN WHO'LL BE LOOKED UP TO BY OTHERS.
I'm excited now. Hurry up and grow, grow.
I'm getting a scholarship this year, too, so I thought I'd get you a gift with the money I made working part-time. What would you like?
Armani? Ferragamo?
Or...I guess Armani would be best.
?
...
You okay? Your face is red.
I'm okay.

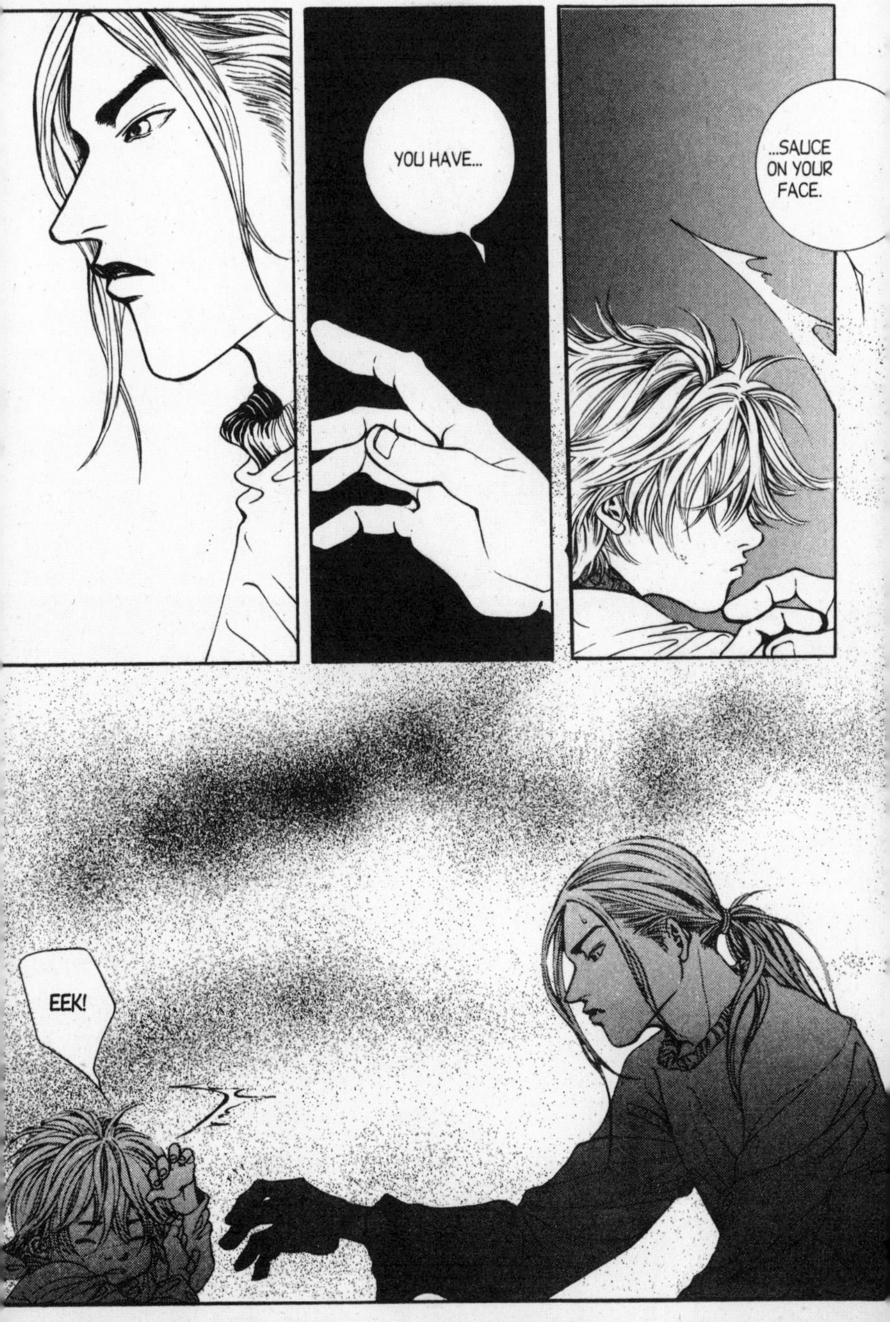
YOU HAVE...
...SAUCE ON YOUR FACE.
EEK!

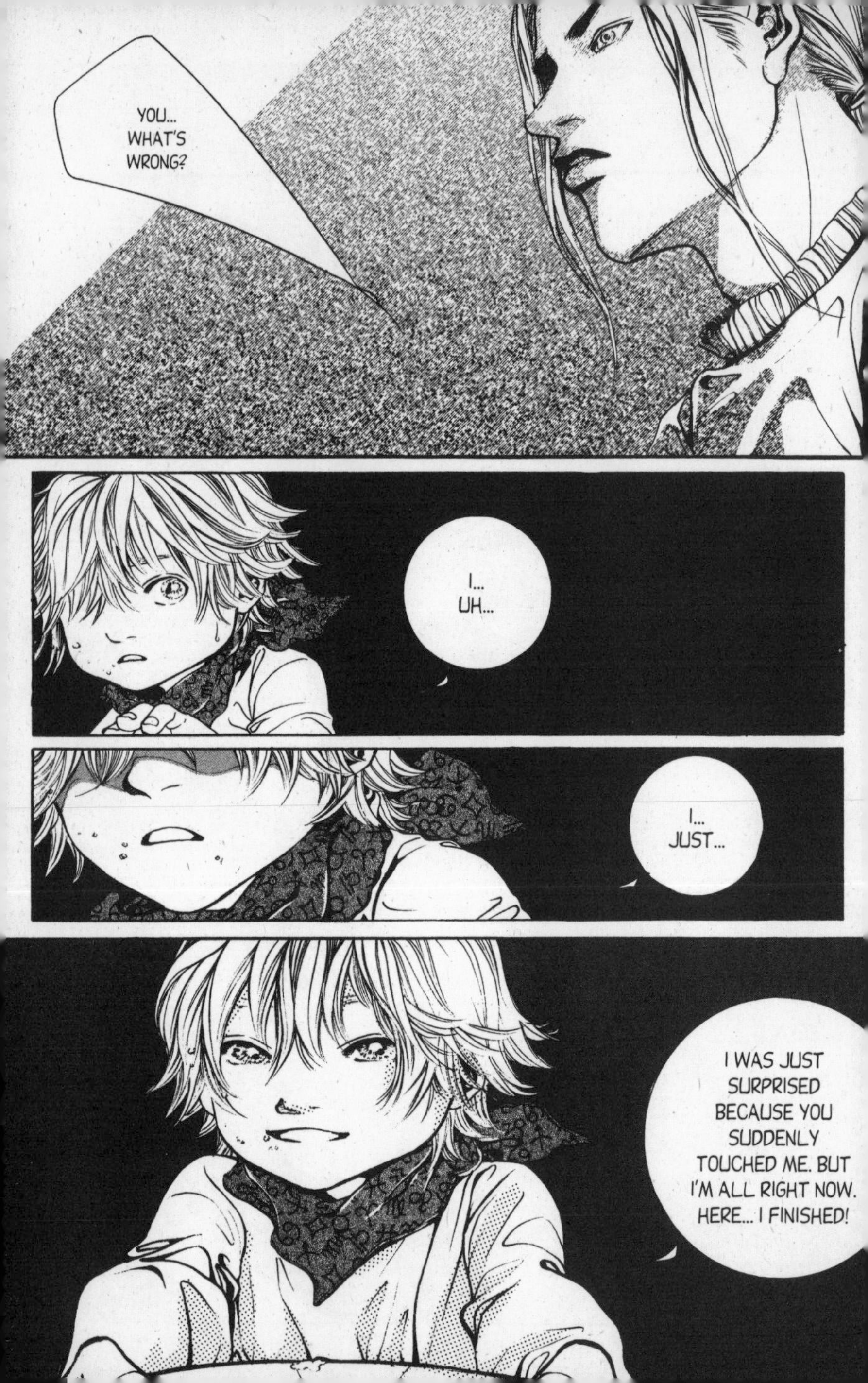
YOU... WHAT'S WRONG?
I... UH...
I... JUST...
I WAS JUST SURPRISED BECAUSE YOU SUDDENLY TOUCHED ME. BUT I'M ALL RIGHT NOW. HERE... I FINISHED!

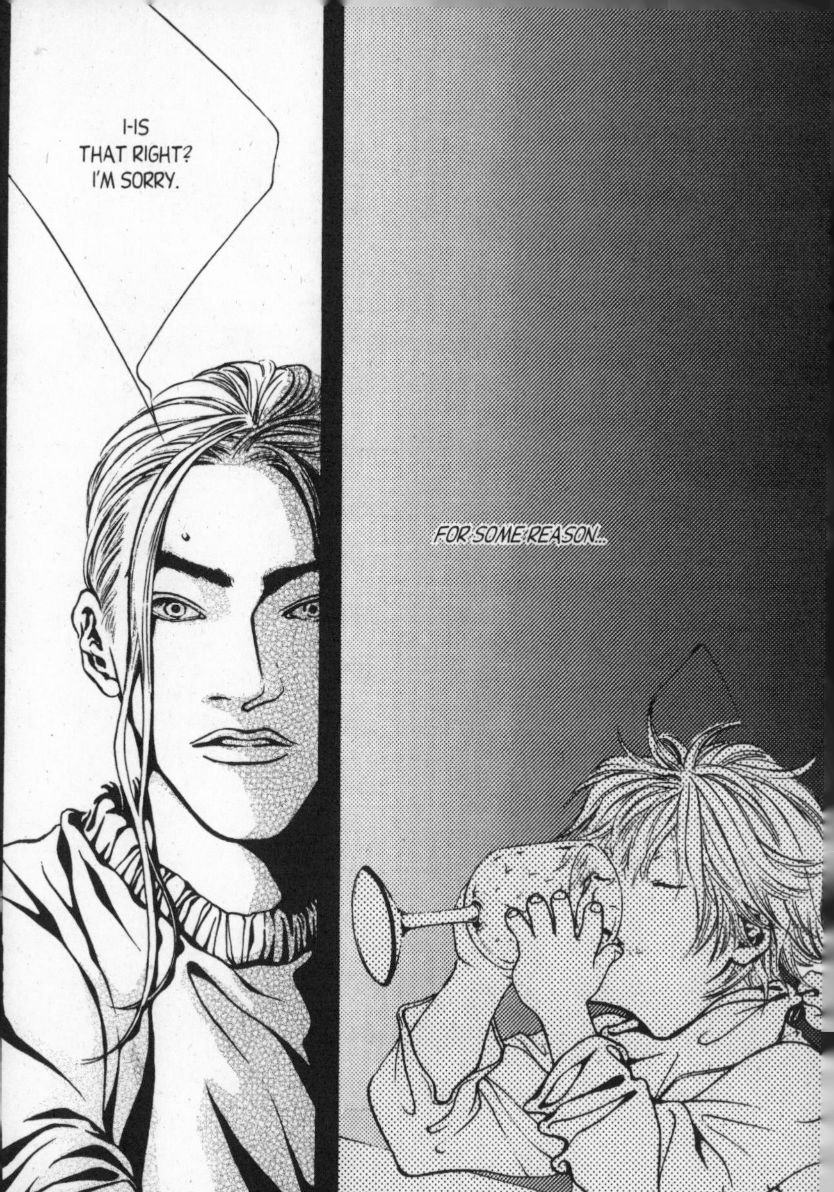
I-IS
THAT RIGHT?
I'M SORRY.
FOR SOME REASON...

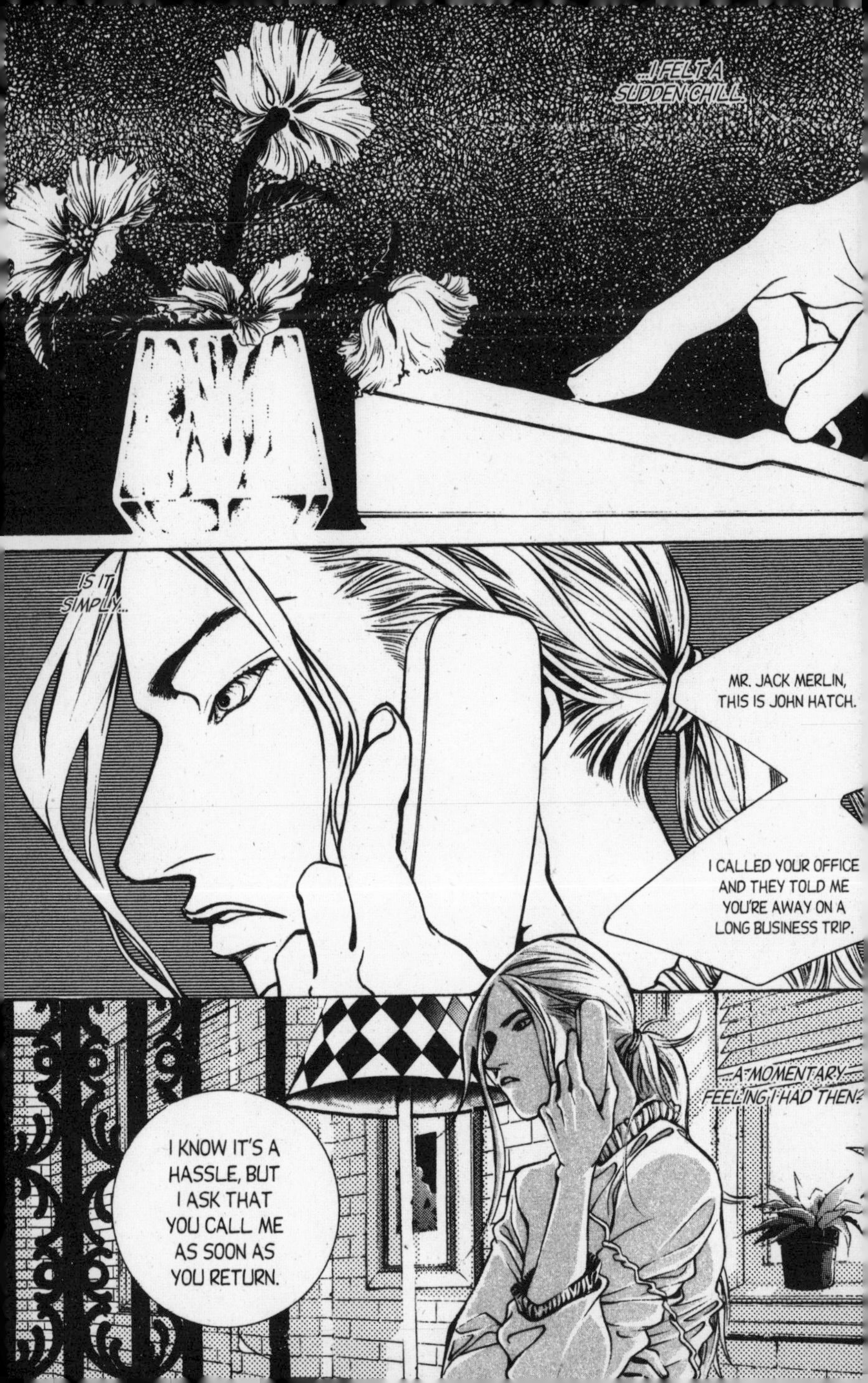
...I FELT A SUDDEN CHILL.
IS IT SIMPLY...
MR. JACK MERLIN, THIS IS JOHN HATCH.
I CALLED YOUR OFFICE AND THEY TOLD ME YOU'RE AWAY ON A LONG BUSINESS TRIP.
I KNOW IT'S A HASSLE, BUT I ASK THAT YOU CALL ME AS SOON AS YOU RETURN.
A MOMENTARY FEELING I HAD THEN?

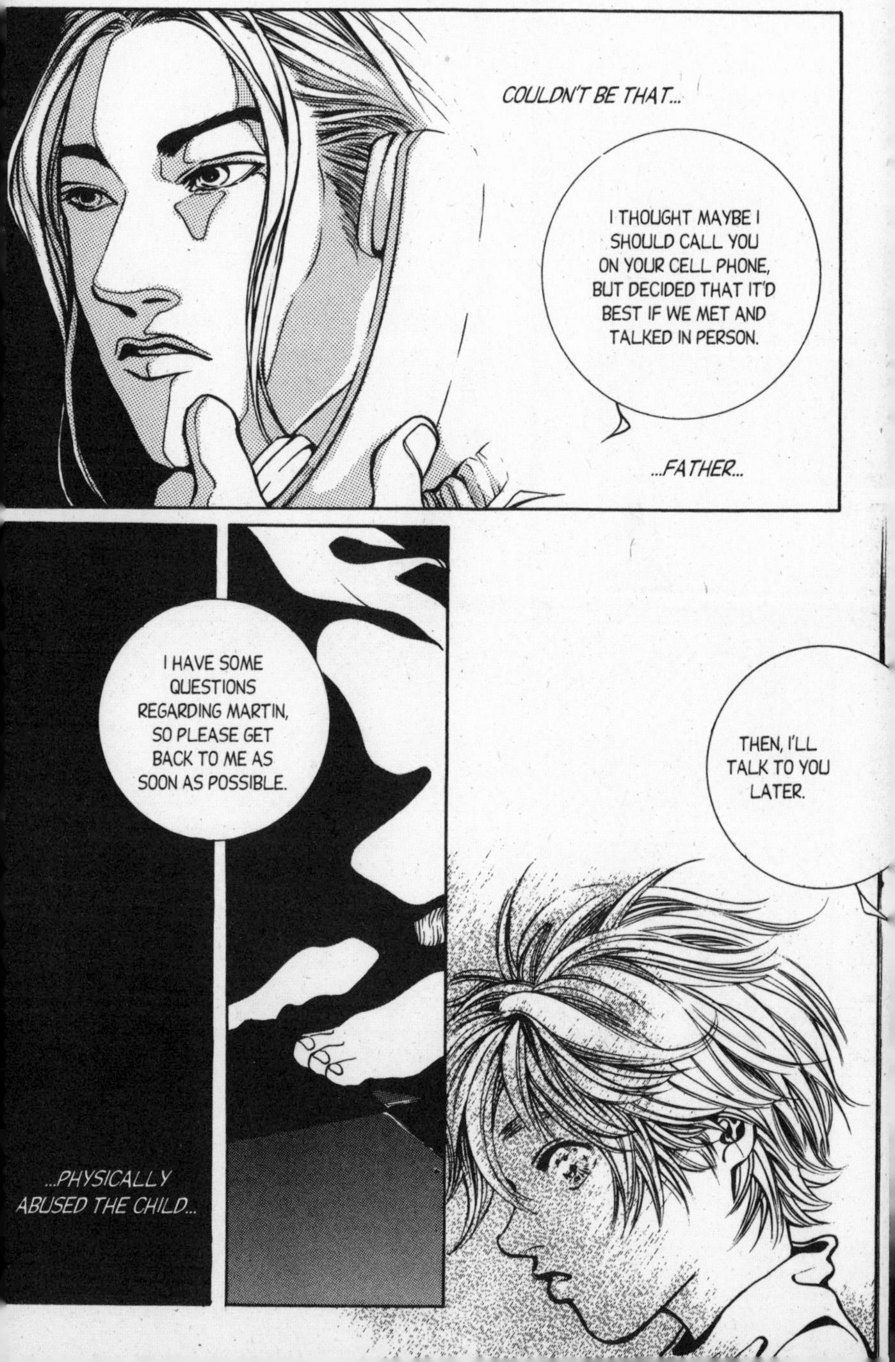
COULDN'T BE THAT...
I THOUGHT MAYBE I SHOULD CALL YOU ON YOUR CELL PHONE, BUT DECIDED THAT IT'D BEST IF WE MET AND TALKED IN PERSON.
...FATHER...
I HAVE SOME QUESTIONS REGARDING MARTIN, SO PLEASE GET BACK TO ME AS SOON AS POSSIBLE.
...PHYSICALLY ABUSED THE CHILD...
THEN, I'LL TALK TO YOU LATER.

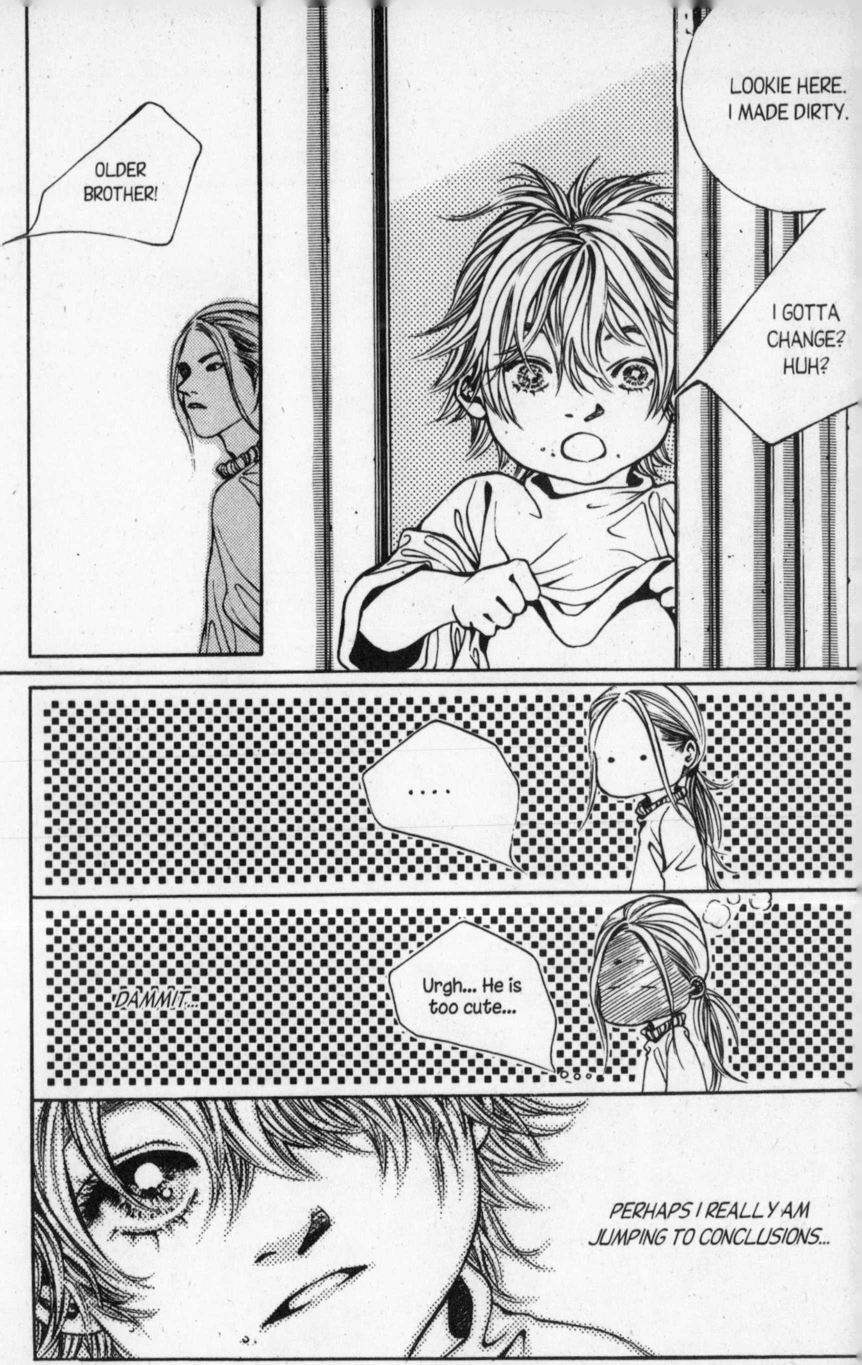
OLDER BROTHER!
LOOKIE HERE. I MADE DIRTY.
I GOTTA CHANGE? HUH?
....
DAMMIT...
Urgh... He is too cute...
PERHAPS I REALLY AM JUMPING TO CONCLUSIONS...

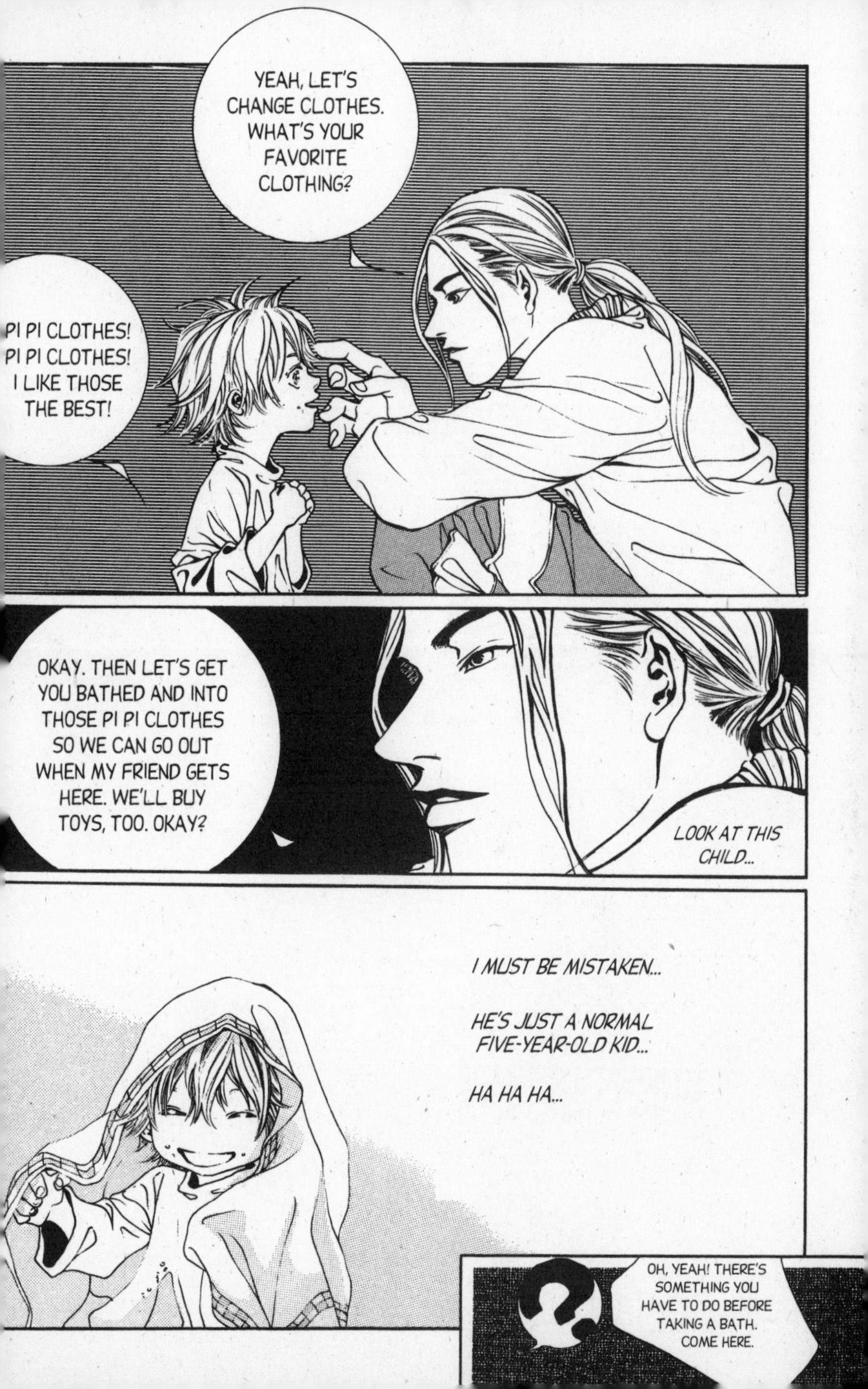
YEAH, LET'S CHANGE CLOTHES. WHAT'S YOUR FAVORITE CLOTHING?
PI PI CLOTHES! PI PI CLOTHES! I LIKE THOSE THE BEST!
OKAY. THEN LET'S GET YOU BATHED AND INTO THOSE PI PI CLOTHES SO WE CAN GO OUT WHEN MY FRIEND GETS HERE. WE'LL BUY TOYS, TOO. OKAY?
LOOK AT THIS CHILD...
I MUST BE MISTAKEN...
HE'S JUST A NORMAL FIVE-YEAR-OLD KID...
HA HA HA...
OH, YEAH! THERE'S SOMETHING YOU HAVE TO DO BEFORE TAKING A BATH. COME HERE.

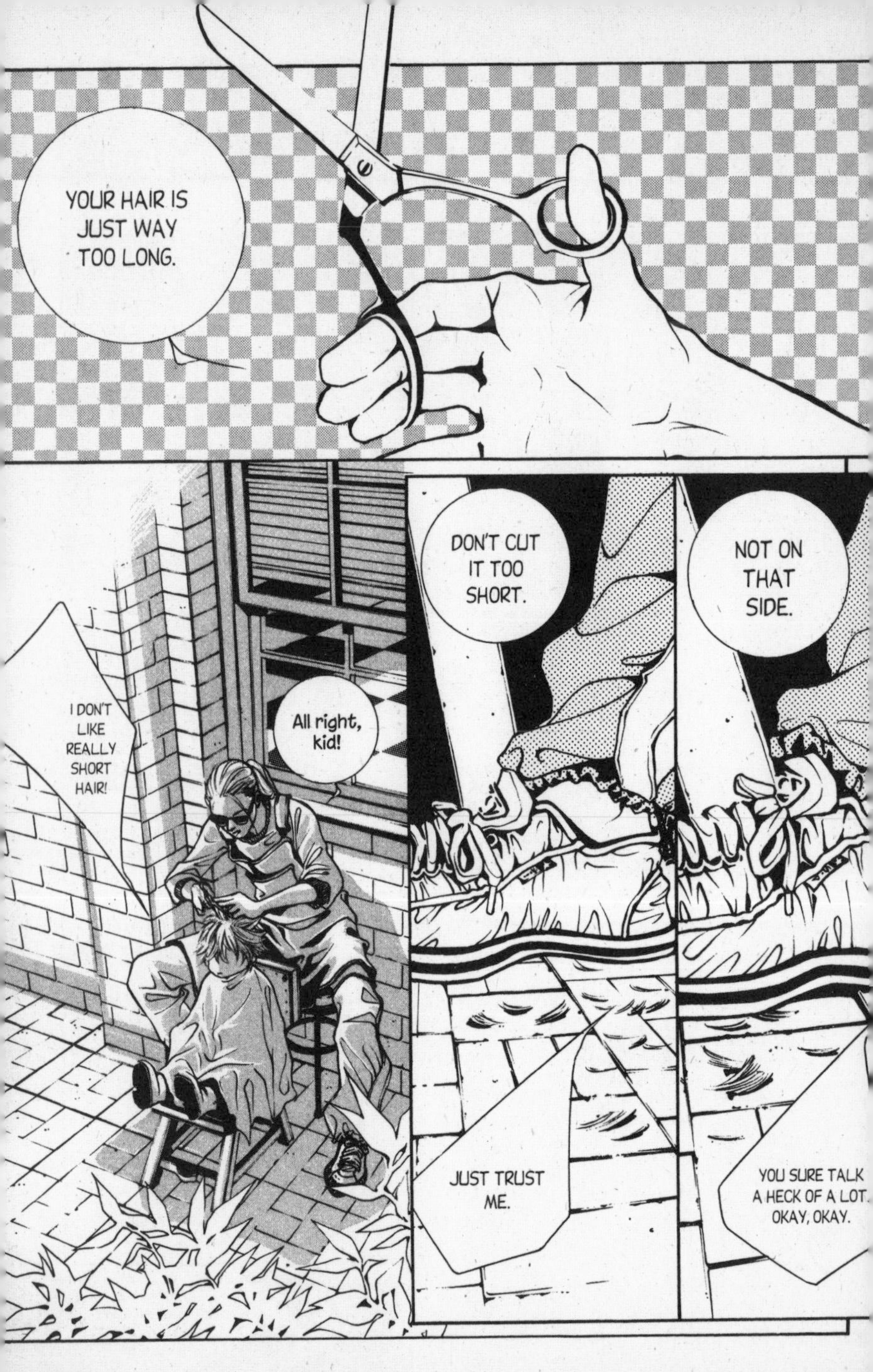
YOUR HAIR IS JUST WAY TOO LONG.
I DON'T LIKE REALLY SHORT HAIR!
All right, kid!
DON'T CUT IT TOO SHORT.
JUST TRUST ME.
NOT ON THAT SIDE.
YOU SURE TALK A HECK OF A LOT. OKAY, OKAY.

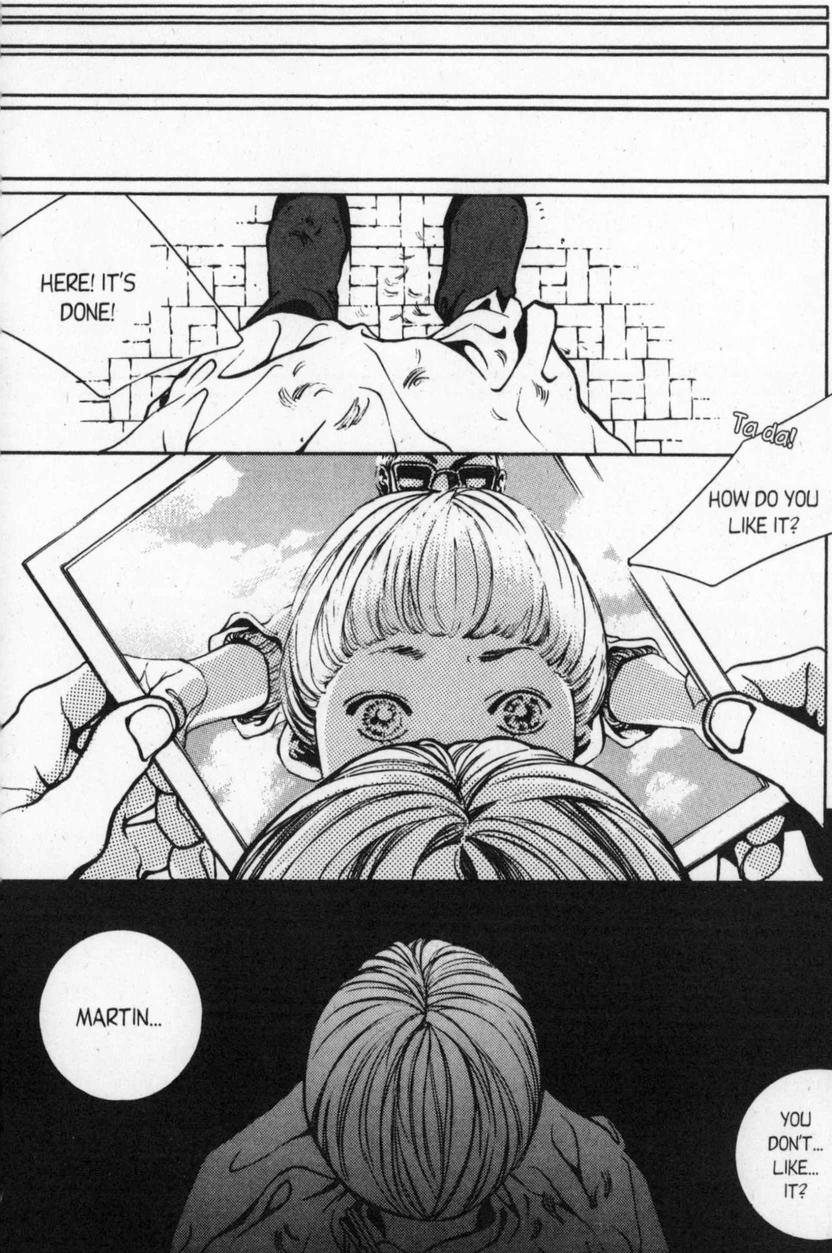
HERE! IT'S DONE!
Ta da!
HOW DO YOU LIKE IT?
MARTIN...
YOU DON'T... LIKE... IT?

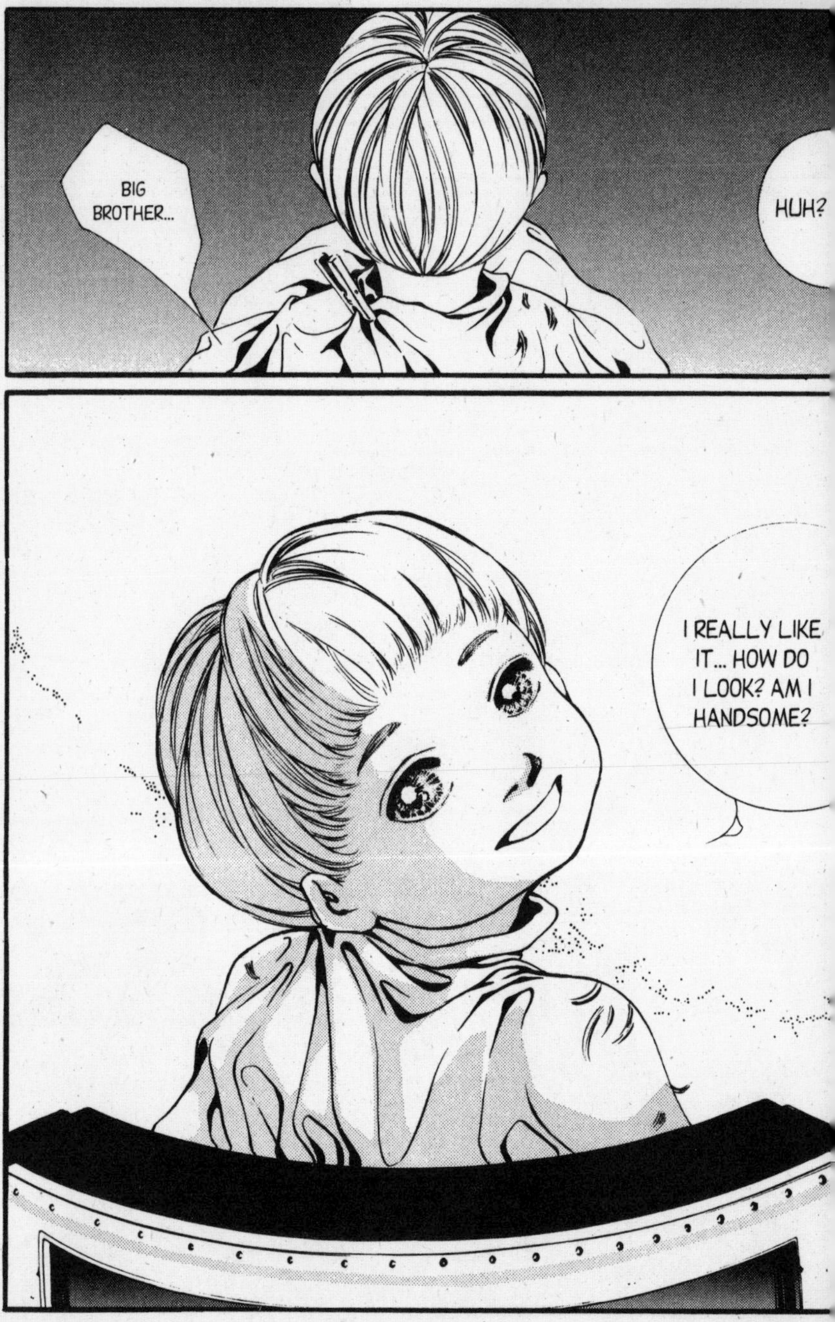
BIG BROTHER...
HUH?
I REALLY LIKE IT... HOW DO I LOOK? AM I HANDSOME?

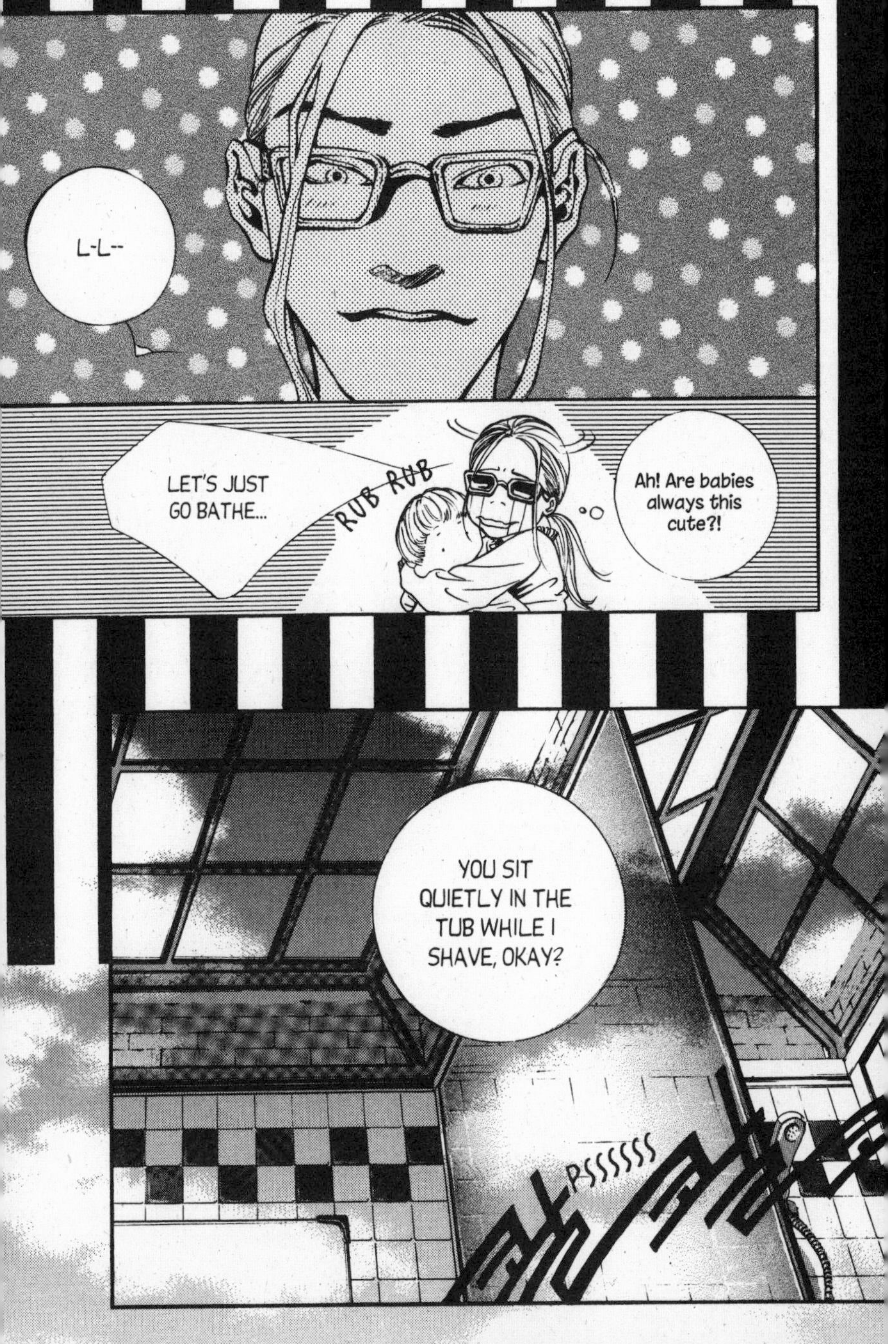
L-L--
LET'S JUST GO BATHE...
RUB RUB
Ah! Are babies always this cute?!
YOU SIT QUIETLY IN THE TUB WHILE I SHAVE, OKAY?
P-SSSSSS

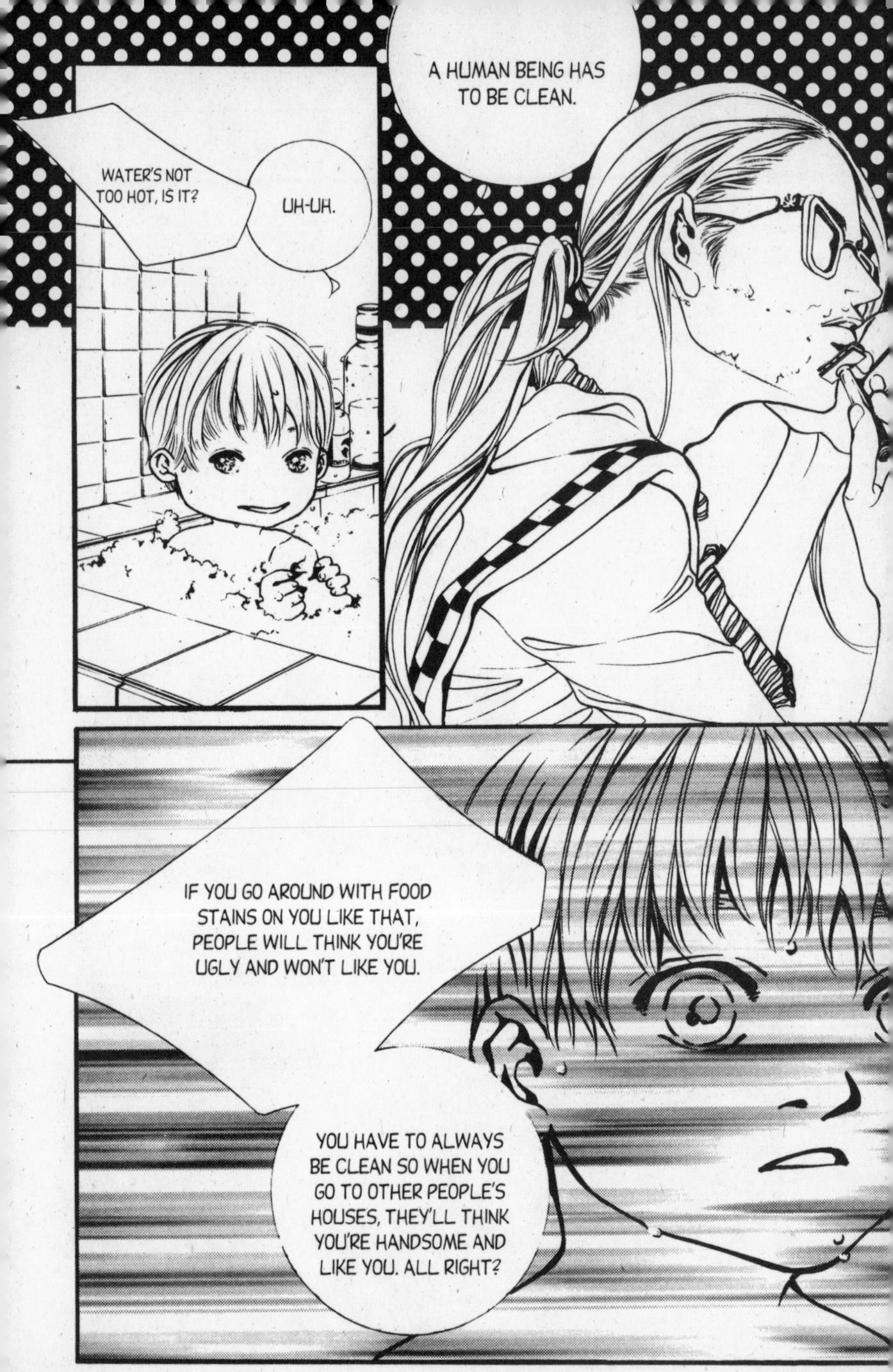
WATER'S NOT TOO HOT, IS IT?
UH-UH.
A HUMAN BEING HAS TO BE CLEAN.
IF YOU GO AROUND WITH FOOD STAINS ON YOU LIKE THAT, PEOPLE WILL THINK YOU'RE UGLY AND WON'T LIKE YOU.
YOU HAVE TO ALWAYS BE CLEAN SO WHEN YOU GO TO OTHER PEOPLE'S HOUSES, THEY'LL THINK YOU'RE HANDSOME AND LIKE YOU. ALL RIGHT?

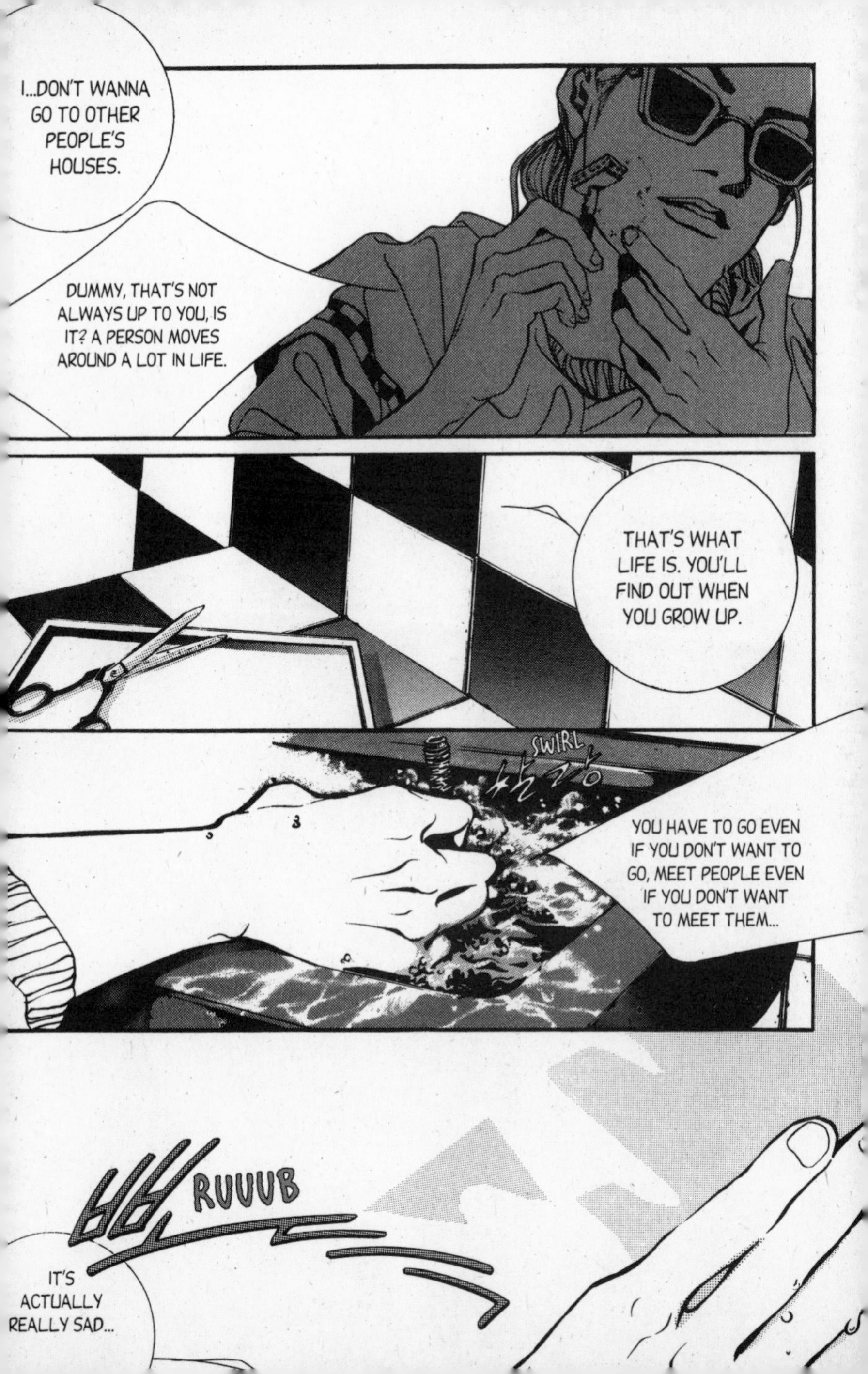
I...DON'T WANNA GO TO OTHER PEOPLE'S HOUSES.
DUMMY, THAT'S NOT ALWAYS UP TO YOU, IS IT? A PERSON MOVES AROUND A LOT IN LIFE.
THAT'S WHAT LIFE IS. YOU'LL FIND OUT WHEN YOU GROW UP.
SWIRL
YOU HAVE TO GO EVEN IF YOU DON'T WANT TO GO, MEET PEOPLE EVEN IF YOU DON'T WANT TO MEET THEM...
RUUUB
IT'S ACTUALLY REALLY SAD...

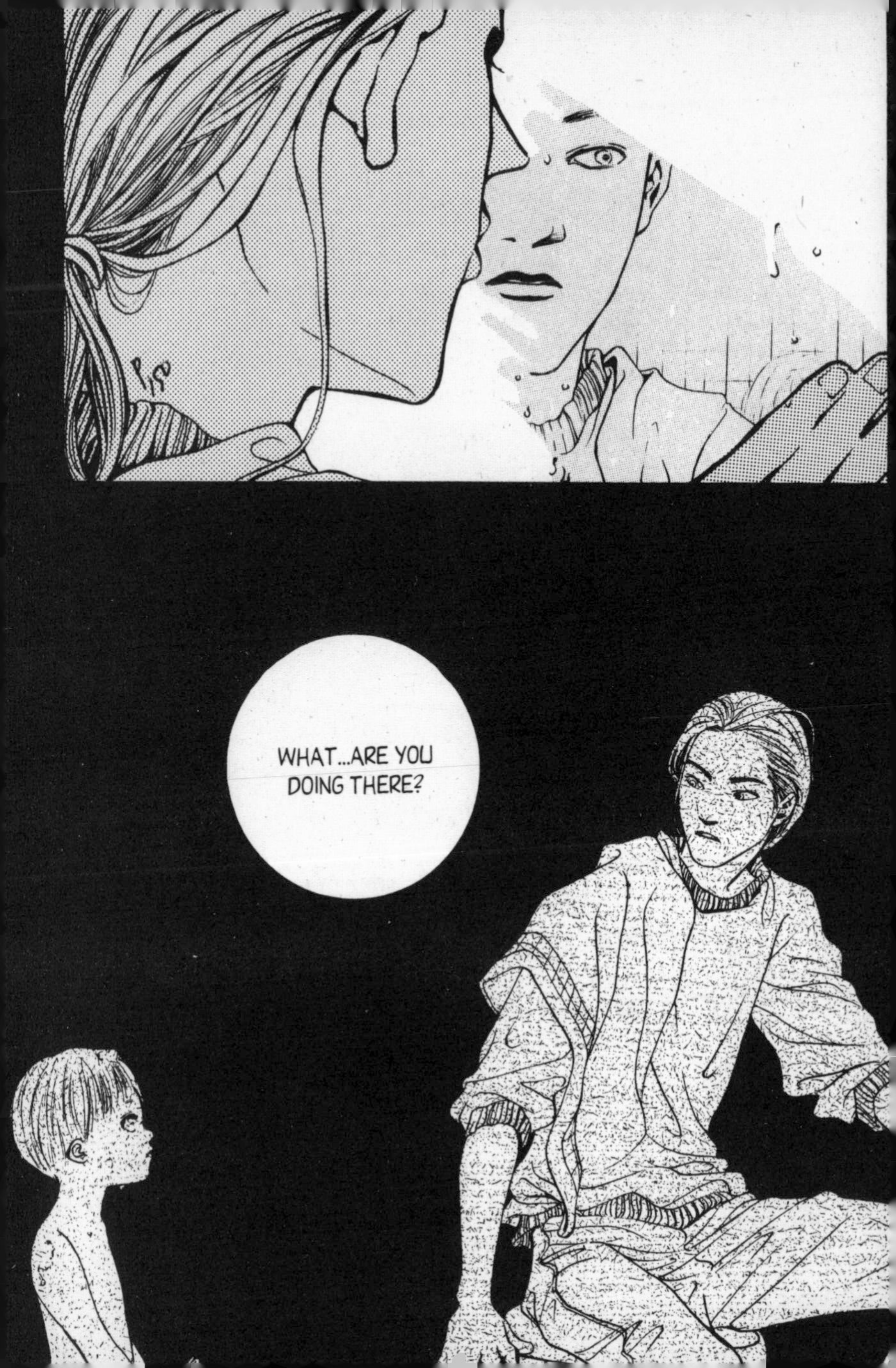
WHAT...ARE YOU DOING THERE?

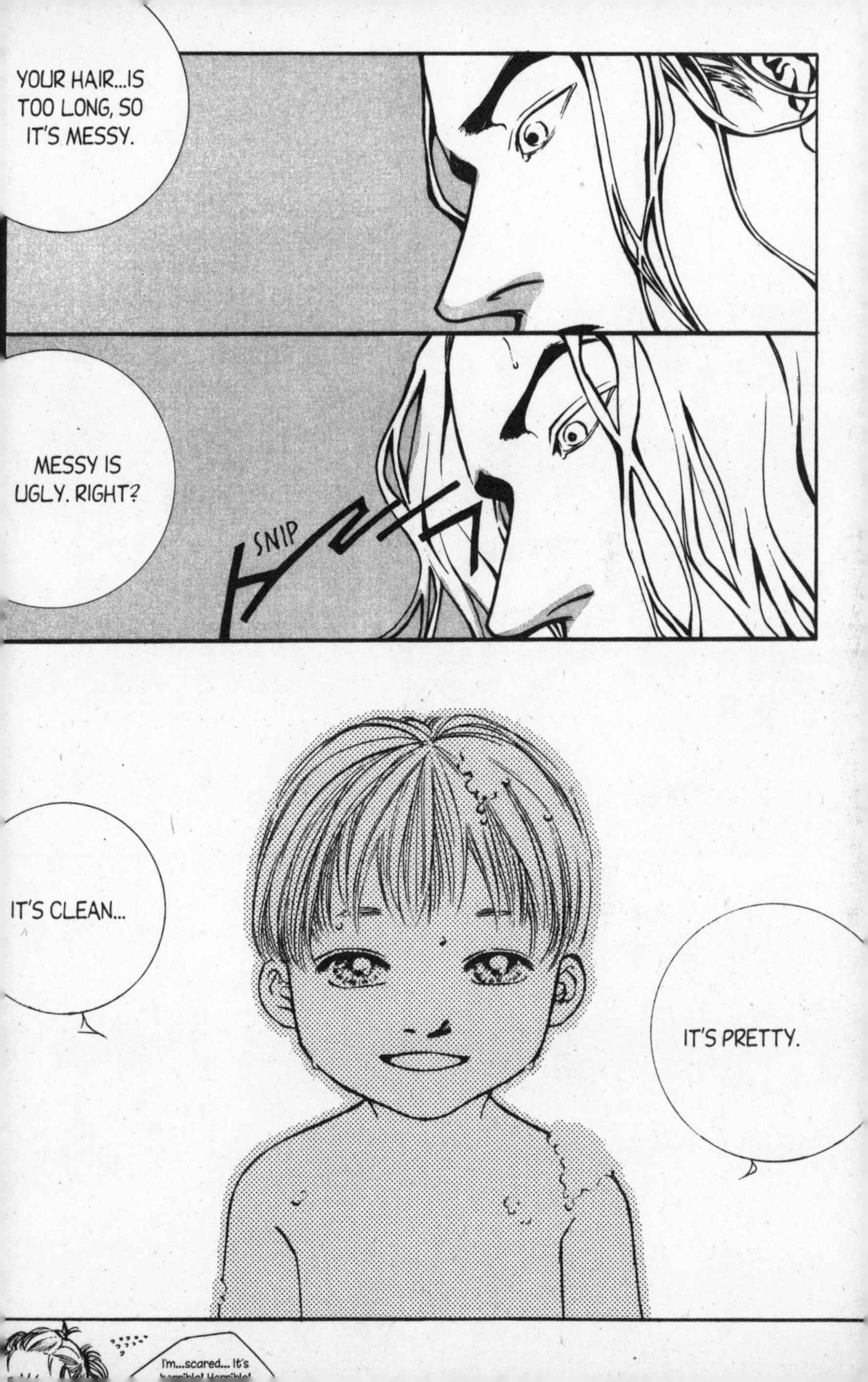
YOUR HAIR...IS TOO LONG, SO IT'S MESSY.
MESSY IS UGLY. RIGHT?
SNIP
IT'S CLEAN...
IT'S PRETTY.
I'm...scared... It's

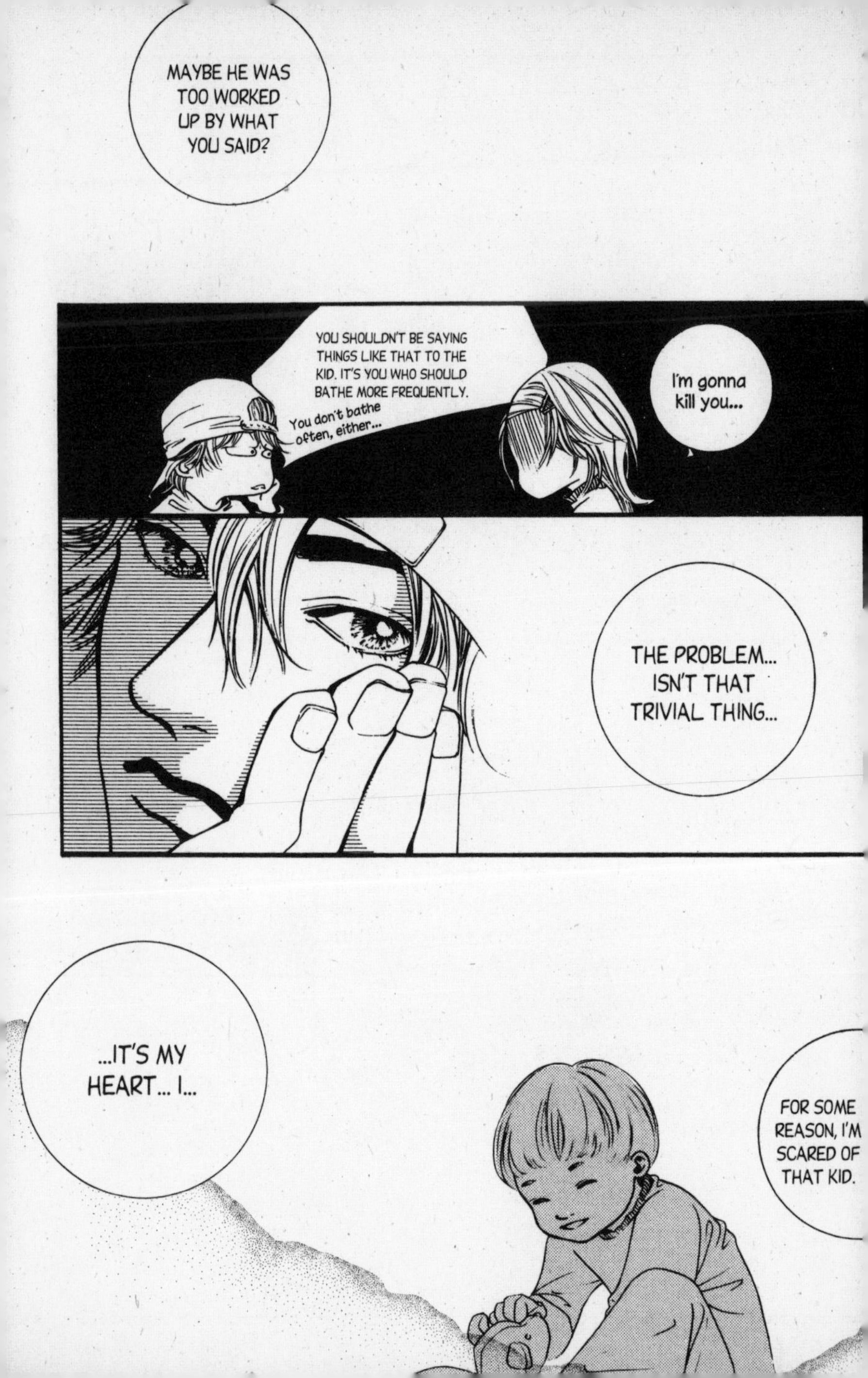
MAYBE HE WAS TOO WORKED UP BY WHAT YOU SAID?
YOU SHOULDN'T BE SAYING THINGS LIKE THAT TO THE KID. IT'S YOU WHO SHOULD BATHE MORE FREQUENTLY.
You don't bathe often, either...
I'm gonna kill you...
THE PROBLEM... ISN'T THAT TRIVIAL THING...
...IT'S MY HEART... I...
FOR SOME REASON, I'M SCARED OF THAT KID.

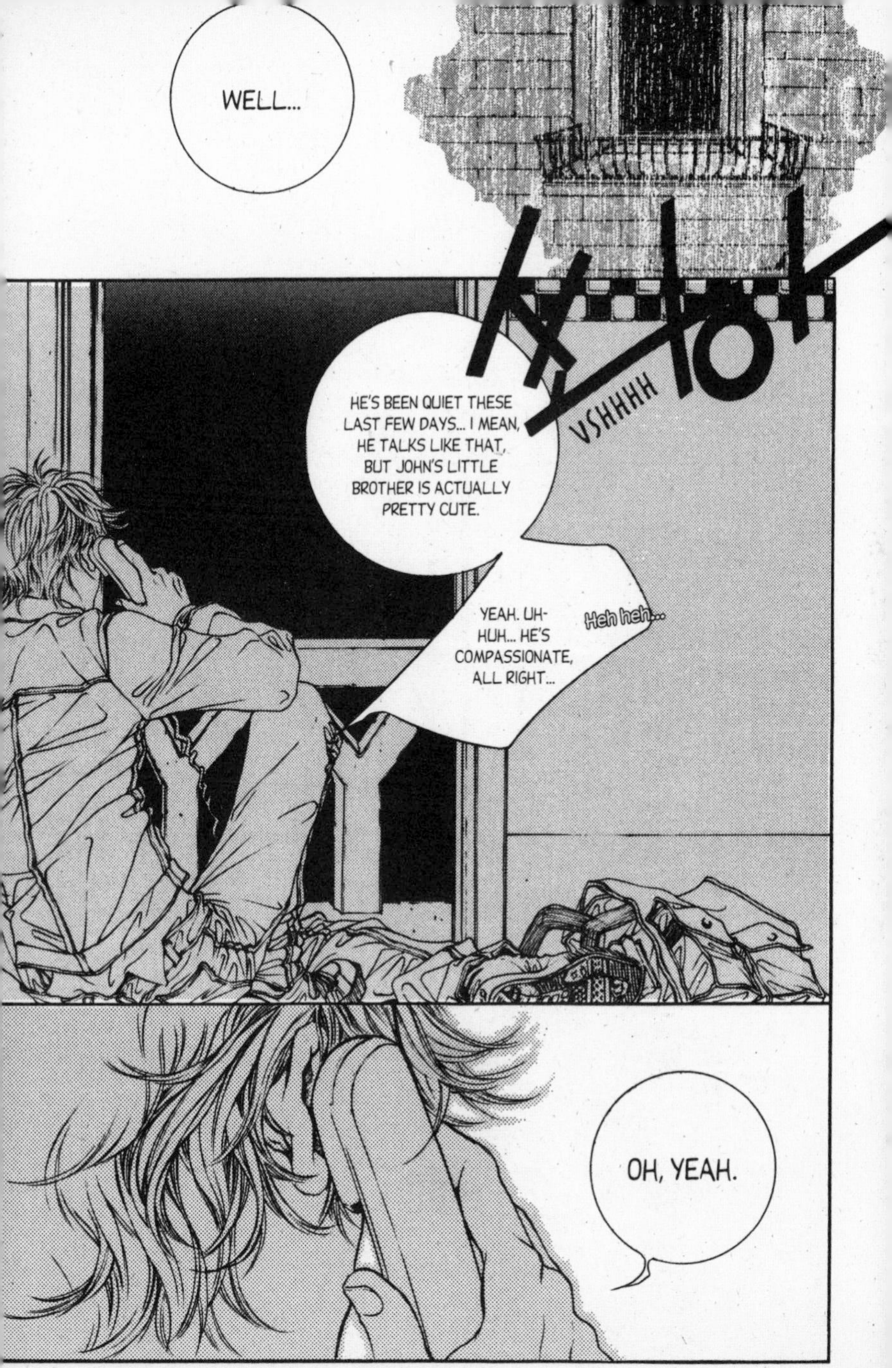
WELL...
VSHHHH
HE'S BEEN QUIET THESE LAST FEW DAYS... I MEAN, HE TALKS LIKE THAT, BUT JOHN'S LITTLE BROTHER IS ACTUALLY PRETTY CUTE.
YEAH. UH-HUH... HE'S COMPASSIONATE, ALL RIGHT...
Heh heh...
OH, YEAH.

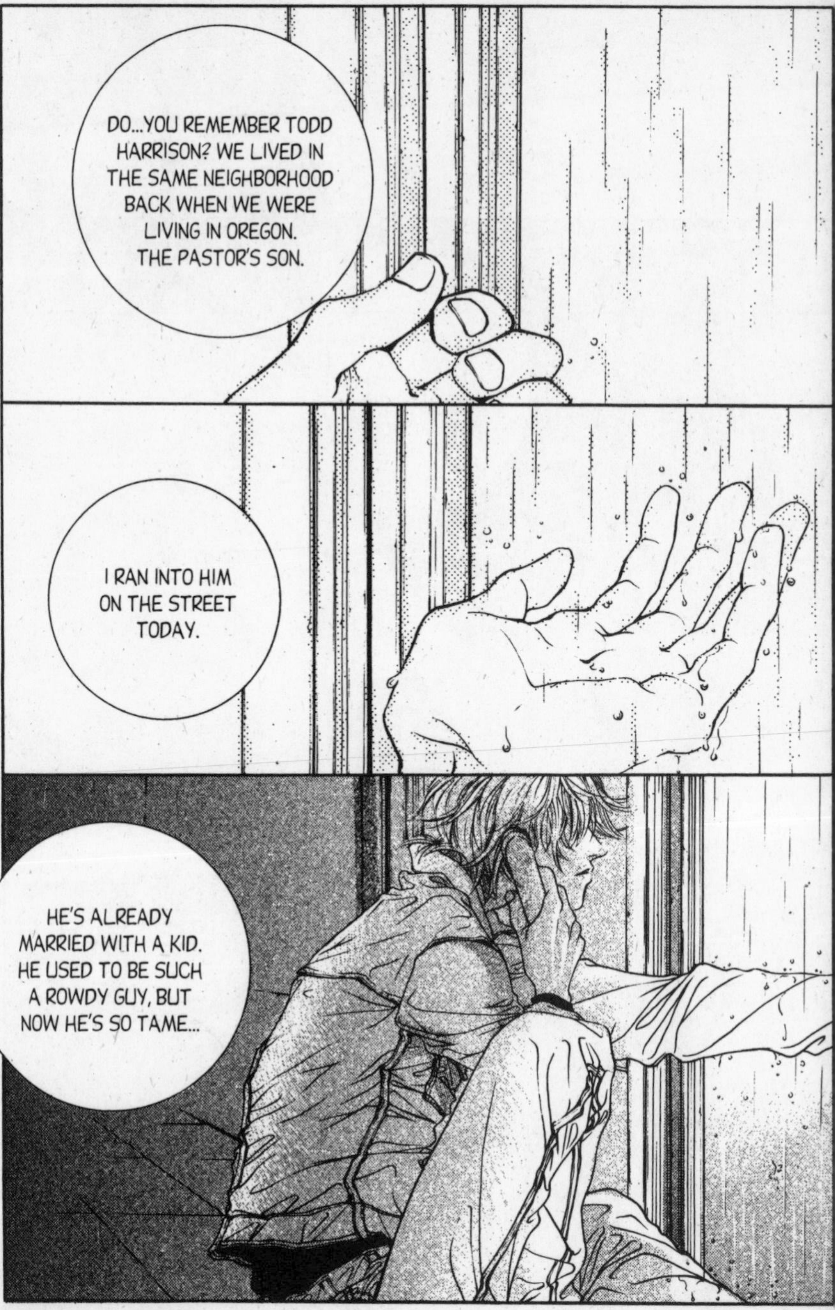
DO...YOU REMEMBER TODD HARRISON? WE LIVED IN THE SAME NEIGHBORHOOD BACK WHEN WE WERE LIVING IN OREGON. THE PASTOR'S SON.
I RAN INTO HIM ON THE STREET TODAY.
HE'S ALREADY MARRIED WITH A KID. HE USED TO BE SUCH A ROWDY GUY, BUT NOW HE'S SO TAME...

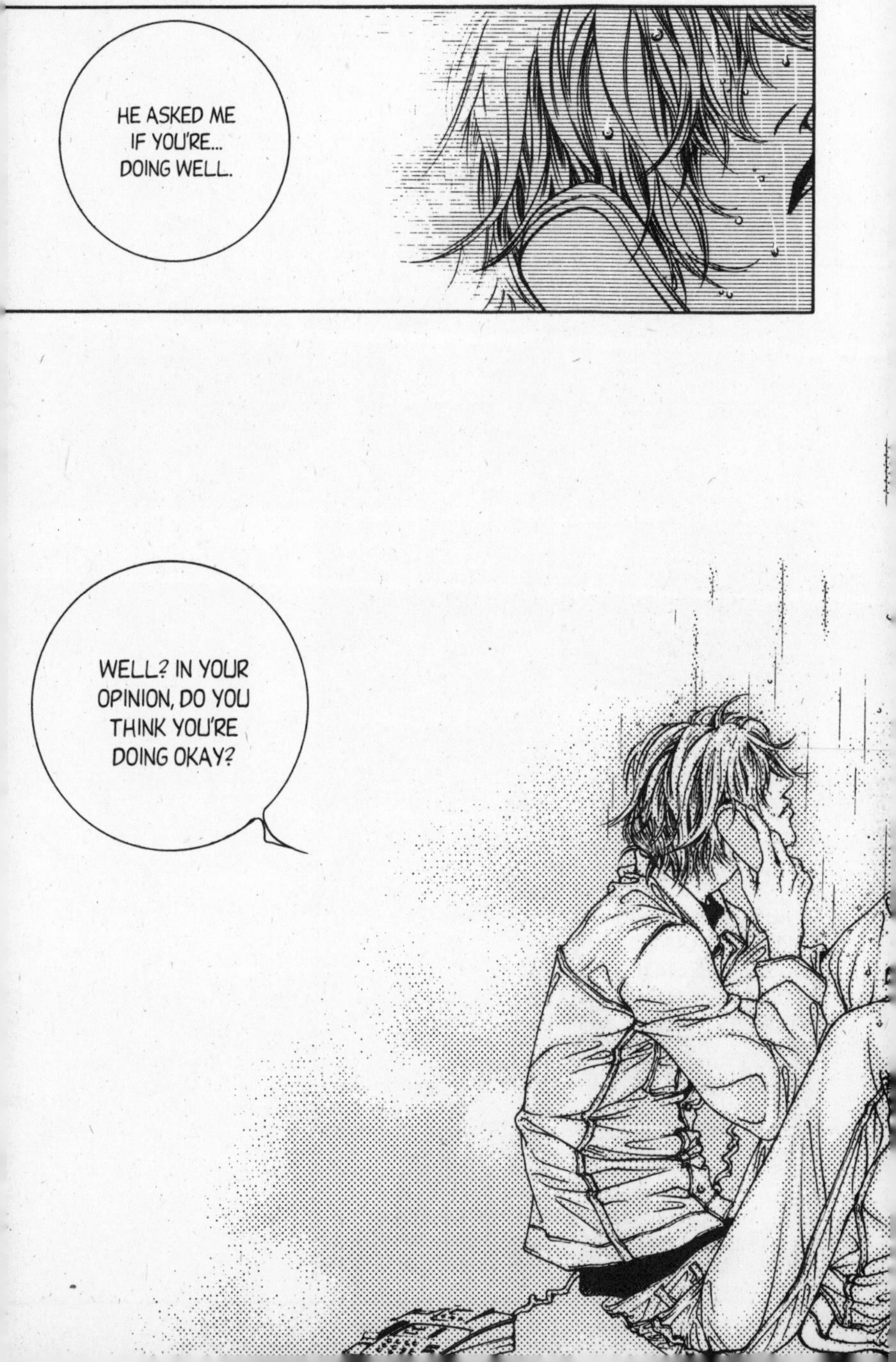
HE ASKED ME IF YOU'RE... DOING WELL.
WELL? IN YOUR OPINION, DO YOU THINK YOU'RE DOING OKAY?

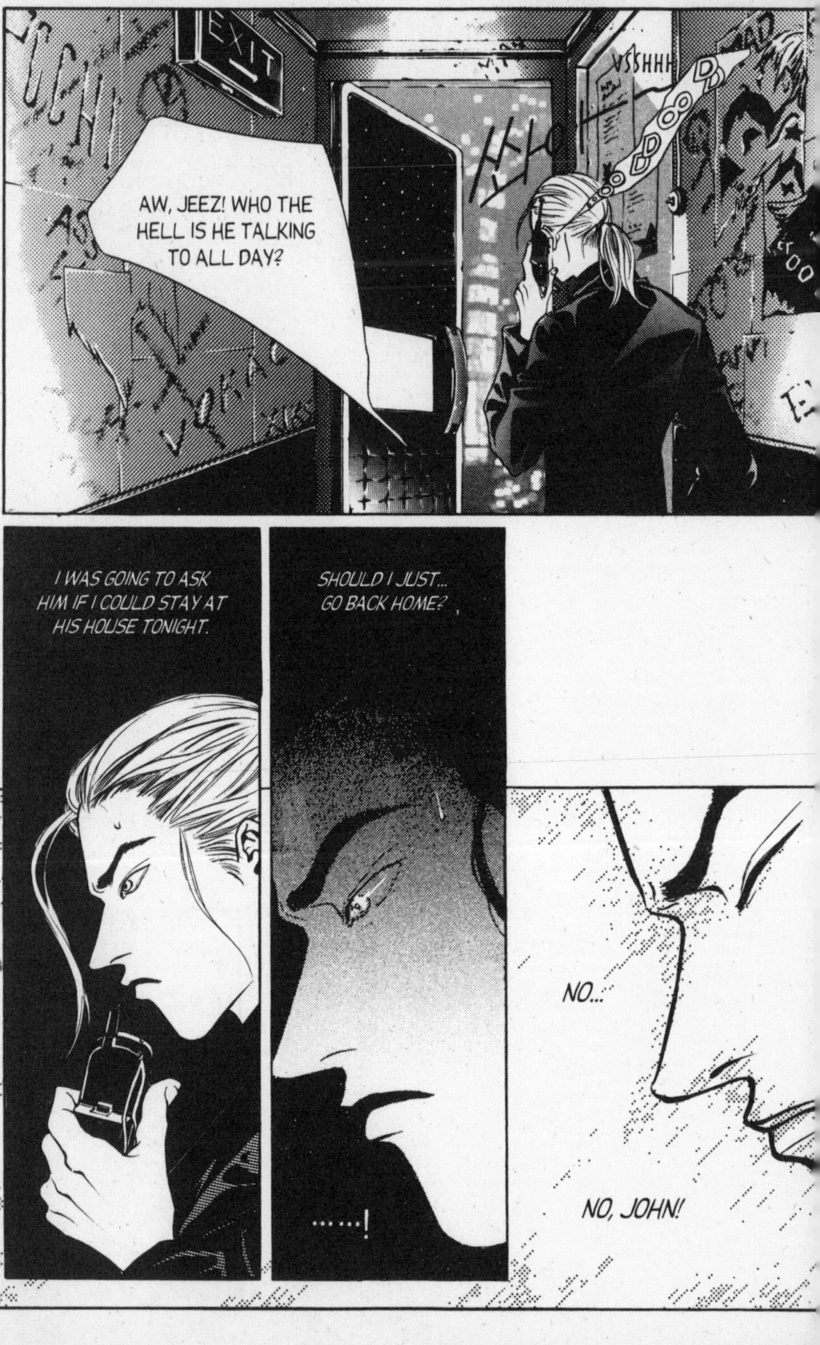

EXIT
VSSHHH
AW, JEEZ! WHO THE HELL IS HE TALKING TO ALL DAY?
I WAS GOING TO ASK HIM IF I COULD STAY AT HIS HOUSE TONIGHT.
SHOULD I JUST... GO BACK HOME?
......!
NO...
NO, JOHN!

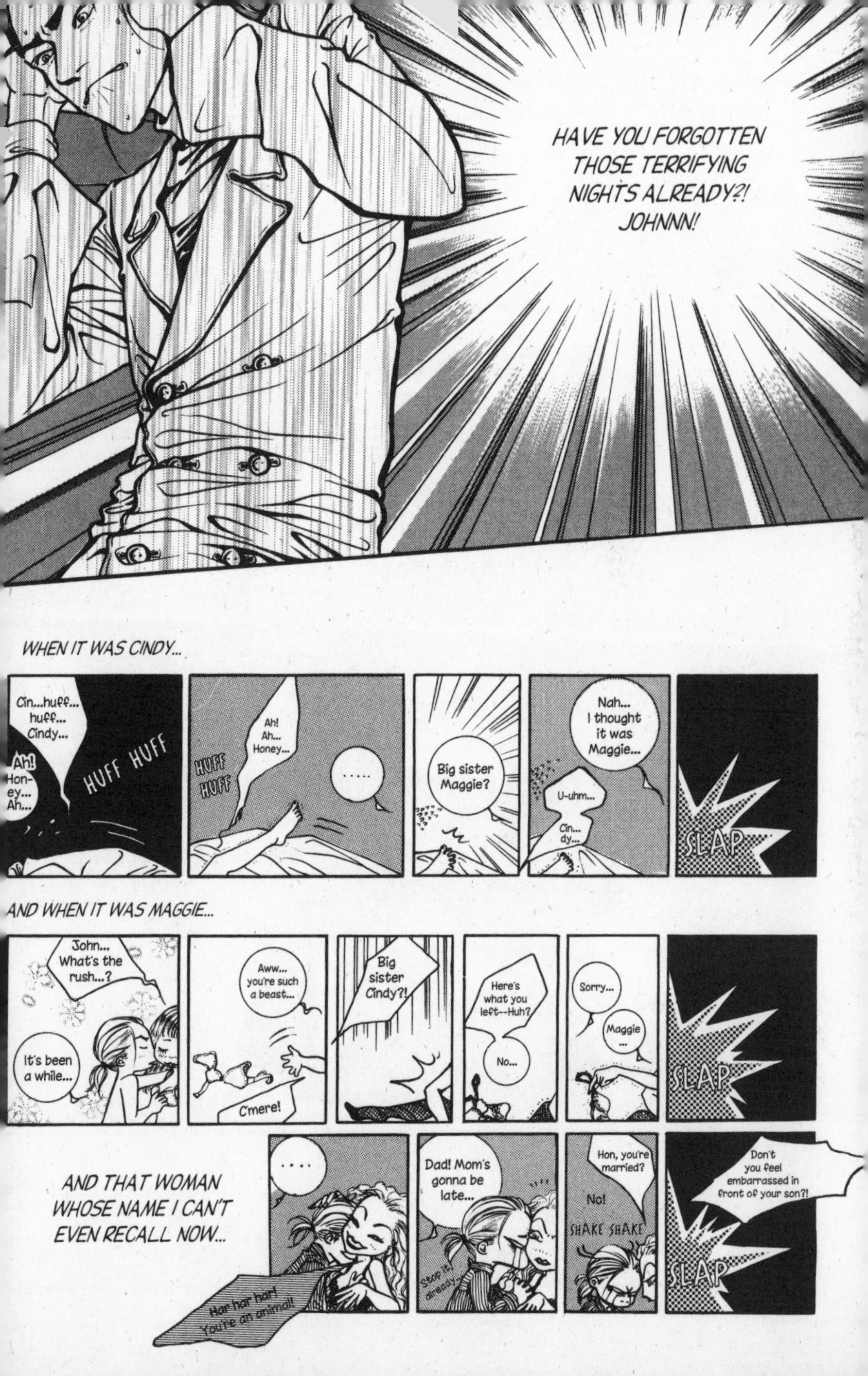
HAVE YOU FORGOTTEN THOSE TERRIFYING NIGHTS ALREADY?! JOHNNN!
WHEN IT WAS CINDY...
Cin...huff... huff... Cindy...
Ah! Honey... Ah...
HUFF HUFF
HUFF HUFF
Ah! Ah... Honey...
.....
Big sister Maggie?
Nah... I thought it was Maggie...
U-uhm...
Cin... dy...
SLAP
AND WHEN IT WAS MAGGIE...
John... What's the rush...?
It's been a while...
Aww... you're such a beast...
C'mere!
Big sister Cindy?!
Here's what you left--Huh?
No...
Sorry...
Maggie ...
SLAP
AND THAT WOMAN WHOSE NAME I CAN'T EVEN RECALL NOW...
....
Har har har! You're an animal!
Dad! Mom's gonna be late...
Stop it already.
Hon, you're married?
No!
SHAKE SHAKE
Don't you feel embarrassed in front of your son?!
SLAP

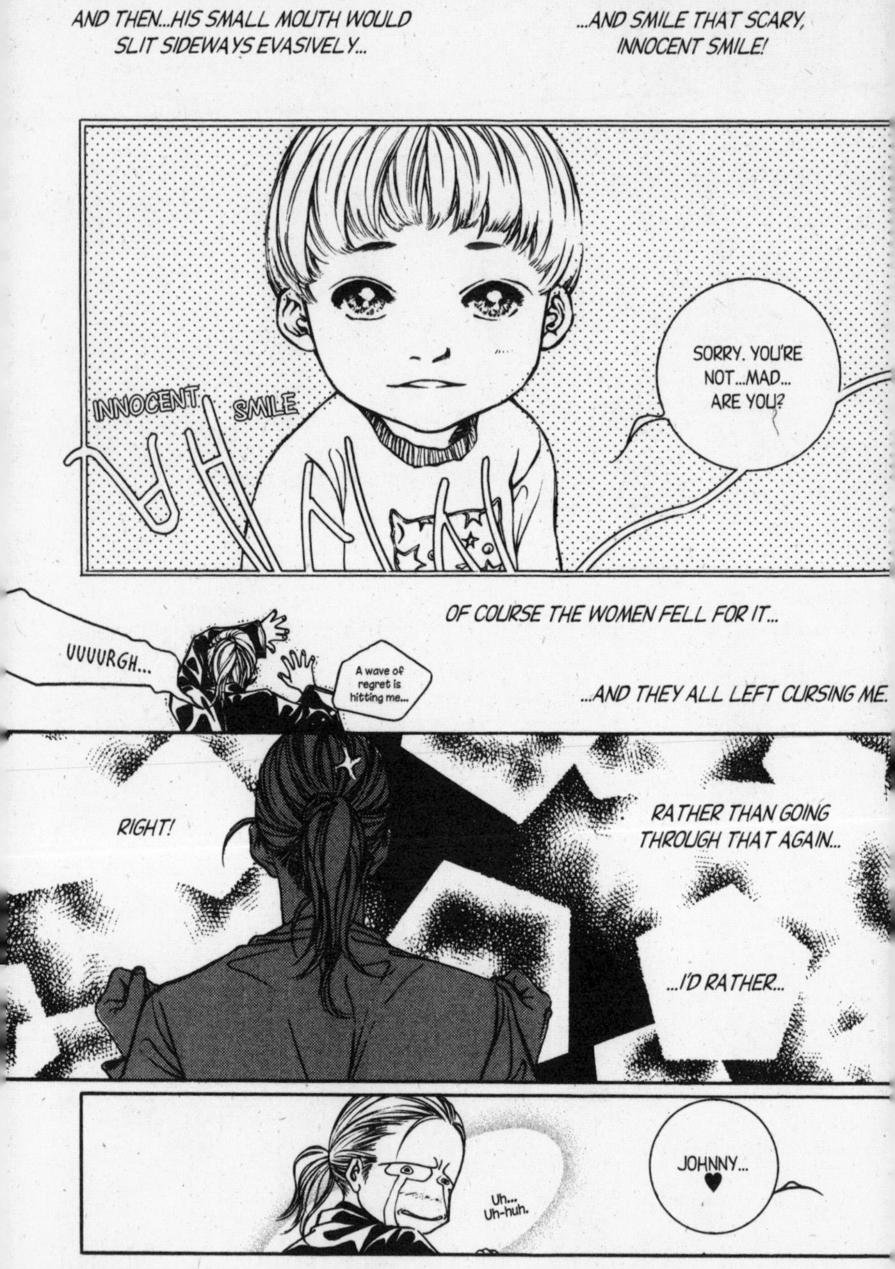
AND THEN...HIS SMALL MOUTH WOULD SLIT SIDEWAYS EVASIVELY...
...AND SMILE THAT SCARY, INNOCENT SMILE!
INNOCENT SMILE
SORRY. YOU'RE NOT...MAD... ARE YOU?
UUUURGH...
A wave of regret is hitting me...
OF COURSE THE WOMEN FELL FOR IT...
...AND THEY ALL LEFT CURSING ME.
RIGHT!
RATHER THAN GOING THROUGH THAT AGAIN...
...I'D RATHER...
Uh... Uh-huh.
JOHNNY... ♥

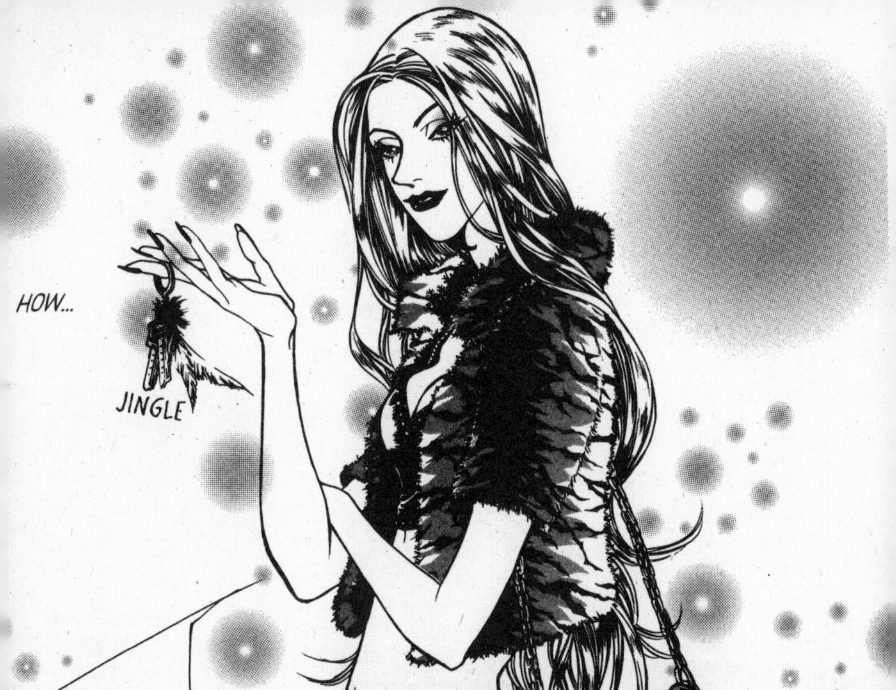
HOW...
JINGLE
MY CAR'S HERE...SO HOW ABOUT IT?
...CAN I PASS UP ON SUCH A SLAMMIN' BODY LIKE THAT?!
I...
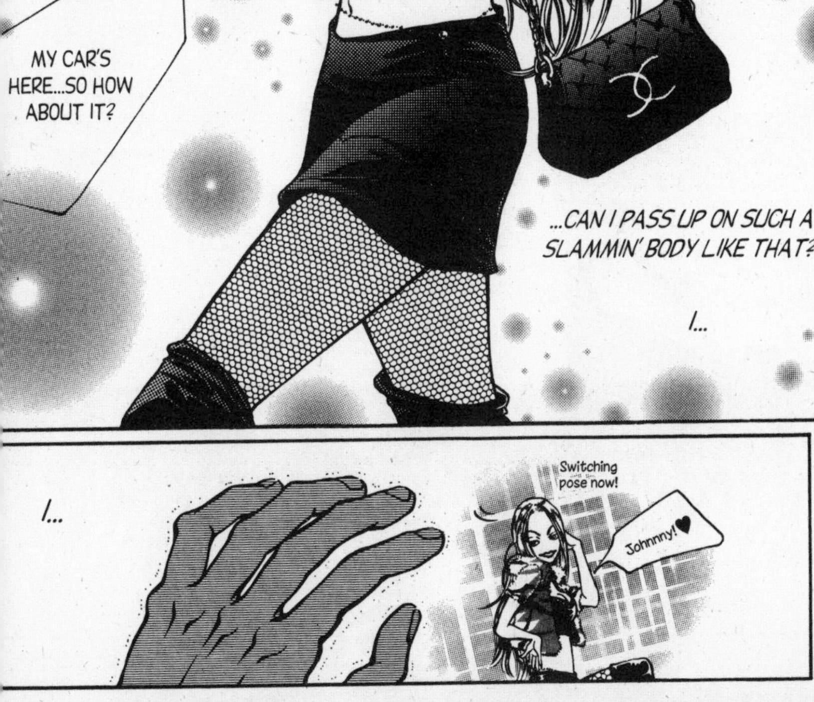
I...
Switching pose now!
Johnnny!♥

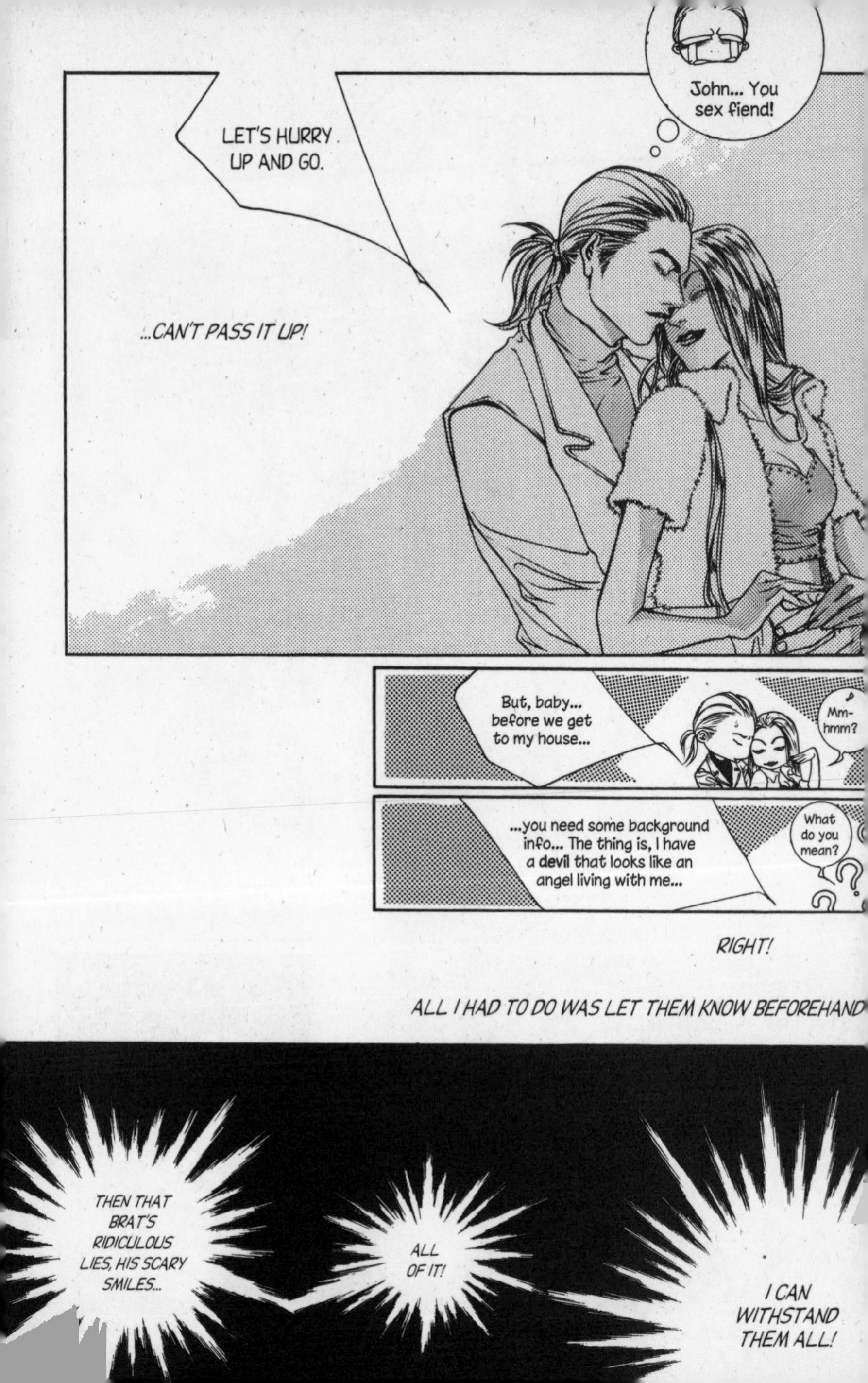
LET'S HURRY UP AND GO.
John... You sex fiend!
...CAN'T PASS IT UP!
But, baby... before we get to my house...
Mm-hmm?
...you need some background info... The thing is, I have a devil that looks like an angel living with me...
What do you mean?
RIGHT!
ALL I HAD TO DO WAS LET THEM KNOW BEFOREHAND
THEN THAT BRAT'S RIDICULOUS LIES, HIS SCARY SMILES...
ALL OF IT!
I CAN WITHSTAND THEM ALL!

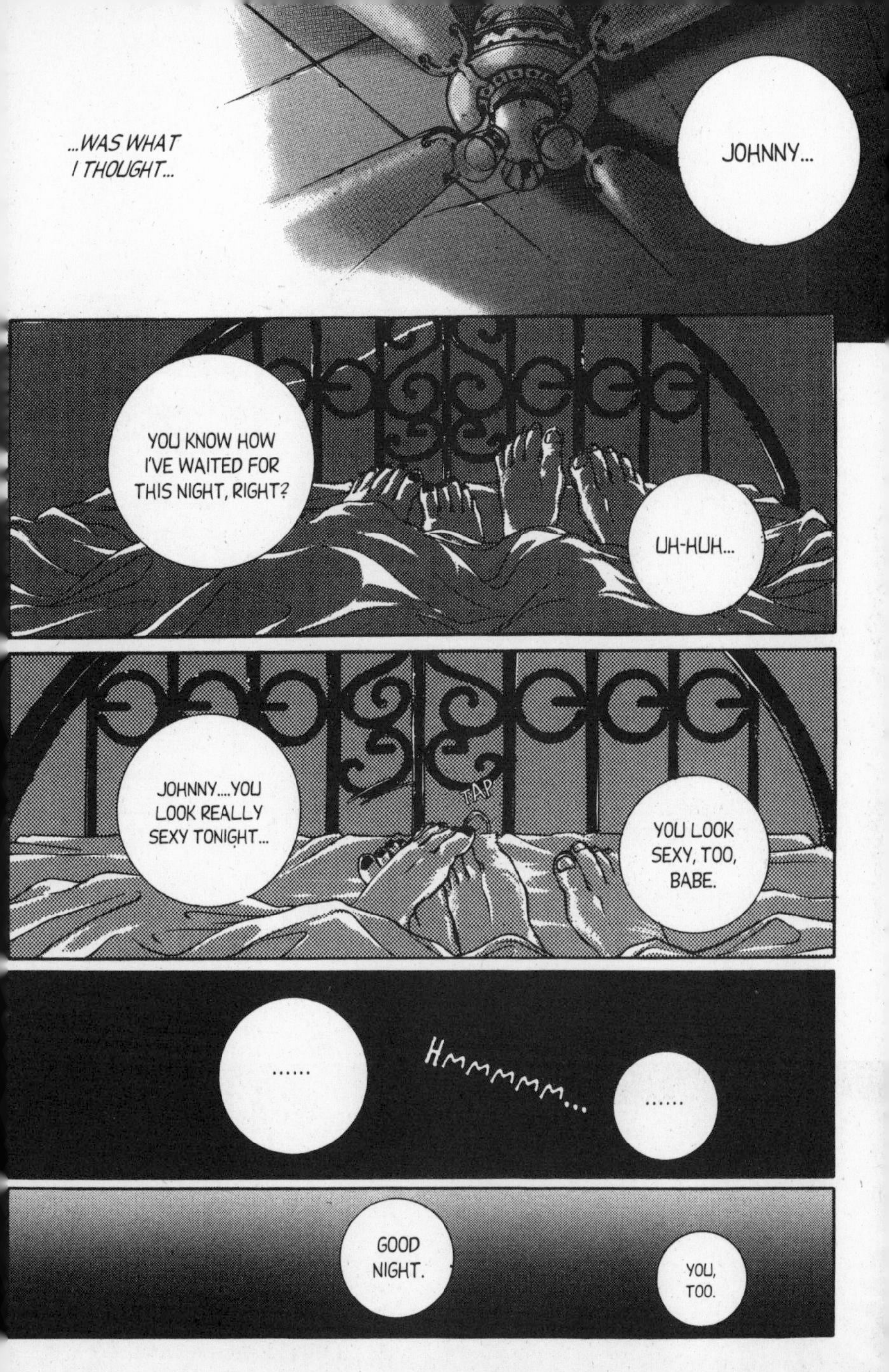
...WAS WHAT I THOUGHT...
JOHNNY...
YOU KNOW HOW I'VE WAITED FOR THIS NIGHT, RIGHT?
UH-HUH...
JOHNNY....YOU LOOK REALLY SEXY TONIGHT...
TAP
YOU LOOK SEXY, TOO, BABE.
......
HMMMMM...
......
GOOD NIGHT.
YOU, TOO.

I WAS THE IDIOT...

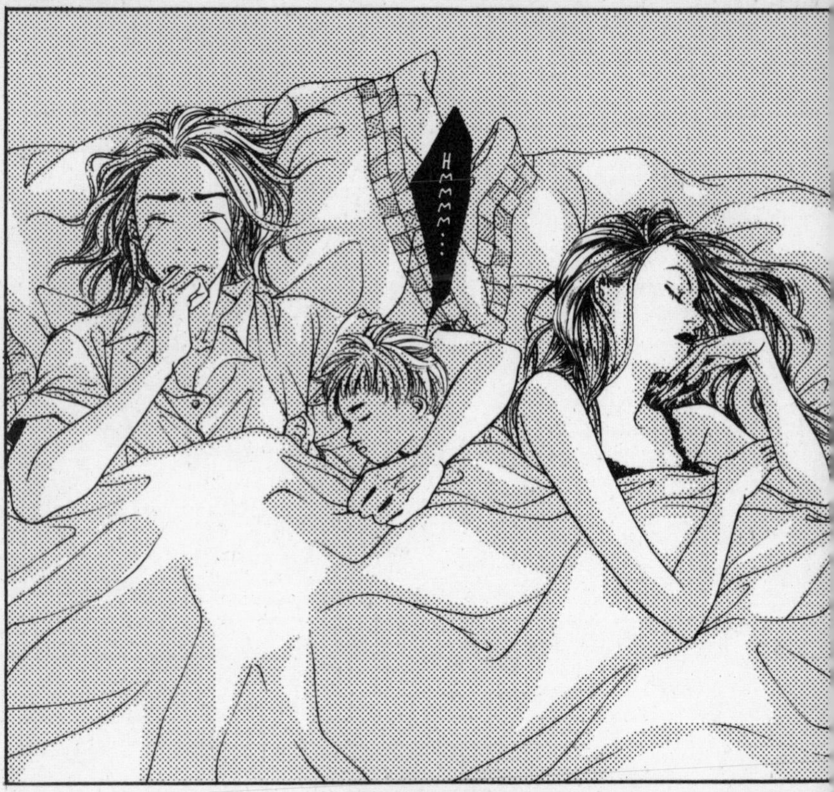
HMMMM...

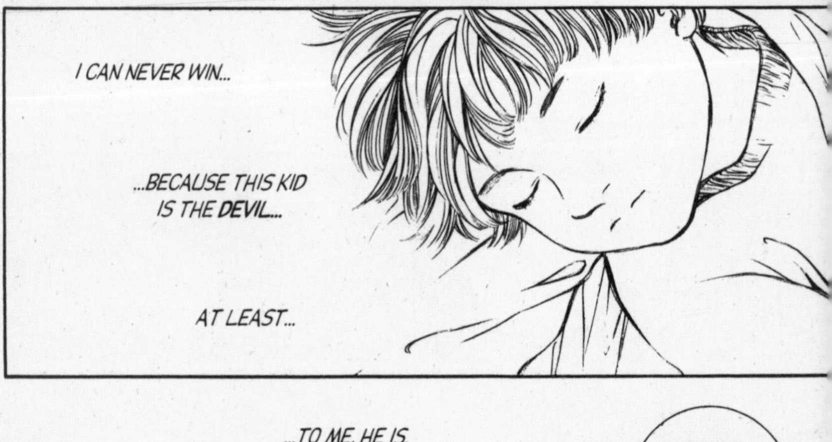
I CAN NEVER WIN...
...BECAUSE THIS KID IS THE **DEVIL**...
AT LEAST...

...TO ME, HE IS.

THIS IS A NEW SONG I'VE COMPOSED OVERNIGHT. IT'S CALLED...

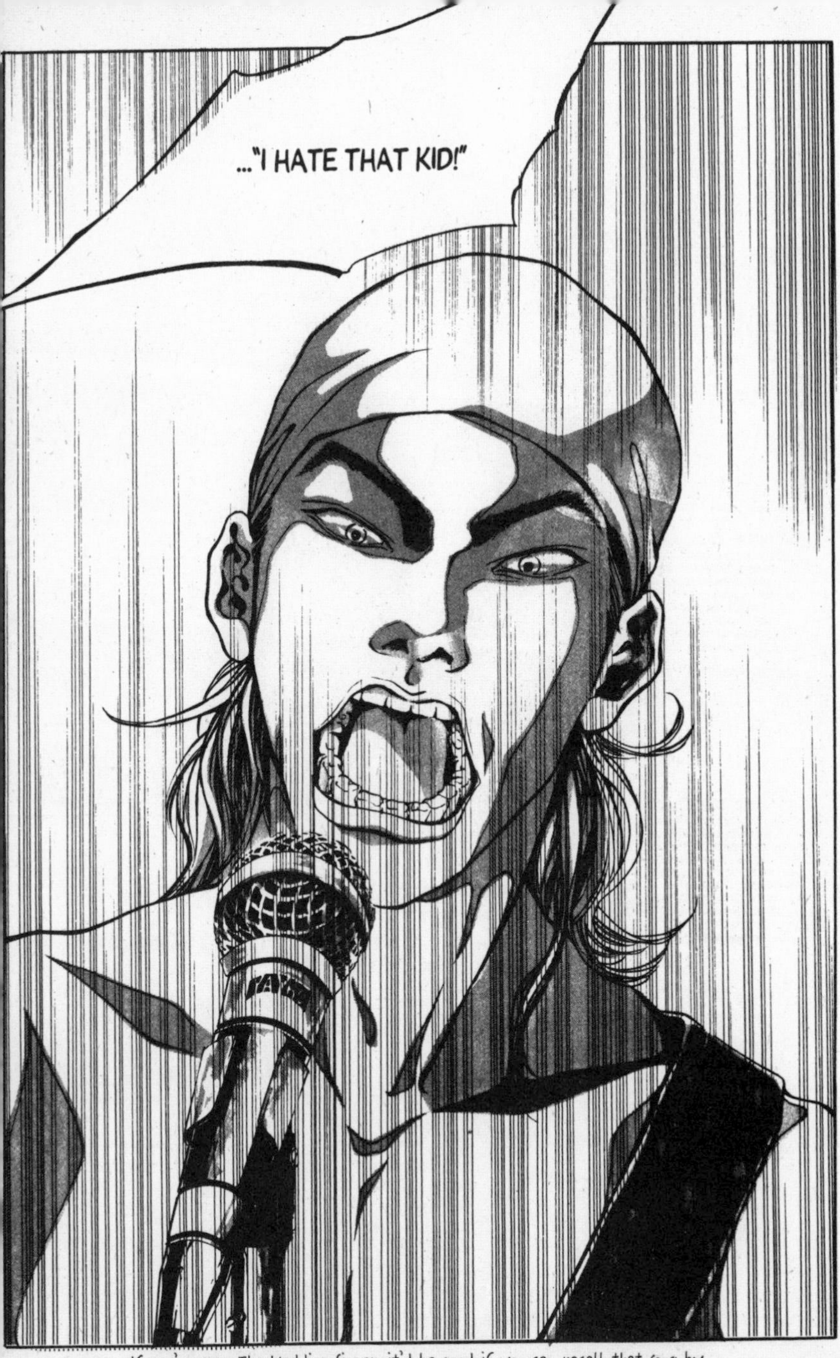
..."I HATE THAT KID!"

If you've seen The Wedding Singer, it'd be good if you can recall that song by Adam Sandler called "Somebody Kill Me." It's just like that, yes!

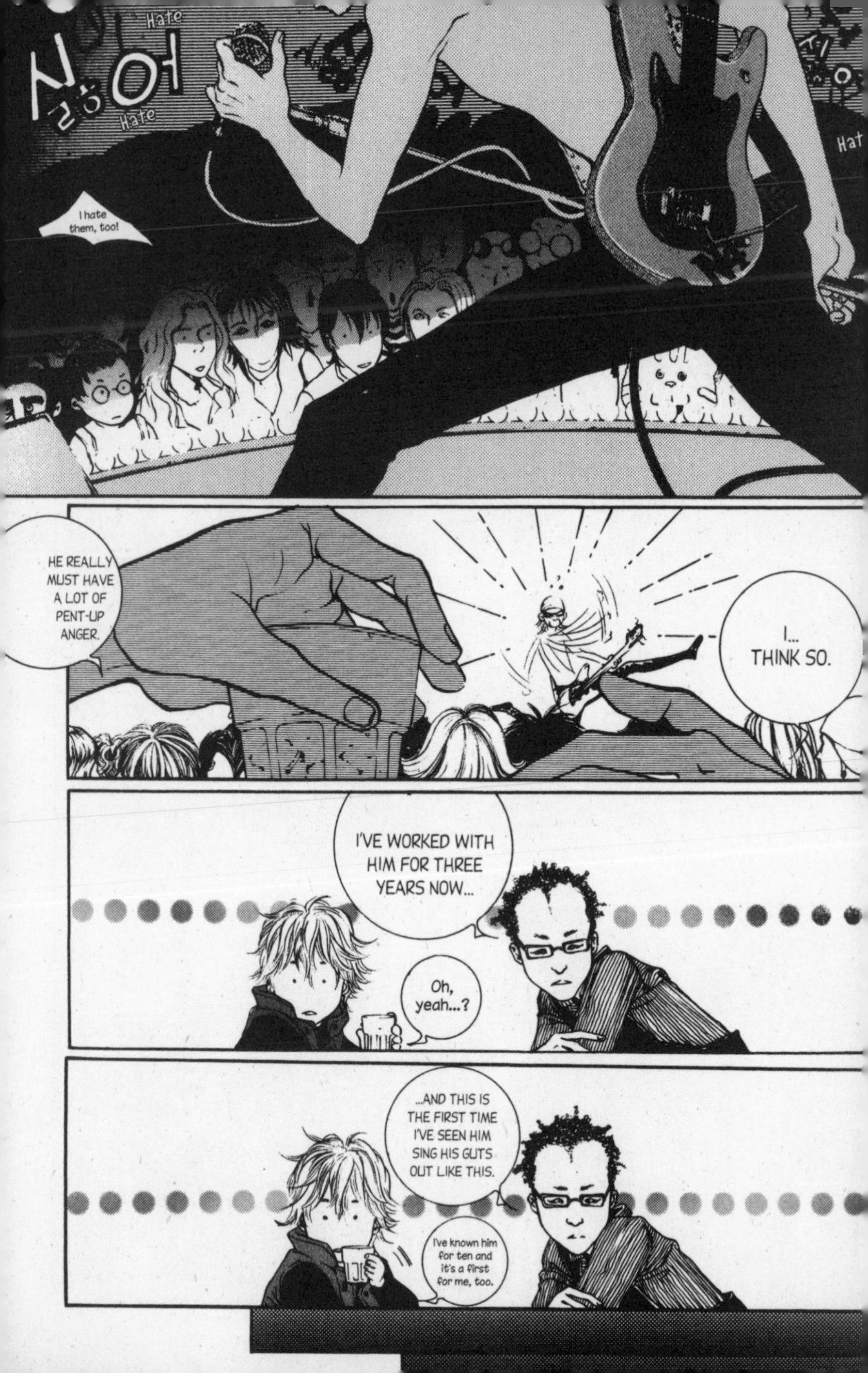
Hate
Hate
I hate them, too!
HE REALLY MUST HAVE A LOT OF PENT-UP ANGER.
I... THINK SO.
I'VE WORKED WITH HIM FOR THREE YEARS NOW...
Oh, yeah...?
...AND THIS IS THE FIRST TIME I'VE SEEN HIM SING HIS GUTS OUT LIKE THIS.
I've known him for ten and it's a first for me, too.

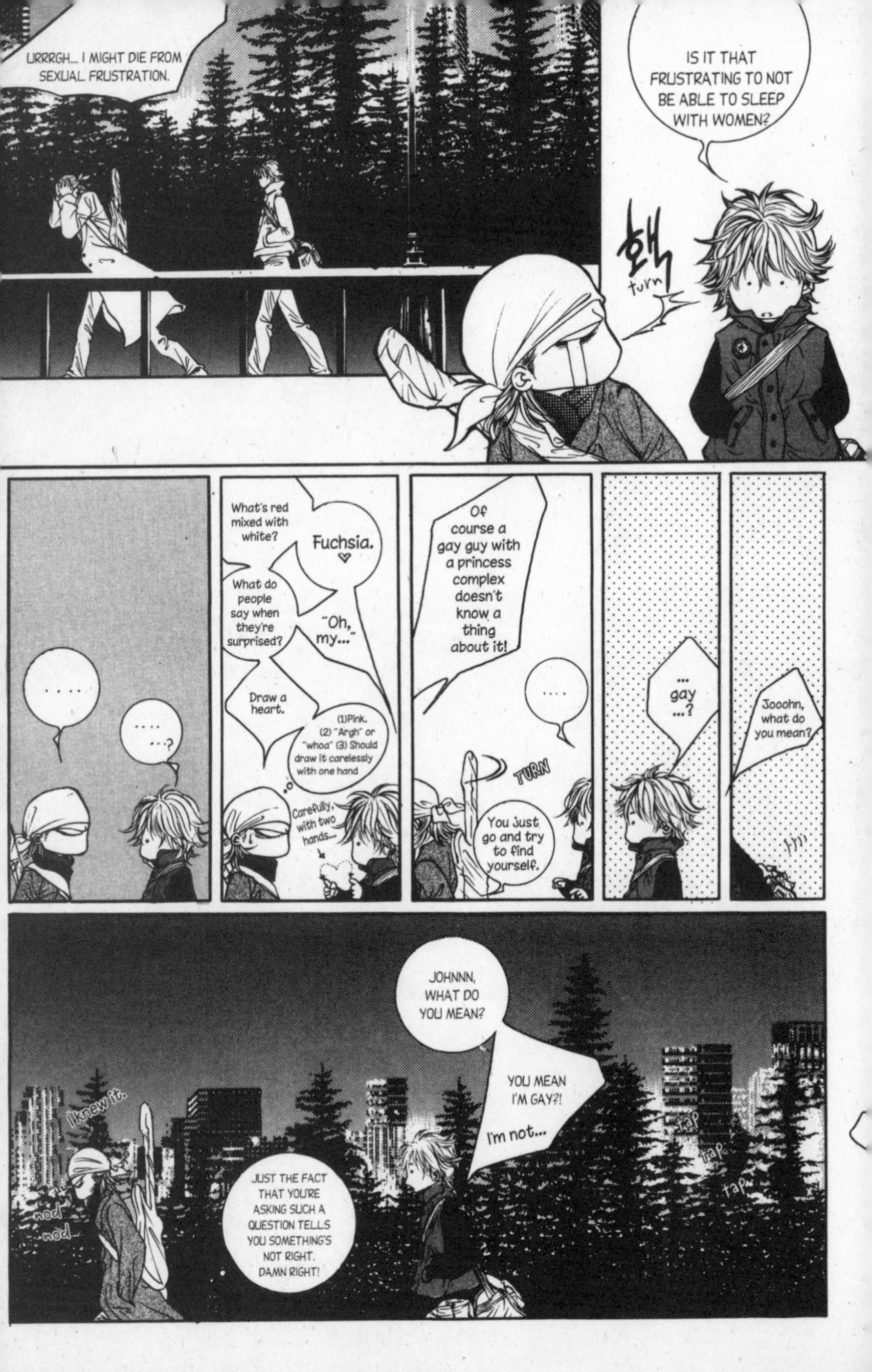
URRRGH... I MIGHT DIE FROM SEXUAL FRUSTRATION.
IS IT THAT FRUSTRATING TO NOT BE ABLE TO SLEEP WITH WOMEN?
홱
turn
.....
....?
What's red mixed with white?
Fuchsia.
What do people say when they're surprised?
"Oh, my..."
Draw a heart.
(1)Pink. (2) "Argh" or "whoa" (3) Should draw it carelessly with one hand
Carefully, with two hands...
Of course a gay guy with a princess complex doesn't know a thing about it!
....
TURN
You just go and try to find yourself.
... gay ...?
Jooohn, what do you mean?
JOHNNN, WHAT DO YOU MEAN?
YOU MEAN I'M GAY?!
I'm not...
I knew it.
nod nod
JUST THE FACT THAT YOU'RE ASKING SUCH A QUESTION TELLS YOU SOMETHING'S NOT RIGHT. DAMN RIGHT!
tap tap tap

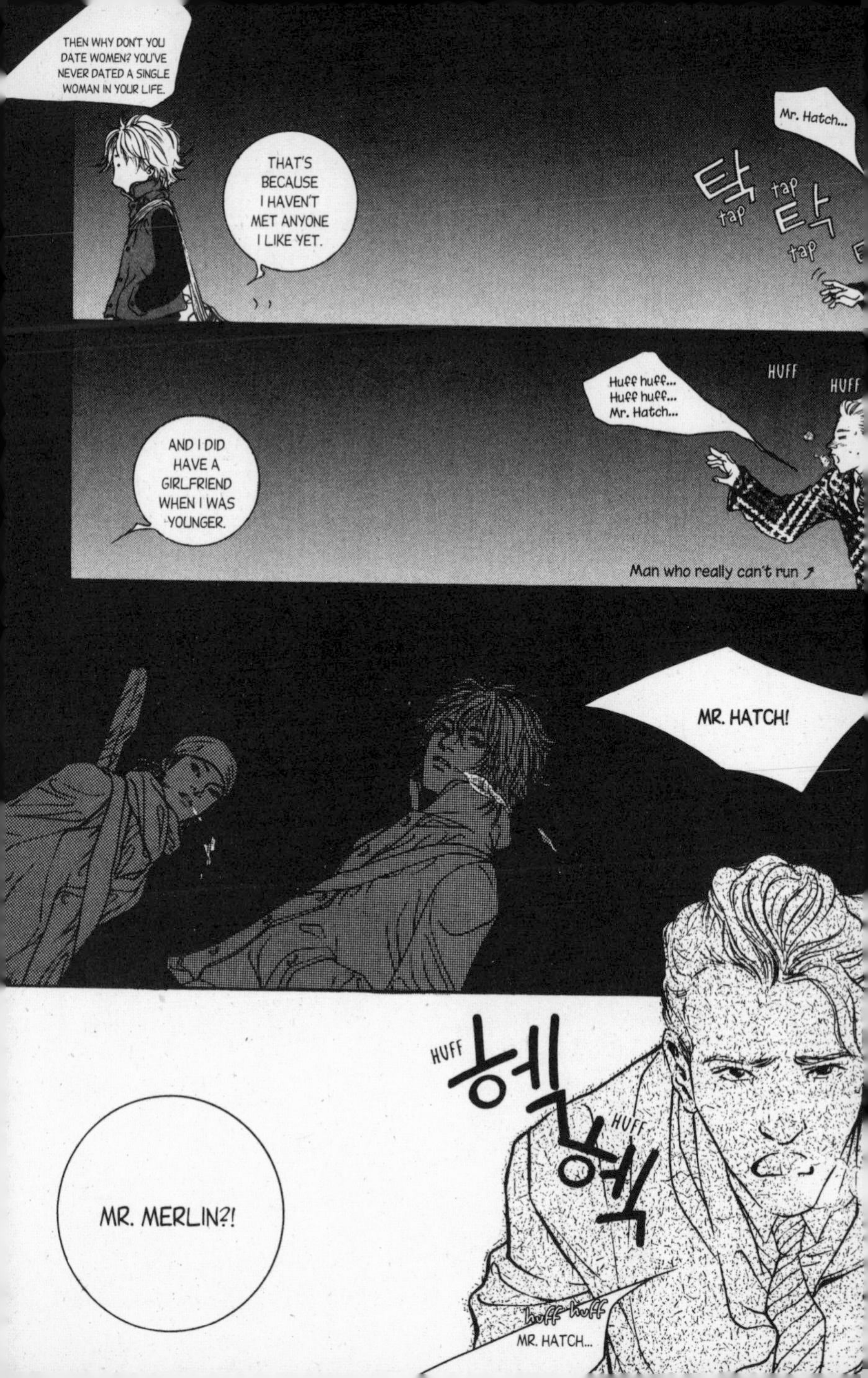
THEN WHY DON'T YOU DATE WOMEN? YOU'VE NEVER DATED A SINGLE WOMAN IN YOUR LIFE.
THAT'S BECAUSE I HAVEN'T MET ANYONE I LIKE YET.
Mr. Hatch...
탁 tap
탁 tap
AND I DID HAVE A GIRLFRIEND WHEN I WAS YOUNGER.
Huff huff... Huff huff... Mr. Hatch...
HUFF
HUFF
Man who really can't run
MR. HATCH!
MR. MERLIN?!
HUFF 헉
HUFF 헉
huff huff
MR. HATCH...

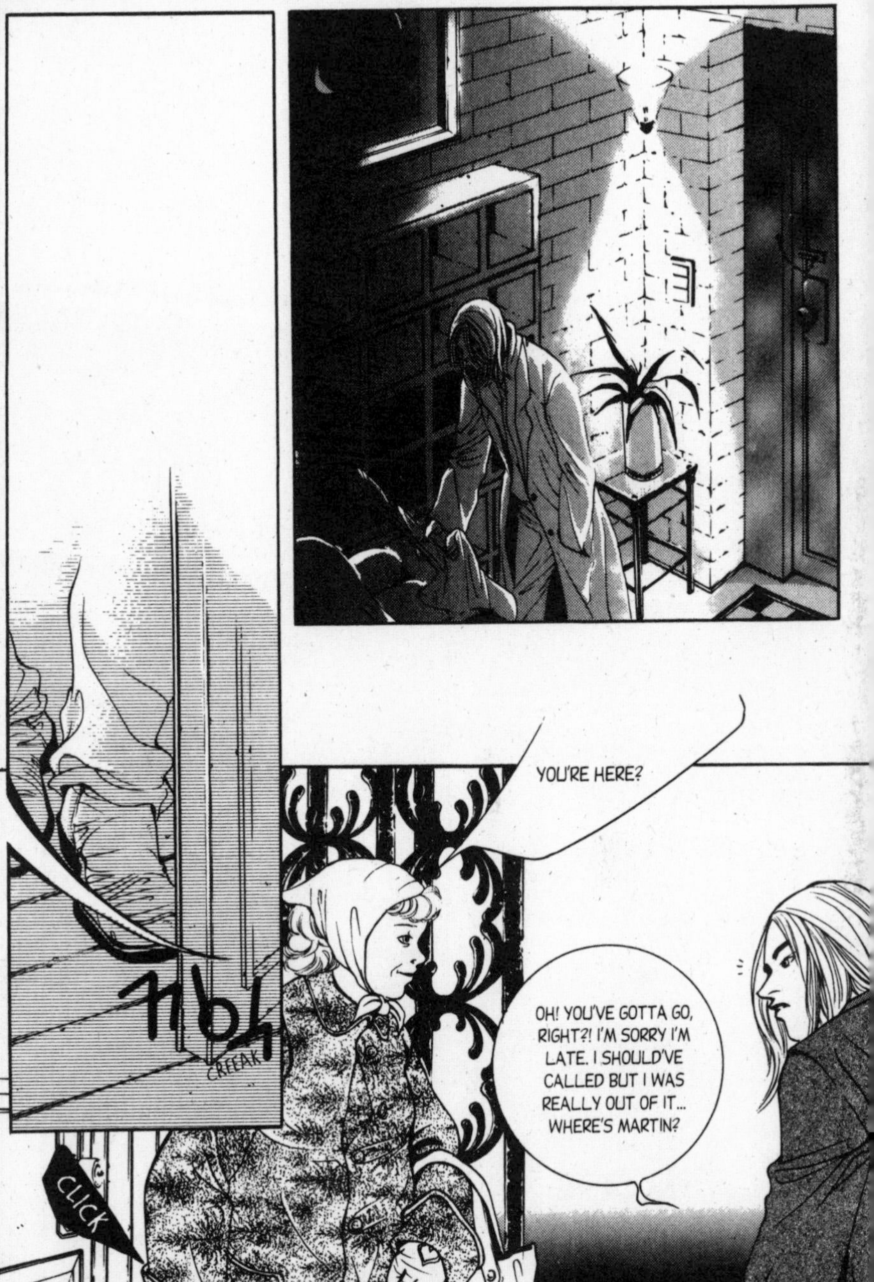
CREEAK
CLICK
YOU'RE HERE?
OH! YOU'VE GOTTA GO, RIGHT?! I'M SORRY I'M LATE. I SHOULD'VE CALLED BUT I WAS REALLY OUT OF IT... WHERE'S MARTIN?

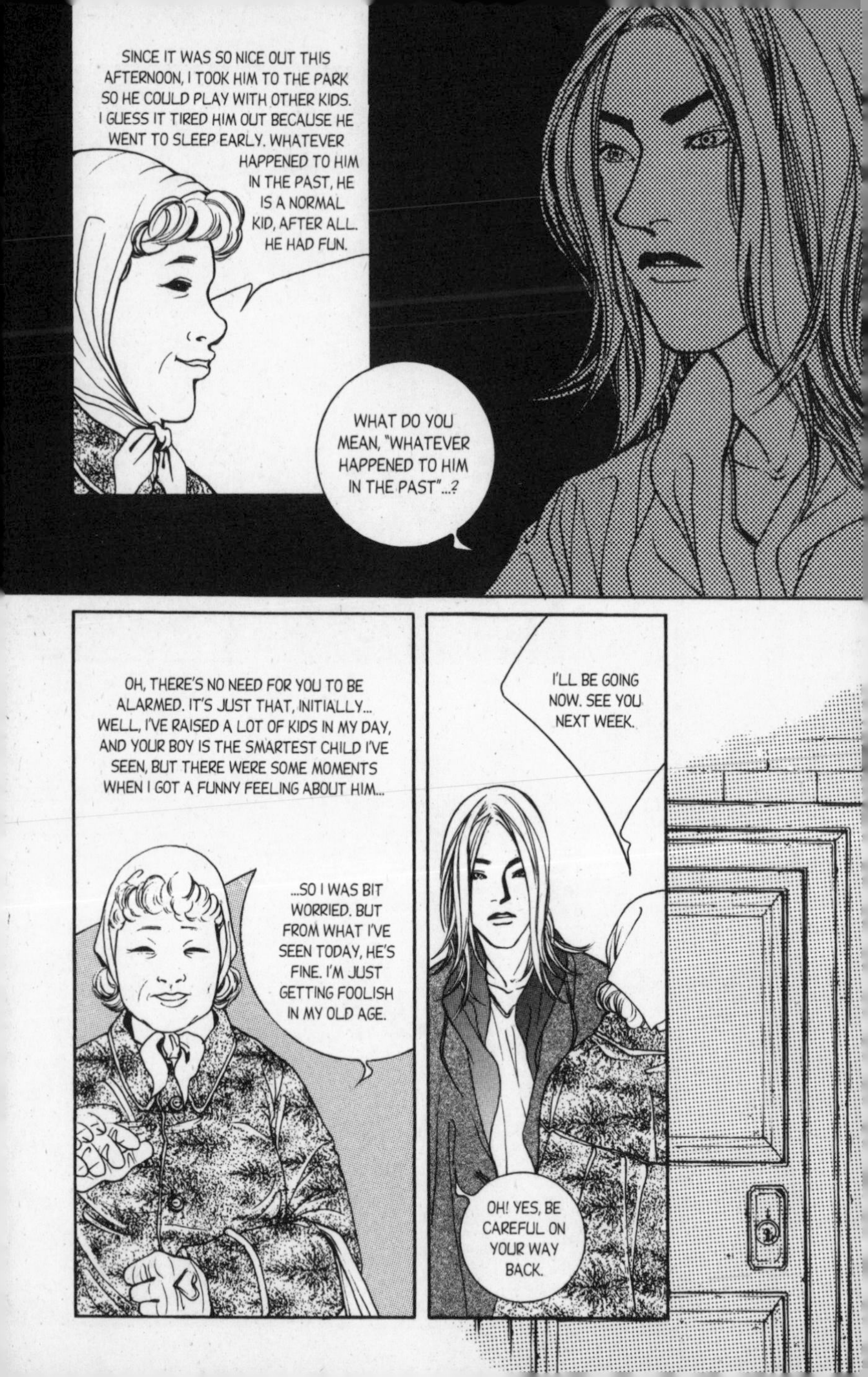
SINCE IT WAS SO NICE OUT THIS AFTERNOON, I TOOK HIM TO THE PARK SO HE COULD PLAY WITH OTHER KIDS. I GUESS IT TIRED HIM OUT BECAUSE HE WENT TO SLEEP EARLY. WHATEVER HAPPENED TO HIM IN THE PAST, HE IS A NORMAL KID, AFTER ALL. HE HAD FUN.
WHAT DO YOU MEAN, "WHATEVER HAPPENED TO HIM IN THE PAST"...?
OH, THERE'S NO NEED FOR YOU TO BE ALARMED. IT'S JUST THAT, INITIALLY... WELL, I'VE RAISED A LOT OF KIDS IN MY DAY, AND YOUR BOY IS THE SMARTEST CHILD I'VE SEEN, BUT THERE WERE SOME MOMENTS WHEN I GOT A FUNNY FEELING ABOUT HIM...
...SO I WAS BIT WORRIED. BUT FROM WHAT I'VE SEEN TODAY, HE'S FINE. I'M JUST GETTING FOOLISH IN MY OLD AGE.
I'LL BE GOING NOW. SEE YOU NEXT WEEK.
OH! YES, BE CAREFUL ON YOUR WAY BACK.

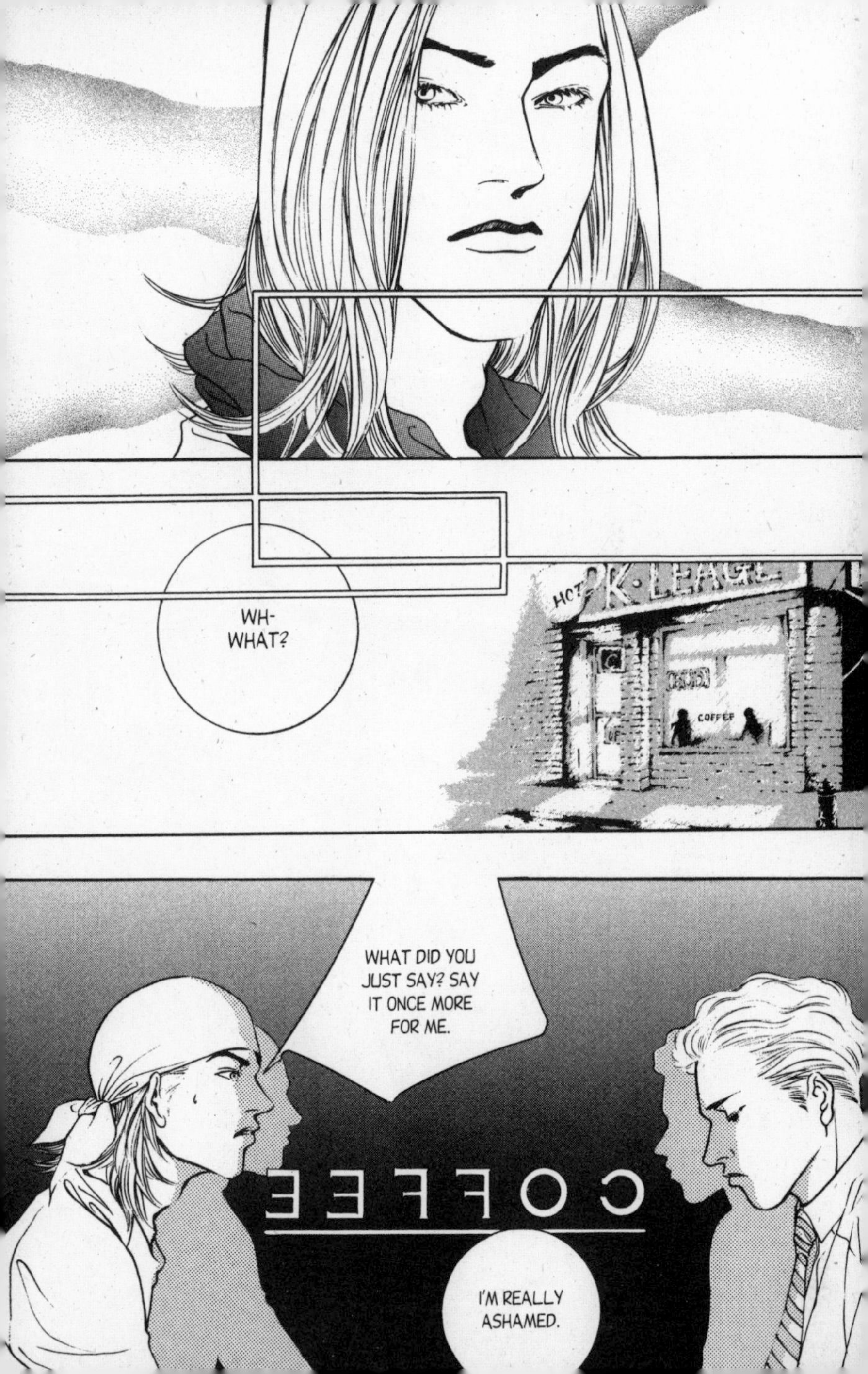
WH-
WHAT?
COFFEE
WHAT DID YOU JUST SAY? SAY IT ONCE MORE FOR ME.
I'M REALLY ASHAMED.

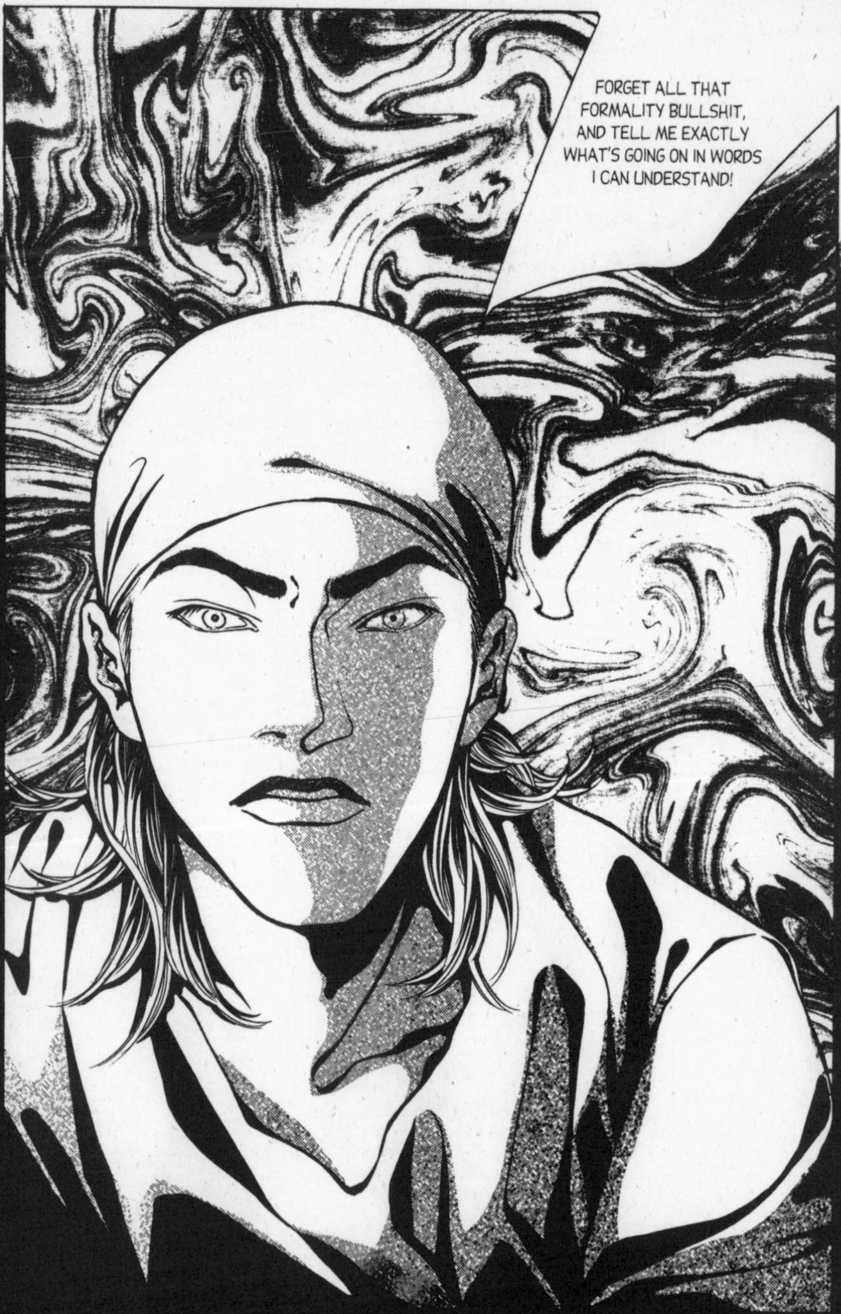
FORGET ALL THAT FORMALITY BULLSHIT, AND TELL ME EXACTLY WHAT'S GOING ON IN WORDS I CAN UNDERSTAND!

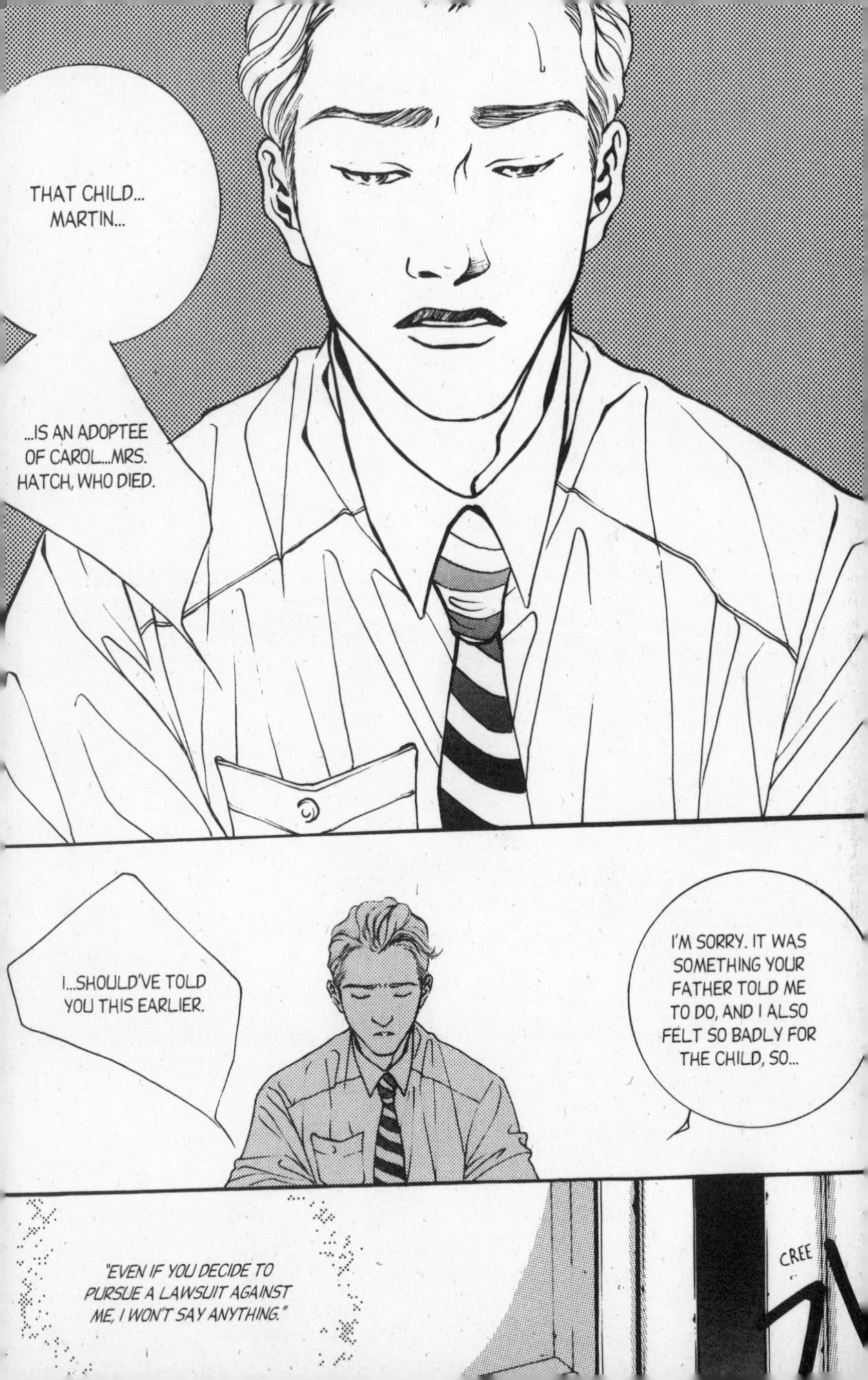
THAT CHILD... MARTIN...
...IS AN ADOPTEE OF CAROL...MRS. HATCH, WHO DIED.
I...SHOULD'VE TOLD YOU THIS EARLIER.
I'M SORRY. IT WAS SOMETHING YOUR FATHER TOLD ME TO DO, AND I ALSO FELT SO BADLY FOR THE CHILD, SO...
"EVEN IF YOU DECIDE TO PURSUE A LAWSUIT AGAINST ME, I WON'T SAY ANYTHING."
CREE

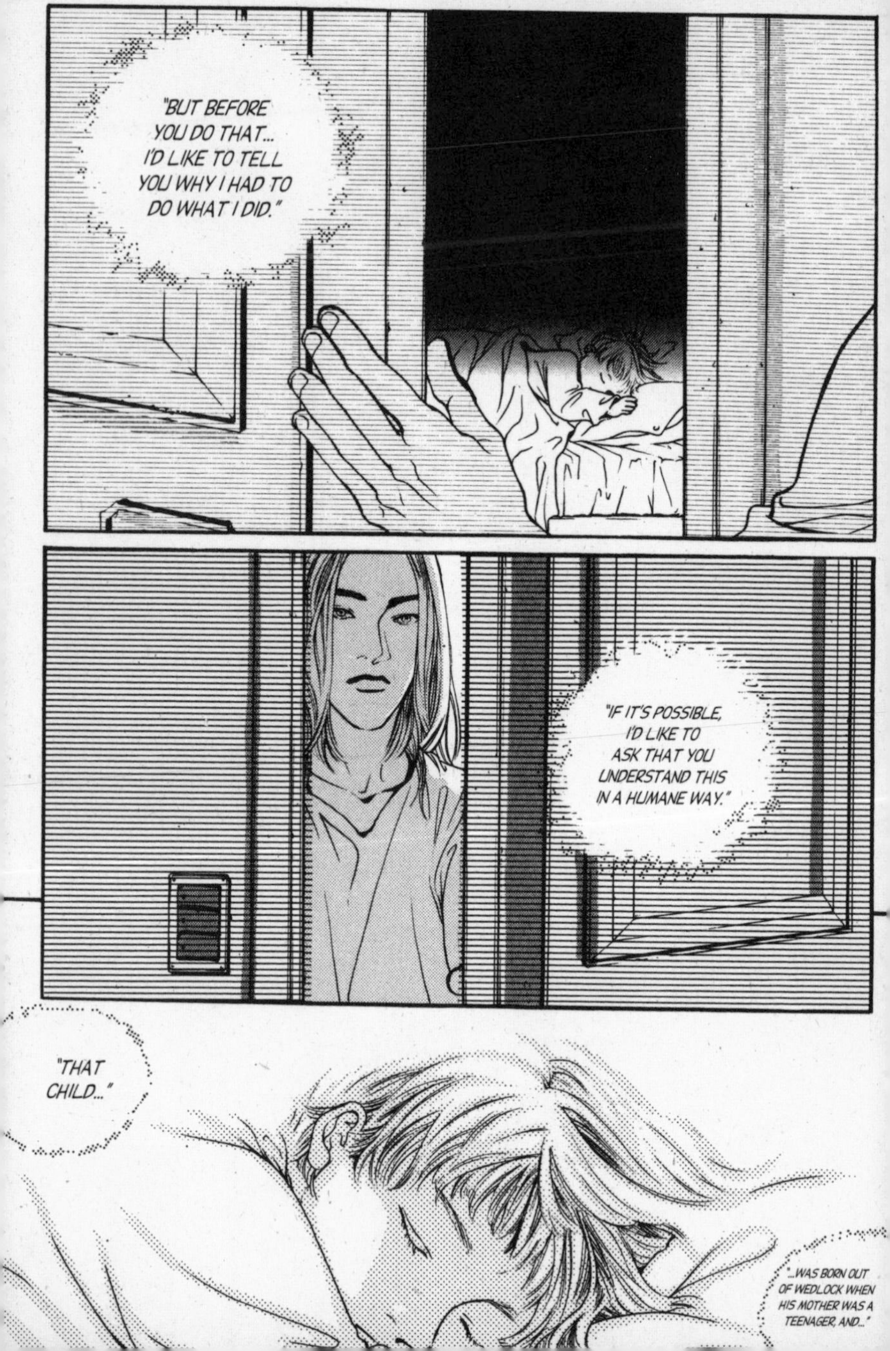
"BUT BEFORE YOU DO THAT... I'D LIKE TO TELL YOU WHY I HAD TO DO WHAT I DID."
"IF IT'S POSSIBLE, I'D LIKE TO ASK THAT YOU UNDERSTAND THIS IN A HUMANE WAY."
"THAT CHILD..."
"...WAS BORN OUT OF WEDLOCK WHEN HIS MOTHER WAS A TEENAGER, AND..."

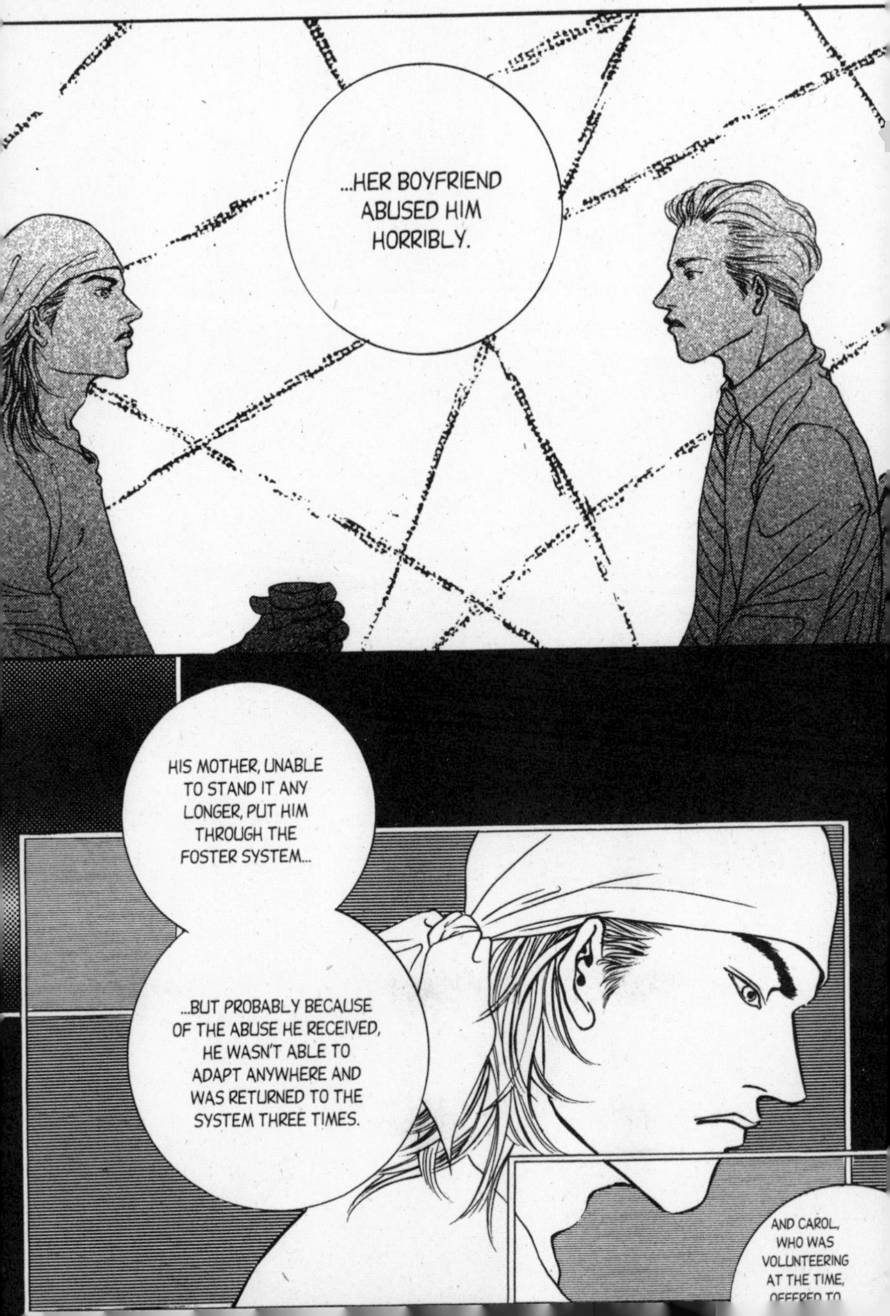
...HER BOYFRIEND ABUSED HIM HORRIBLY.
HIS MOTHER, UNABLE TO STAND IT ANY LONGER, PUT HIM THROUGH THE FOSTER SYSTEM...
...BUT PROBABLY BECAUSE OF THE ABUSE HE RECEIVED, HE WASN'T ABLE TO ADAPT ANYWHERE AND WAS RETURNED TO THE SYSTEM THREE TIMES.
AND CAROL, WHO WAS VOLUNTEERING AT THE TIME,

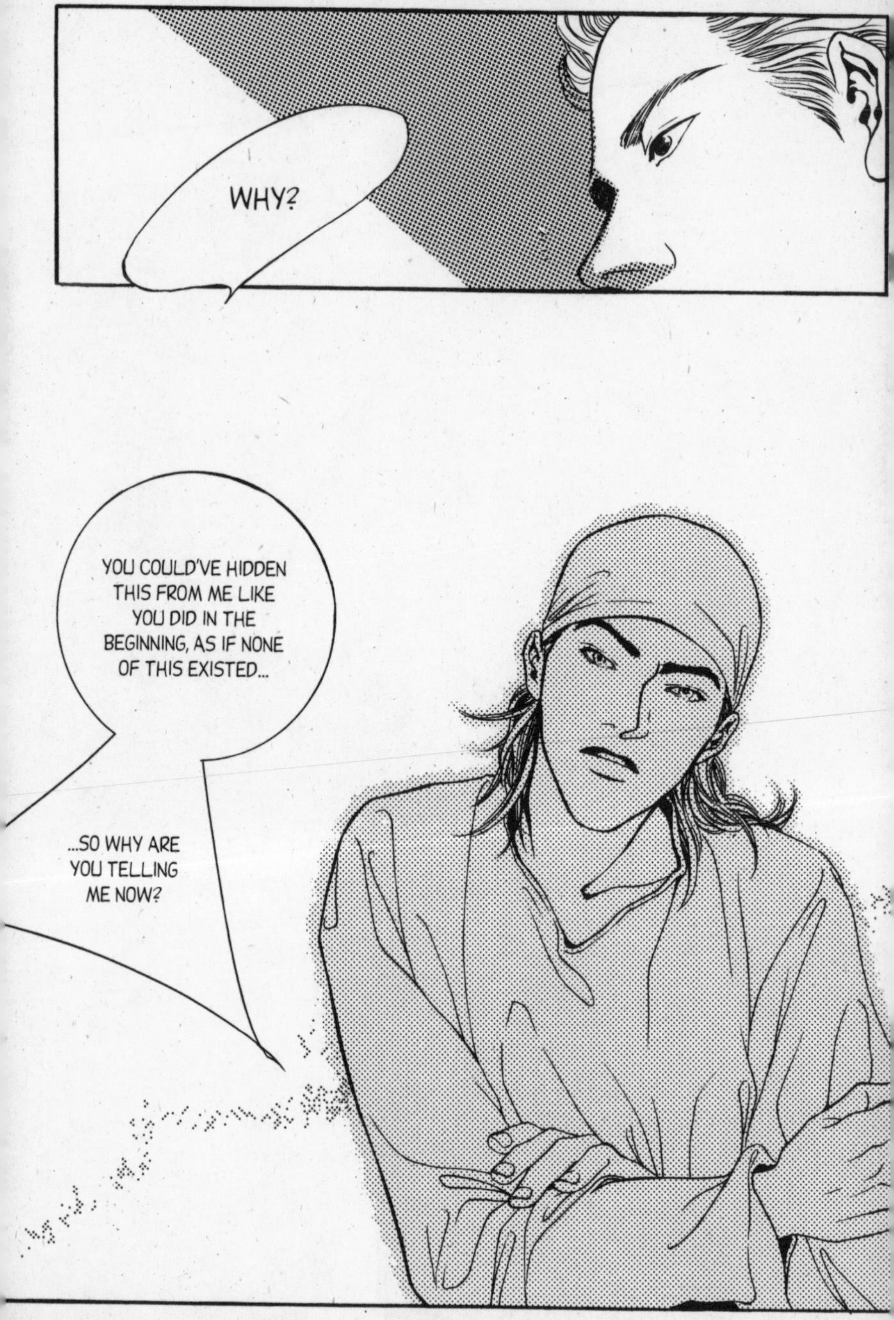
WHY?
YOU COULD'VE HIDDEN THIS FROM ME LIKE YOU DID IN THE BEGINNING, AS IF NONE OF THIS EXISTED...
...SO WHY ARE YOU TELLING ME NOW?

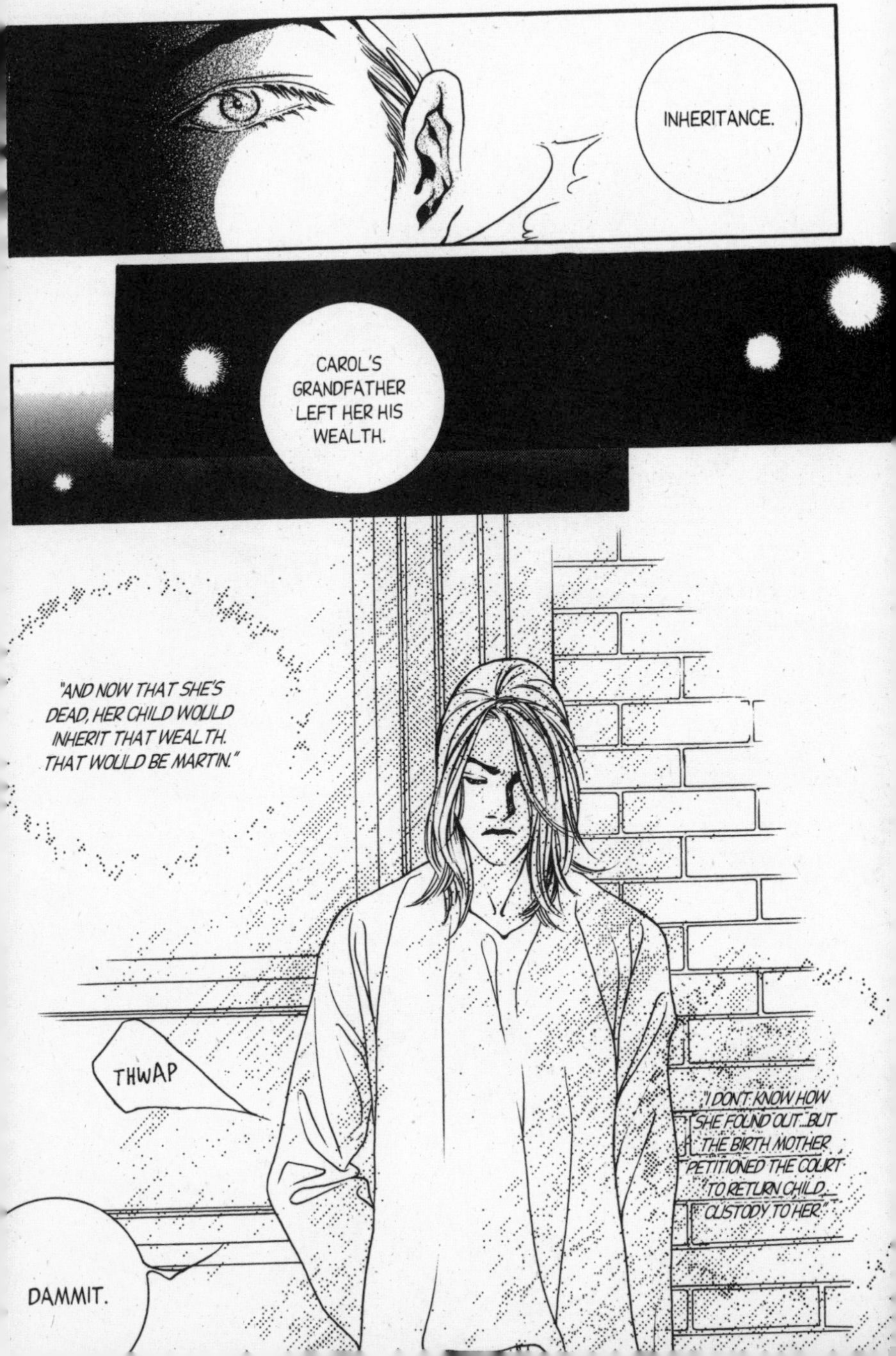
INHERITANCE.
CAROL'S GRANDFATHER LEFT HER HIS WEALTH.
"AND NOW THAT SHE'S DEAD, HER CHILD WOULD INHERIT THAT WEALTH. THAT WOULD BE MARTIN."
THWAP
"I DON'T KNOW HOW SHE FOUND OUT...BUT THE BIRTH MOTHER PETITIONED THE COURT TO RETURN CHILD CUSTODY TO HER."
DAMMIT.

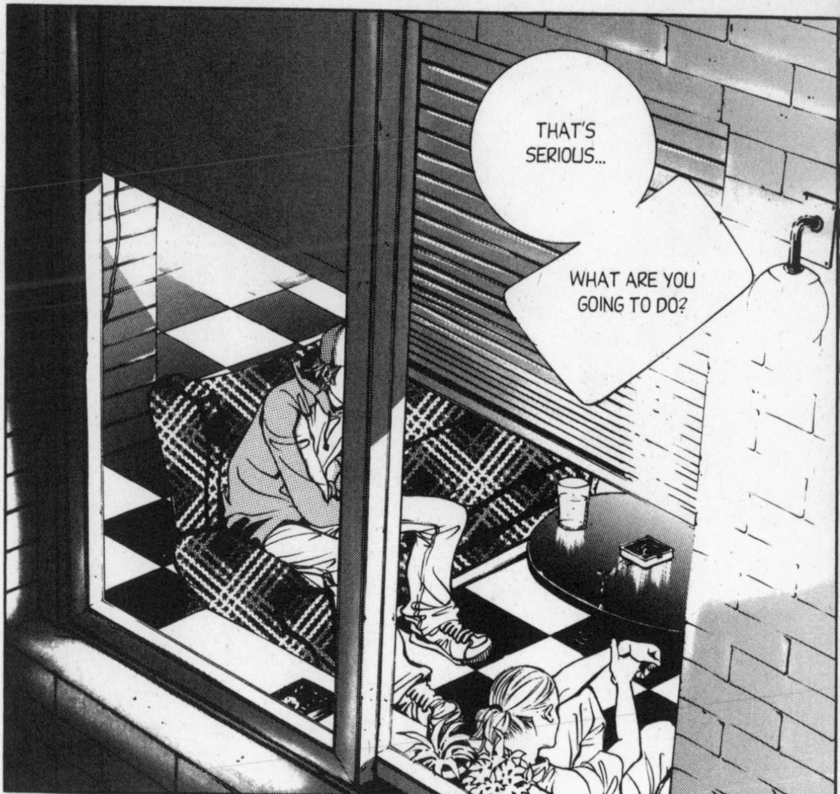
THAT'S SERIOUS...
WHAT ARE YOU GOING TO DO?

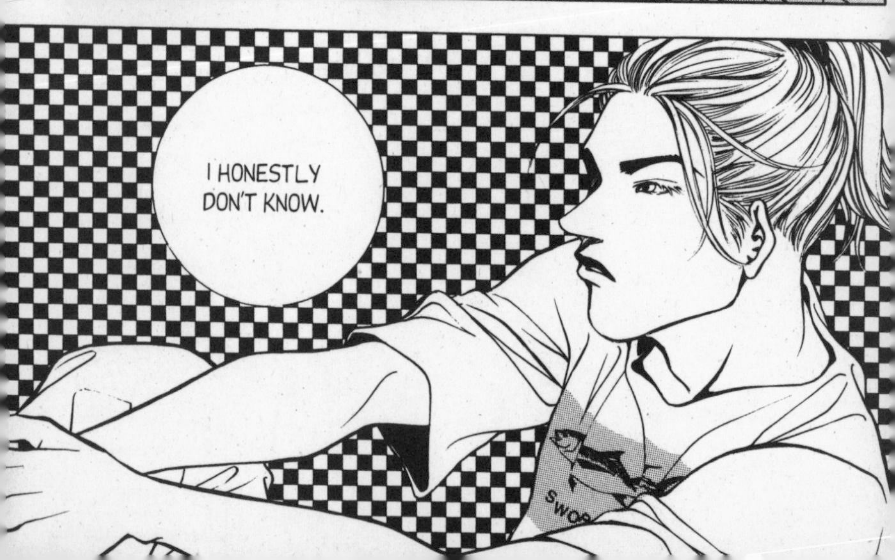
I HONESTLY DON'T KNOW.

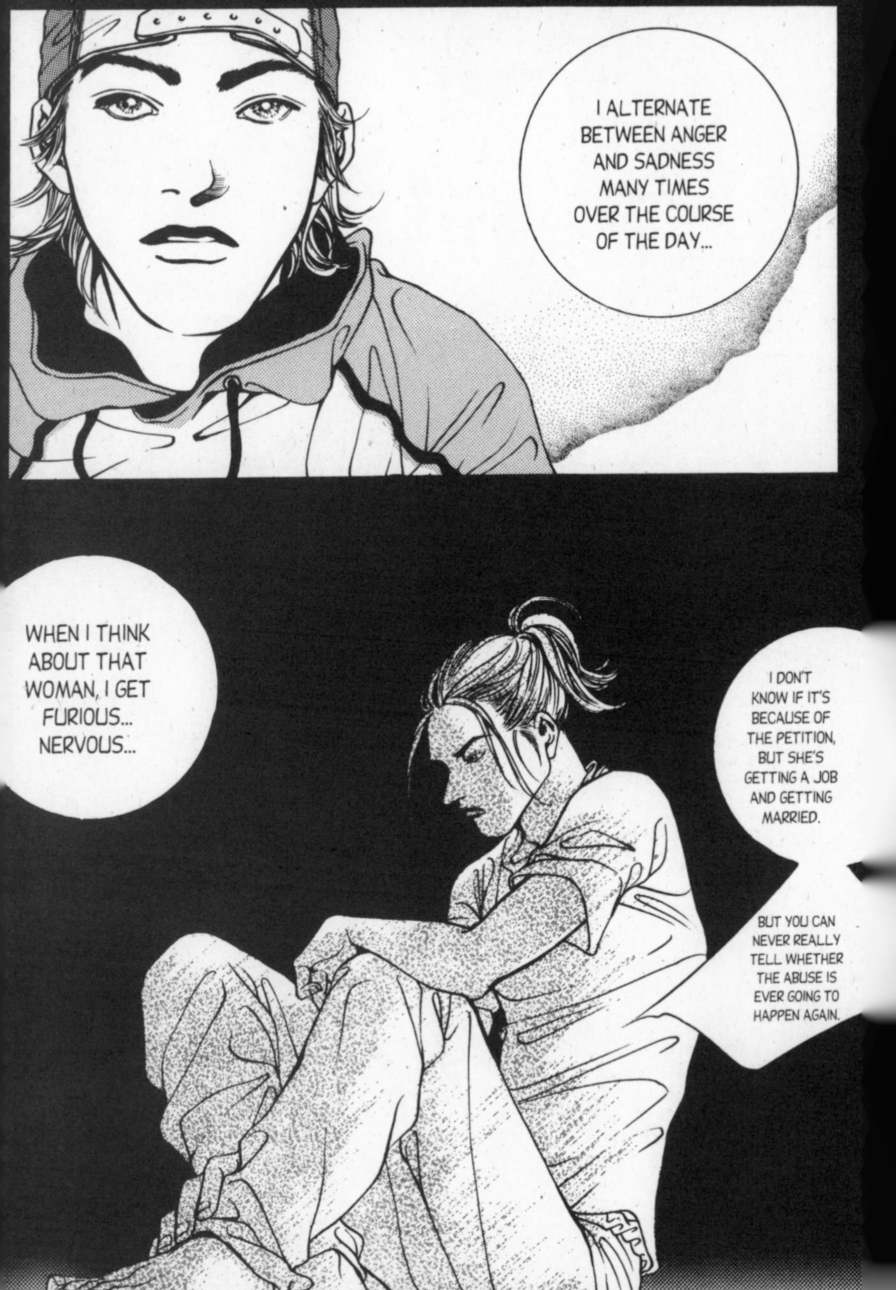
I ALTERNATE BETWEEN ANGER AND SADNESS MANY TIMES OVER THE COURSE OF THE DAY...
WHEN I THINK ABOUT THAT WOMAN, I GET FURIOUS... NERVOUS...
I DON'T KNOW IF IT'S BECAUSE OF THE PETITION, BUT SHE'S GETTING A JOB AND GETTING MARRIED.
BUT YOU CAN NEVER REALLY TELL WHETHER THE ABUSE IS EVER GOING TO HAPPEN AGAIN.

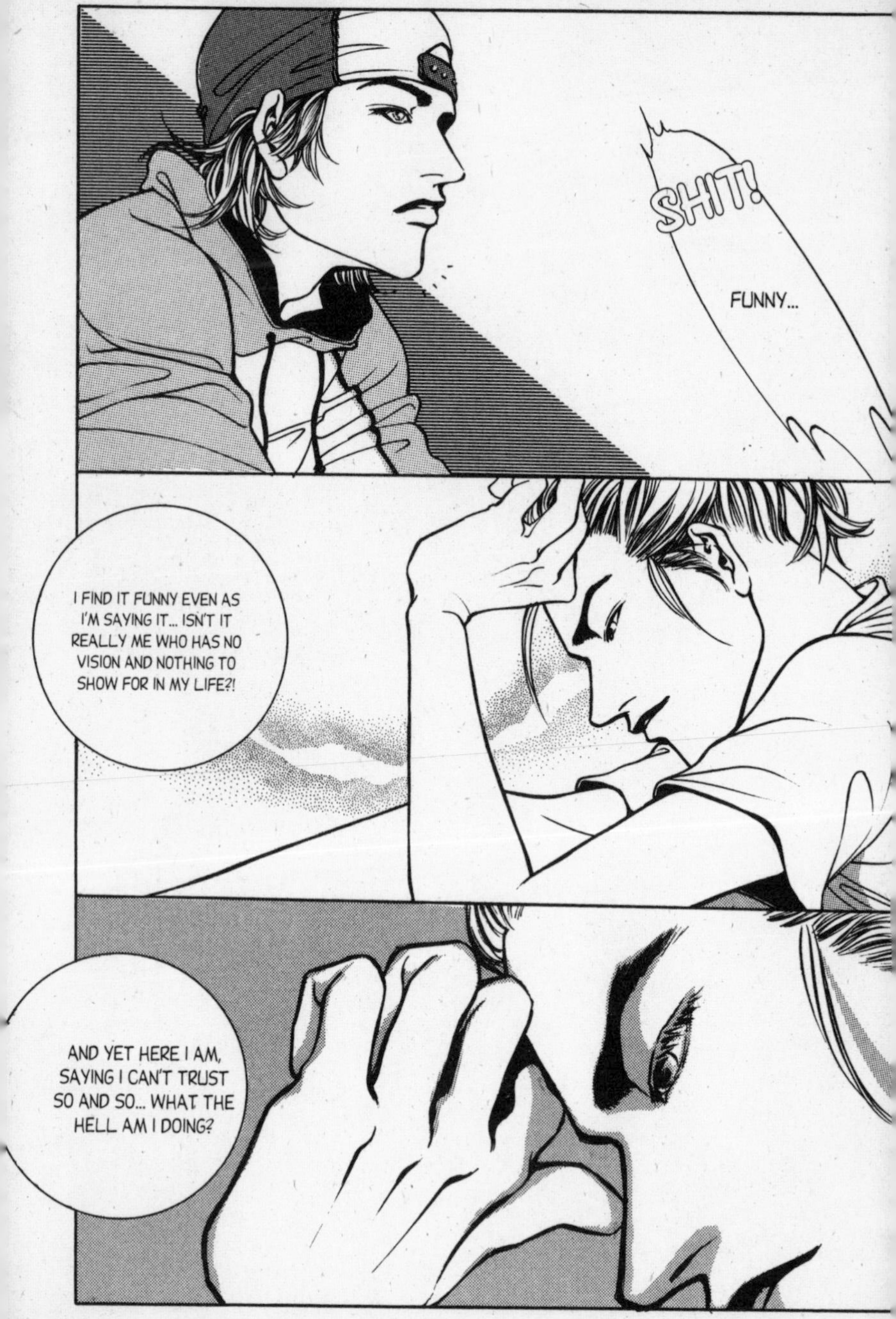
SHIT!
FUNNY...
I FIND IT FUNNY EVEN AS I'M SAYING IT... ISN'T IT REALLY ME WHO HAS NO VISION AND NOTHING TO SHOW FOR IN MY LIFE?!
AND YET HERE I AM, SAYING I CAN'T TRUST SO AND SO... WHAT THE HELL AM I DOING?

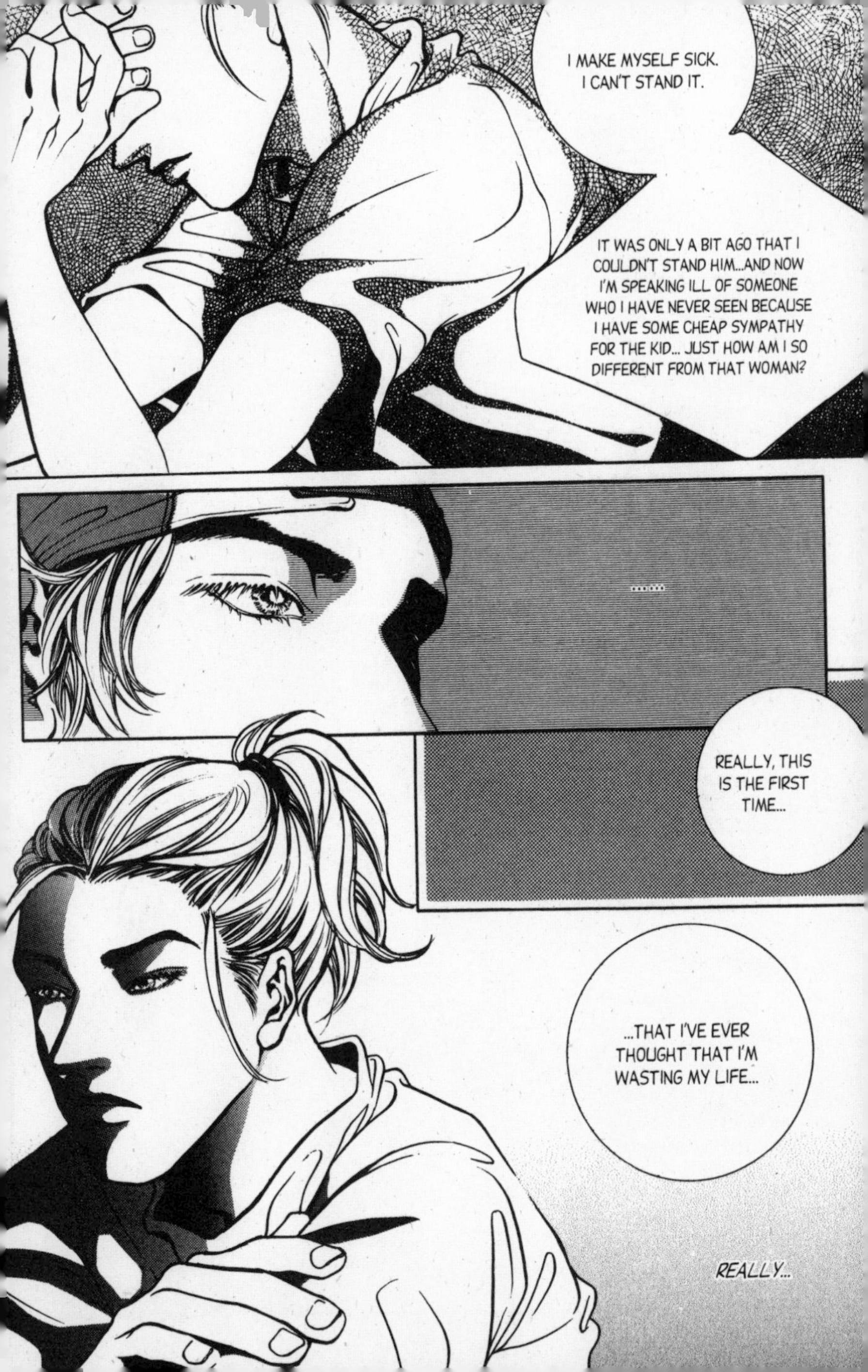
I MAKE MYSELF SICK.
I CAN'T STAND IT.
IT WAS ONLY A BIT AGO THAT I COULDN'T STAND HIM...AND NOW I'M SPEAKING ILL OF SOMEONE WHO I HAVE NEVER SEEN BECAUSE I HAVE SOME CHEAP SYMPATHY FOR THE KID... JUST HOW AM I SO DIFFERENT FROM THAT WOMAN?
......
REALLY, THIS IS THE FIRST TIME...
...THAT I'VE EVER THOUGHT THAT I'M WASTING MY LIFE...
REALLY...

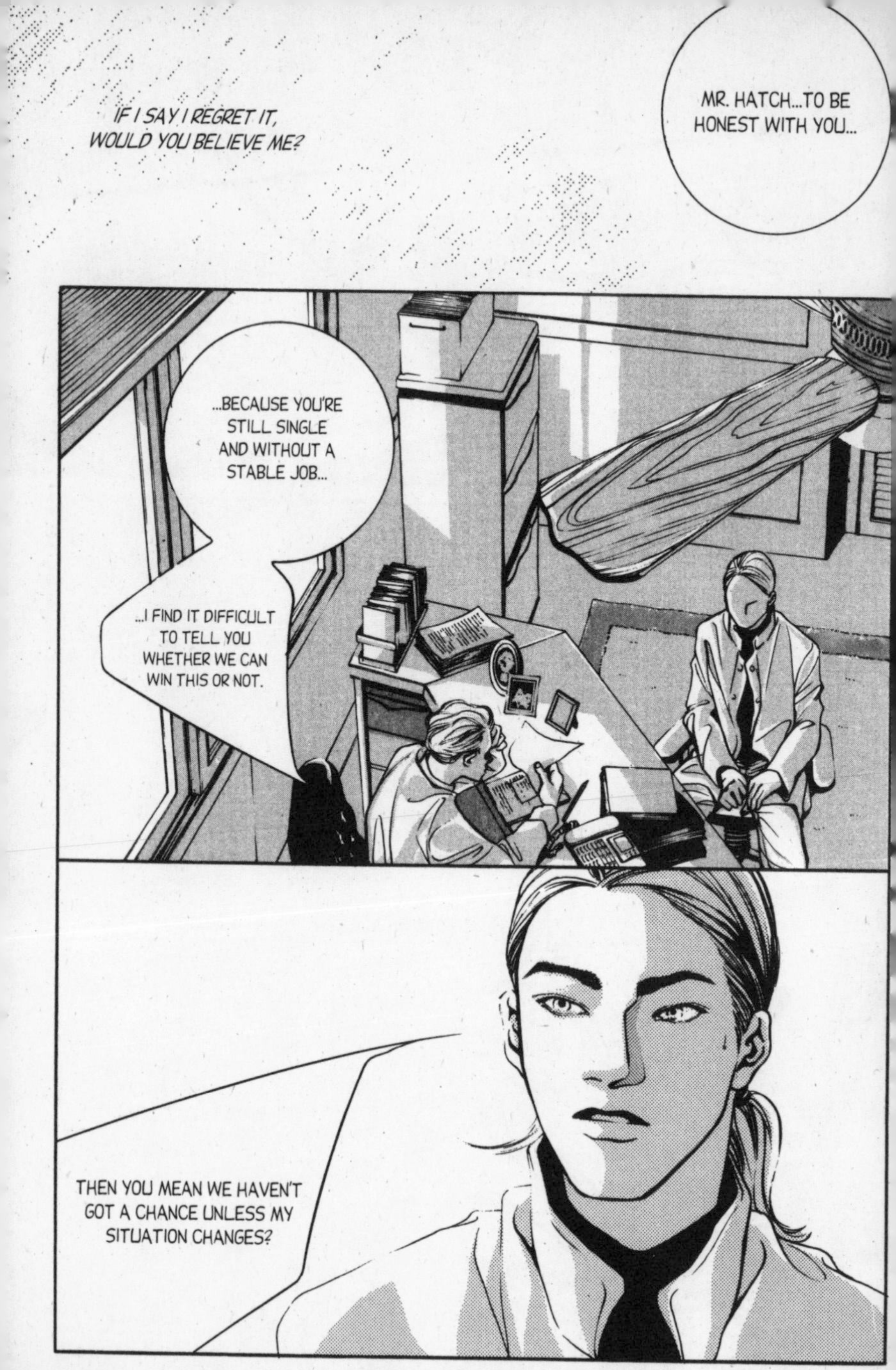
IF I SAY I REGRET IT, WOULD YOU BELIEVE ME?
MR. HATCH...TO BE HONEST WITH YOU...
...BECAUSE YOU'RE STILL SINGLE AND WITHOUT A STABLE JOB...
...I FIND IT DIFFICULT TO TELL YOU WHETHER WE CAN WIN THIS OR NOT.
THEN YOU MEAN WE HAVEN'T GOT A CHANCE UNLESS MY SITUATION CHANGES?

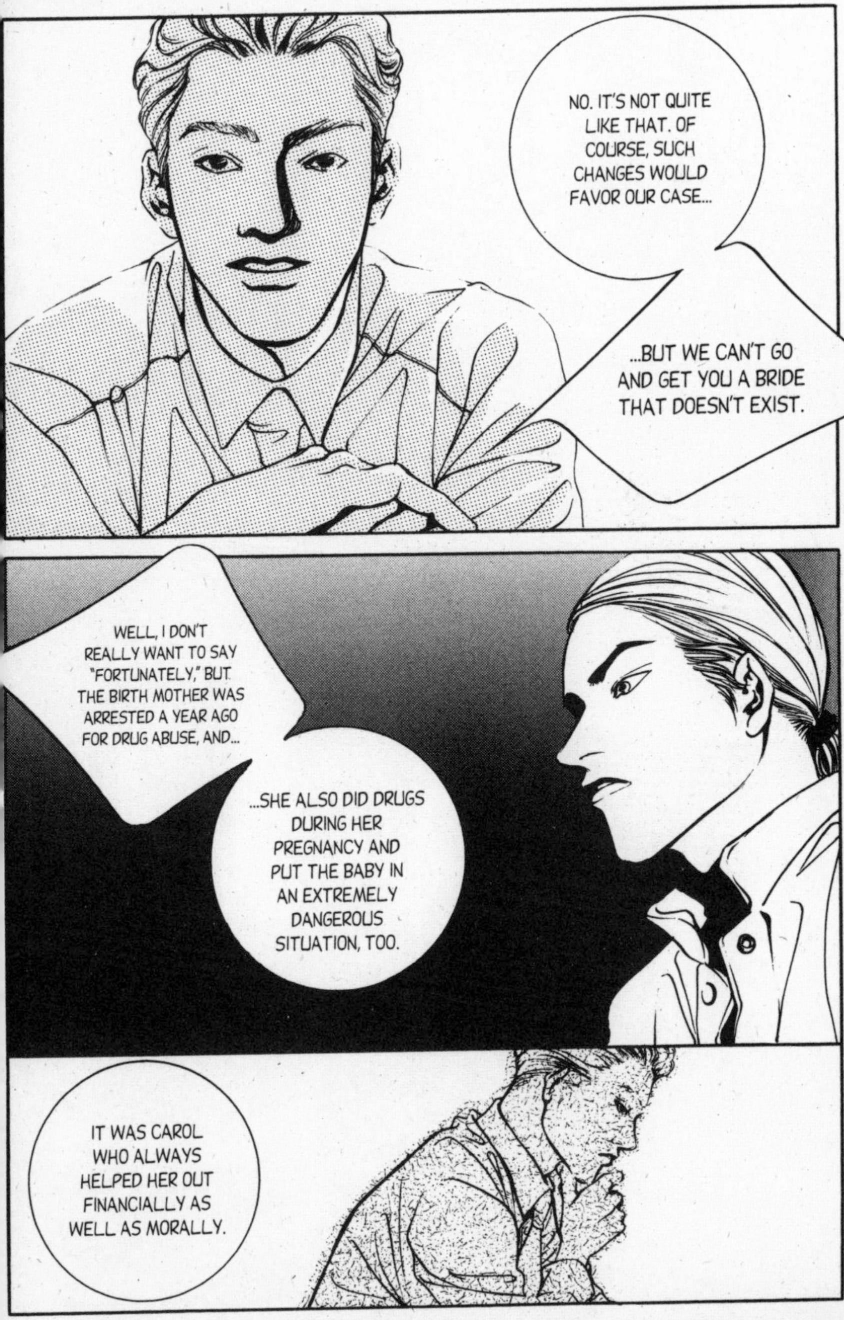
NO. IT'S NOT QUITE LIKE THAT. OF COURSE, SUCH CHANGES WOULD FAVOR OUR CASE...
...BUT WE CAN'T GO AND GET YOU A BRIDE THAT DOESN'T EXIST.
WELL, I DON'T REALLY WANT TO SAY "FORTUNATELY," BUT THE BIRTH MOTHER WAS ARRESTED A YEAR AGO FOR DRUG ABUSE, AND...
...SHE ALSO DID DRUGS DURING HER PREGNANCY AND PUT THE BABY IN AN EXTREMELY DANGEROUS SITUATION, TOO.
IT WAS CAROL WHO ALWAYS HELPED HER OUT FINANCIALLY AS WELL AS MORALLY.

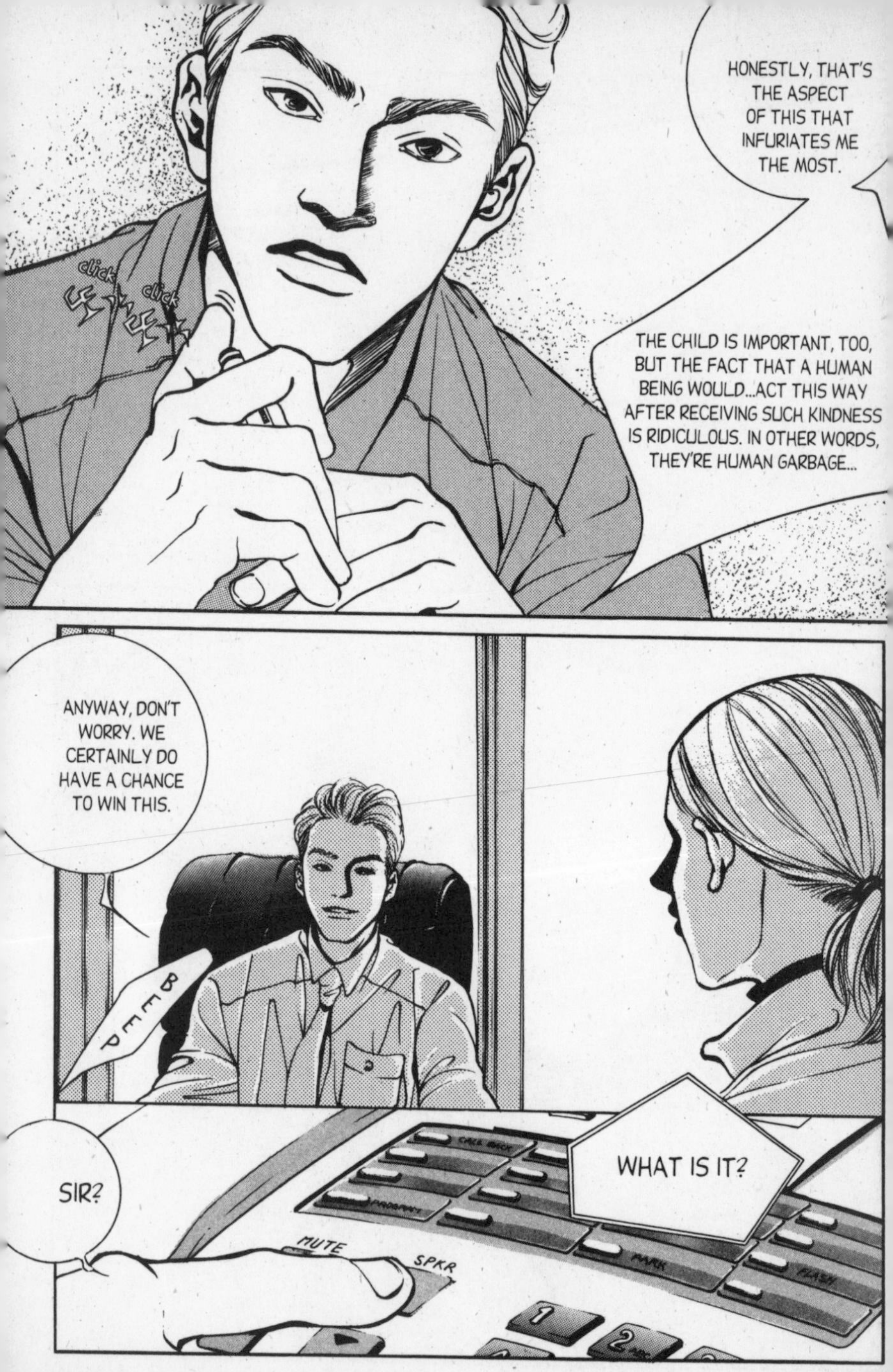

HONESTLY, THAT'S THE ASPECT OF THIS THAT INFURIATES ME THE MOST.
click click
THE CHILD IS IMPORTANT, TOO, BUT THE FACT THAT A HUMAN BEING WOULD...ACT THIS WAY AFTER RECEIVING SUCH KINDNESS IS RIDICULOUS. IN OTHER WORDS, THEY'RE HUMAN GARBAGE...
ANYWAY, DON'T WORRY. WE CERTAINLY DO HAVE A CHANCE TO WIN THIS.
BEEP
SIR?
WHAT IS IT?
MUTE
SPKR

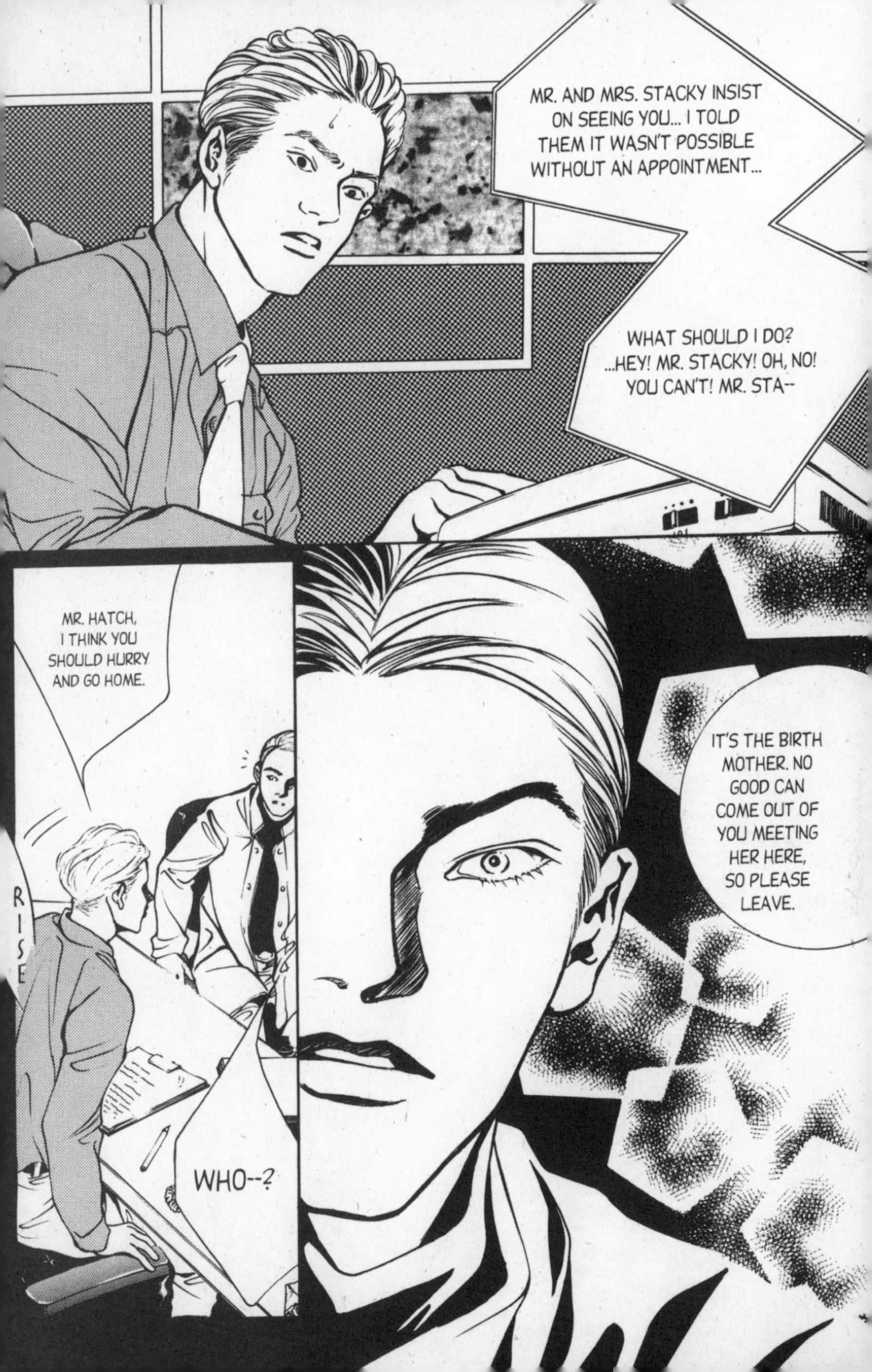
MR. AND MRS. STACKY INSIST ON SEEING YOU... I TOLD THEM IT WASN'T POSSIBLE WITHOUT AN APPOINTMENT...
WHAT SHOULD I DO? ...HEY! MR. STACKY! OH, NO! YOU CAN'T! MR. STA--
MR. HATCH, I THINK YOU SHOULD HURRY AND GO HOME.
RISE
WHO--?
IT'S THE BIRTH MOTHER. NO GOOD CAN COME OUT OF YOU MEETING HER HERE, SO PLEASE LEAVE.

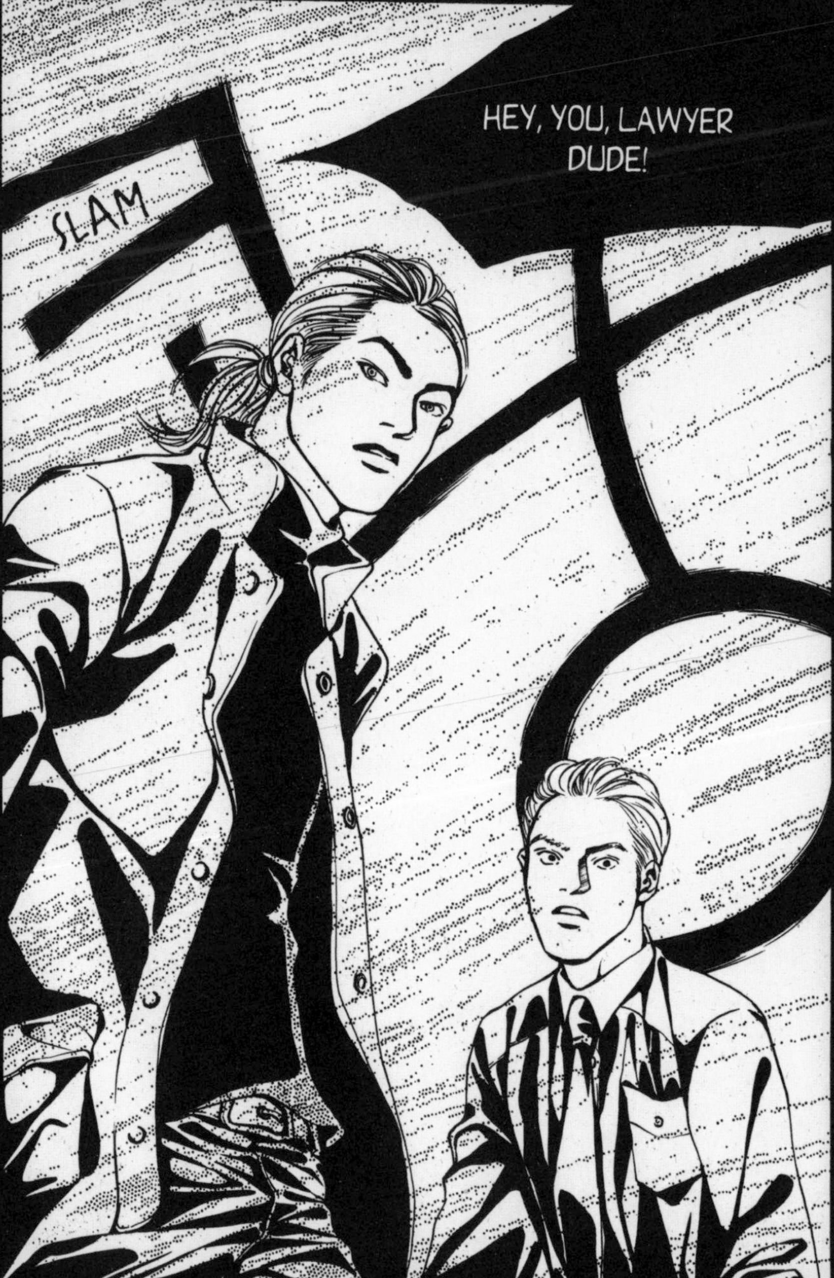
SLAM
HEY, YOU, LAWYER DUDE!

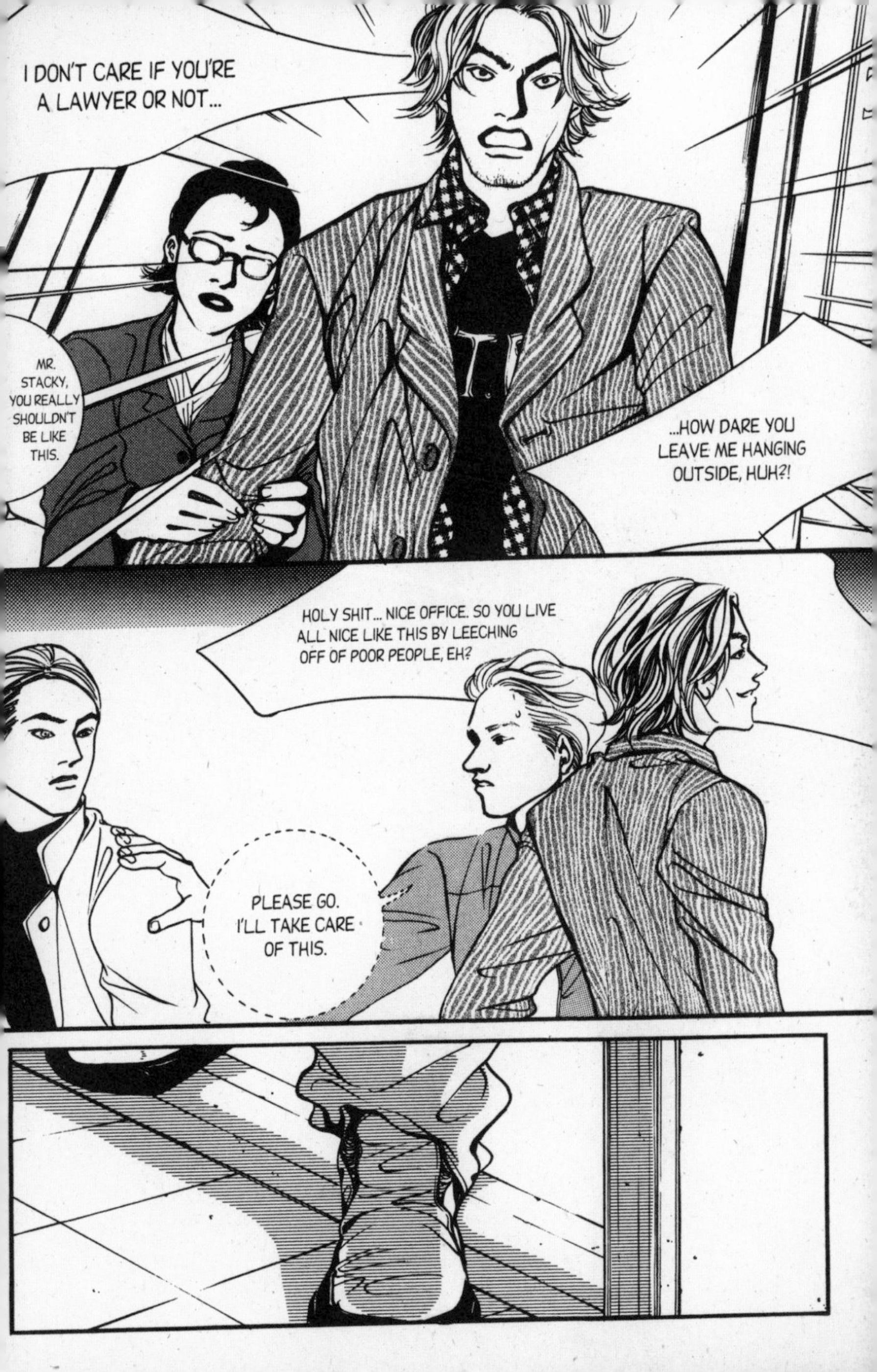
I DON'T CARE IF YOU'RE A LAWYER OR NOT...
MR. STACKY, YOU REALLY SHOULDN'T BE LIKE THIS.
...HOW DARE YOU LEAVE ME HANGING OUTSIDE, HUH?!
HOLY SHIT... NICE OFFICE. SO YOU LIVE ALL NICE LIKE THIS BY LEECHING OFF OF POOR PEOPLE, EH?
PLEASE GO. I'LL TAKE CARE OF THIS.

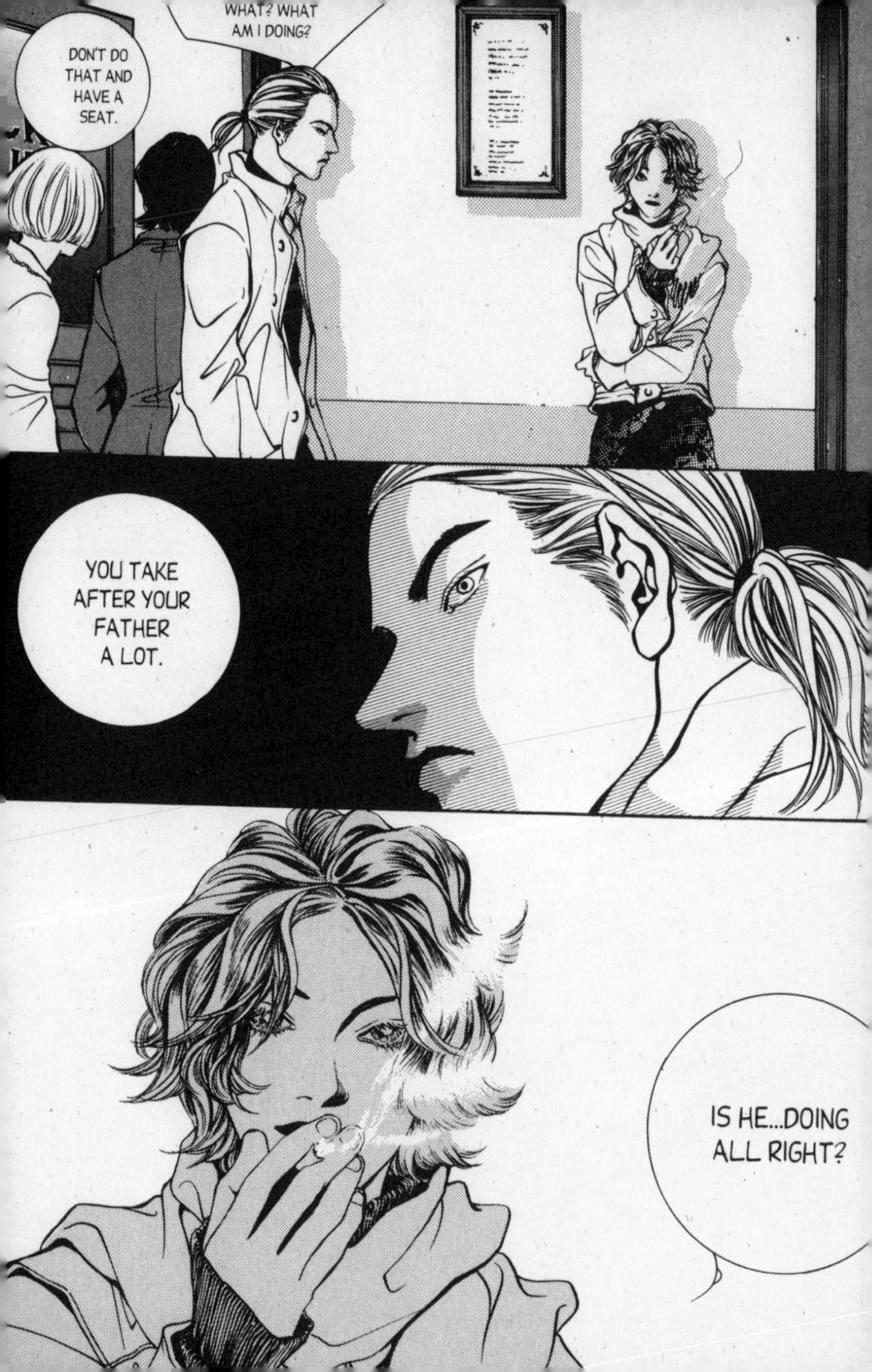
DON'T DO THAT AND HAVE A SEAT.
WHAT? WHAT AM I DOING?
YOU TAKE AFTER YOUR FATHER A LOT.
IS HE...DOING ALL RIGHT?

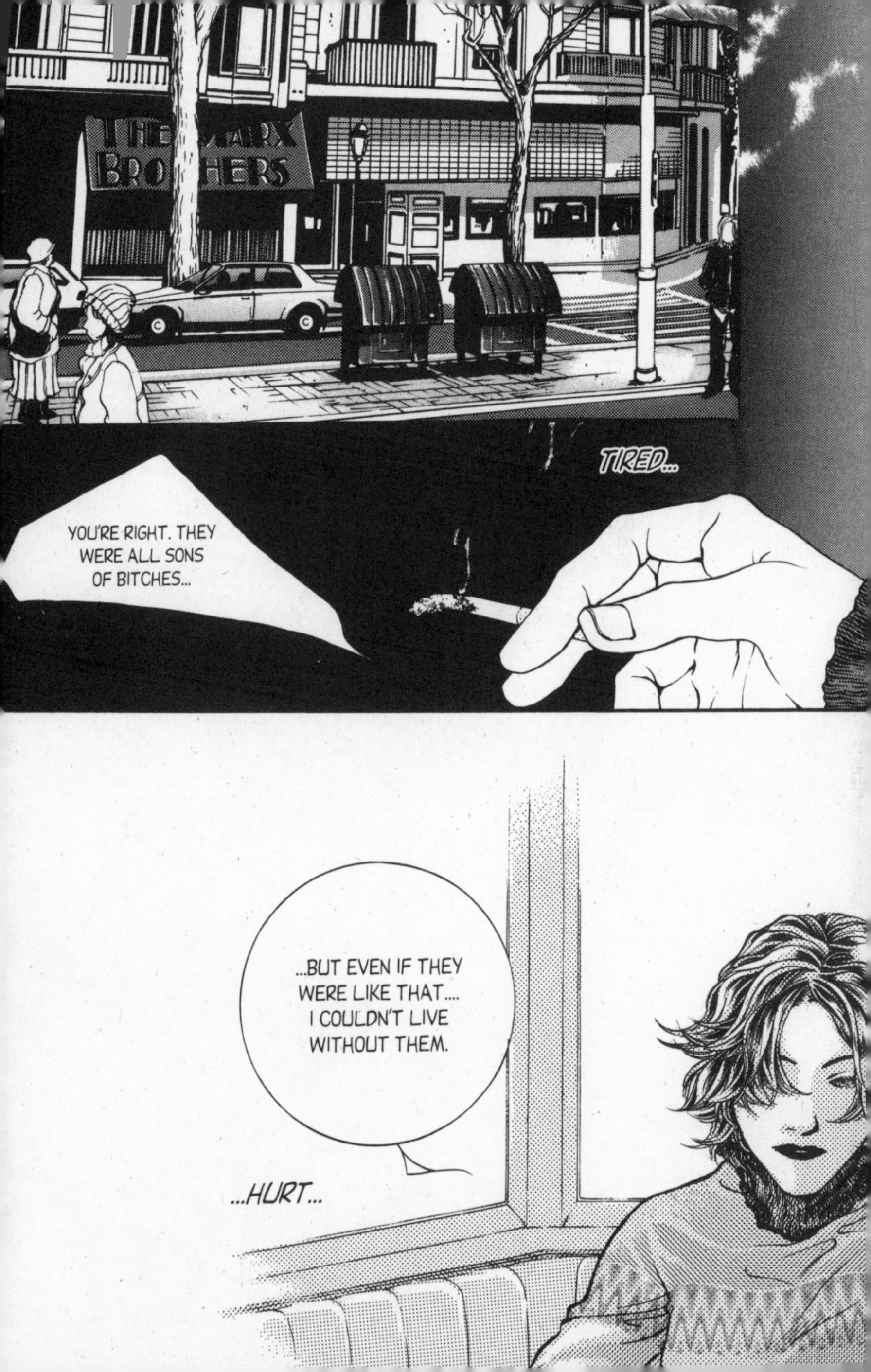
YOU'RE RIGHT. THEY WERE ALL SONS OF BITCHES...
TIRED...
...BUT EVEN IF THEY WERE LIKE THAT.... I COULDN'T LIVE WITHOUT THEM.
...HURT...

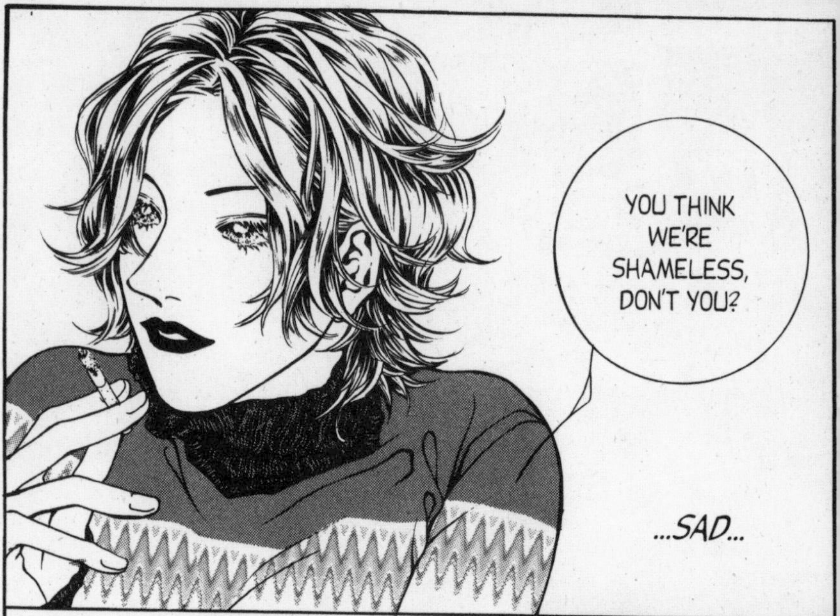
YOU THINK WE'RE SHAMELESS, DON'T YOU?
...SAD...

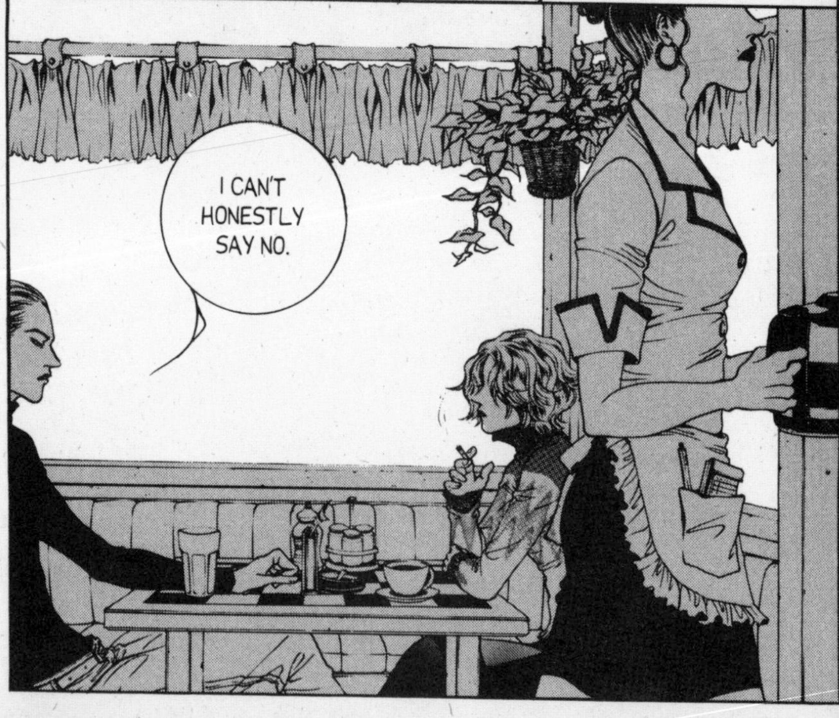
I CAN'T HONESTLY SAY NO.

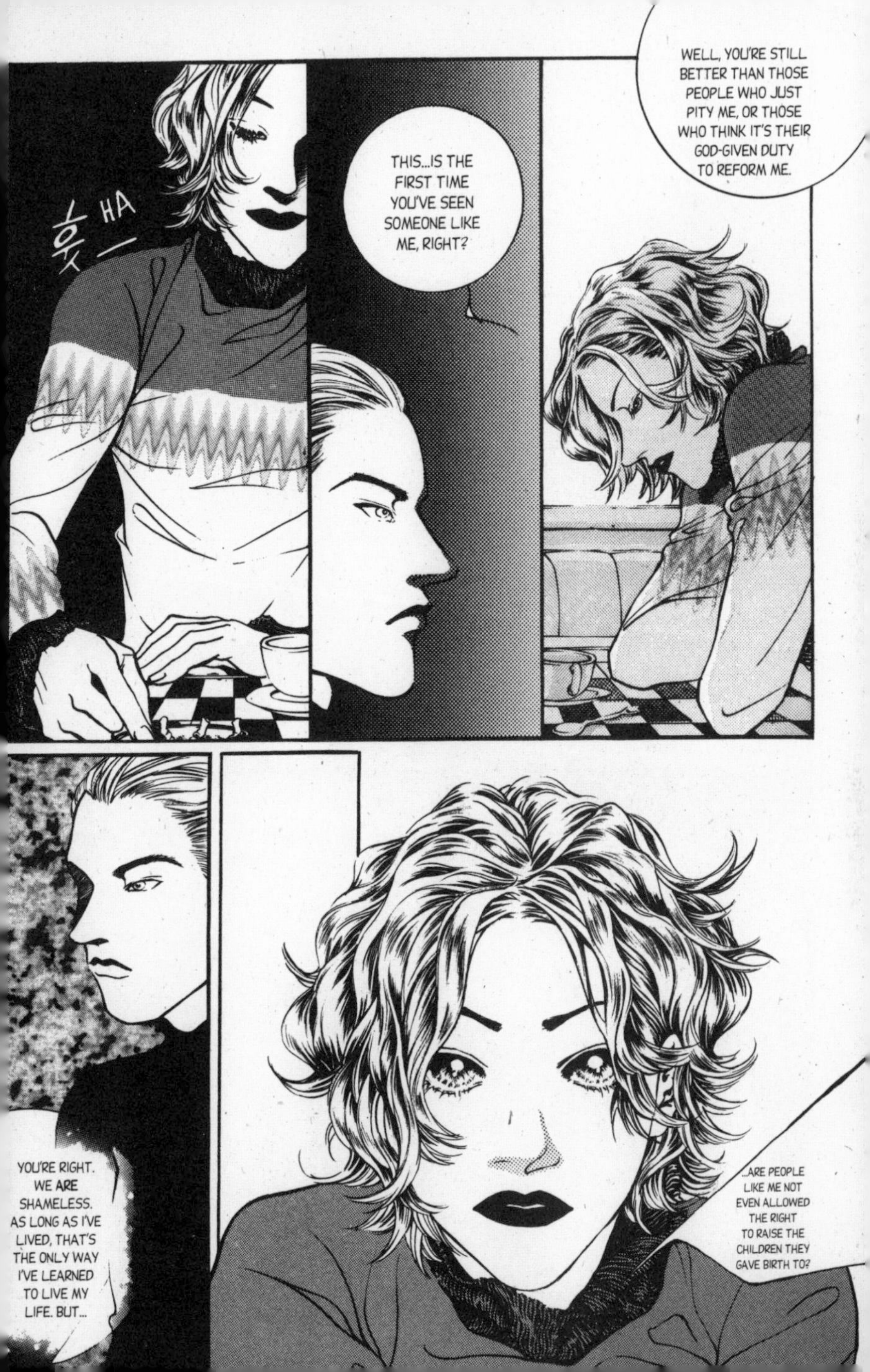
HA
THIS...IS THE FIRST TIME YOU'VE SEEN SOMEONE LIKE ME, RIGHT?
WELL, YOU'RE STILL BETTER THAN THOSE PEOPLE WHO JUST PITY ME, OR THOSE WHO THINK IT'S THEIR GOD-GIVEN DUTY TO REFORM ME.
YOU'RE RIGHT. WE ARE SHAMELESS. AS LONG AS I'VE LIVED, THAT'S THE ONLY WAY I'VE LEARNED TO LIVE MY LIFE. BUT...
...ARE PEOPLE LIKE ME NOT EVEN ALLOWED THE RIGHT TO RAISE THE CHILDREN THEY GAVE BIRTH TO?

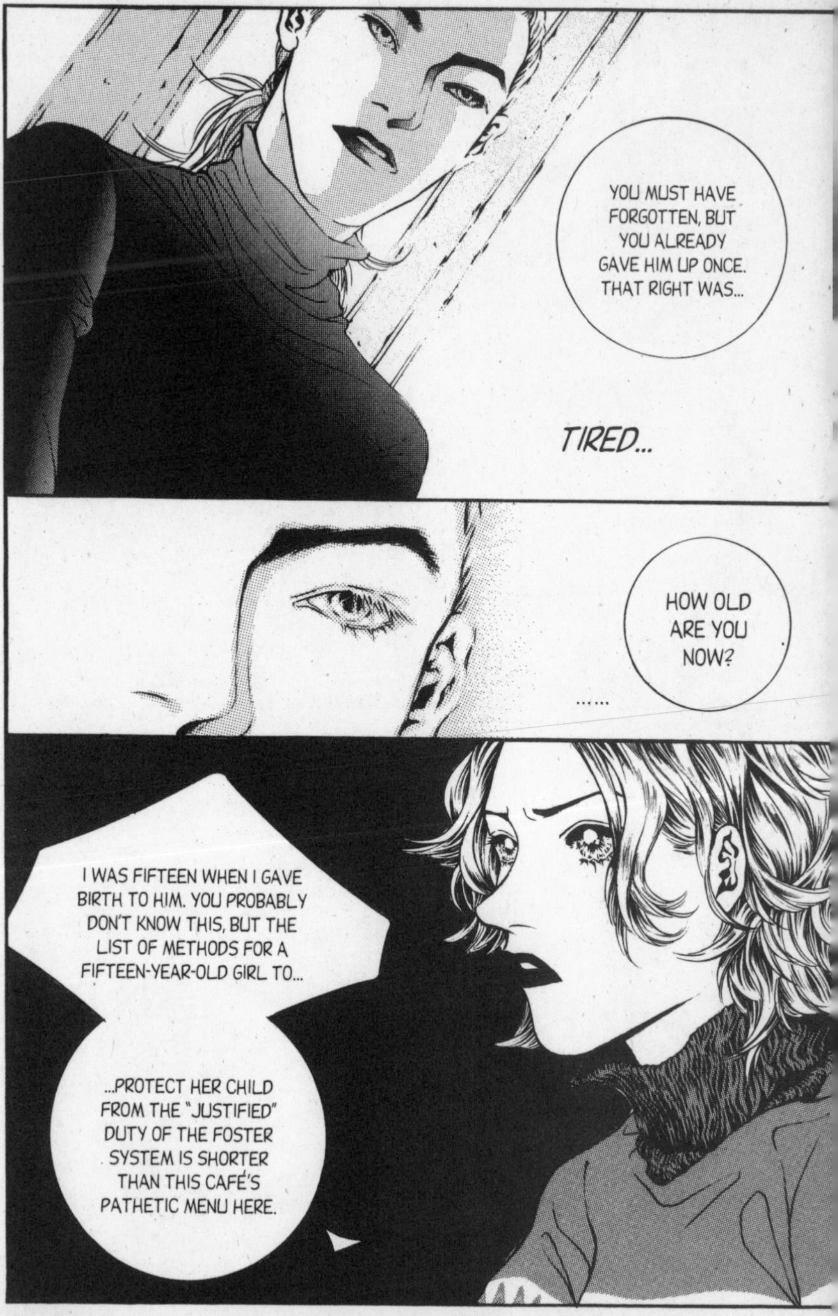

YOU MUST HAVE FORGOTTEN, BUT YOU ALREADY GAVE HIM UP ONCE. THAT RIGHT WAS...
TIRED...
HOW OLD ARE YOU NOW?
......
I WAS FIFTEEN WHEN I GAVE BIRTH TO HIM. YOU PROBABLY DON'T KNOW THIS, BUT THE LIST OF METHODS FOR A FIFTEEN-YEAR-OLD GIRL TO...
...PROTECT HER CHILD FROM THE "JUSTIFIED" DUTY OF THE FOSTER SYSTEM IS SHORTER THAN THIS CAFÉ'S PATHETIC MENU HERE.

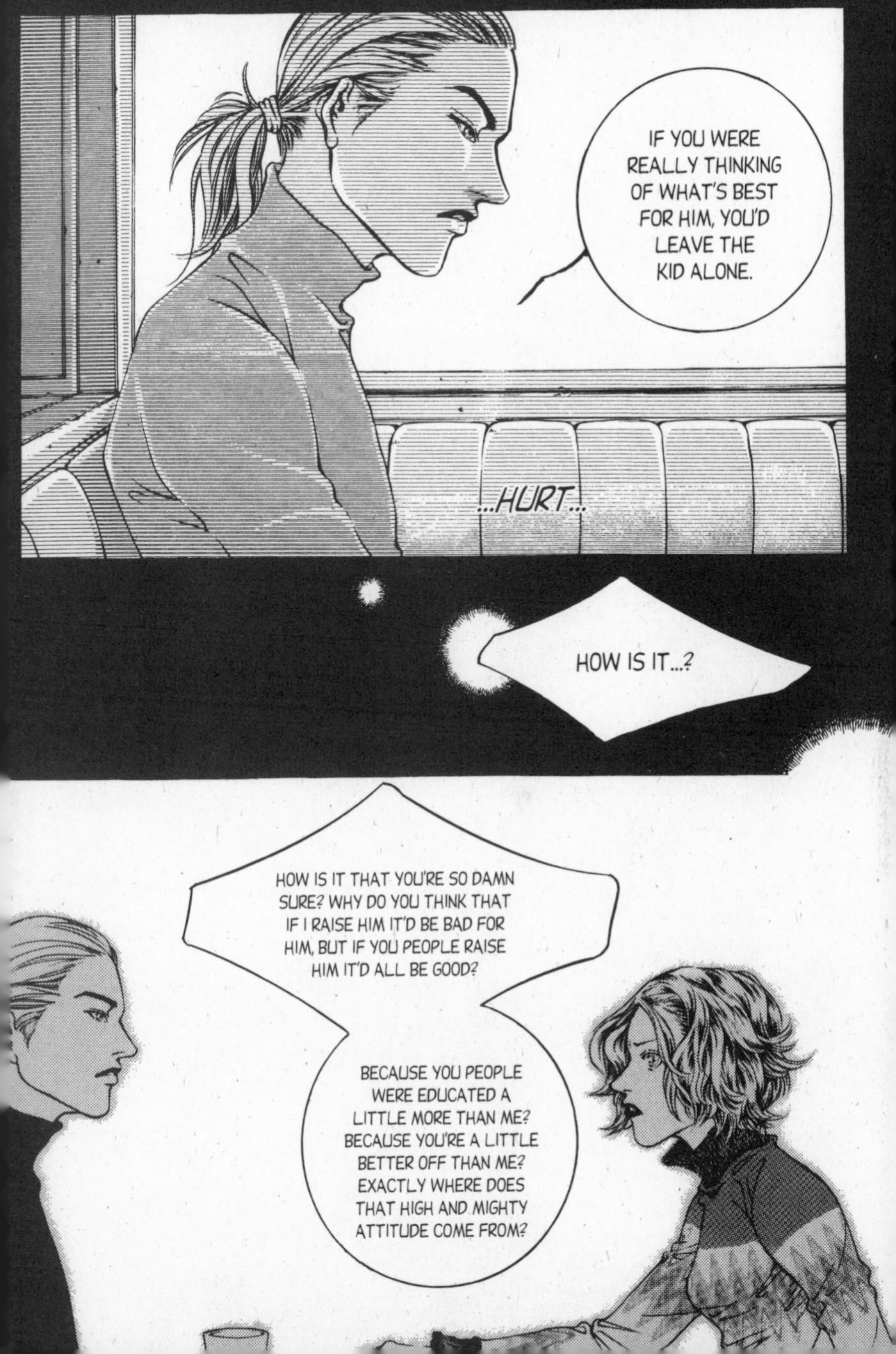
IF YOU WERE REALLY THINKING OF WHAT'S BEST FOR HIM, YOU'D LEAVE THE KID ALONE.
...HURT...
HOW IS IT...?
HOW IS IT THAT YOU'RE SO DAMN SURE? WHY DO YOU THINK THAT IF I RAISE HIM IT'D BE BAD FOR HIM, BUT IF YOU PEOPLE RAISE HIM IT'D ALL BE GOOD?
BECAUSE YOU PEOPLE WERE EDUCATED A LITTLE MORE THAN ME? BECAUSE YOU'RE A LITTLE BETTER OFF THAN ME? EXACTLY WHERE DOES THAT HIGH AND MIGHTY ATTITUDE COME FROM?

AND YOU? WHAT ABOUT YOU?
SAY IT'S BECAUSE OF THE MONEY!
HOW IS IT THAT THIS WELLSPRING OF MOTHERLY LOVE THAT HAS BEEN CURIOUSLY ABSENT FOR ALL THESE YEARS IS SUDDENLY OVERFLOWING LIKE THIS? DON'T YOU THINK OUR THOUGHTS ABOUT YOU ARE JUSTIFIED?
THAT'S A MORE ACCURATE PORTRAYAL OF HOW YOU REALLY ARE!
DON'T TRY TO MAKE SOME UNCHARACTERISTICALLY DIGNIFIED EXCUSE AND JUST SPEAK HONESTLY.

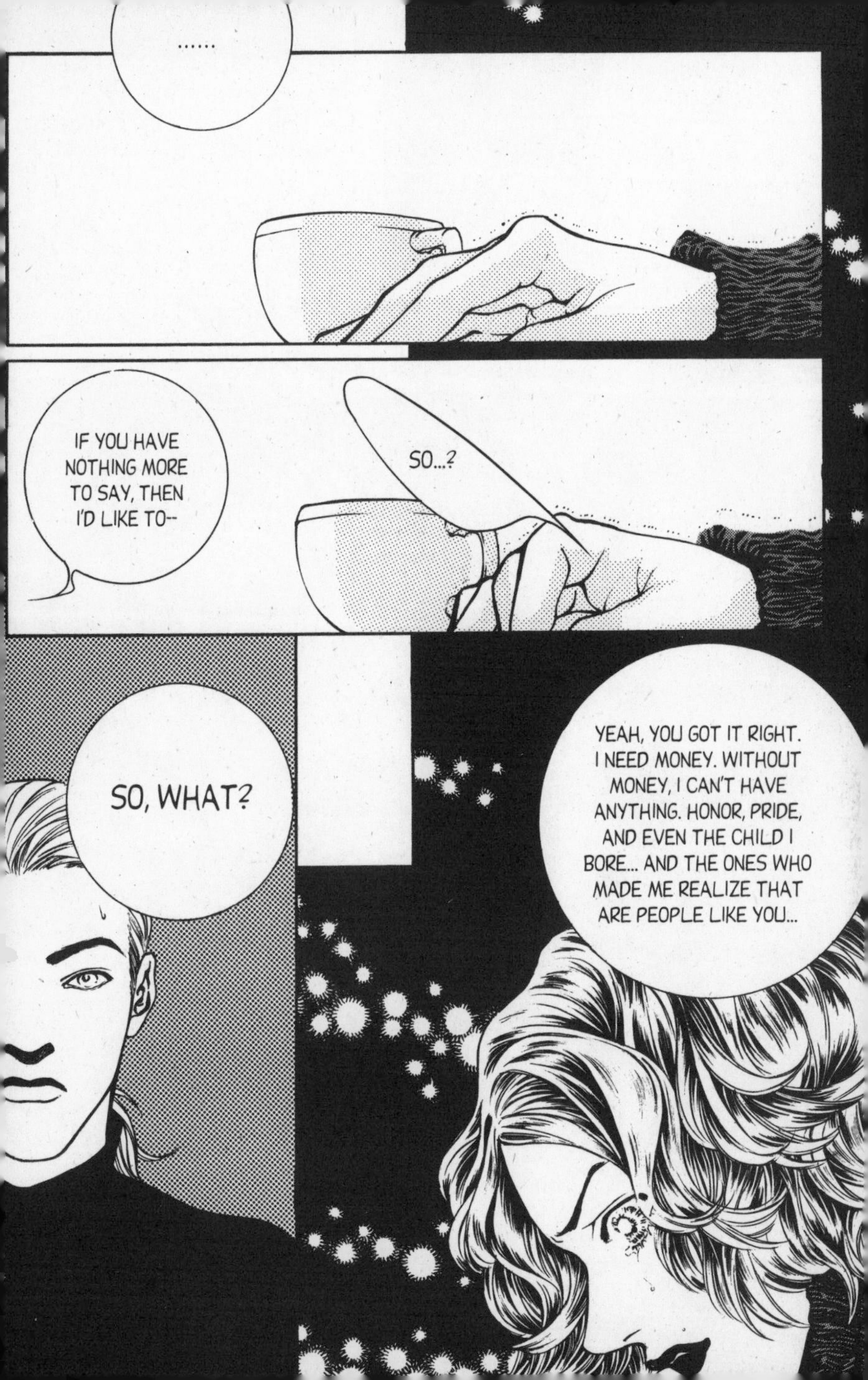
......
IF YOU HAVE NOTHING MORE TO SAY, THEN I'D LIKE TO--
SO...?
SO, WHAT?
YEAH, YOU GOT IT RIGHT. I NEED MONEY. WITHOUT MONEY, I CAN'T HAVE ANYTHING. HONOR, PRIDE, AND EVEN THE CHILD I BORE... AND THE ONES WHO MADE ME REALIZE THAT ARE PEOPLE LIKE YOU...

THAT DAY... THEY SAT ME AND MY CHILD DOWN...AND REALLY, IN JUST A FEW MINUTES, SO SIMPLY...THEY DEEMED ME A FAILURE, A PERVERT, AND A SOCIAL OUTCAST.
I...HAD JUST CALLED THE POLICE BECAUSE I COULDN'T STAND TO HAVE MY CHILD GET BEATEN UP BY THAT SON OF A BITCH... I REALLY HAD NO IDEA THAT I'D LOSE HIM...
IT'S ALL BECAUSE I'M POOR... IF ONLY I HAD MONEY... IF ONLY I COULD'VE GONE TO COURT...
PLEASE... PLEASE, I BEG YOU. RETURN MY CHILD TO ME...

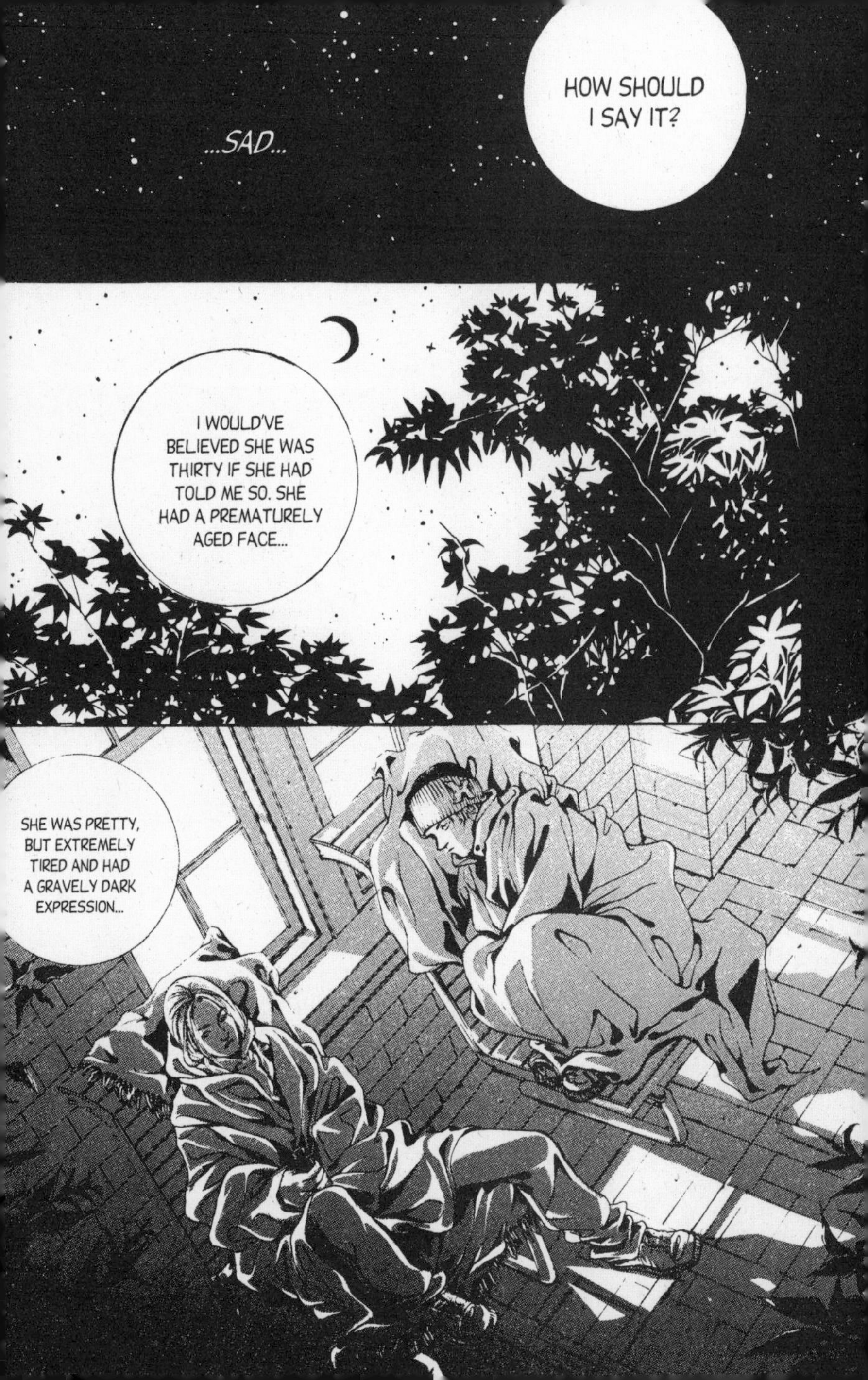
...SAD...
HOW SHOULD I SAY IT?
I WOULD'VE BELIEVED SHE WAS THIRTY IF SHE HAD TOLD ME SO. SHE HAD A PREMATURELY AGED FACE...
SHE WAS PRETTY, BUT EXTREMELY TIRED AND HAD A GRAVELY DARK EXPRESSION...

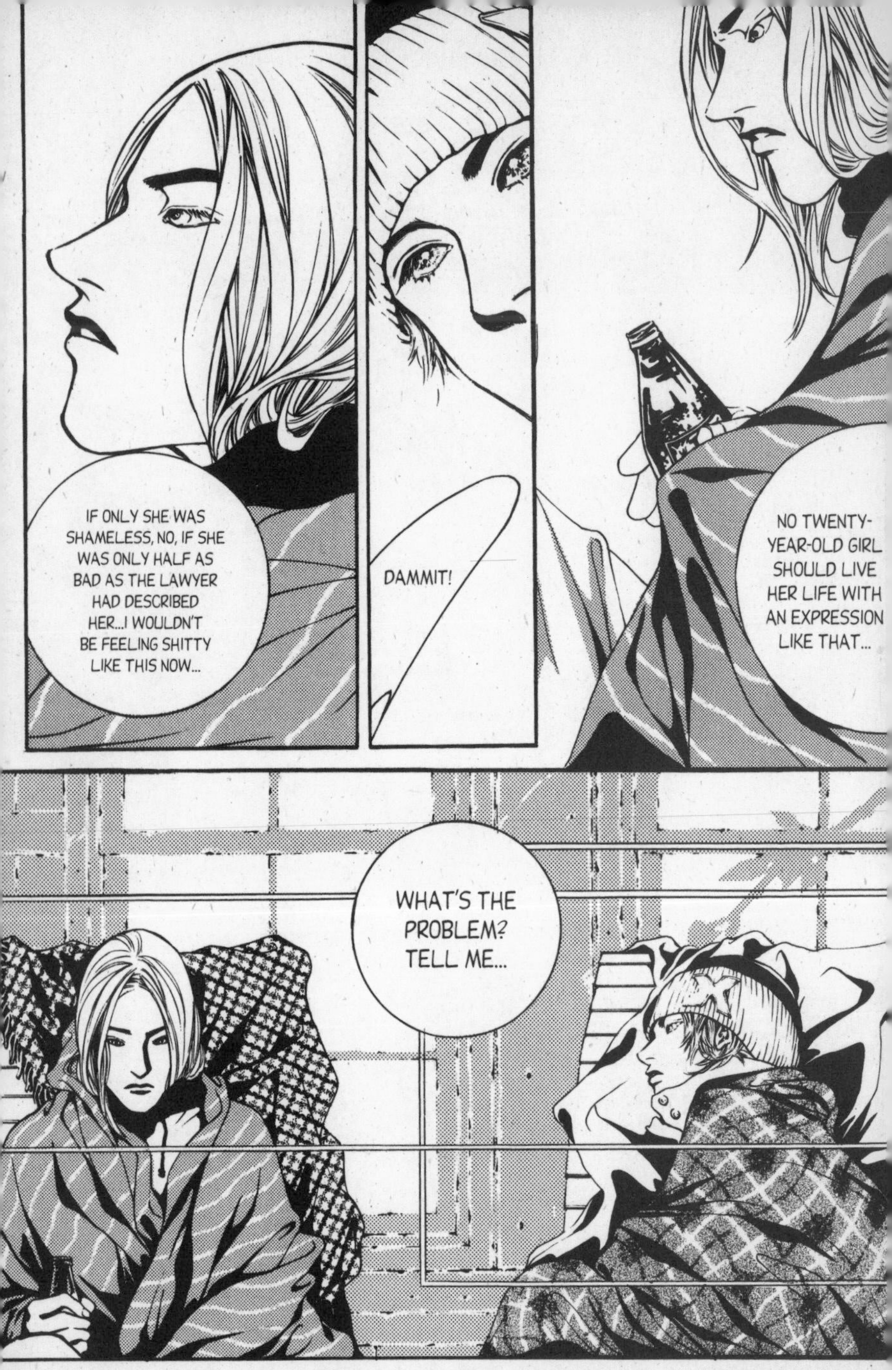
IF ONLY SHE WAS SHAMELESS, NO, IF SHE WAS ONLY HALF AS BAD AS THE LAWYER HAD DESCRIBED HER...I WOULDN'T BE FEELING SHITTY LIKE THIS NOW...
DAMMIT!
NO TWENTY-YEAR-OLD GIRL SHOULD LIVE HER LIFE WITH AN EXPRESSION LIKE THAT...
WHAT'S THE PROBLEM? TELL ME...

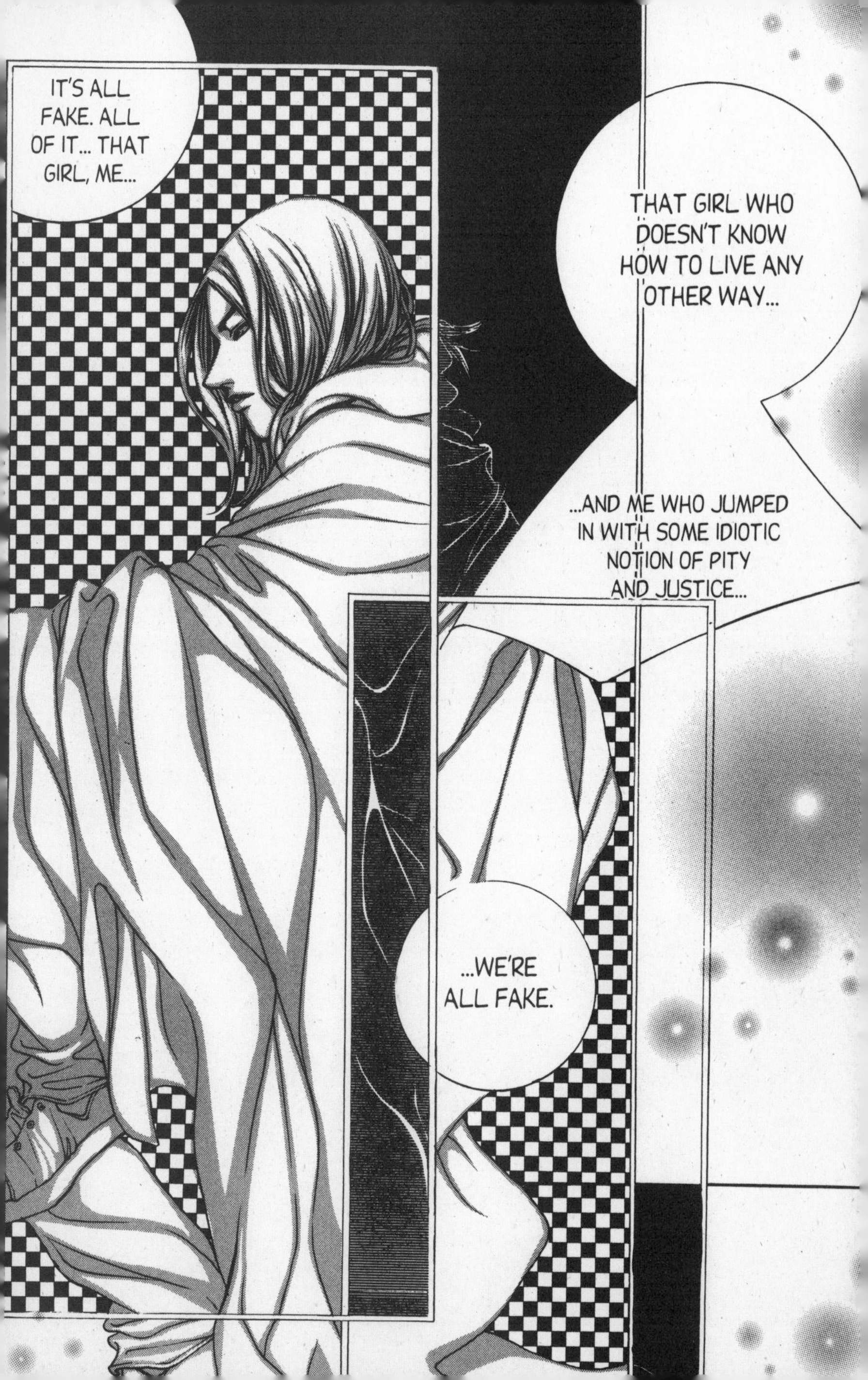
IT'S ALL FAKE. ALL OF IT... THAT GIRL, ME...
THAT GIRL WHO DOESN'T KNOW HOW TO LIVE ANY OTHER WAY...
...AND ME WHO JUMPED IN WITH SOME IDIOTIC NOTION OF PITY AND JUSTICE...
...WE'RE ALL FAKE.

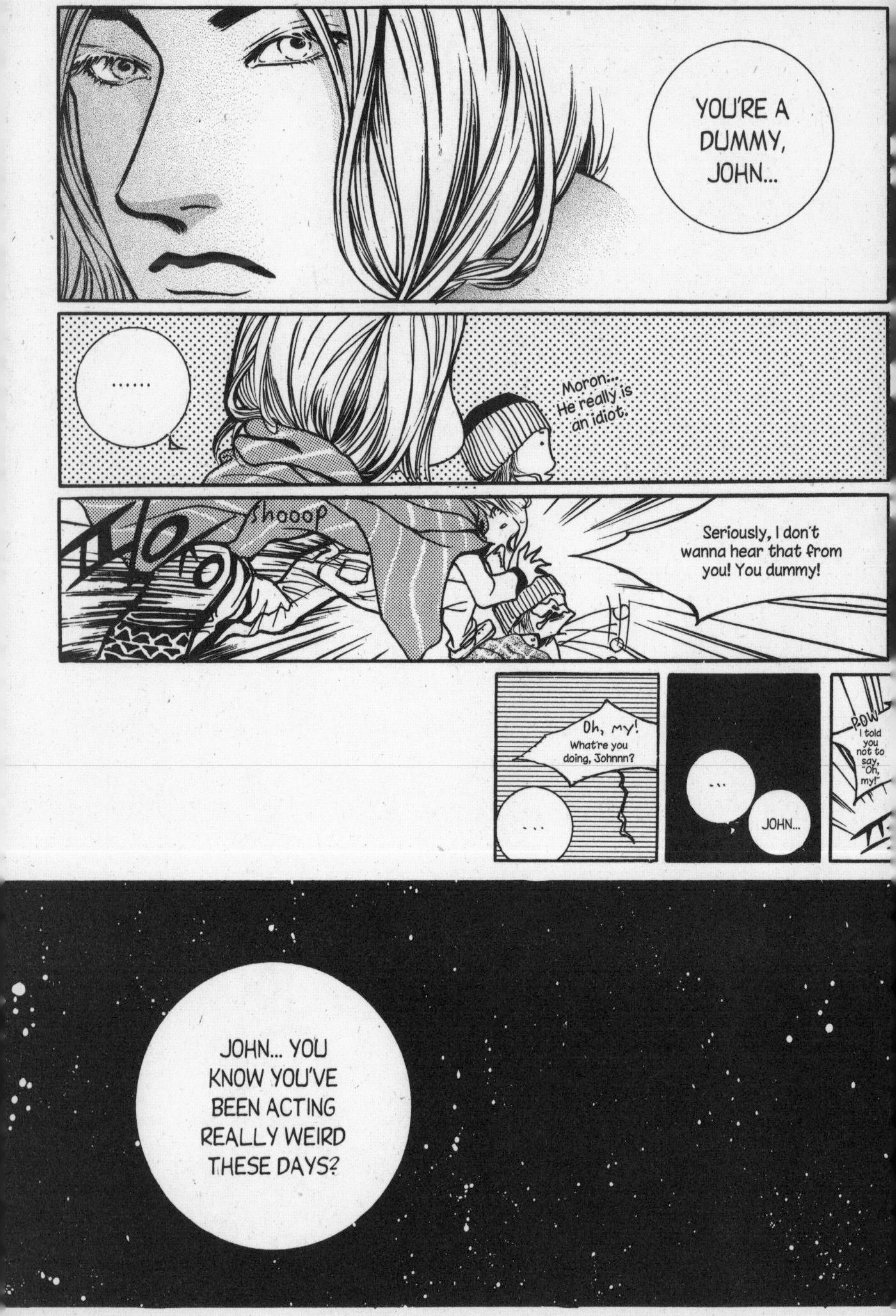
YOU'RE A DUMMY, JOHN...
......
Moron... He really is an idiot.
shooop
Seriously, I don't wanna hear that from you! You dummy!
Oh, my! What're you doing, Johnnn?
...
...
JOHN...
POW
I told you not to say, "Oh, my!"
JOHN... YOU KNOW YOU'VE BEEN ACTING REALLY WEIRD THESE DAYS?

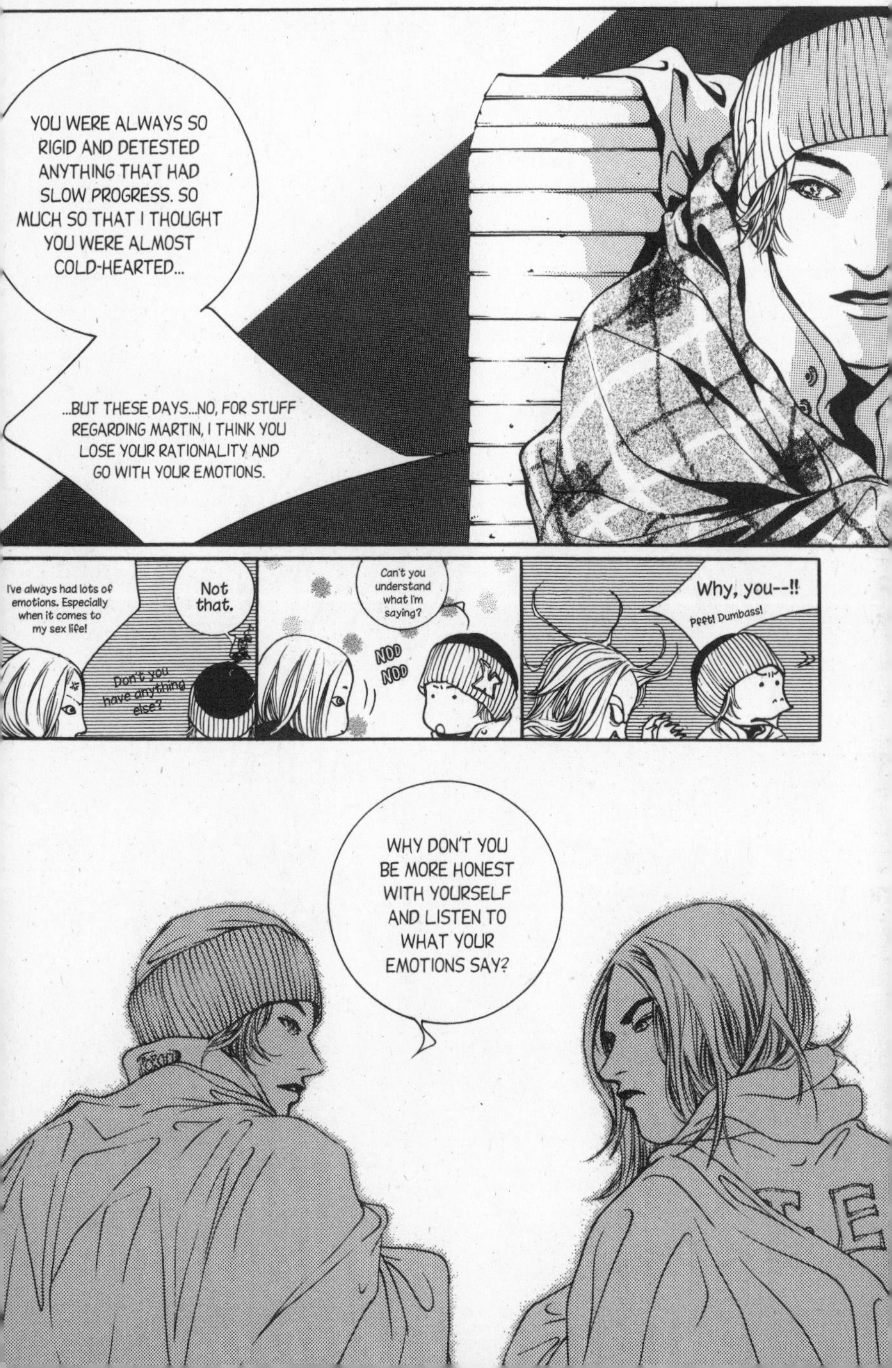
YOU WERE ALWAYS SO RIGID AND DETESTED ANYTHING THAT HAD SLOW PROGRESS. SO MUCH SO THAT I THOUGHT YOU WERE ALMOST COLD-HEARTED...
...BUT THESE DAYS...NO, FOR STUFF REGARDING MARTIN, I THINK YOU LOSE YOUR RATIONALITY AND GO WITH YOUR EMOTIONS.
I've always had lots of emotions. Especially when it comes to my sex life!
Not that.
Don't you have anything else?
Can't you understand what I'm saying?
NOD NOD
Why, you--!!
Pfft! Dumbass!
WHY DON'T YOU BE MORE HONEST WITH YOURSELF AND LISTEN TO WHAT YOUR EMOTIONS SAY?

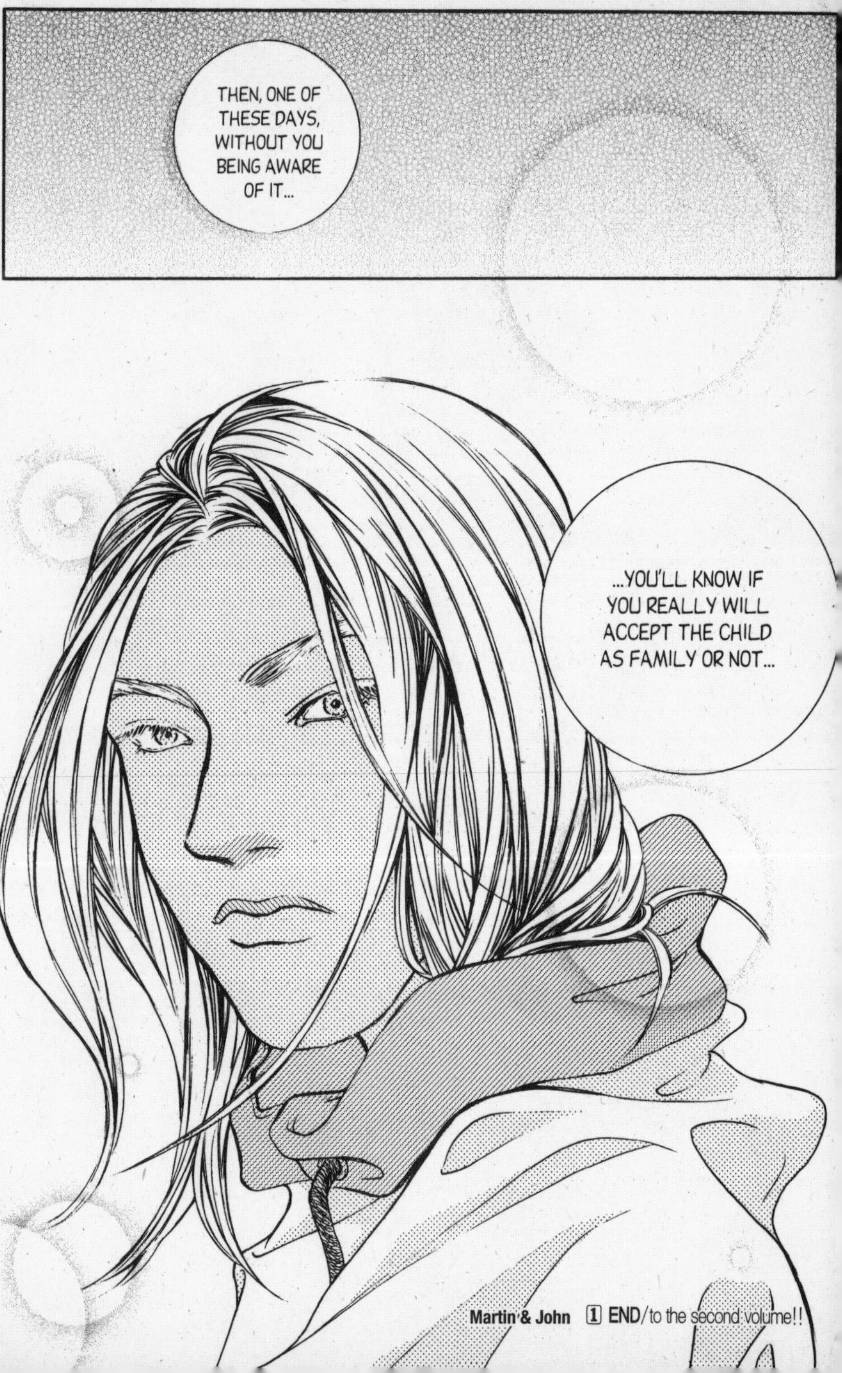
THEN, ONE OF THESE DAYS, WITHOUT YOU BEING AWARE OF IT...
...YOU'LL KNOW IF YOU REALLY WILL ACCEPT THE CHILD AS FAMILY OR NOT...
Martin & John 1 **END**/to the second volume!!

In The Next Volume Of

Martin & John

The story of John and
his step-brother Martin continues...
What kind of secret is the little boy hiding,
and will John still want to fight to keep
him after he finds out the truth?

And then...
Two more Martin's, two more Johns...
What does life have in store for all of them?

TOKYOPOP®.com
WHERE MANGA LIVES!
JOIN the TOKYOPOP community:
www.TOKYOPOP.com
COME AND PREVIEW THE HOTTEST MANGA AROUND!
CREATE...
UPLOAD...
DOWNLOAD...
BLOG...
CHAT...
VOTE...
LIVE!!!!
WWW.TOKYOPOP.COM HAS:
• Exclusives
• News
• Contests
• Games
• Rising Stars of Manga
• iManga
• and more...
TOKYOPOP :: Leading the Manga Revolution for 10 Years and Beyond
http://www.TOKYOPOP.com/
Where else?
TOKYOPOP
STARS
ART
LIFE
MOBILE
SHOP
HOT
POP-CAST
Now with long lasting flavor
WATCH HERE!
MOST RECENT
MOST POPPED
TP FEATURES
TOKYOPOP.COM 2.0
NOW LIVE!
THE MANGA REVOLUTION • LEADING • THE MANGA REVOLUTION • LEADING
漫画革命
© Branded Entertainment LLC, TOKYOPOP Inc., and Russell Productions, Inc.

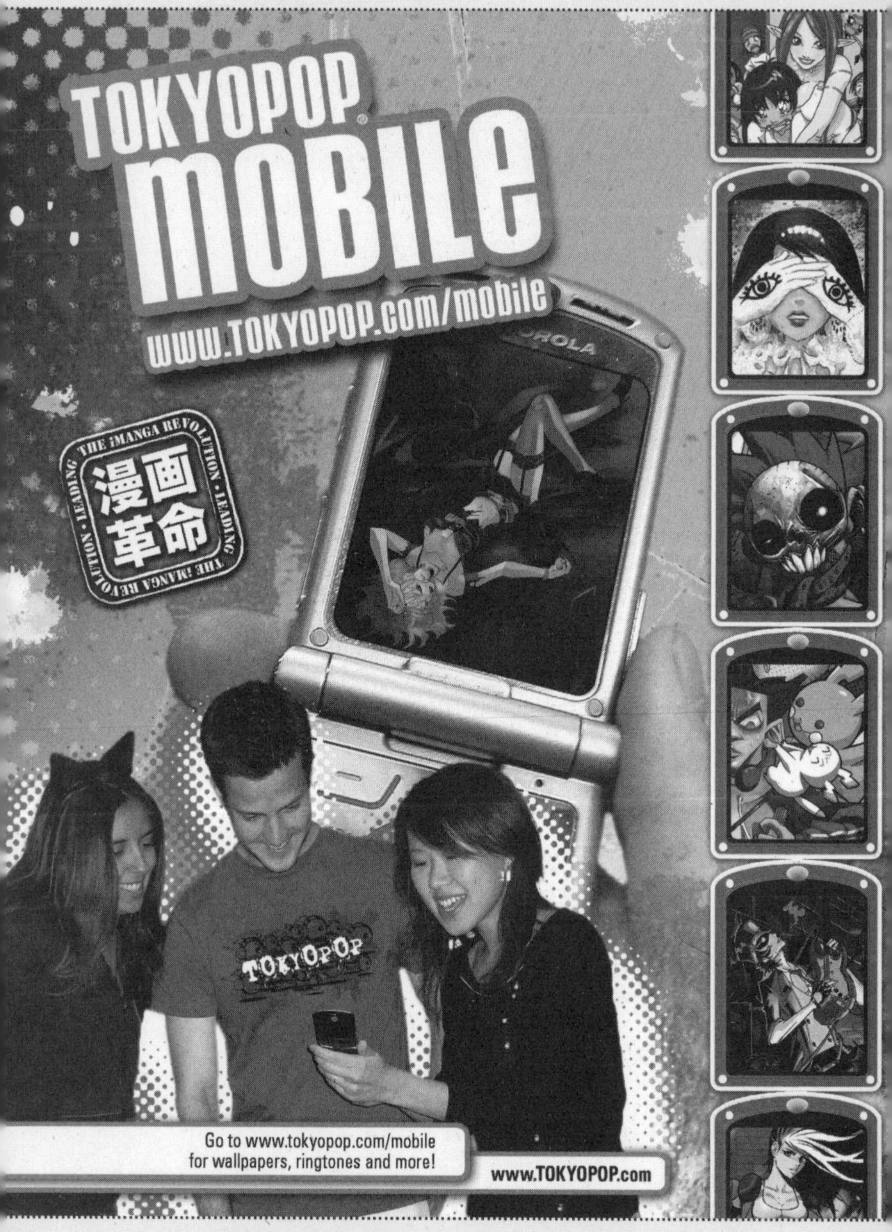
TOKYOPOP
MOBILE
www.TOKYOPOP.com/mobile
THE MANGA REVOLUTION · LEADING · THE MANGA REVOLUTION · LEADING
漫画革命
TOKYOPOP
Go to www.tokyopop.com/mobile
for wallpapers, ringtones and more!
www.TOKYOPOP.com

CHIBI VAMPIRE
MANGA BY YUNA KAGESAKI, NOVEL BY TOHRU KAI AND YUNA KAGESAKI

The HILARIOUS adventures of

chibi
Vampire

TOKYOPOP®

Created By:
Yuna Kagesaki

9

As Karin and Kenta's official first date continues, Anju shows up to keep an eye on the clumsy couple. When Kenta tells Karin how he really feels, will it destroy their relationship? Also, the new girl in town, Yuriya, begins snooping around in search of vampires. Why is she trying to uncover Karin's identity, and what secrets of her own is she hiding?

chibi
Vampire™ ⁓ Inspired the

FOR MORE INFORMATION VISIT: